JOHNNY HIRO

JOHNN

Y HIRO

{ Half Asian, All Hero }

Fred Chao

greytones by Dylan Babb
letters by Jesse Post

TOR®

A Tom Doherty Associates Book
New York

JOHNNY HIRO: HALF ASIAN, ALL HERO

Copyright © 2009 by Fred Chao

Originally published as *Johnny Hiro*, issues 1–3 (2007, 2008), previously collected with new material as *Johnny Hiro* by AdHouse Books (2009). Excerpt published in *Best American Comics 2010* from Houghton Mifflin Harcourt (2010).

A Tor Book
Published by Tom Doherty Associates, LLC
175 Fifth Avenue
New York, NY 10010

www.tor-forge.com

Tor® is a registered trademark of Tom Doherty Associates, LLC.

ISBN 978-0-7653-2937-0

First Tor Edition: July 2012

Printed in the United States of America

0 9 8 7 6 5 4 3 2 1

For Dylan,

whose grace and clumsy have inspired
so much within these pages

A-Yo, this rap game got me in a figure 4 leglock
I lock and love but that lock is submissive
the ref holdin' my arm like I'm gonna pass out
but never ever in this world I gonna tap out.
And you can never put words or explain perseverance
or what it takes just to shit this rap out.
And yeah left to get a degree
and a house, wife and kid ain't far-fetched
but for now, yo, it's our sketch.
And my first foot forward is my best step
and I ain't trying to deny the fact: I'm trying to earn to live a better life
but it's a life hanging with its bread and butter knife.
Well you gotta perfect it just to get it right.
And man, once you get it right it leads to longer nights
and longer nights, man, just leads to make or break
'cause chasing a dream's a bitch when you wide awake.

                           —The Alias Brothers, "Gone Head"

Perhaps one day I will be able to tell you what I have learned of the eye
and the romance it carries on, quietly and in a most halting manner,
with the veiled beauty of the world.

                           —Ethan Canin, *Carry Me Across the Water*

うらにわにいるおおきいなとかげ

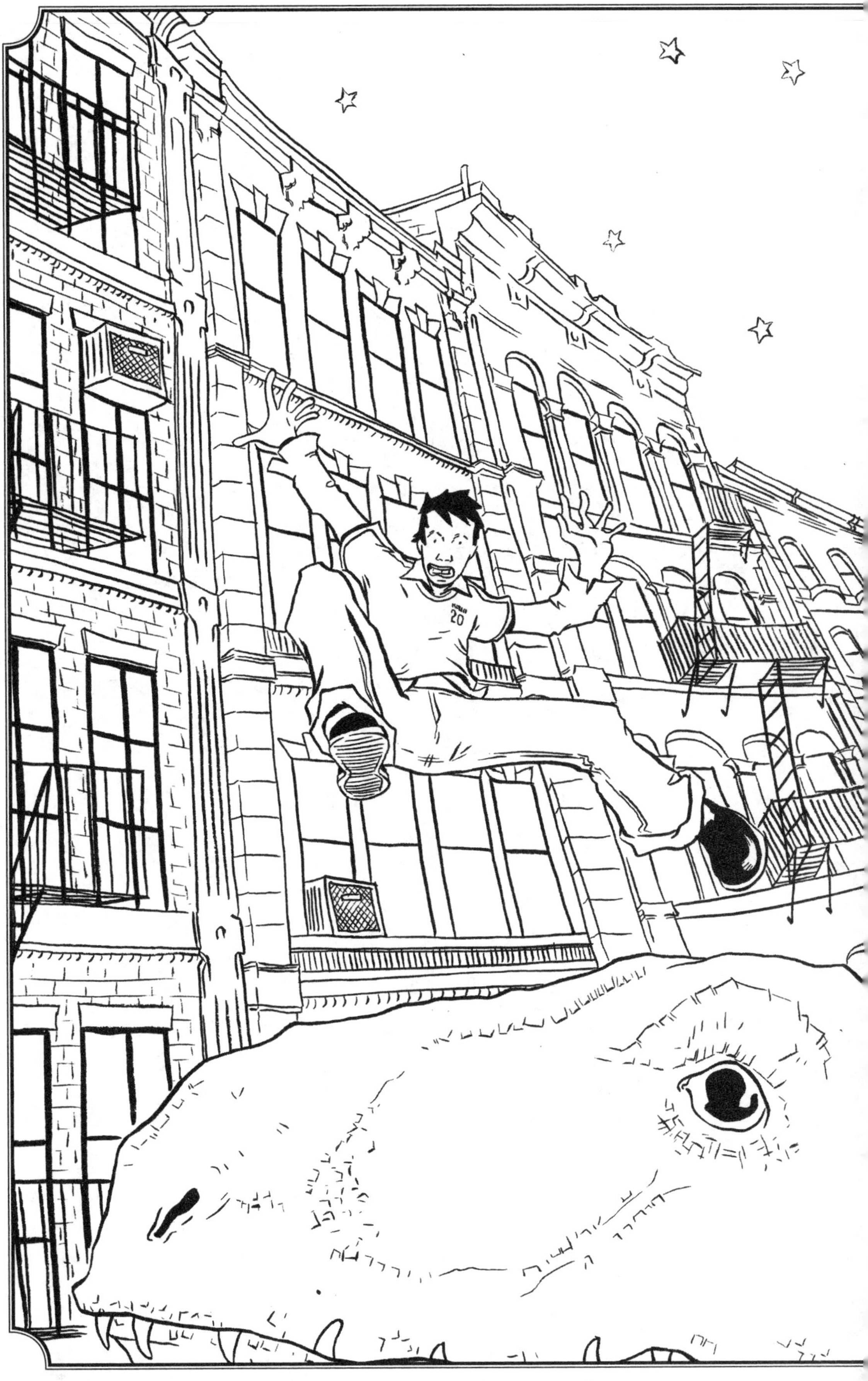
20

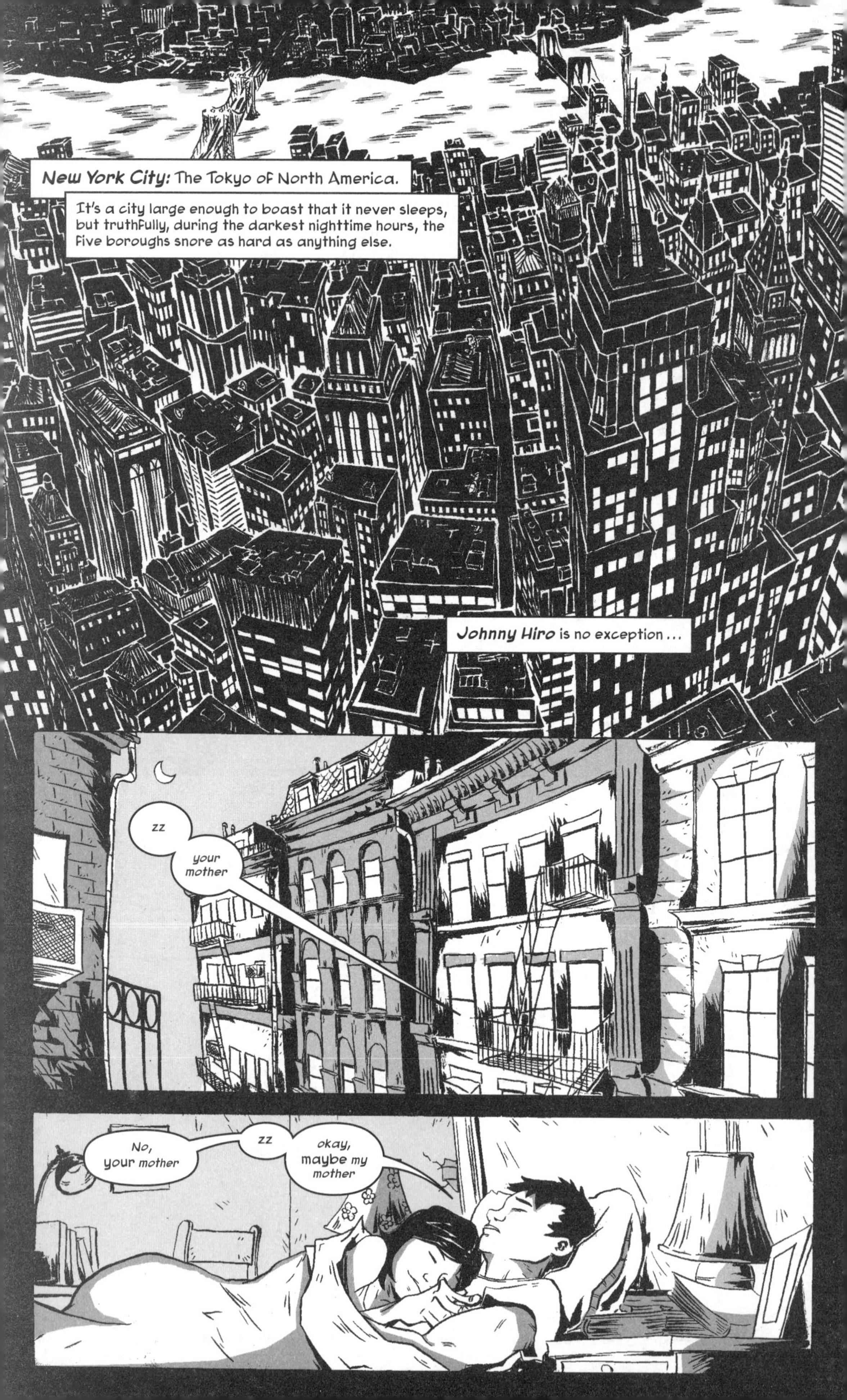
New York City: The Tokyo of North America.
It's a city large enough to boast that it never sleeps, but truthfully, during the darkest nighttime hours, the five boroughs snore as hard as anything else.
Johnny Hiro is no exception ...
zz
your mother
No, your mother
zz
okay, maybe my mother

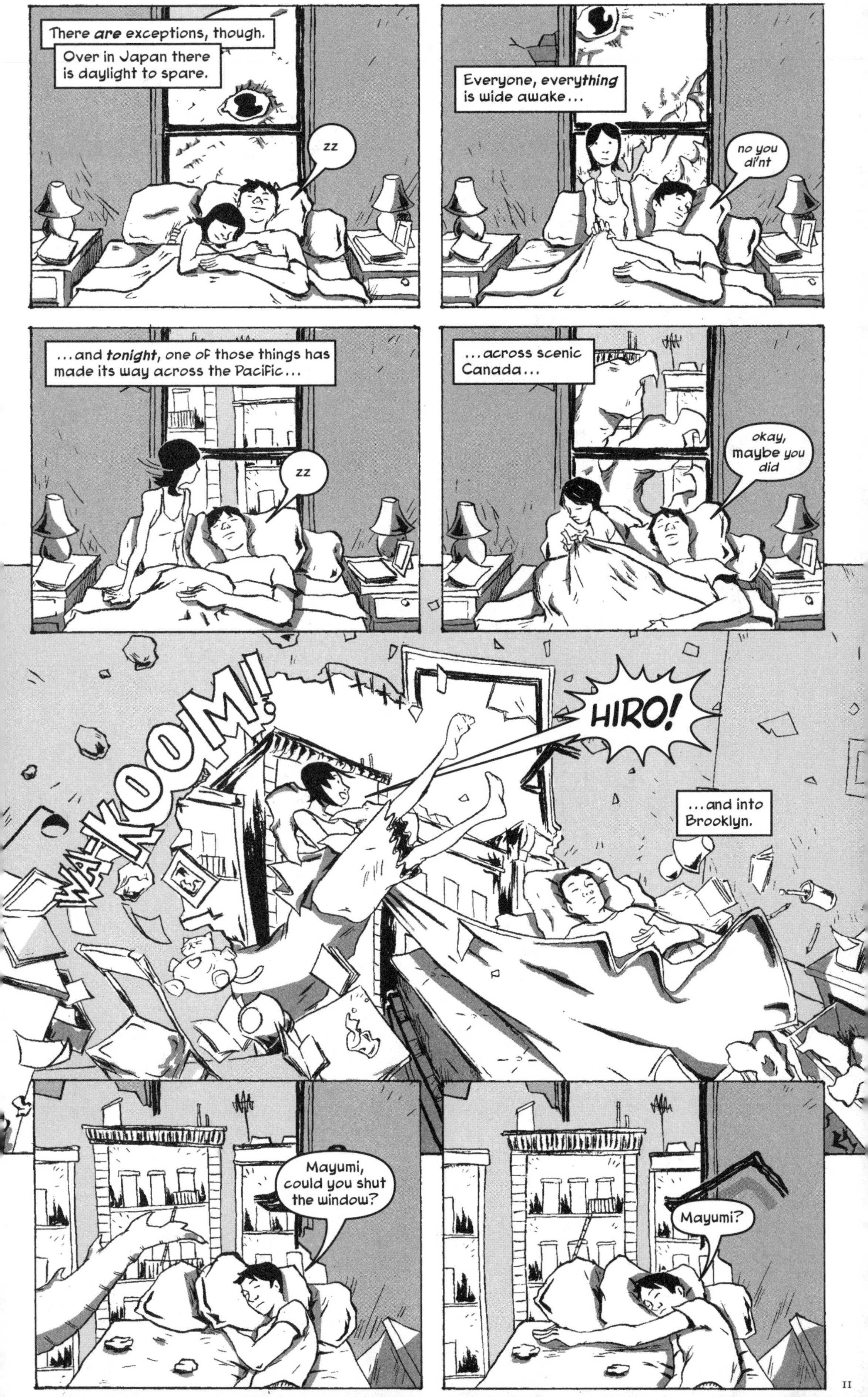
There **are** exceptions, though.
Over in Japan there is daylight to spare.
zz
Everyone, every*thing* is wide awake...
no you di'nt
...and **tonight**, one of those things has made its way across the Pacific...
zz
...across scenic Canada...
okay, maybe you did
WA-KOOM!!
HIRO!
...and into Brooklyn.
Mayumi, could you shut the window?
Mayumi?

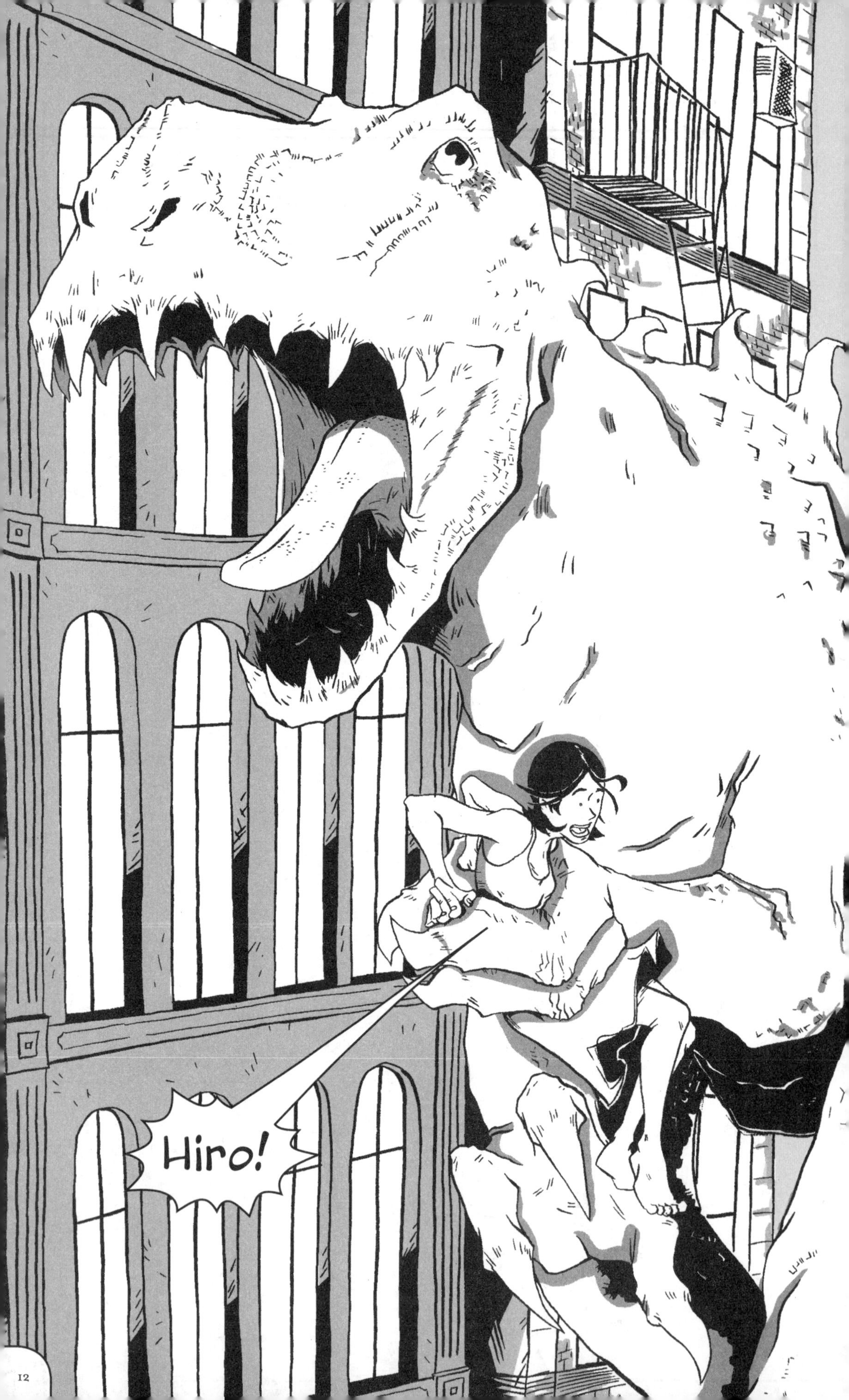
Hiro!

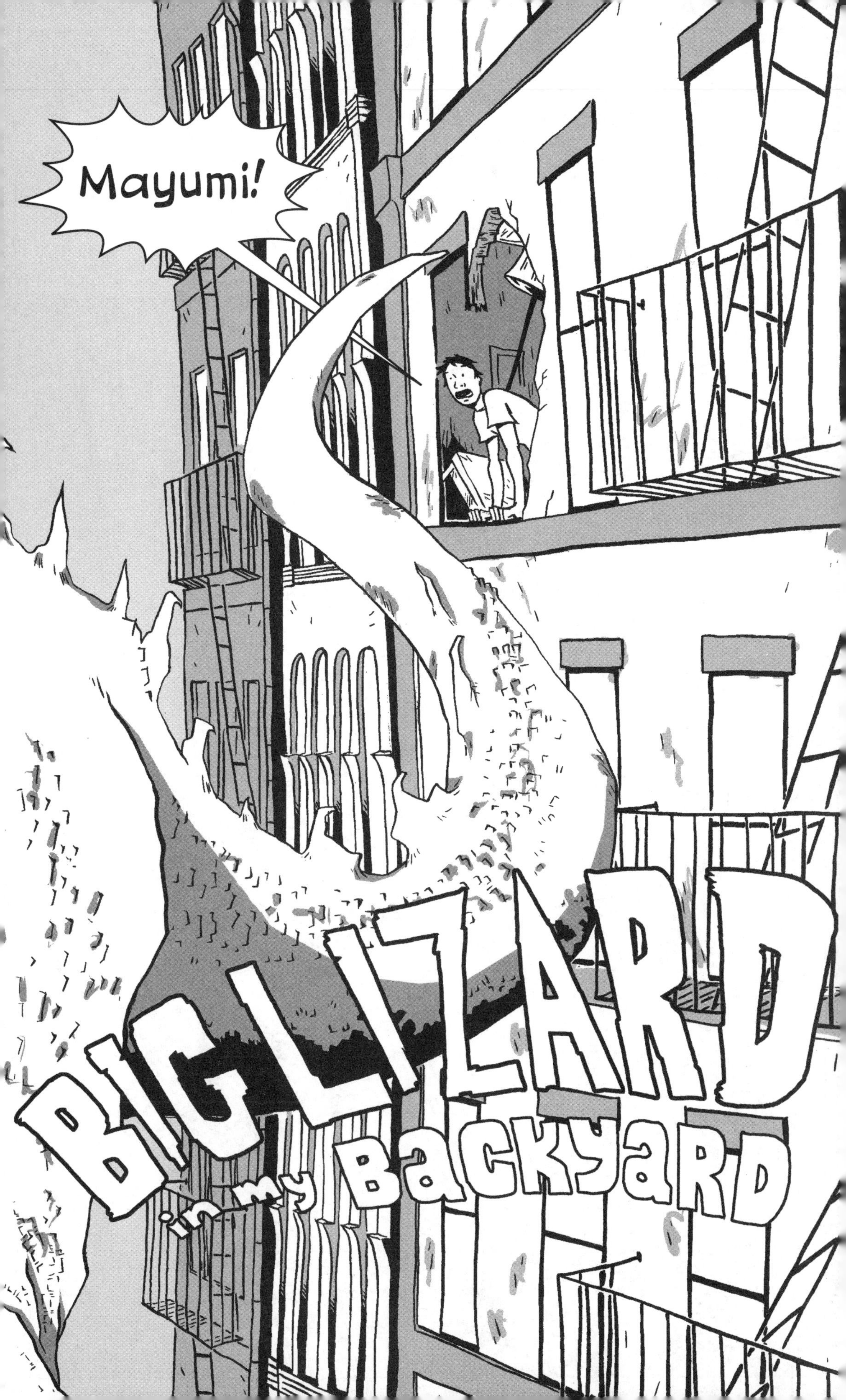
Mayumi!
BIG LIZARD in my BACKYARD

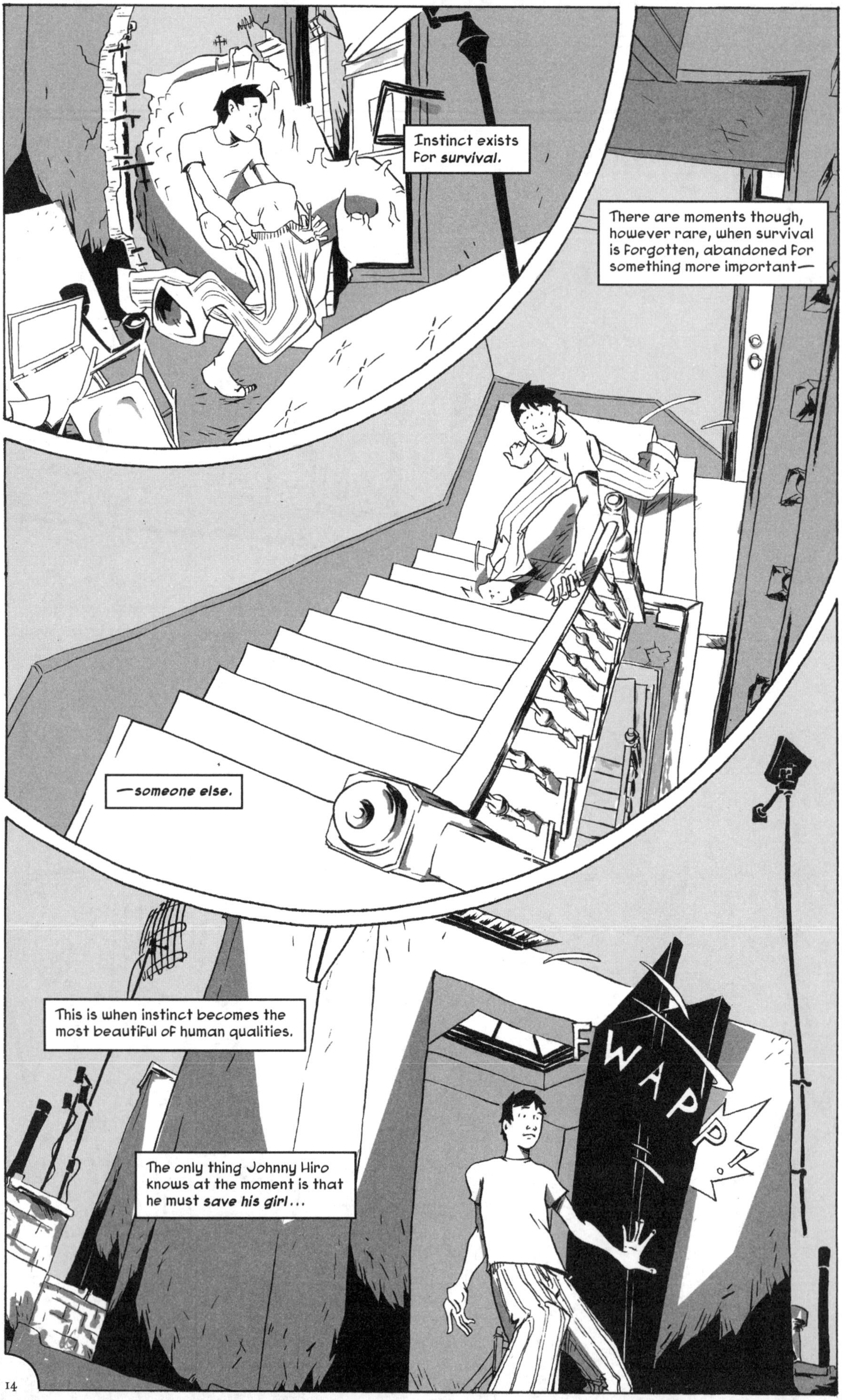
Instinct exists for *survival*.
There are moments though, however rare, when survival is forgotten, abandoned for something more important—
—*someone else.*
This is when instinct becomes the most beautiful of human qualities.
FWAPP!
The only thing Johnny Hiro knows at the moment is that he must *save his girl*...

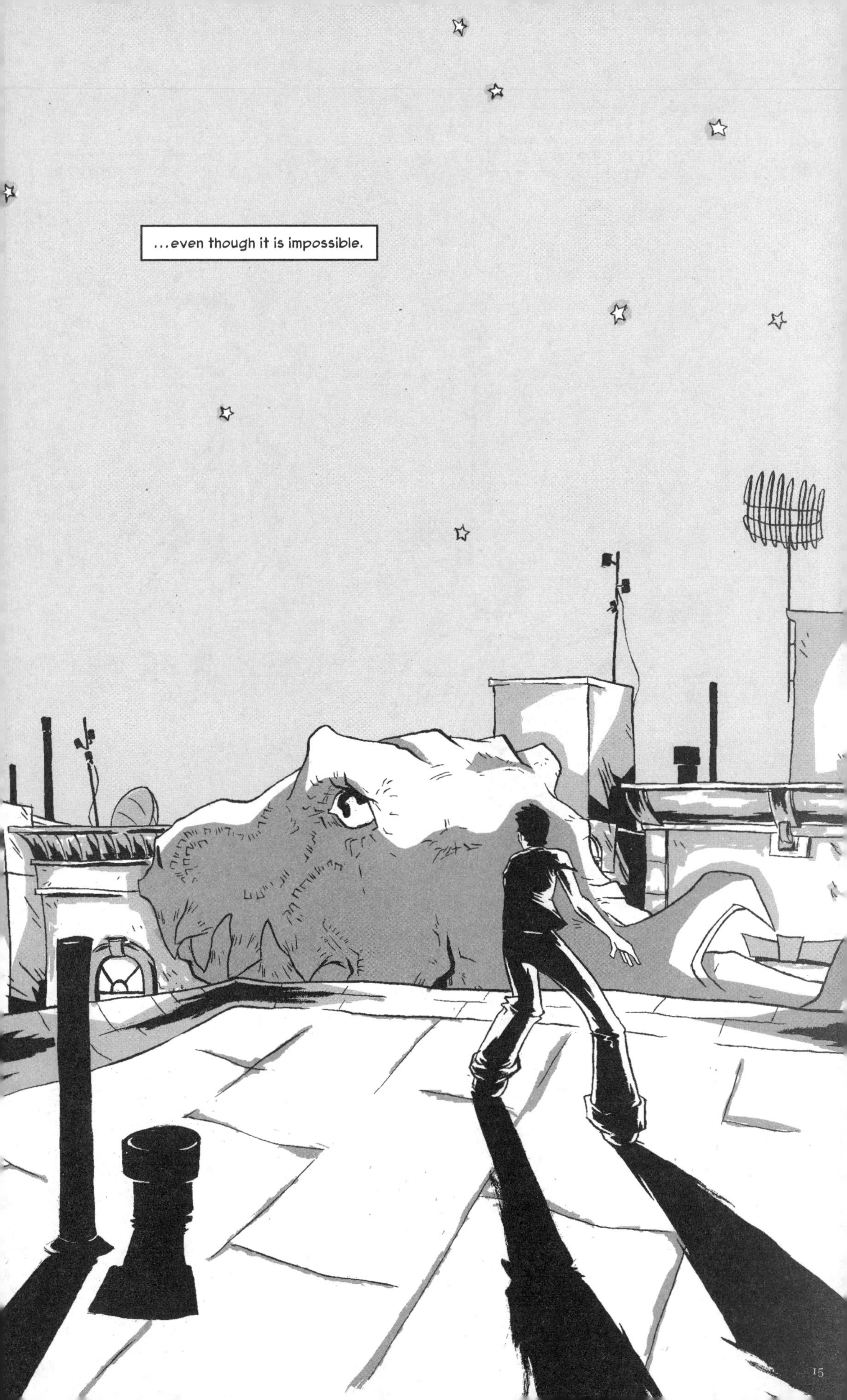
...even though it is impossible.

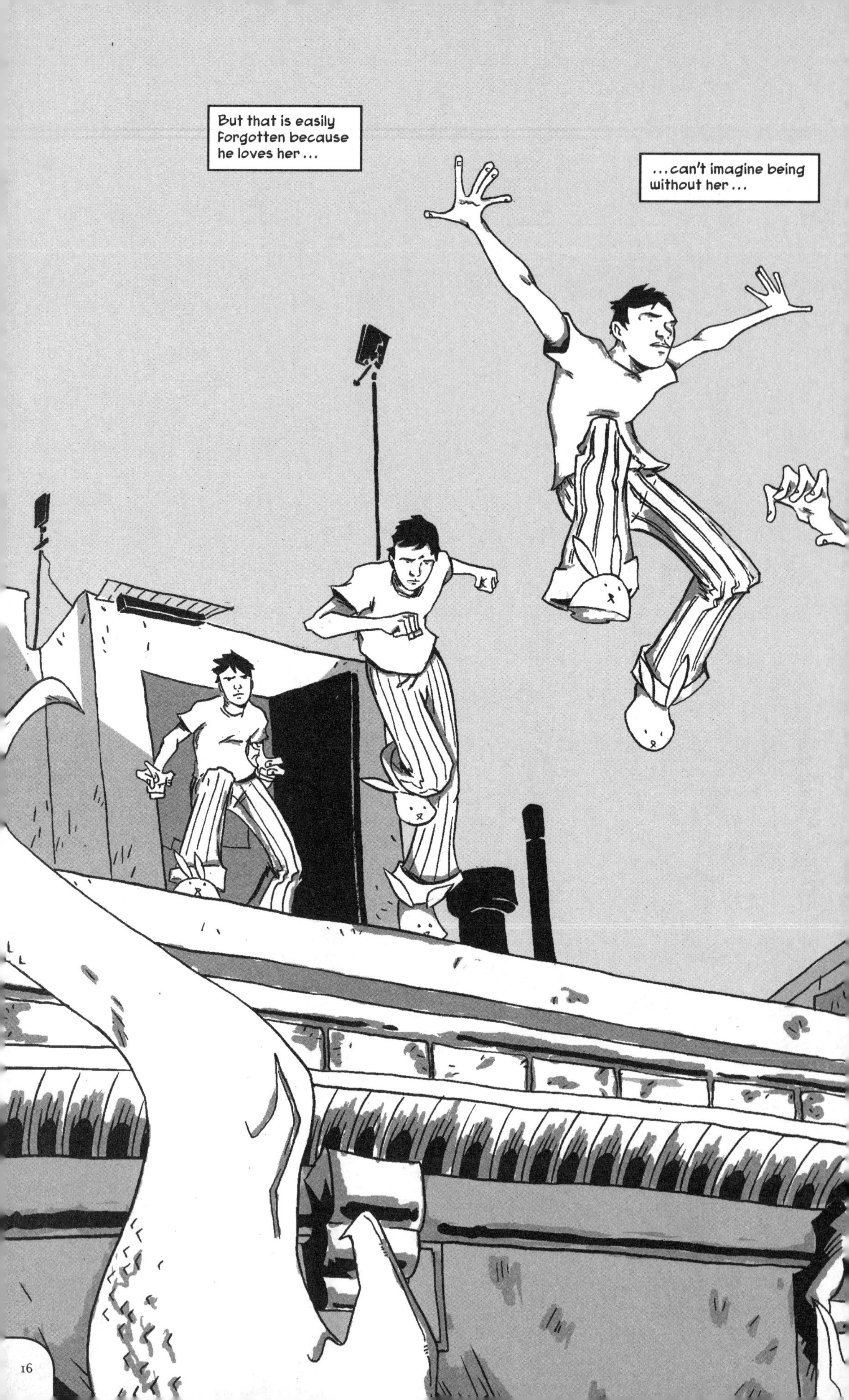
But that is easily forgotten because he loves her . . .
. . . can't imagine being without her . . .

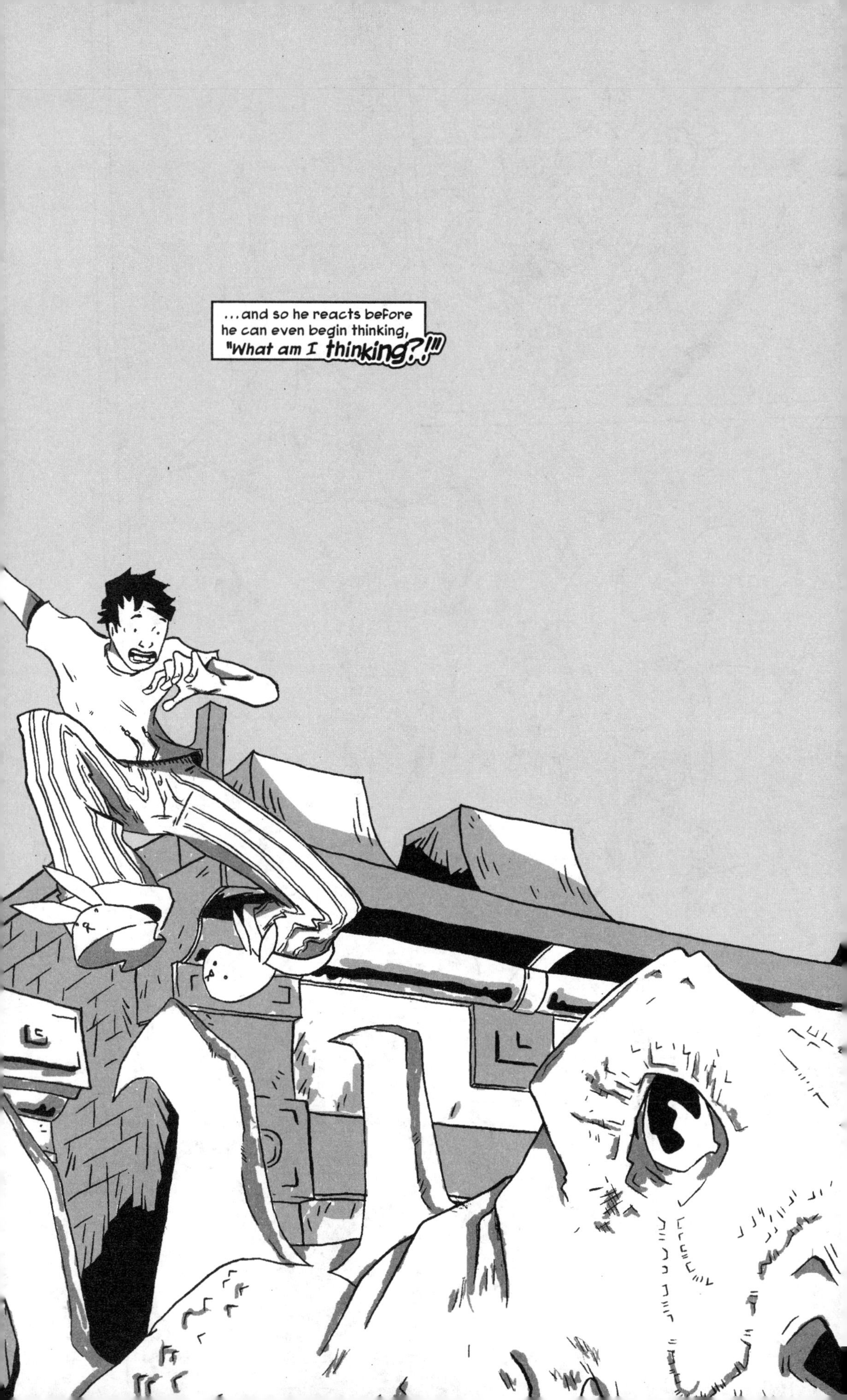
...and so he reacts before he can even begin thinking, "What am I thinking?!"

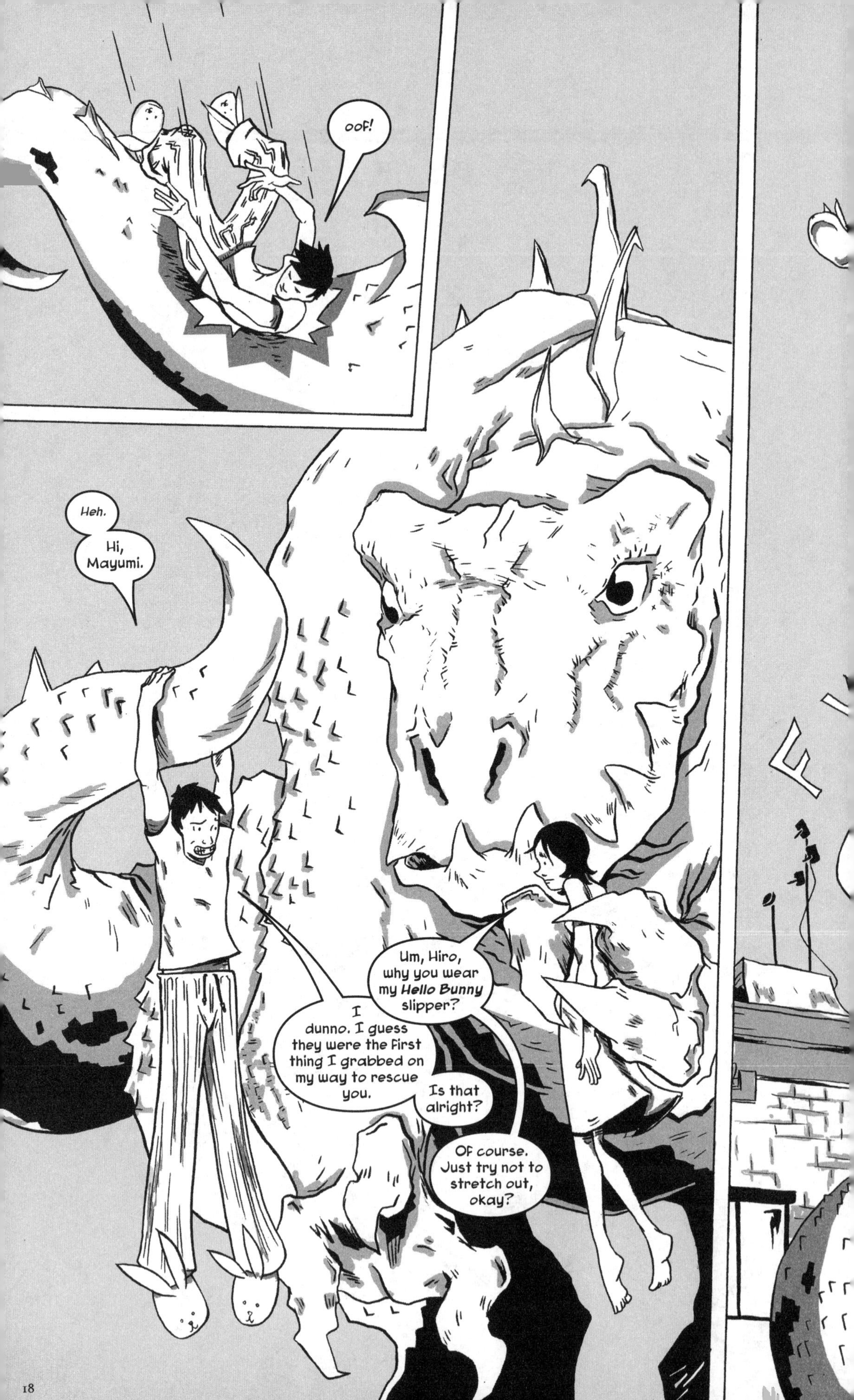
oof!
Heh.
Hi, Mayumi.
Um, Hiro, why you wear my *Hello Bunny* slipper?
I dunno. I guess they were the first thing I grabbed on my way to rescue you.
Is that alright?
Of course. Just try not to stretch out, okay?

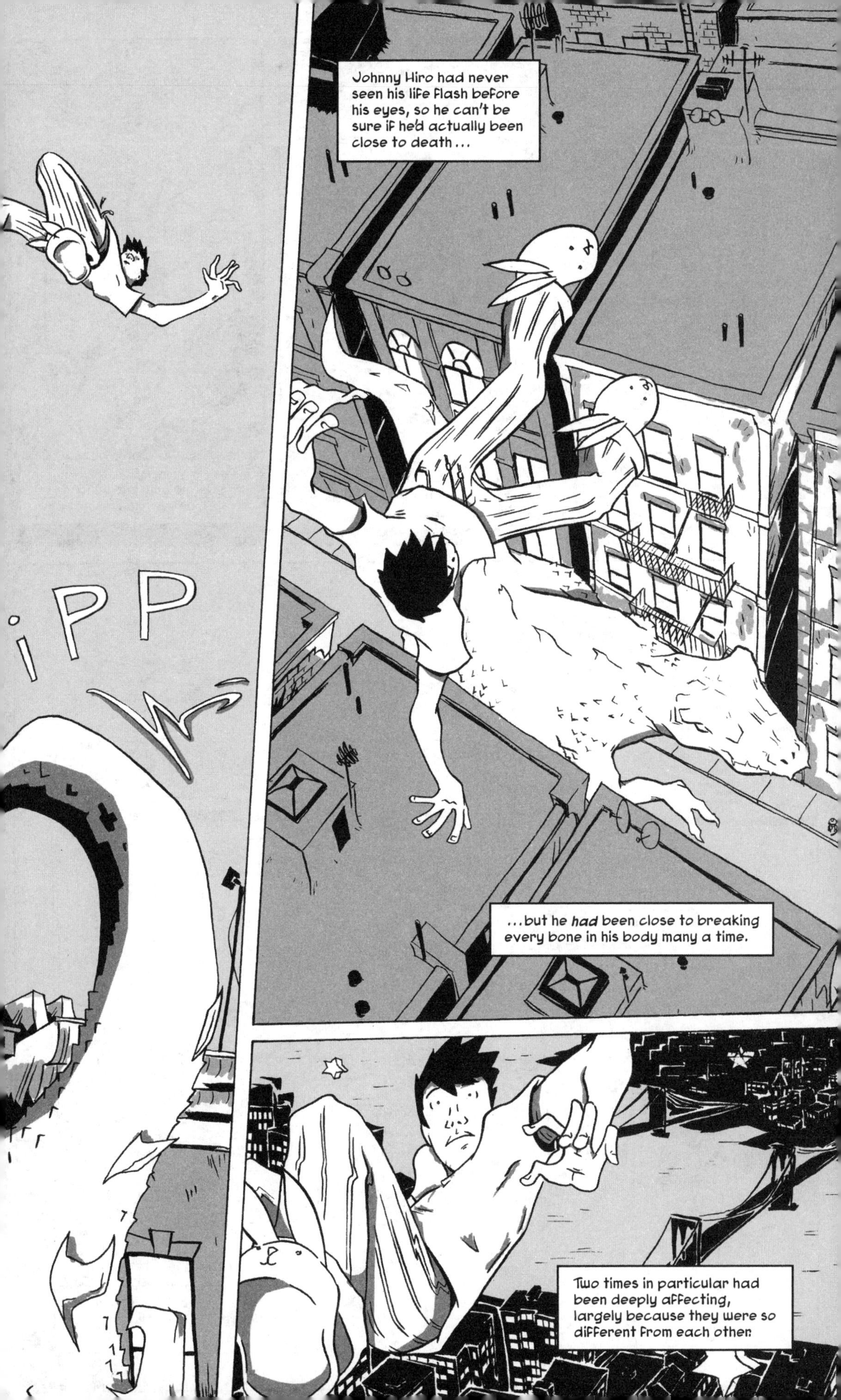
Johnny Hiro had never seen his life flash before his eyes, so he can't be sure if he'd actually been close to death...
...but he *had* been close to breaking every bone in his body many a time.
Two times in particular had been deeply affecting, largely because they were so different from each other.

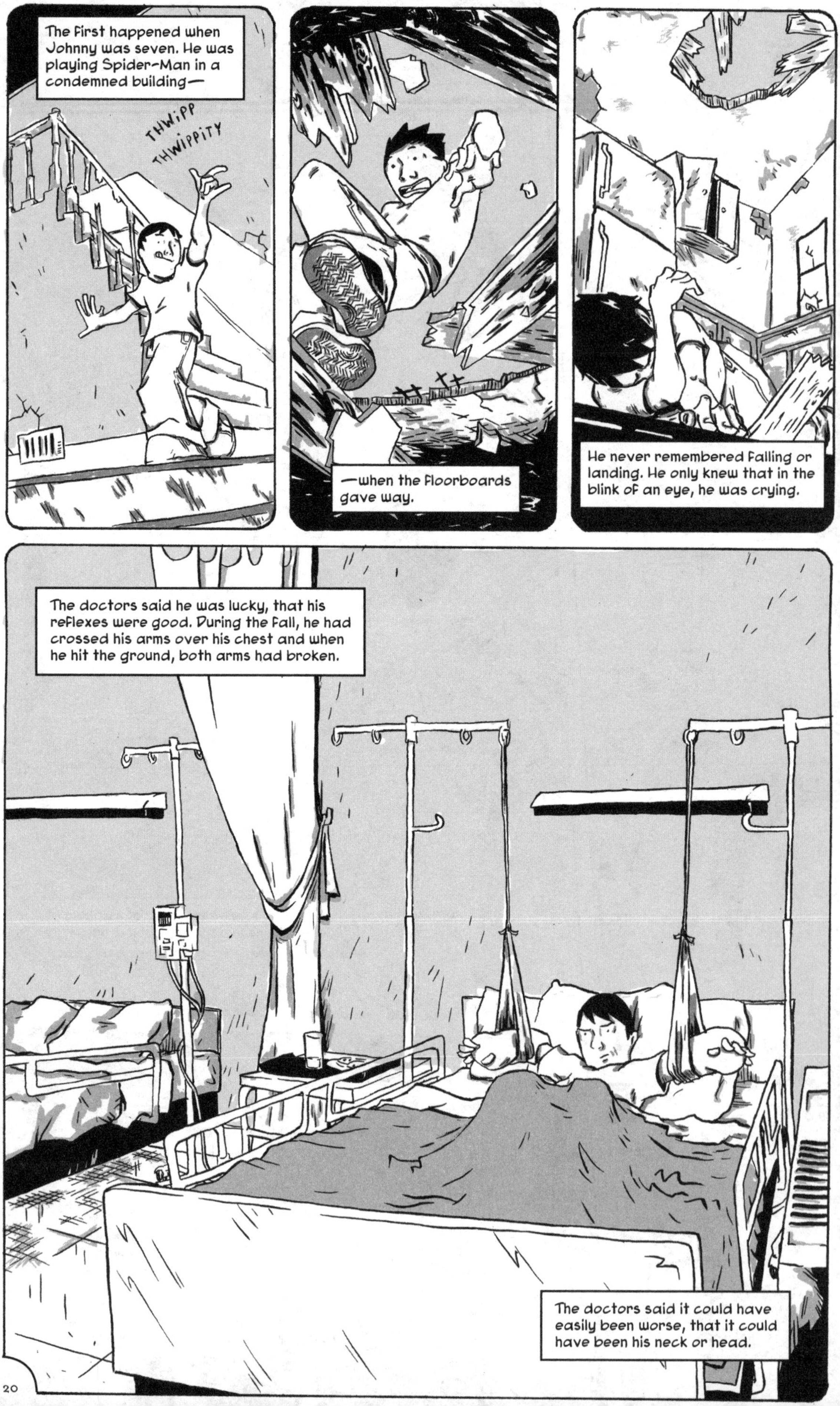
The first happened when Johnny was seven. He was playing Spider-Man in a condemned building—
THWiPP
THWiPPiTY
—when the floorboards gave way.
He never remembered falling or landing. He only knew that in the blink of an eye, he was crying.
The doctors said he was lucky, that his reflexes were good. During the fall, he had crossed his arms over his chest and when he hit the ground, both arms had broken.
The doctors said it could have easily been worse, that it could have been his neck or head.

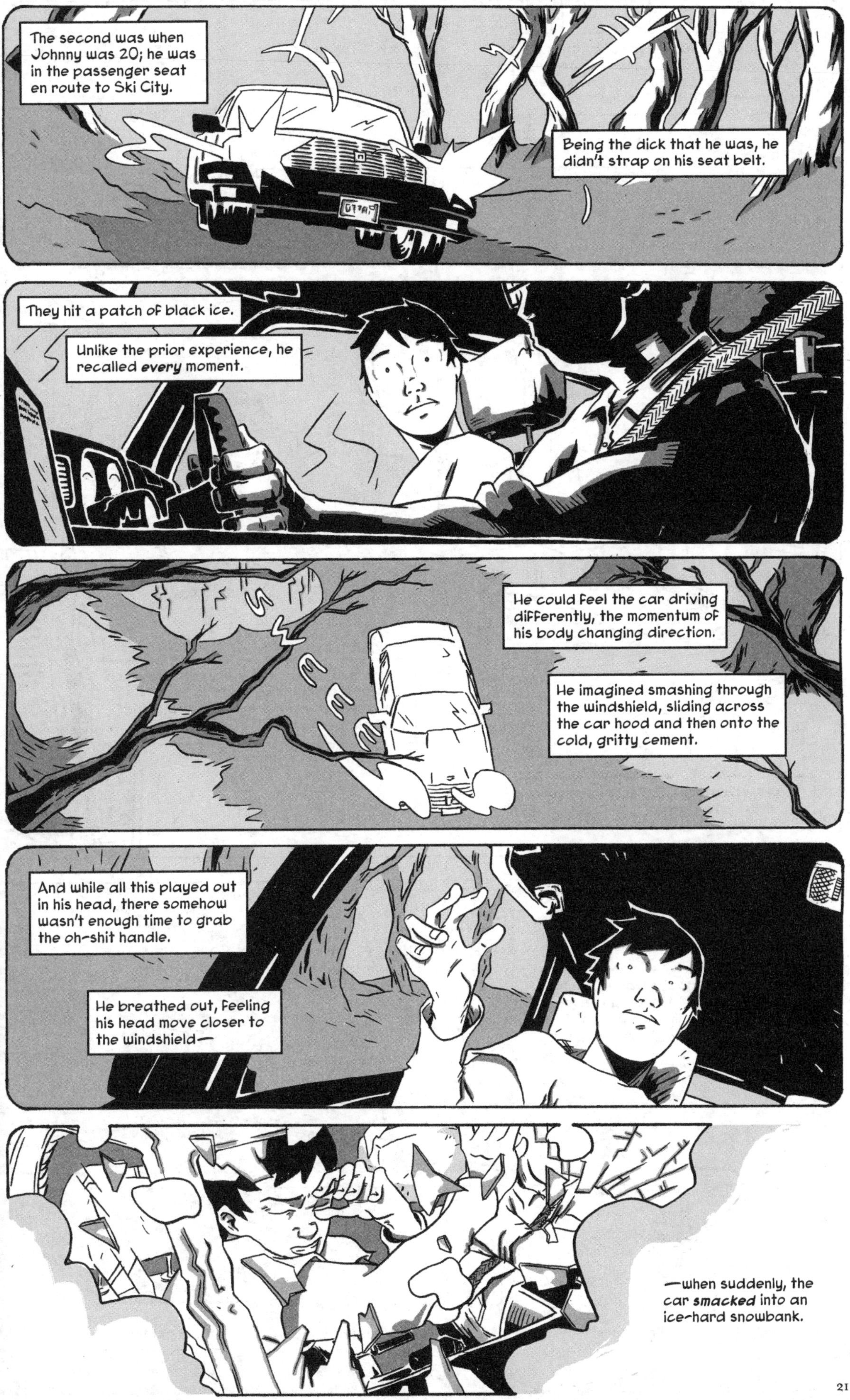
The second was when Johnny was 20; he was in the passenger seat en route to Ski City.
Being the dick that he was, he didn't strap on his seat belt.
They hit a patch of black ice.
Unlike the prior experience, he recalled *every* moment.
He could feel the car driving differently, the momentum of his body changing direction.
He imagined smashing through the windshield, sliding across the car hood and then onto the cold, gritty cement.
And while all this played out in his head, there somehow wasn't enough time to grab the oh-shit handle.
He breathed out, feeling his head move closer to the windshield—
—when suddenly, the car ***smacked*** into an ice-hard snowbank.

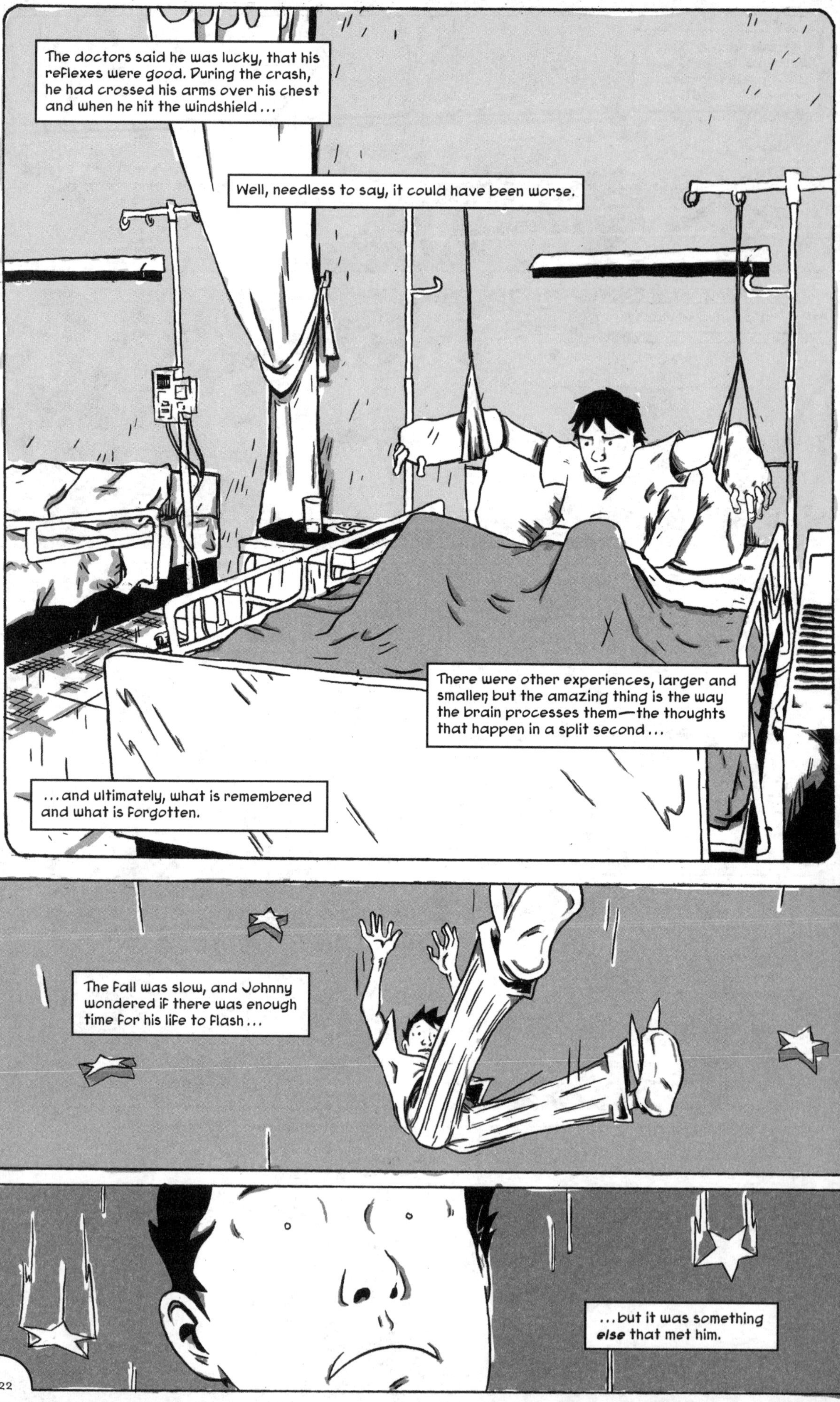
The doctors said he was lucky, that his reflexes were good. During the crash, he had crossed his arms over his chest and when he hit the windshield...
Well, needless to say, it could have been worse.
There were other experiences, larger and smaller, but the amazing thing is the way the brain processes them—the thoughts that happen in a split second...
...and ultimately, what is remembered and what is forgotten.
The fall was slow, and Johnny wondered if there was enough time for his life to flash...
...but it was something ***else*** that met him.

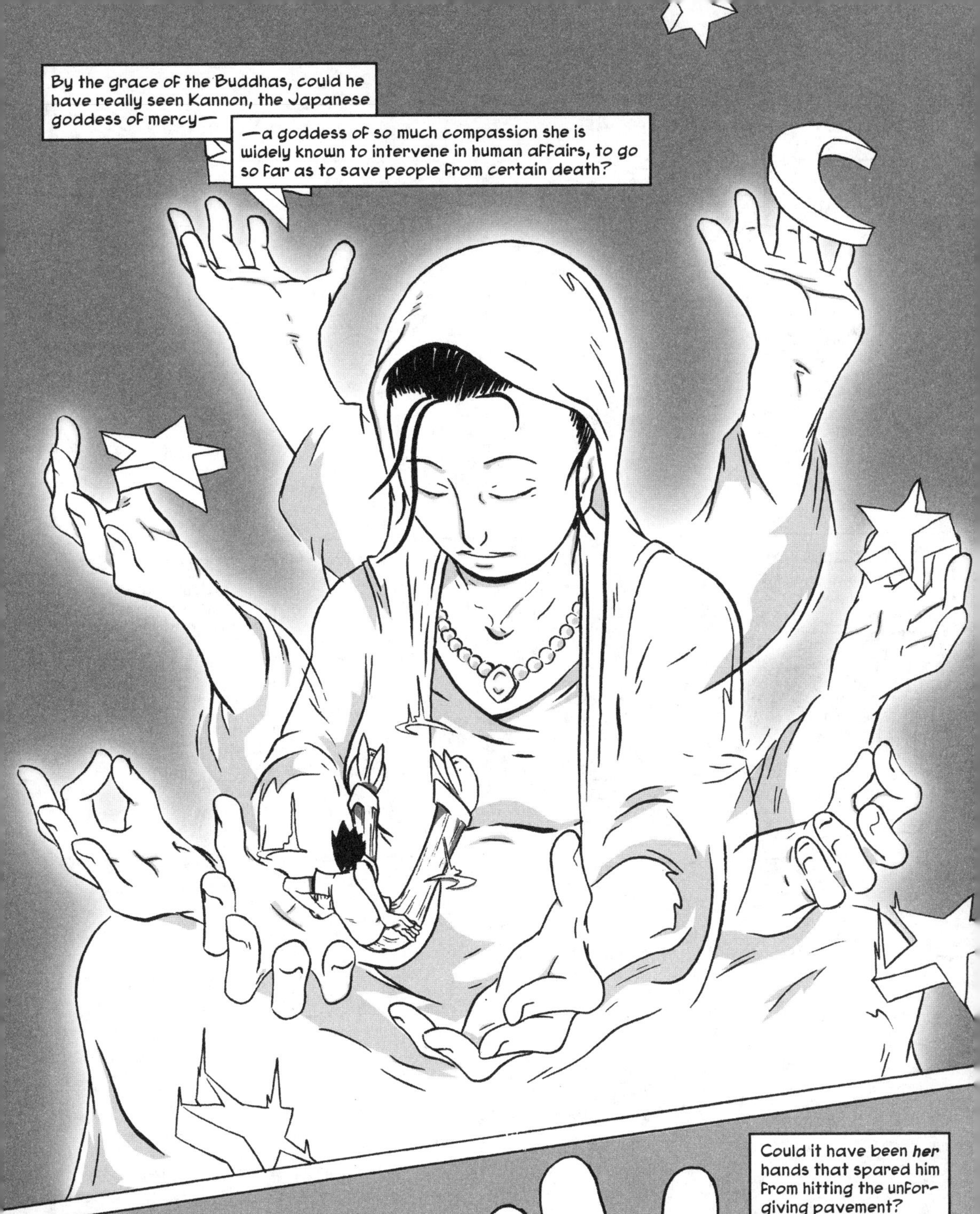
By the grace of the Buddhas, could he have really seen Kannon, the Japanese goddess of mercy—
—a goddess of so much compassion she is widely known to intervene in human affairs, to go so far as to save people from certain death?
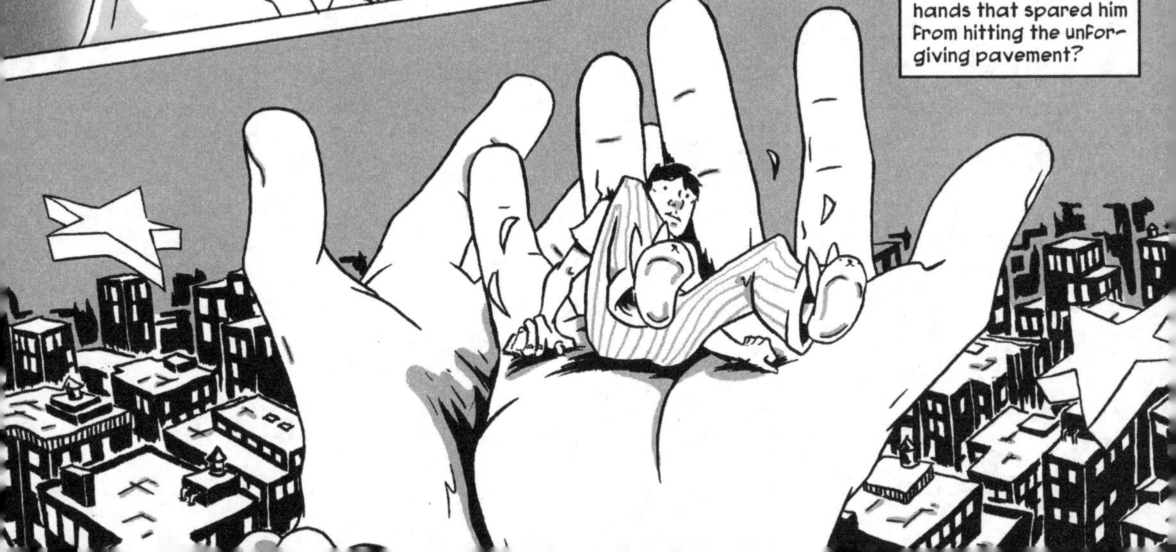
Could it have been *her* hands that spared him from hitting the unfor-giving pavement?

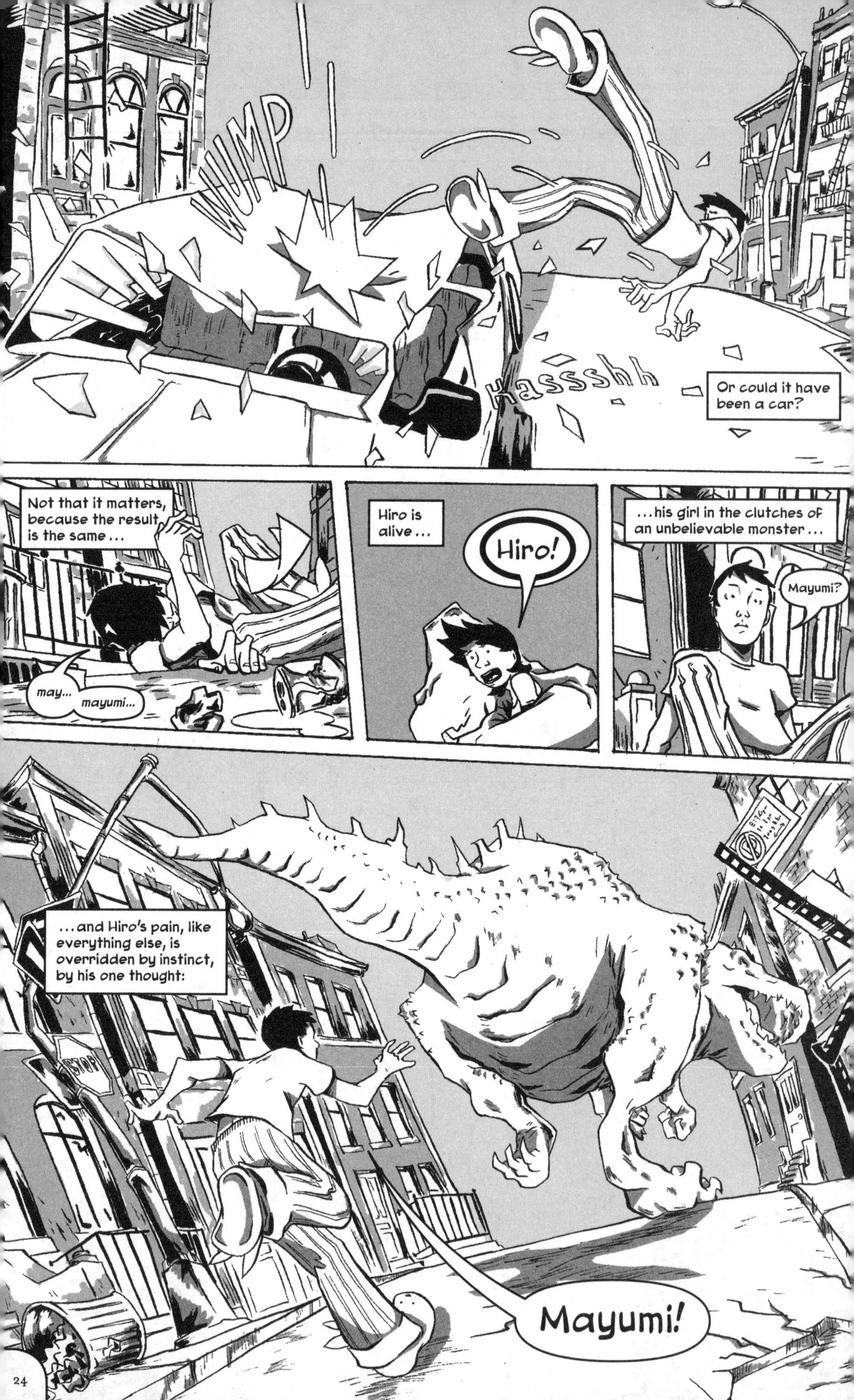
WUMP
kassshh
Or could it have been a car?
Not that it matters, because the result is the same . . .
may... mayumi...
Hiro is alive . . .
Hiro!
. . . his girl in the clutches of an unbelievable monster . . .
Mayumi?
. . . and Hiro's pain, like everything else, is overridden by instinct, by his one thought:
STOP
Mayumi!

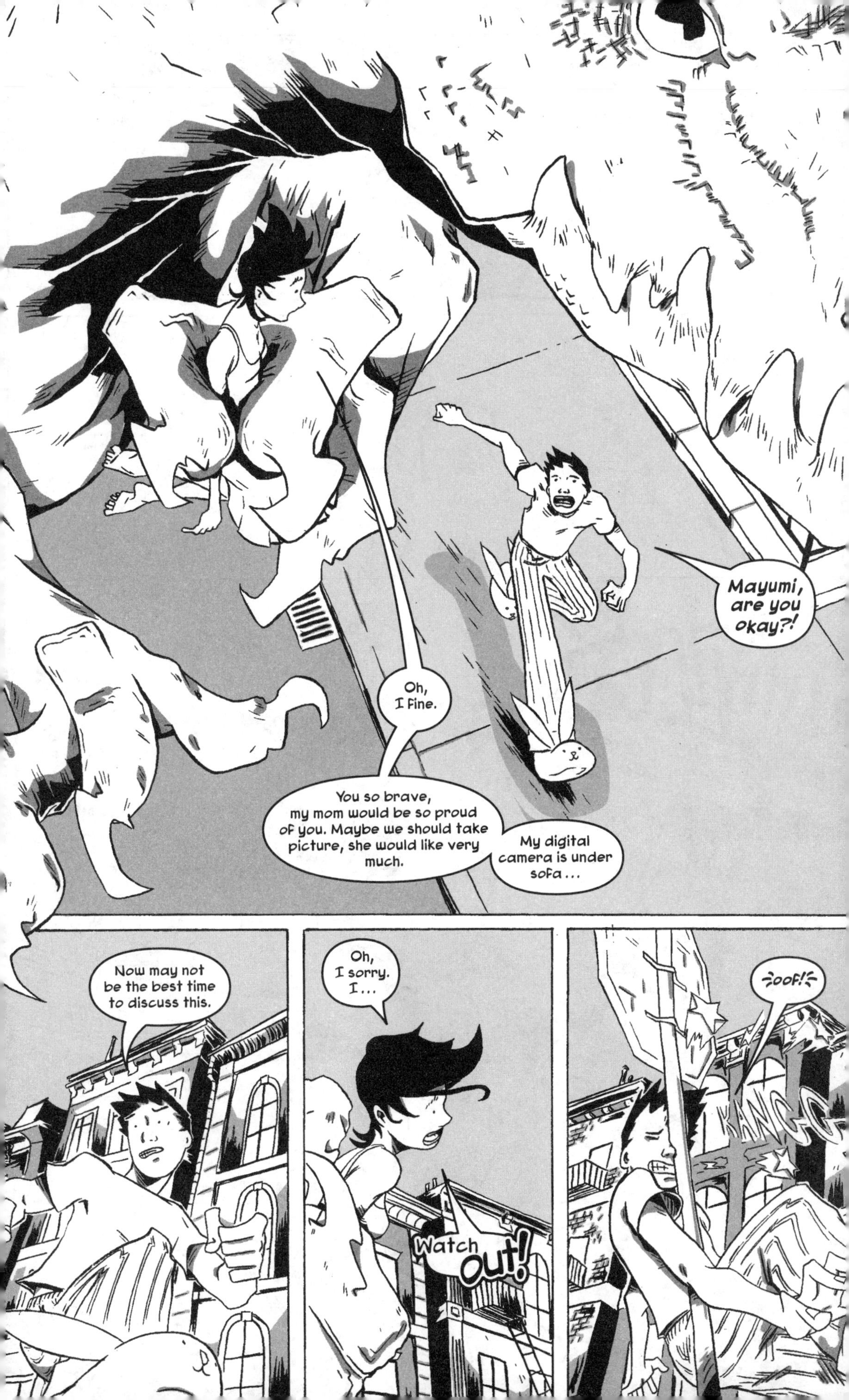
Mayumi, are you okay?!
Oh, I fine.
You so brave, my mom would be so proud of you. Maybe we should take picture, she would like very much.
My digital camera is under sofa...
Now may not be the best time to discuss this.
Oh, I sorry. I...
Watch out!
oof!

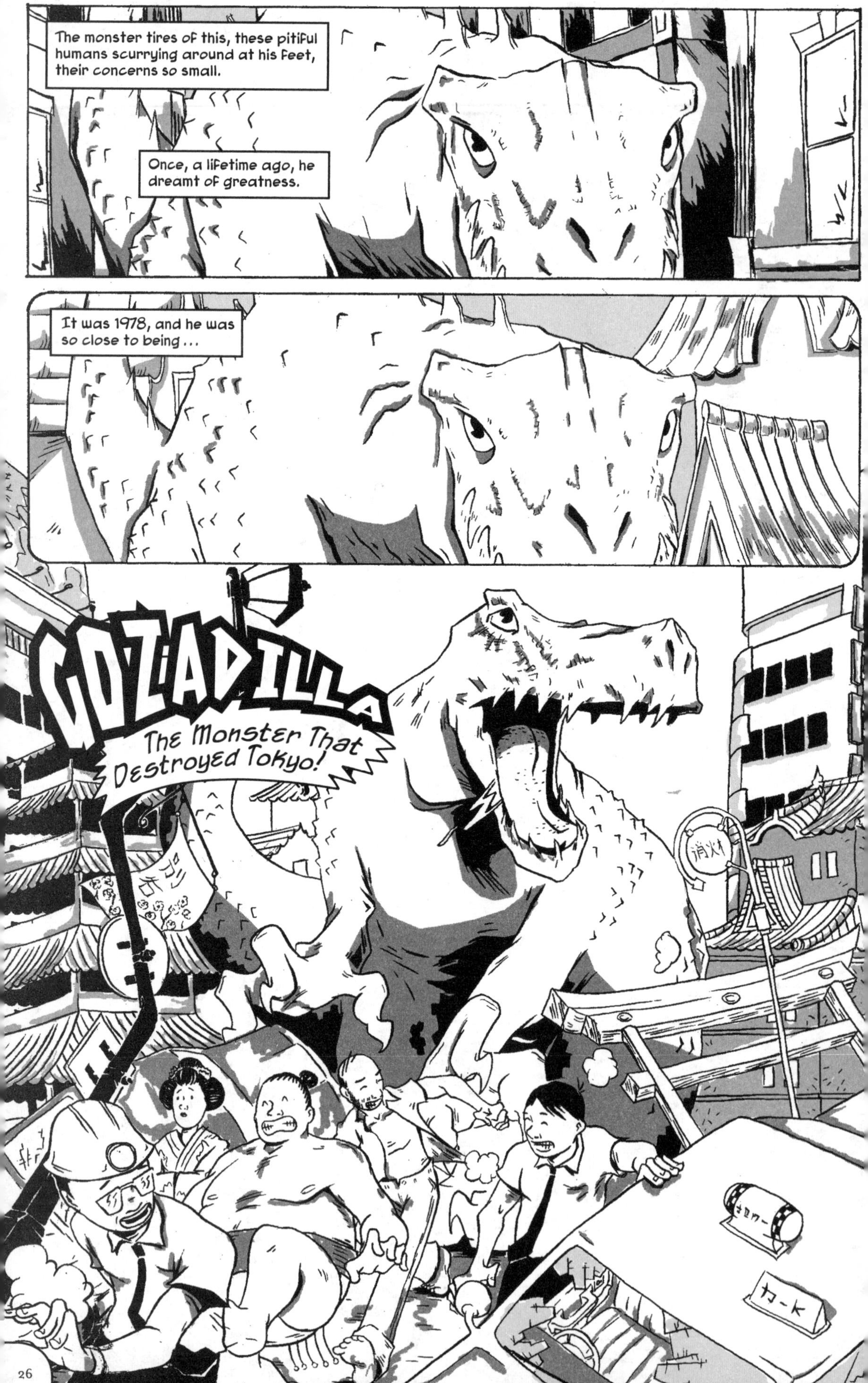
The monster tires of this, these pitiful humans scurrying around at his feet, their concerns so small.
Once, a lifetime ago, he dreamt of greatness.
It was 1978, and he was so close to being...
GOZADILLA
The Monster That Destroyed Tokyo!

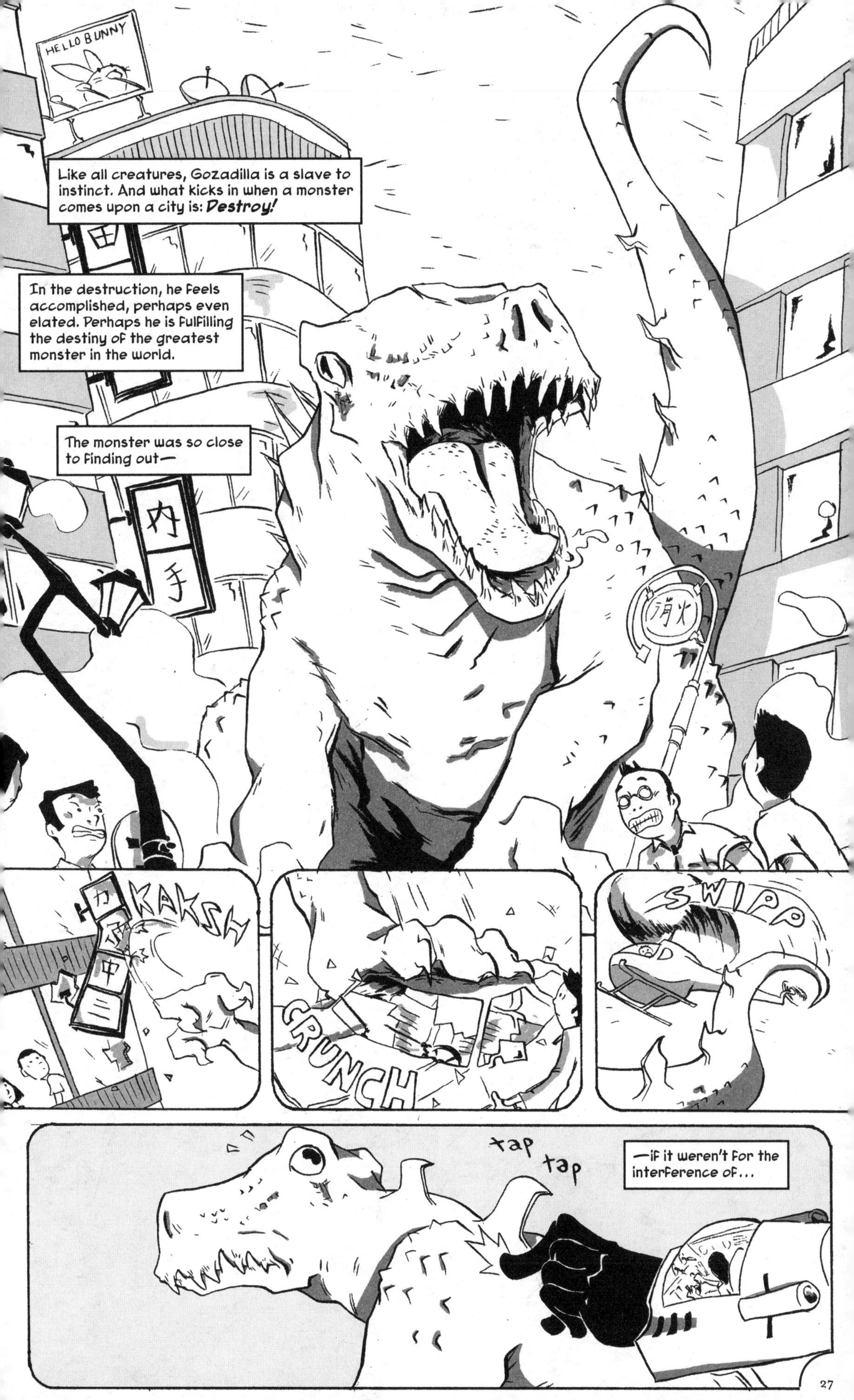
HELLO BUNNY
Like all creatures, Gozadilla is a slave to instinct. And what kicks in when a monster comes upon a city is: Destroy!
In the destruction, he feels accomplished, perhaps even elated. Perhaps he is fulfilling the destiny of the greatest monster in the world.
The monster was so close to finding out—
内
手
消火
KAKSH
CRUNCH
SWIPP
tap
tap
—if it weren't for the interference of...

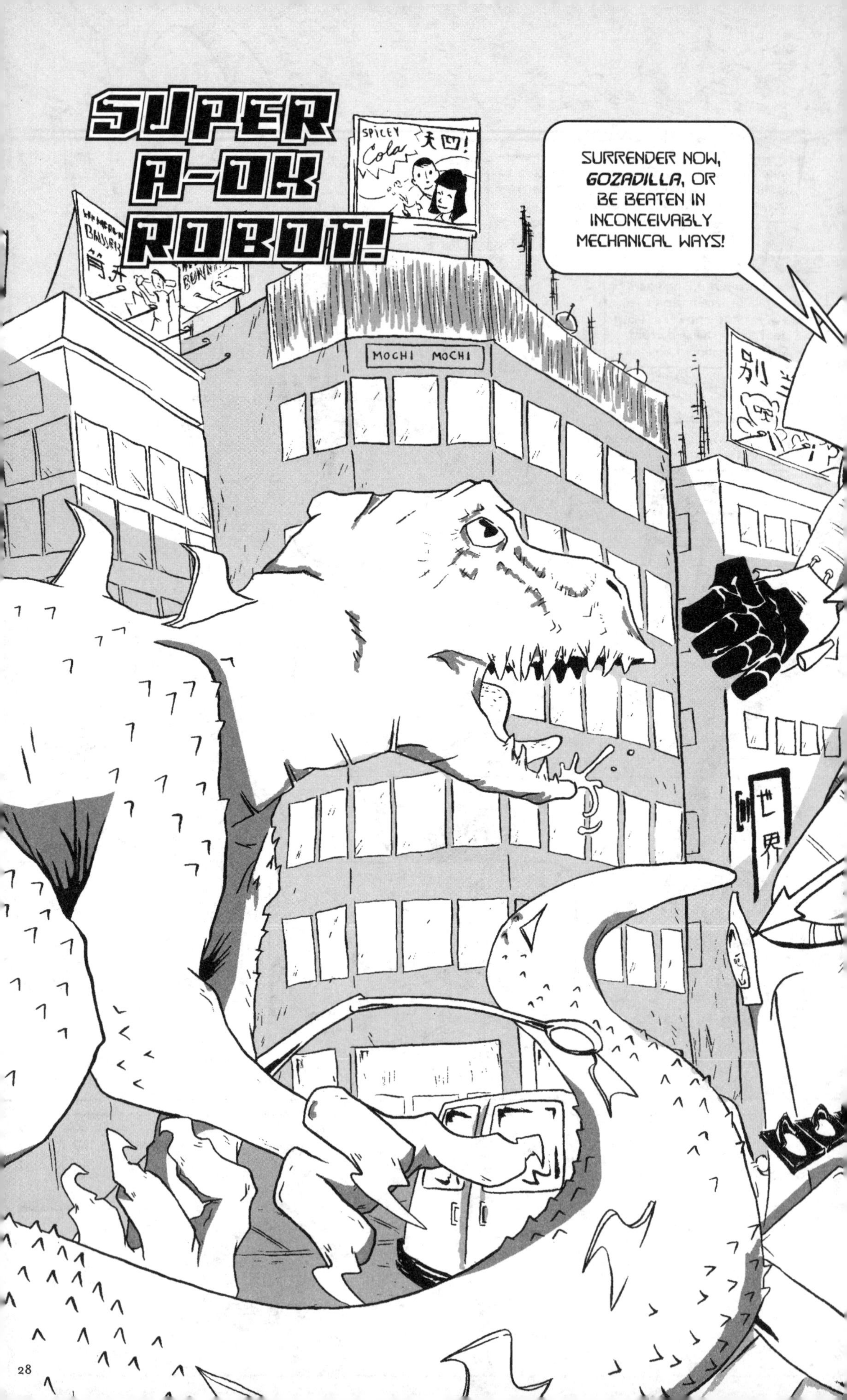
SUPER A-OK ROBOT!
SPICEY Cola
MOCHI MOCHI
SURRENDER NOW, *GOZADILLA*, OR BE BEATEN IN INCONCEIVABLY MECHANICAL WAYS!

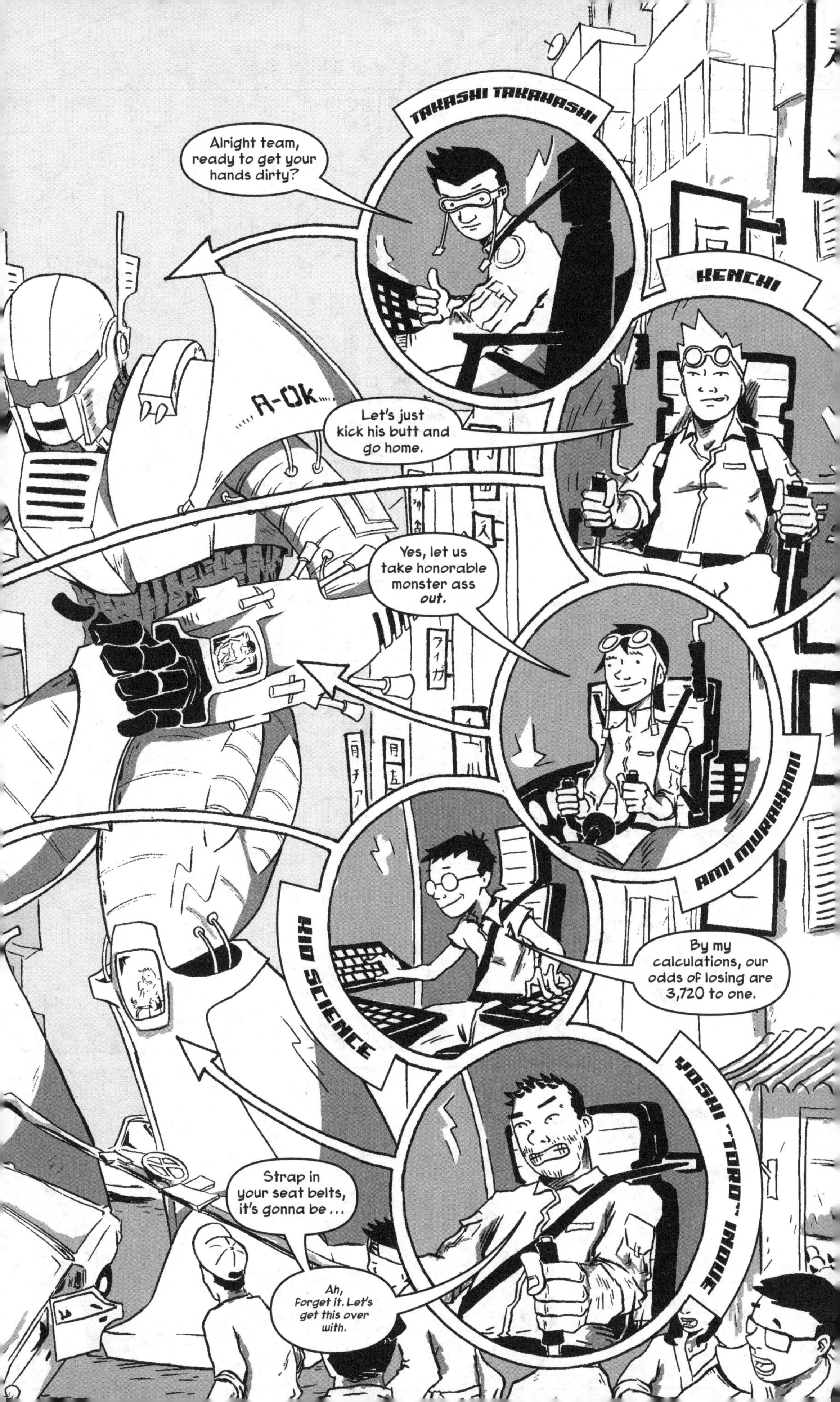

TAKASHI TAKAHASHI
Alright team, ready to get your hands dirty?
KENCHI
A-Ok
Let's just kick his butt and go home.
Yes, let us take honorable monster ass out.
AMI MURAKAMI
KID SCIENCE
By my calculations, our odds of losing are 3,720 to one.
YOSHI "TORO" INOUE
Strap in your seat belts, it's gonna be . . .
Ah, forget it. Let's get this over with.

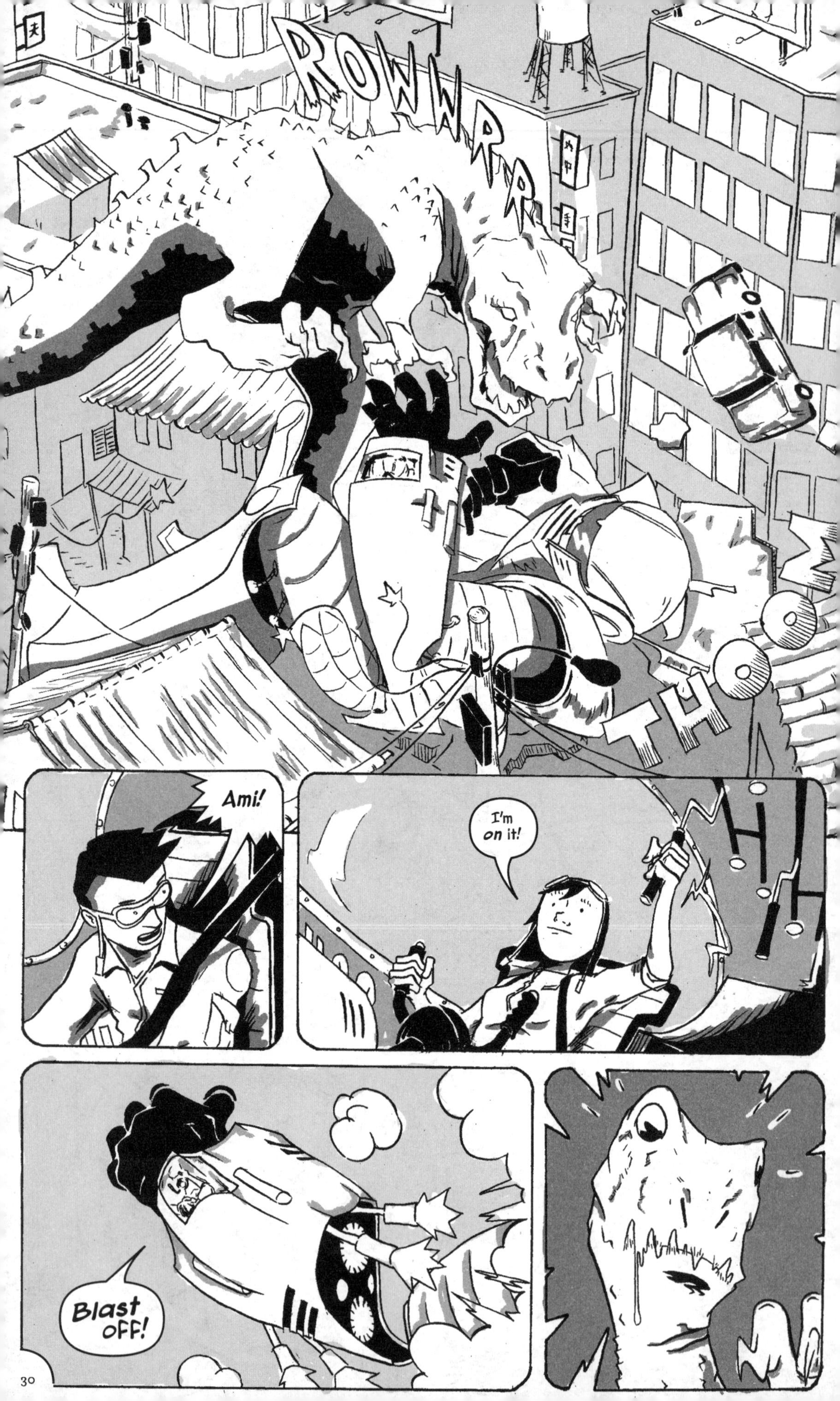
ROWWRR
THOOM
Ami!
I'm on it!
Blast OFF!

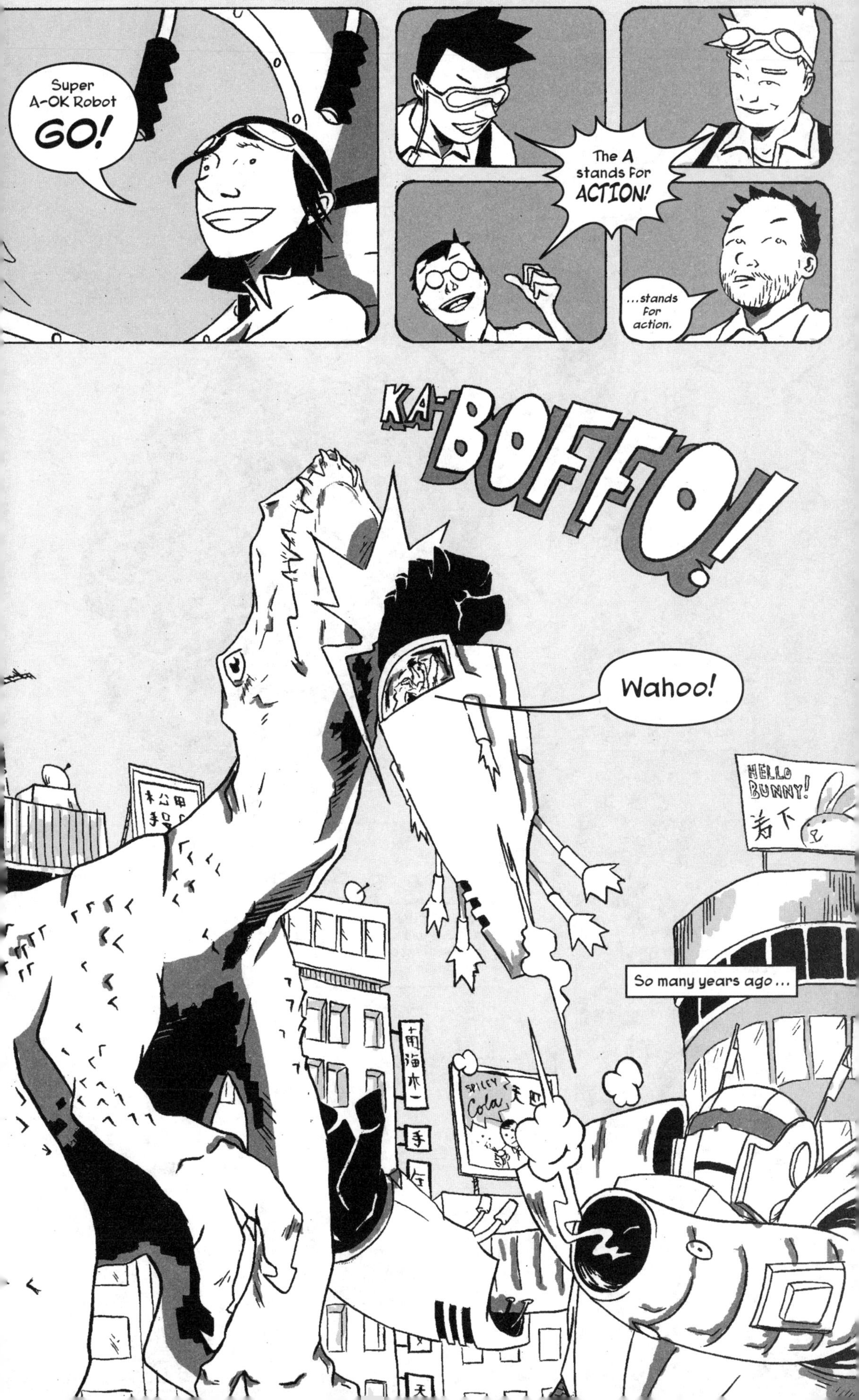
Super A-OK Robot GO!
The A stands for ACTION!
...stands for action.
KA-BOFFO!
Wahoo!
HELLO BUNNY!
SPILEY Cola
So many years ago...

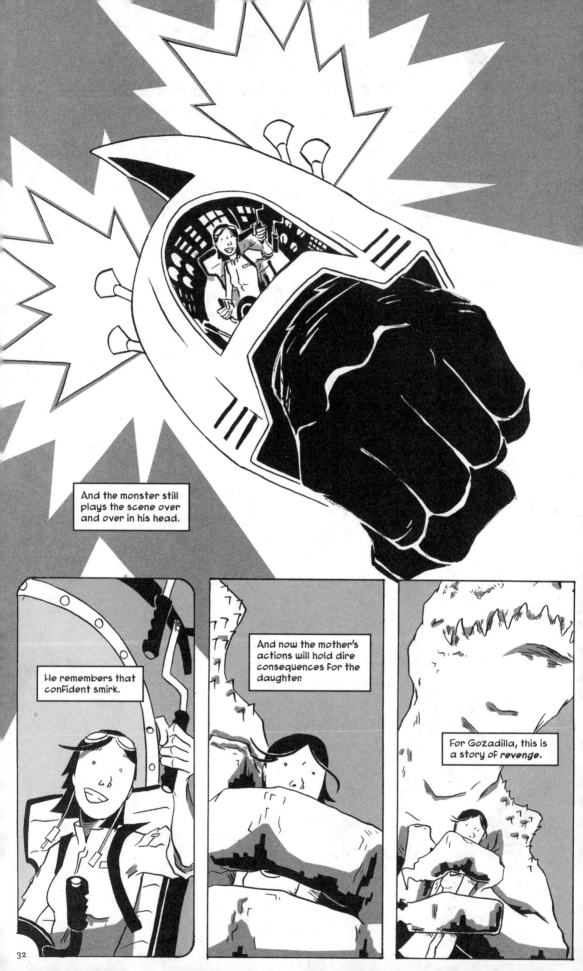

And the monster still plays the scene over and over in his head.

He remembers that confident smirk.

And now the mother's actions will hold dire consequences for the daughter.

For Gozadilla, this is a story of *revenge*.

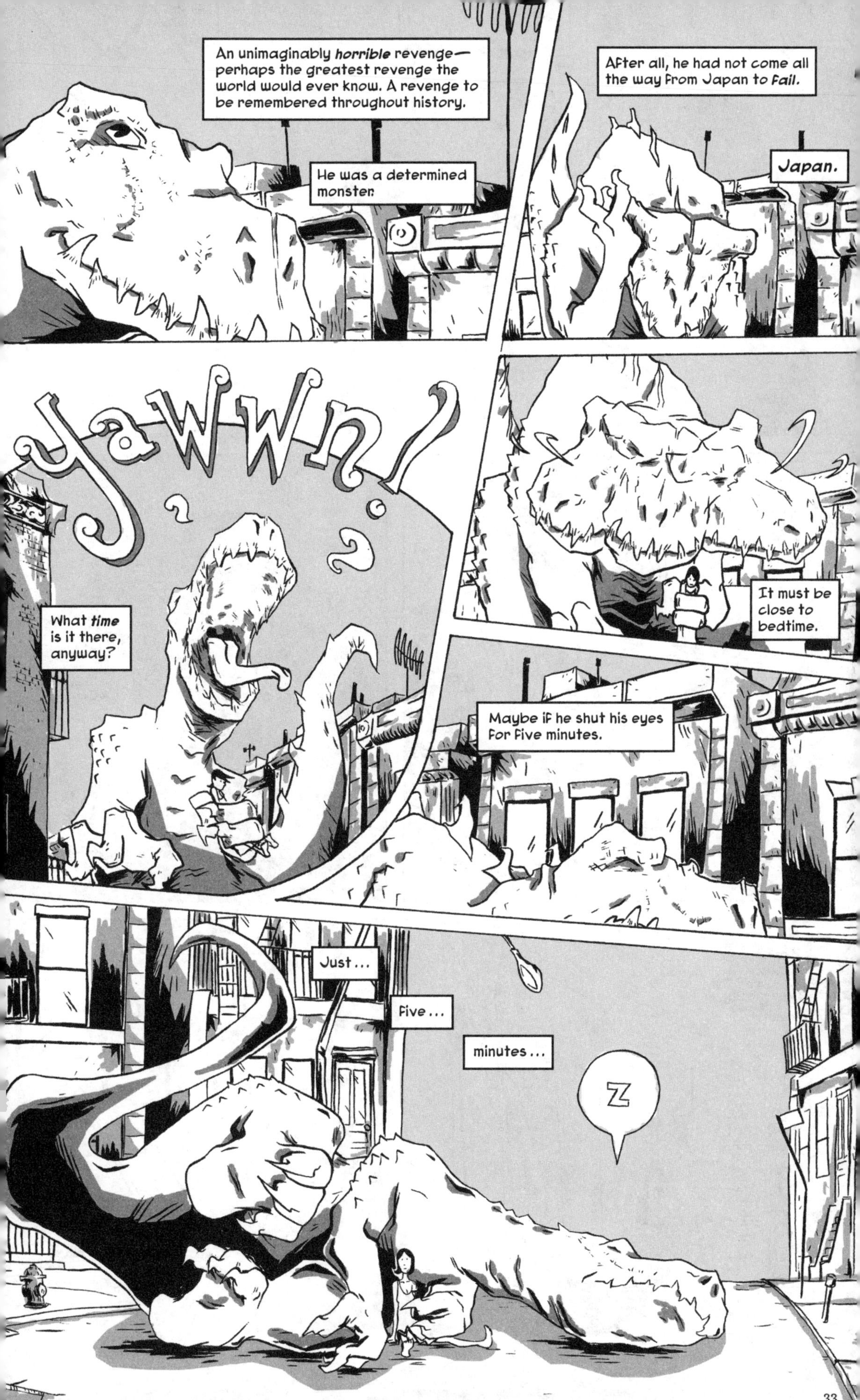

An unimaginably *horrible* revenge—perhaps the greatest revenge the world would ever know. A revenge to be remembered throughout history.
He was a determined monster.
After all, he had not come all the way from Japan to *fail.*
Japan.
YAWWN!
What *time* is it there, anyway?
It must be close to bedtime.
Maybe if he shut his eyes for five minutes.
Just...
five...
minutes...
Z

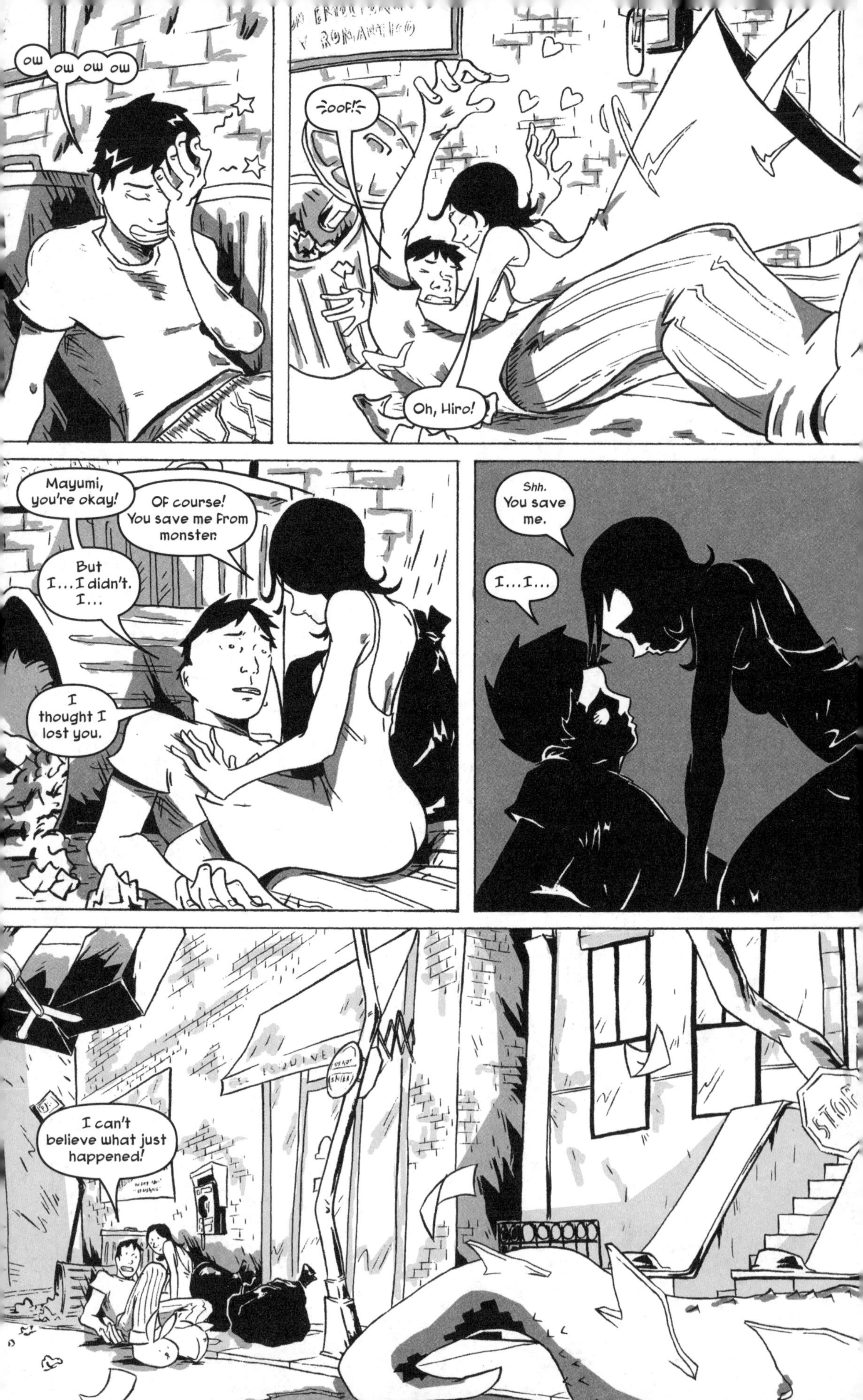
ow
ow ow ow
OOF!
Oh, Hiro!
Mayumi, you're okay!
Of course! You save me from monster.
But I... I didn't. I...
I thought I lost you.
Shh. You save me.
I... I...
I can't believe what just happened!

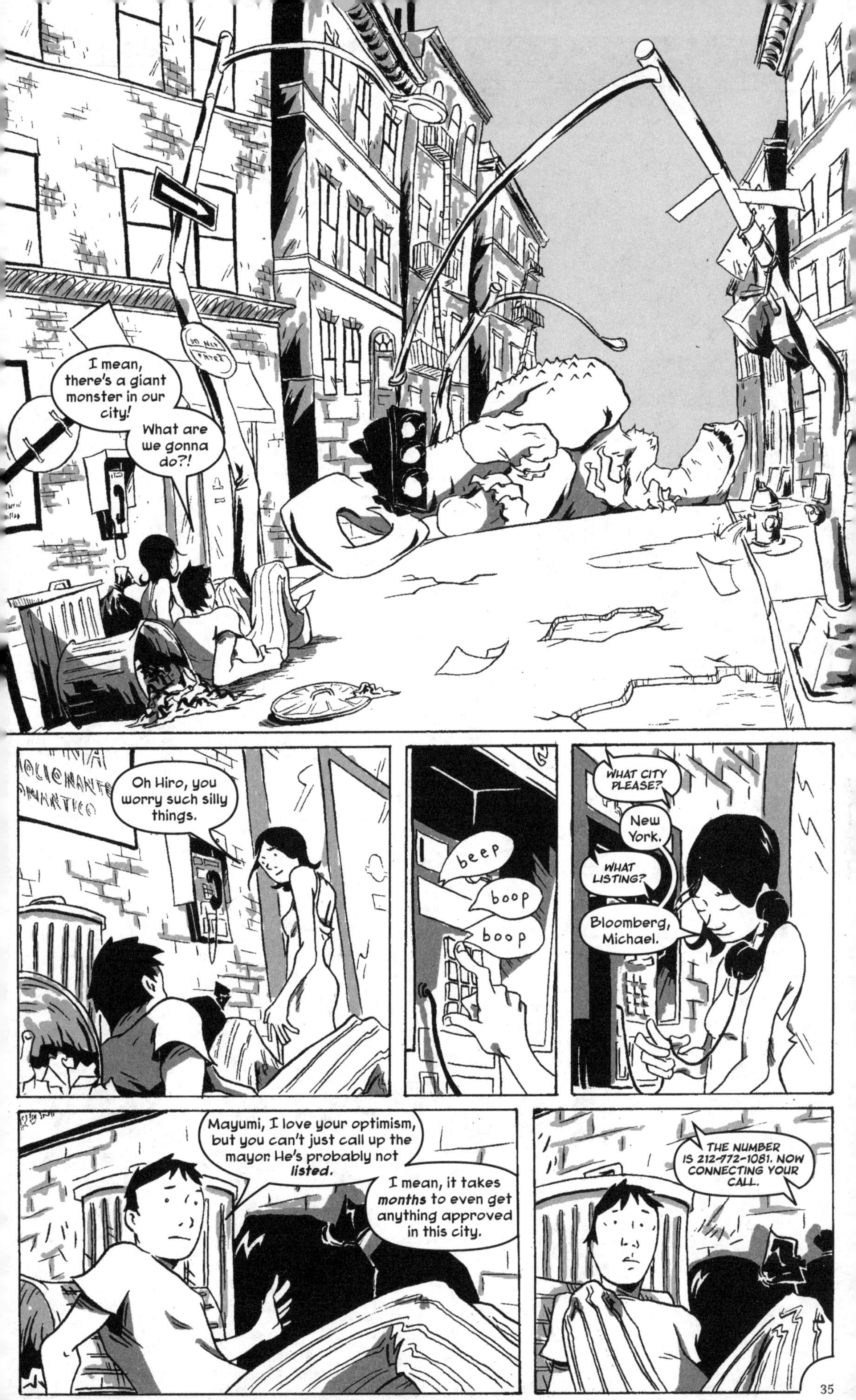
I mean, there's a giant monster in our city!
What are we gonna do?!
Oh Hiro, you worry such silly things.
beep
boop
boop
WHAT CITY PLEASE?
New York.
WHAT LISTING?
Bloomberg, Michael.
Mayumi, I love your optimism, but you can't just call up the mayor. He's probably not *listed*.
I mean, it takes *months* to even get anything approved in this city.
THE NUMBER IS 212-772-1081. NOW CONNECTING YOUR CALL.

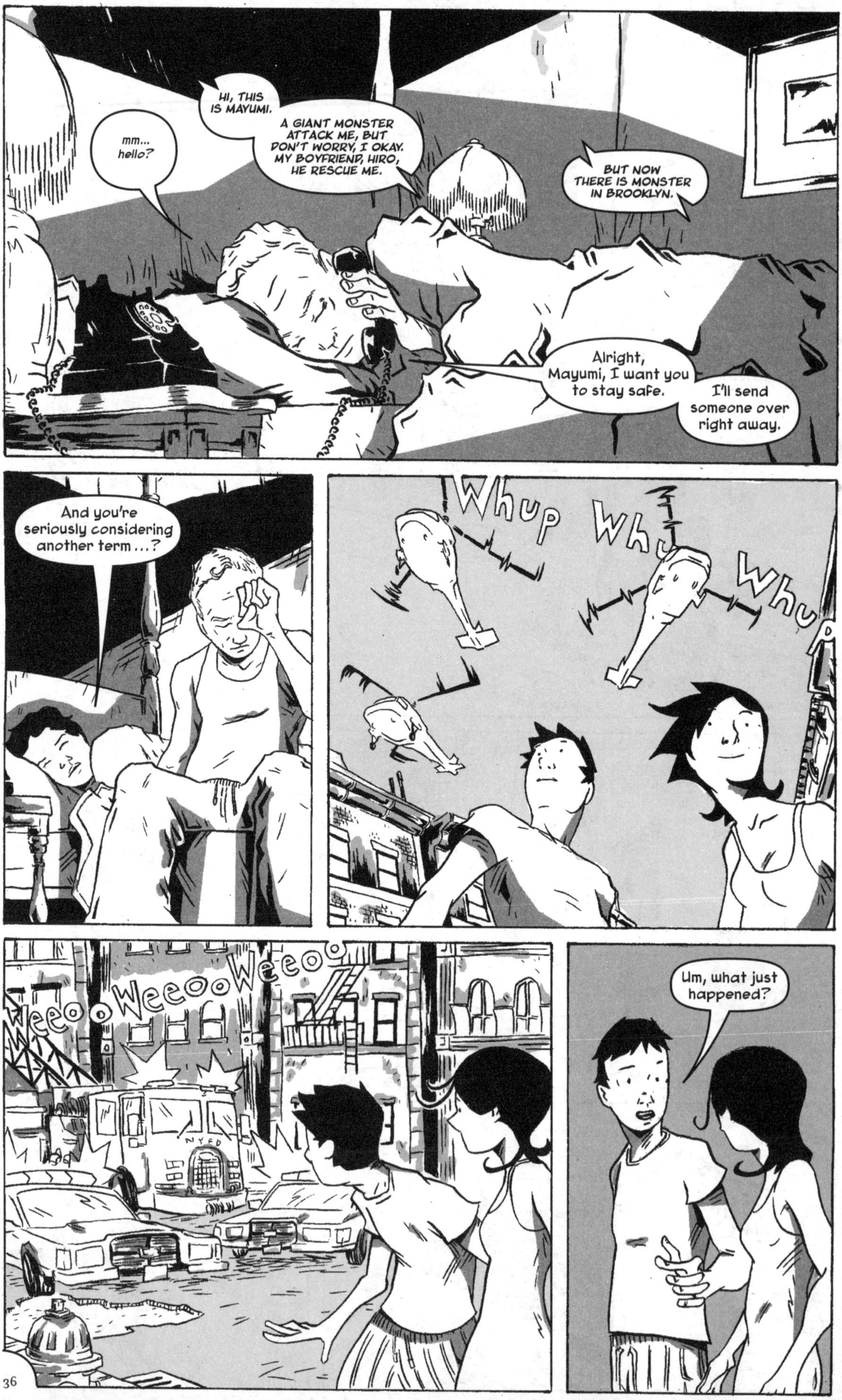
mm... hello?
HI, THIS IS MAYUMI.
A GIANT MONSTER ATTACK ME, BUT DON'T WORRY, I OKAY. MY BOYFRIEND, HIRO, HE RESCUE ME.
BUT NOW THERE IS MONSTER IN BROOKLYN.
Alright, Mayumi, I want you to stay safe.
I'll send someone over right away.
And you're seriously considering another term ...?
Whup
Whup
Weeo
Weeoo
Weeoo
NYFD
Um, what just happened?

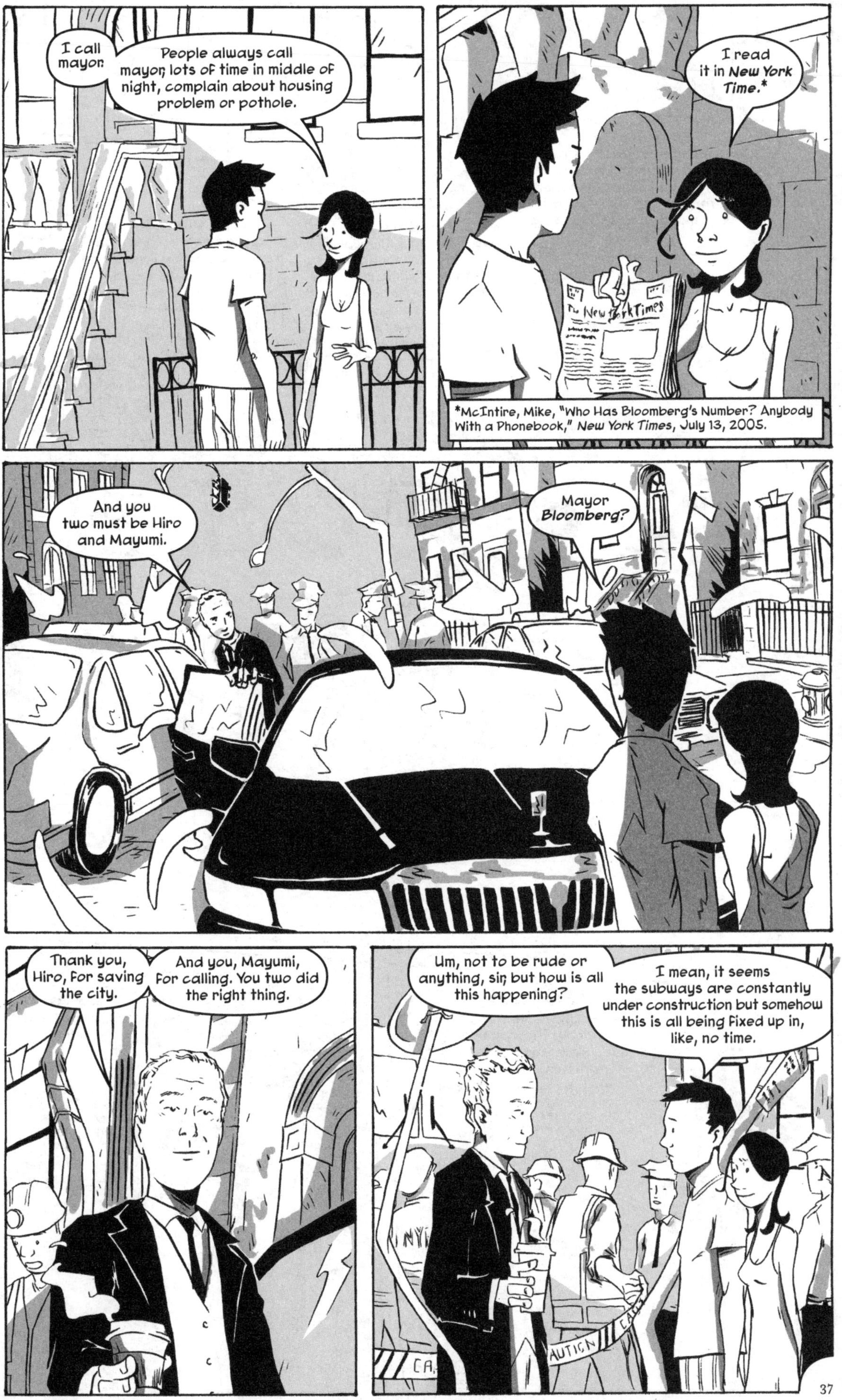
I call mayor.
People always call mayor, lots of time in middle of night, complain about housing problem or pothole.
I read it in New York Time.*
The New York Times
*McIntire, Mike, "Who Has Bloomberg's Number? Anybody With a Phonebook," New York Times, July 13, 2005.
And you two must be Hiro and Mayumi.
Mayor Bloomberg?
Thank you, Hiro, for saving the city.
And you, Mayumi, for calling. You two did the right thing.
Um, not to be rude or anything, sir, but how is all this happening?
I mean, it seems the subways are constantly under construction but somehow this is all being fixed up in, like, no time.

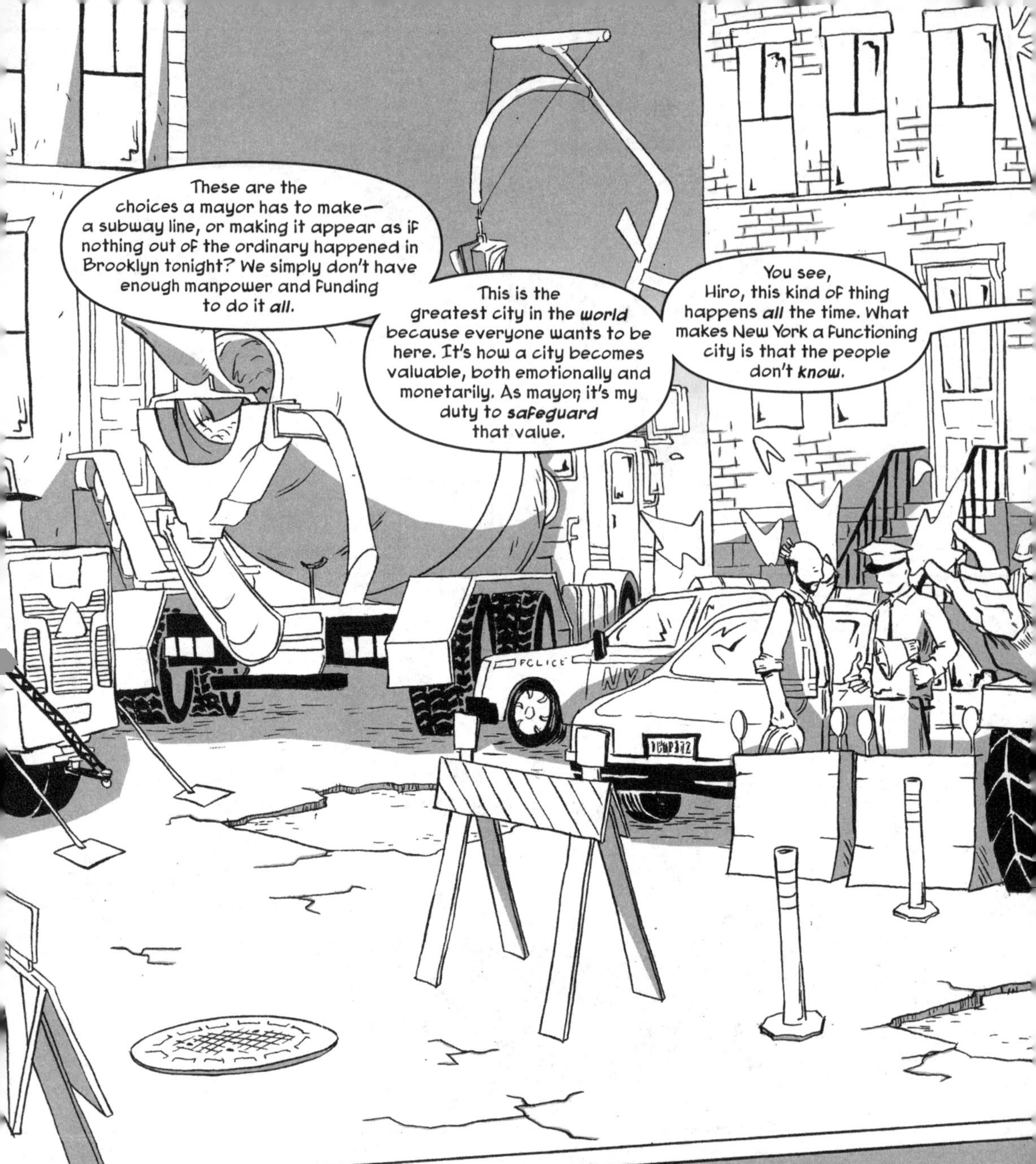
These are the choices a mayor has to make—a subway line, or making it appear as if nothing out of the ordinary happened in Brooklyn tonight? We simply don't have enough manpower and funding to do it *all*.
This is the greatest city in the *world* because everyone wants to be here. It's how a city becomes valuable, both emotionally and monetarily. As mayor, it's my duty to *safeguard* that value.
You see, Hiro, this kind of thing happens *all* the time. What makes New York a functioning city is that the people don't *know*.
POLICE
NYP

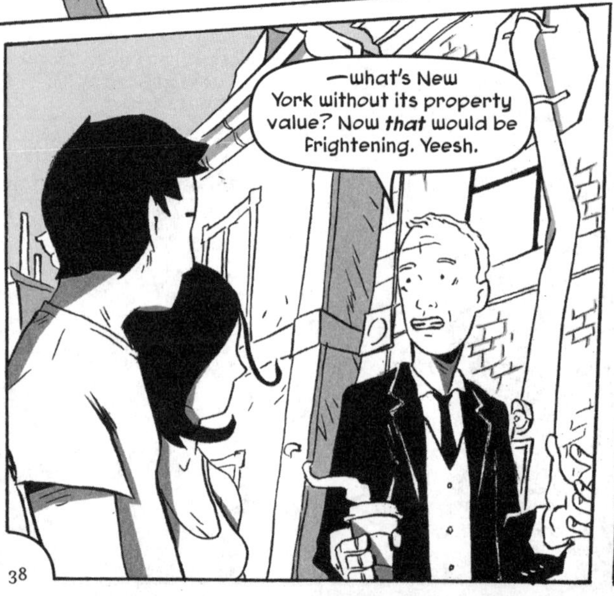
—what's New York without its property value? Now *that* would be frightening. Yeesh.

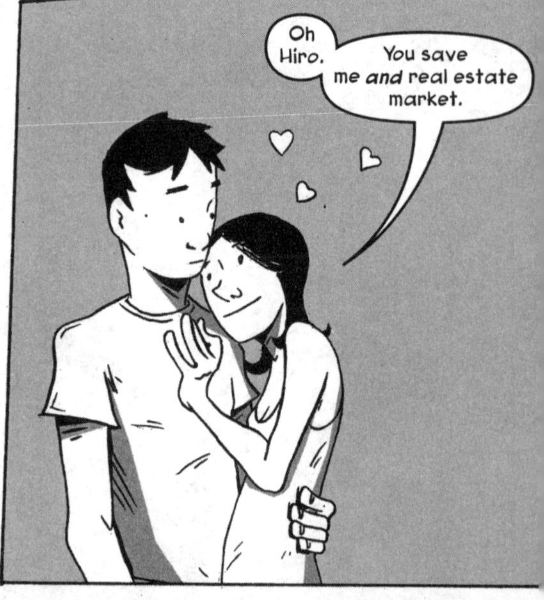
Oh Hiro.
You save me *and* real estate market.

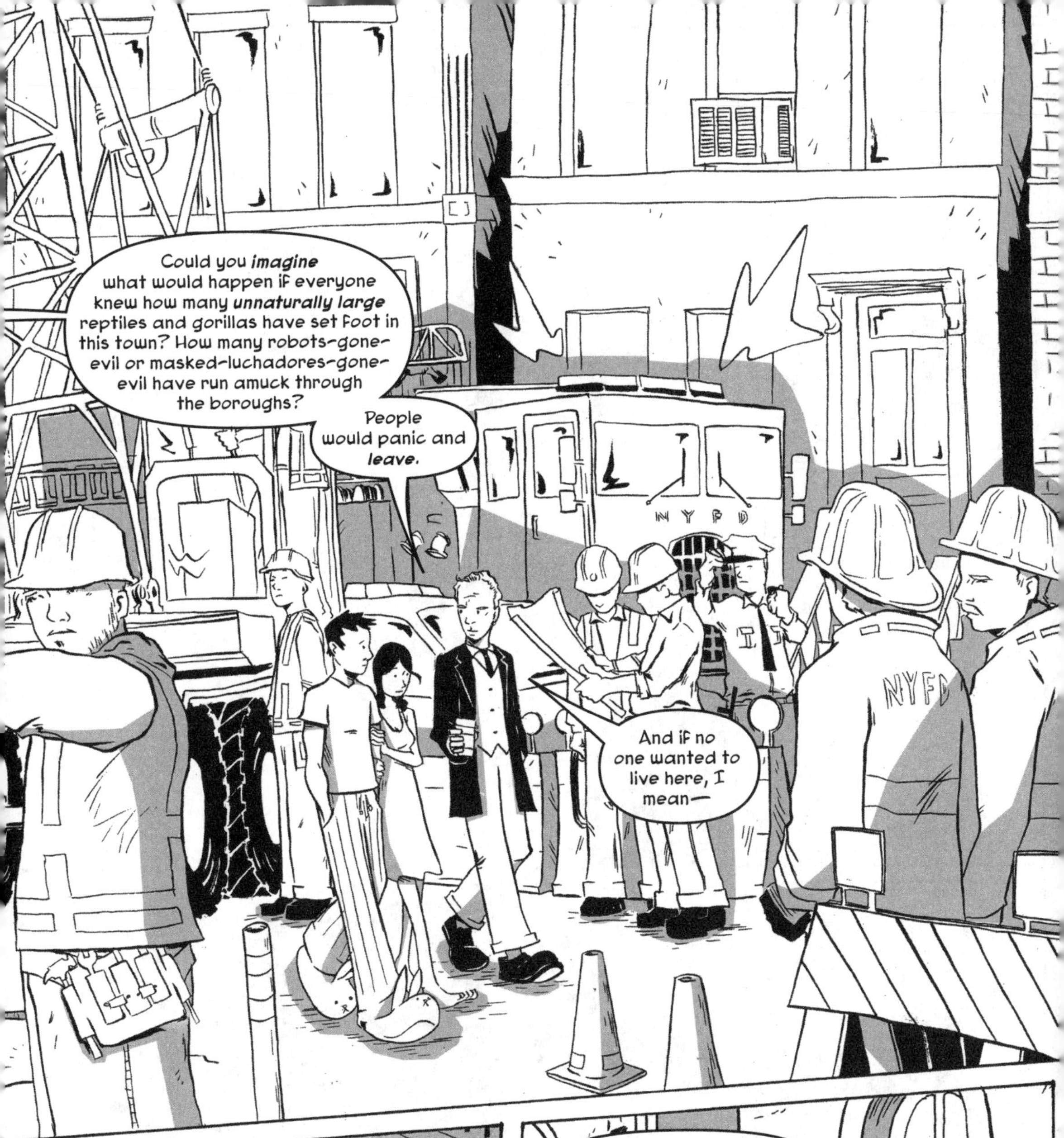
Could you *imagine* what would happen if everyone knew how many *unnaturally large* reptiles and gorillas have set foot in this town? How many robots-gone-evil or masked-luchadores-gone-evil have run amuck through the boroughs?
People would panic and *leave.*
NYPD
NYFD
And if no one wanted to live here, I mean—

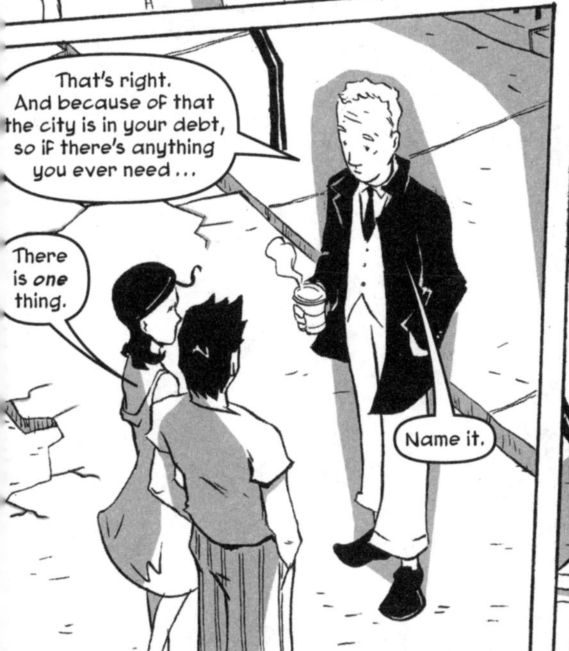
That's right. And because of that the city is in your debt, so if there's anything you ever need . . .
There is *one* thing.
Name it.

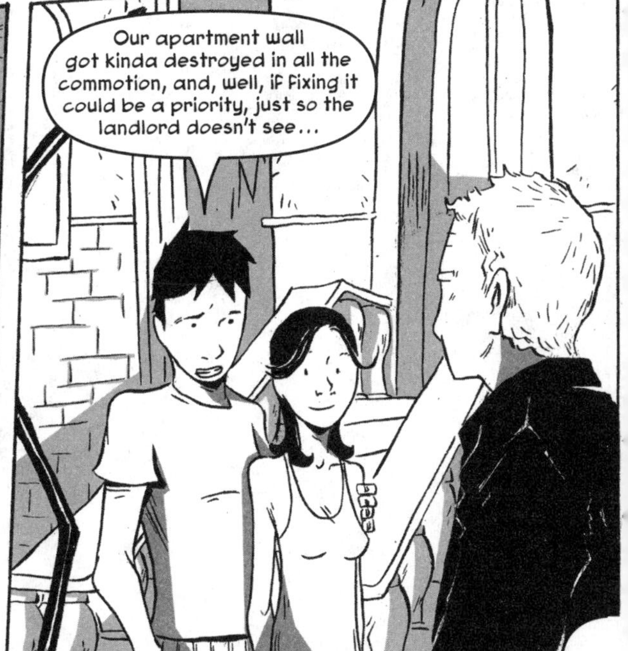
Our apartment wall got kinda destroyed in all the commotion, and, well, if fixing it could be a priority, just so the landlord doesn't see . . .

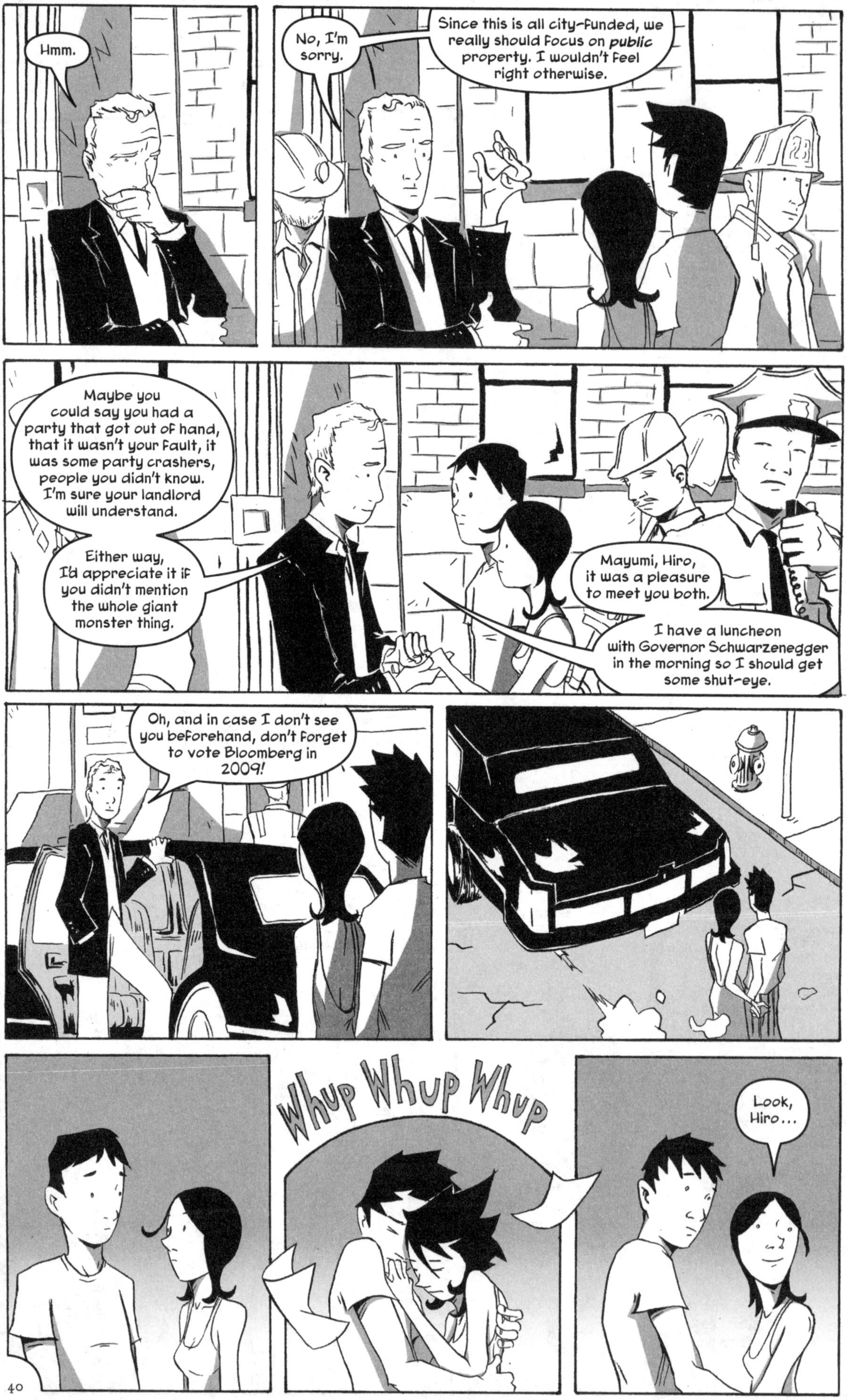
Hmm.
No, I'm sorry.
Since this is all city-funded, we really should focus on *public* property. I wouldn't feel right otherwise.
Maybe you could say you had a party that got out of hand, that it wasn't your fault, it was some party crashers, people you didn't know. I'm sure your landlord will understand.
Either way, I'd appreciate it if you didn't mention the whole giant monster thing.
Mayumi, Hiro, it was a pleasure to meet you both.
I have a luncheon with Governor Schwarzenegger in the morning so I should get some shut-eye.
Oh, and in case I don't see you beforehand, don't forget to vote Bloomberg in 2009!
Whup Whup Whup
Look, Hiro...

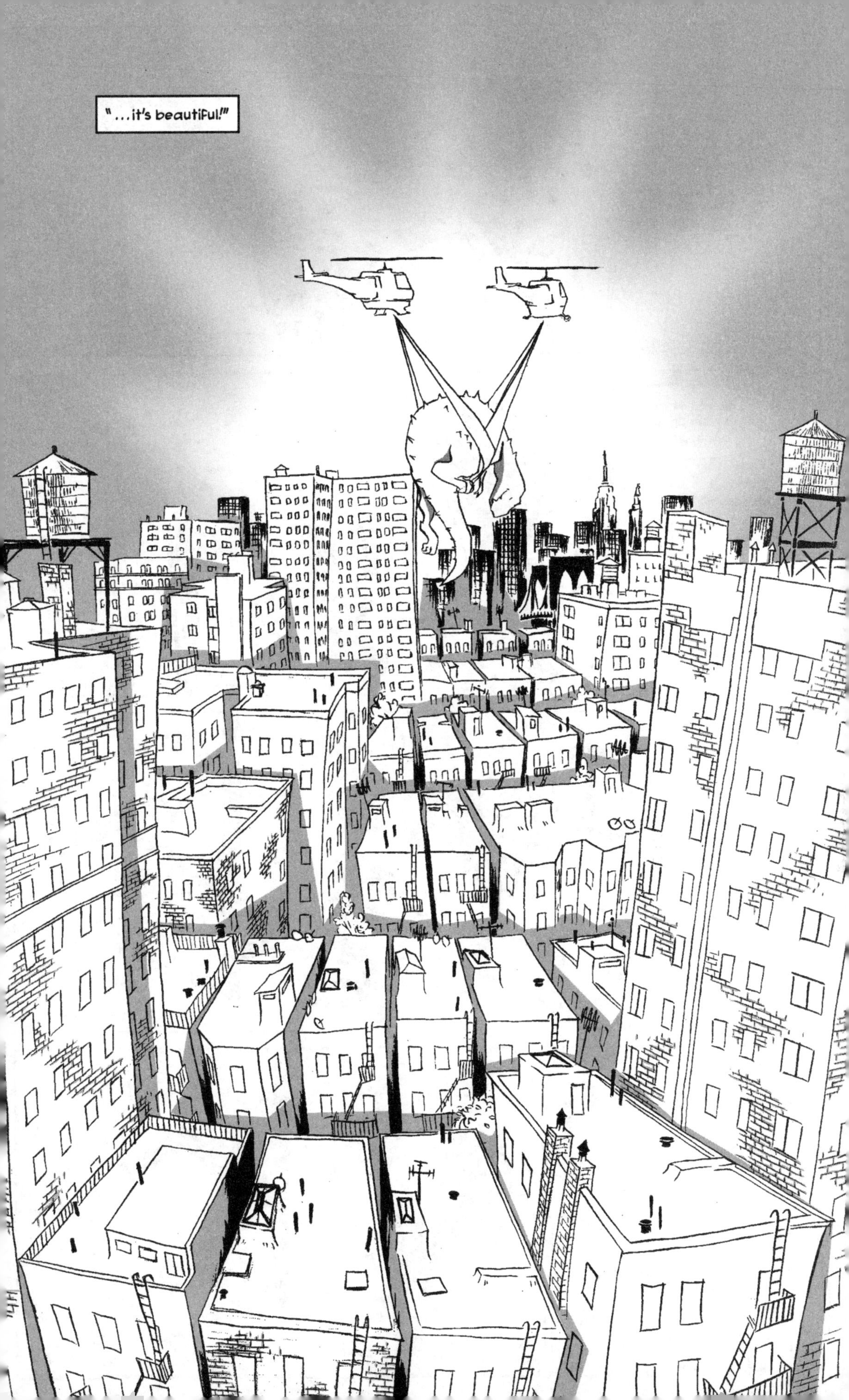
"...it's beautiful!"

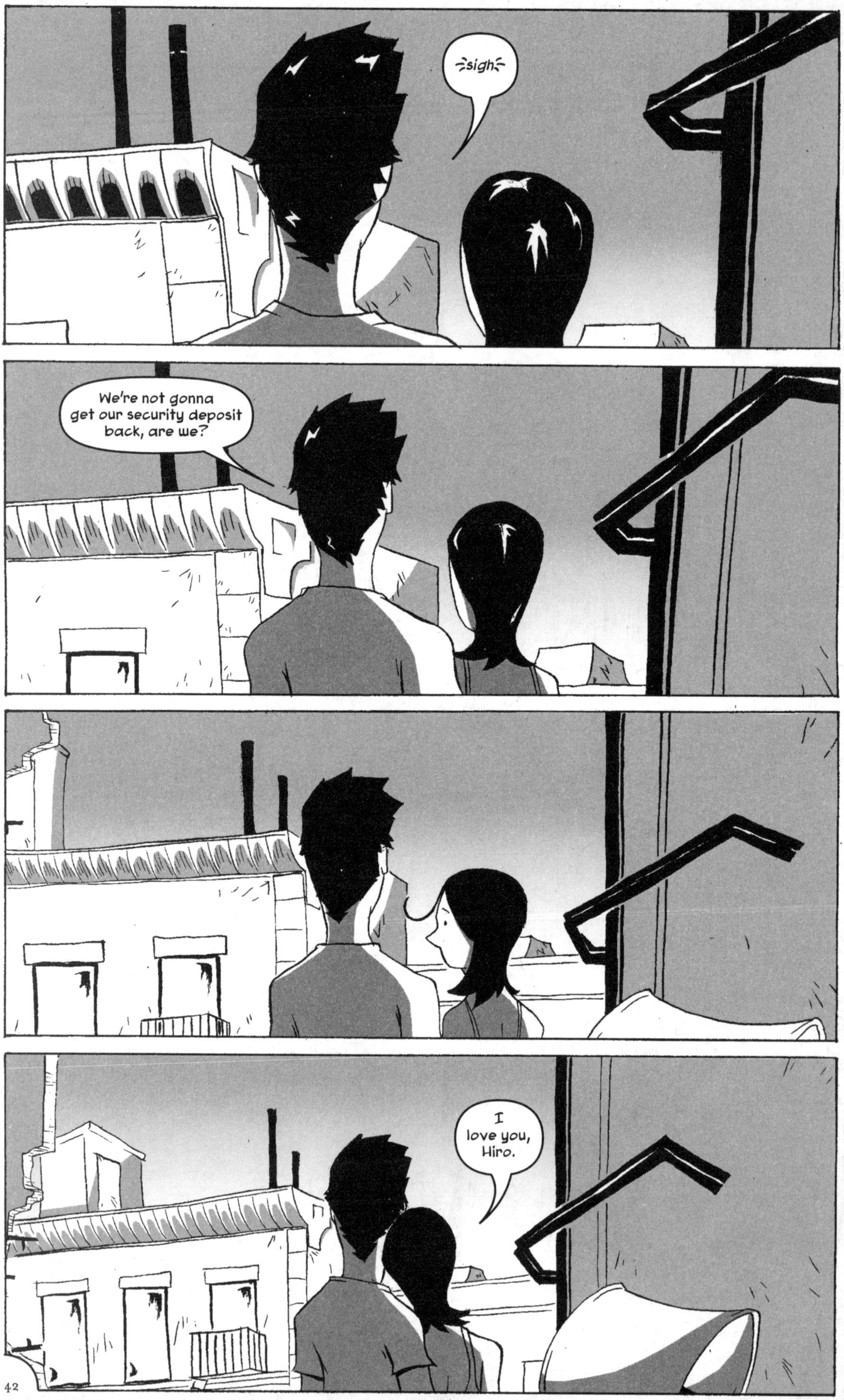
sigh
We're not gonna get our security deposit back, are we?
I love you, Hiro.

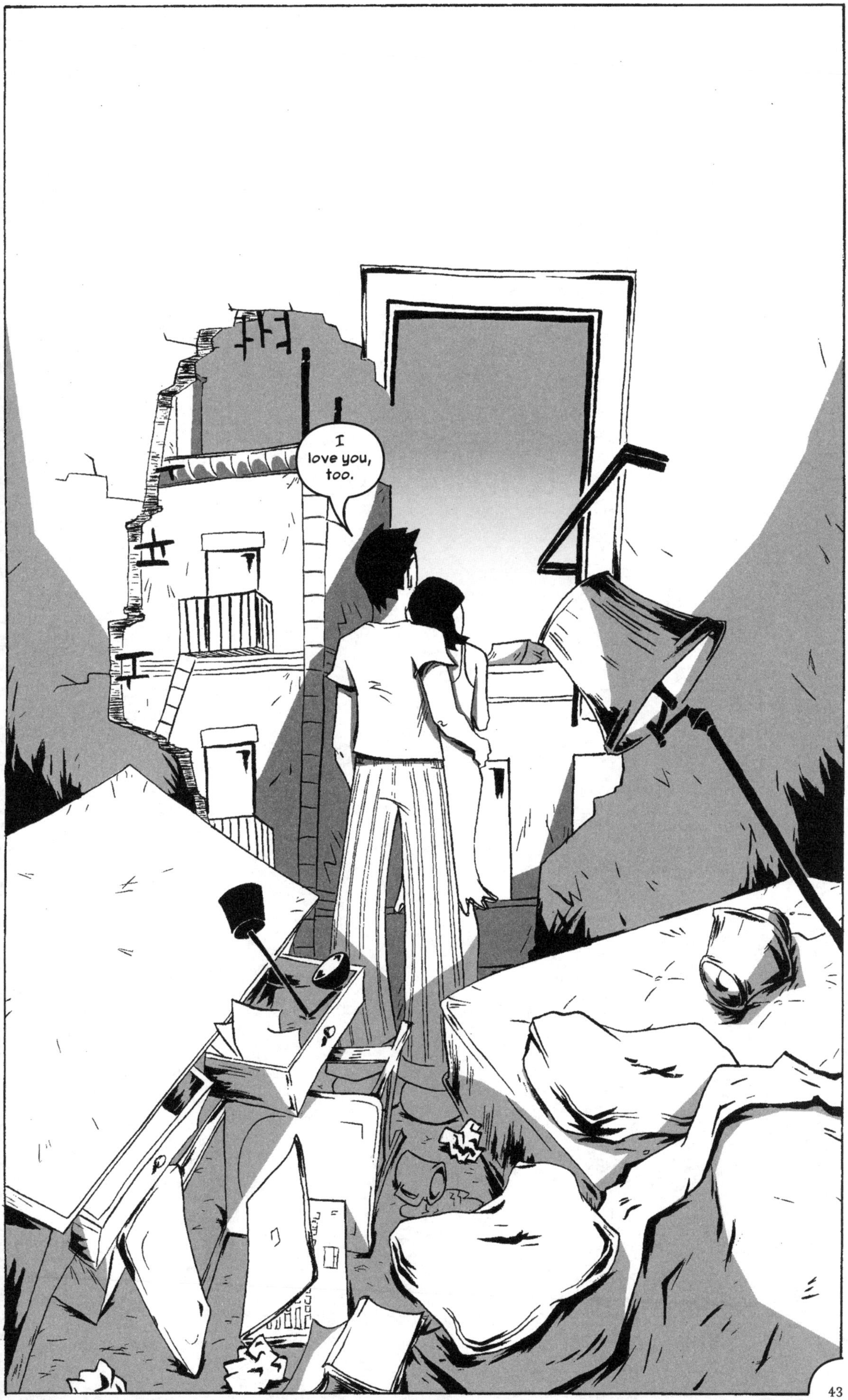
I love you, too.

いせえびのそうぎょう

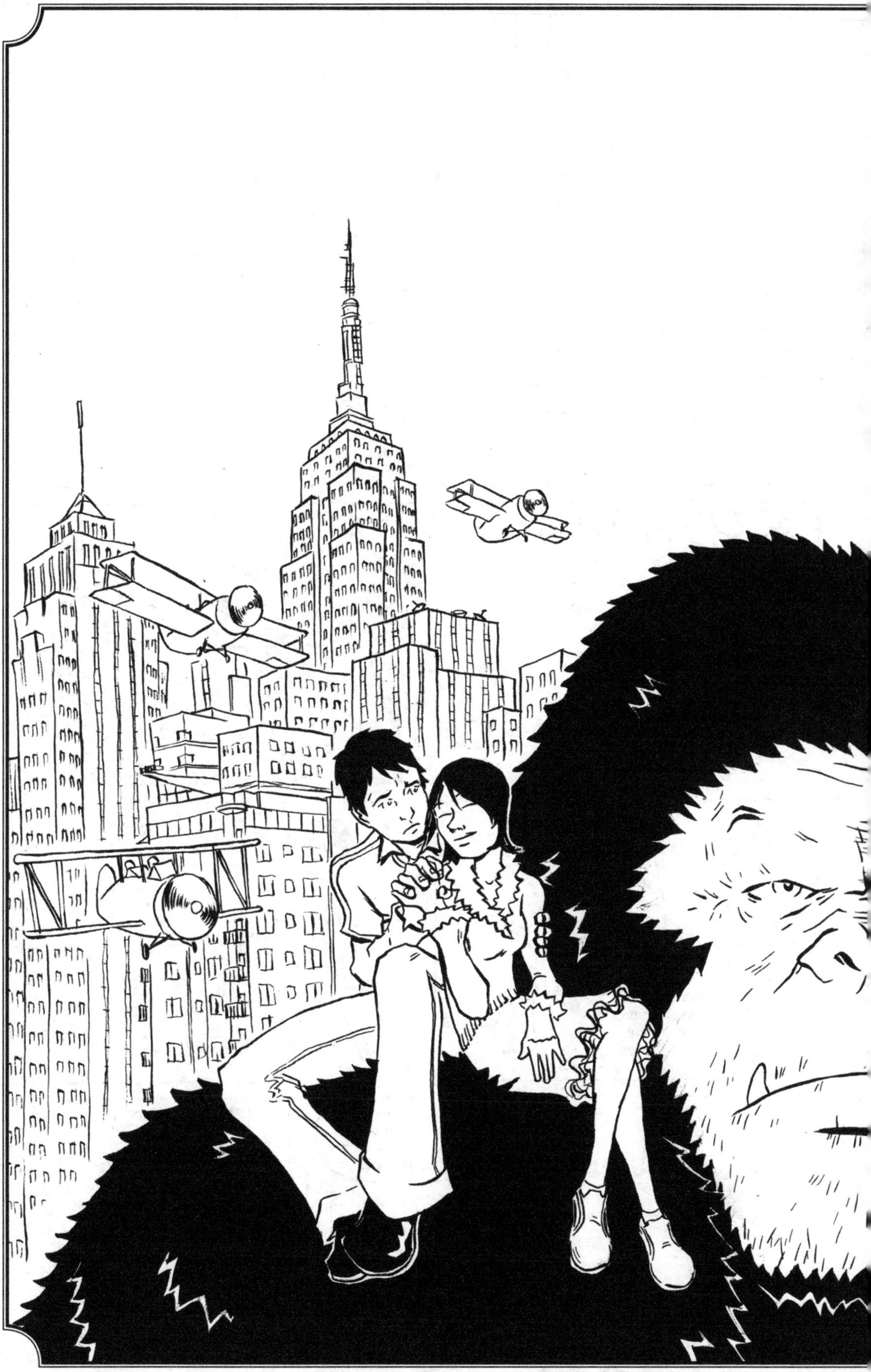

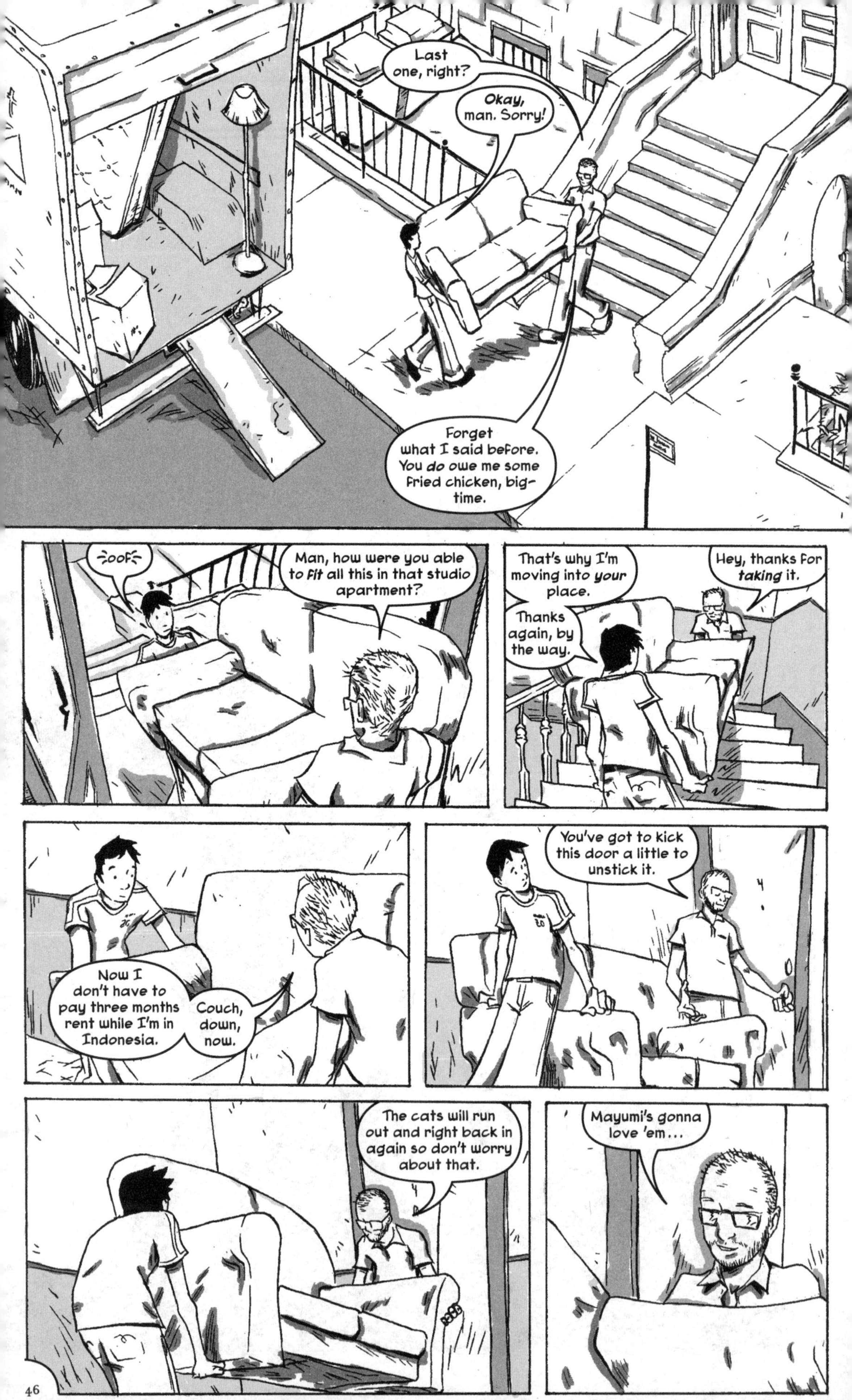

Last one, right?
Okay, man. Sorry!
Forget what I said before. You do owe me some fried chicken, big-time.
oof
Man, how were you able to fit all this in that studio apartment?
That's why I'm moving into your place.
Hey, thanks for taking it.
Thanks again, by the way.
Now I don't have to pay three months rent while I'm in Indonesia.
Couch, down, now.
You've got to kick this door a little to unstick it.
The cats will run out and right back in again so don't worry about that.
Mayumi's gonna love 'em...

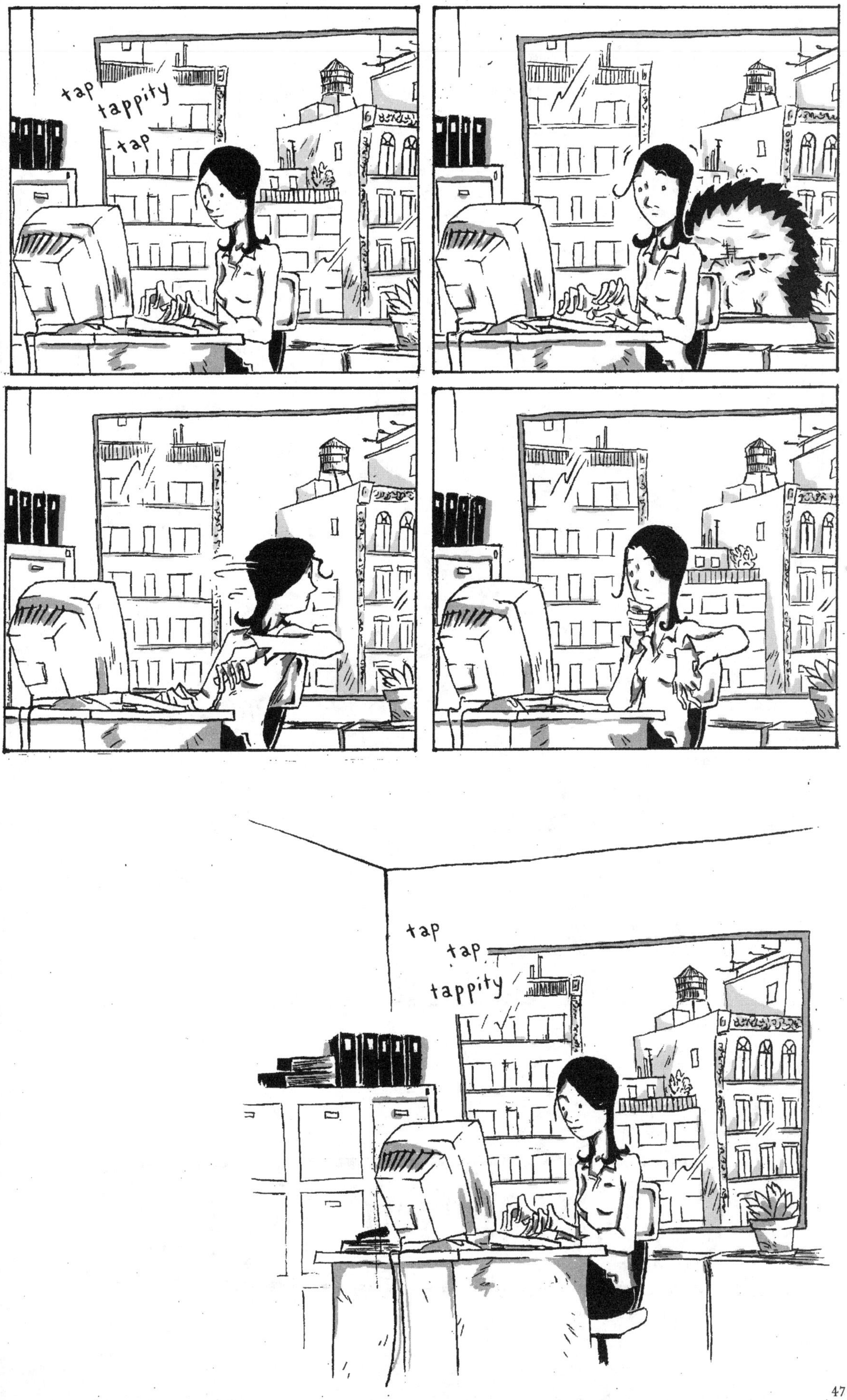
tap
tappity
tap
tap
tap
tappity

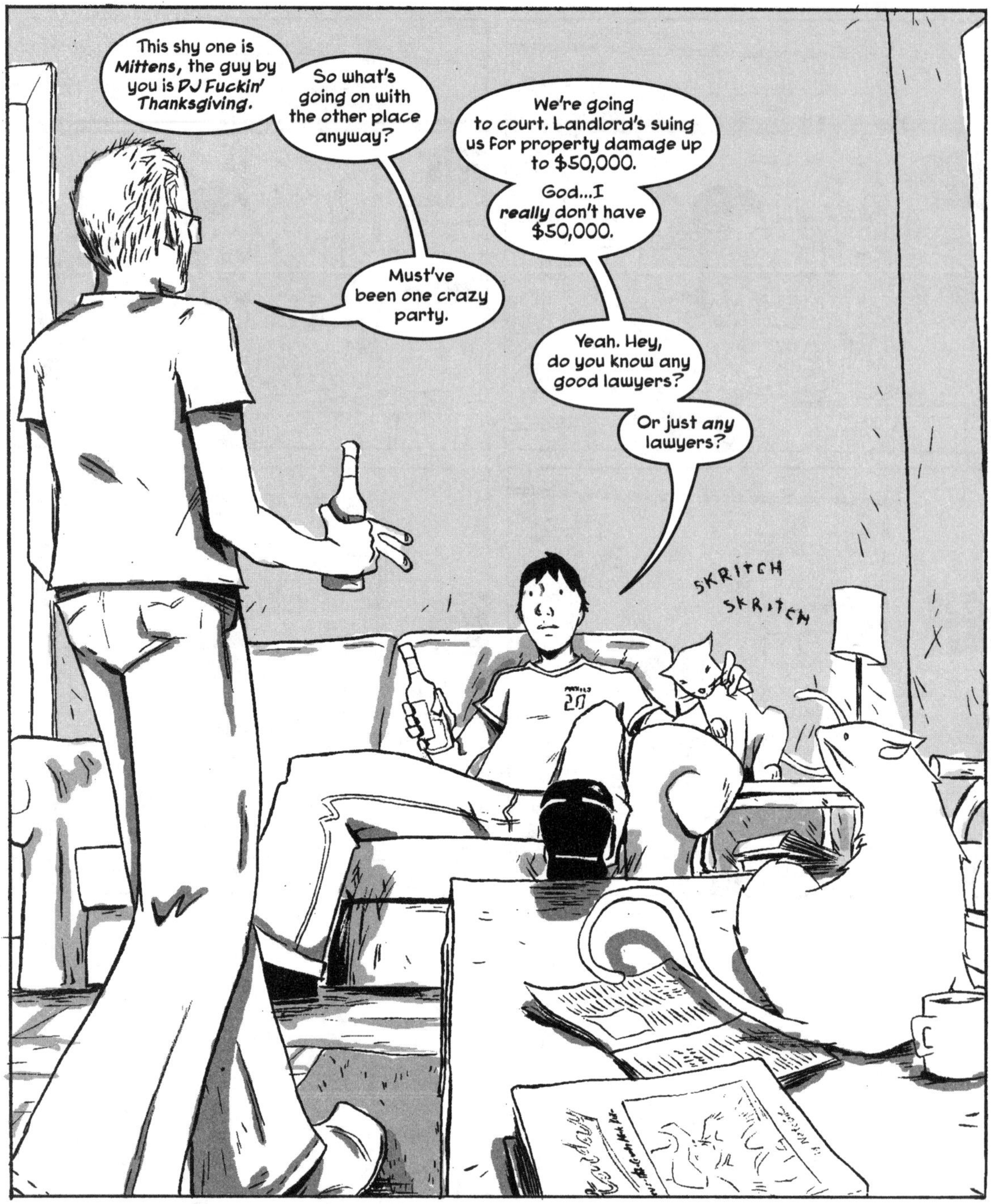
This shy one is *Mittens*, the guy by you is *DJ Fuckin' Thanksgiving*.
So what's going on with the other place anyway?
We're going to court. Landlord's suing us for property damage up to $50,000.
God...I *really* don't have $50,000.
Must've been one crazy party.
Yeah. Hey, do you know any good lawyers?
Or just *any* lawyers?
SKRITCH SKRITCH

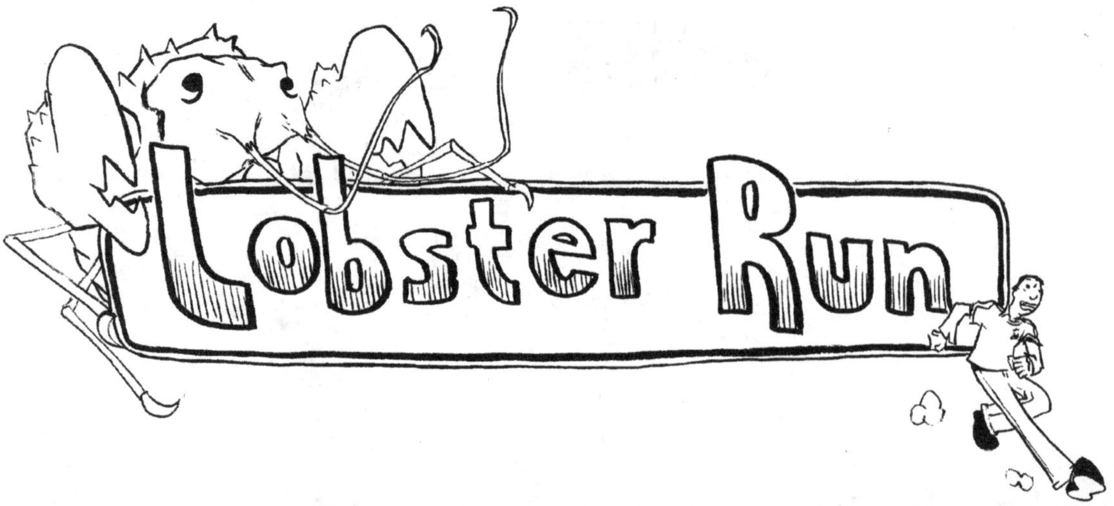
Lobster Run

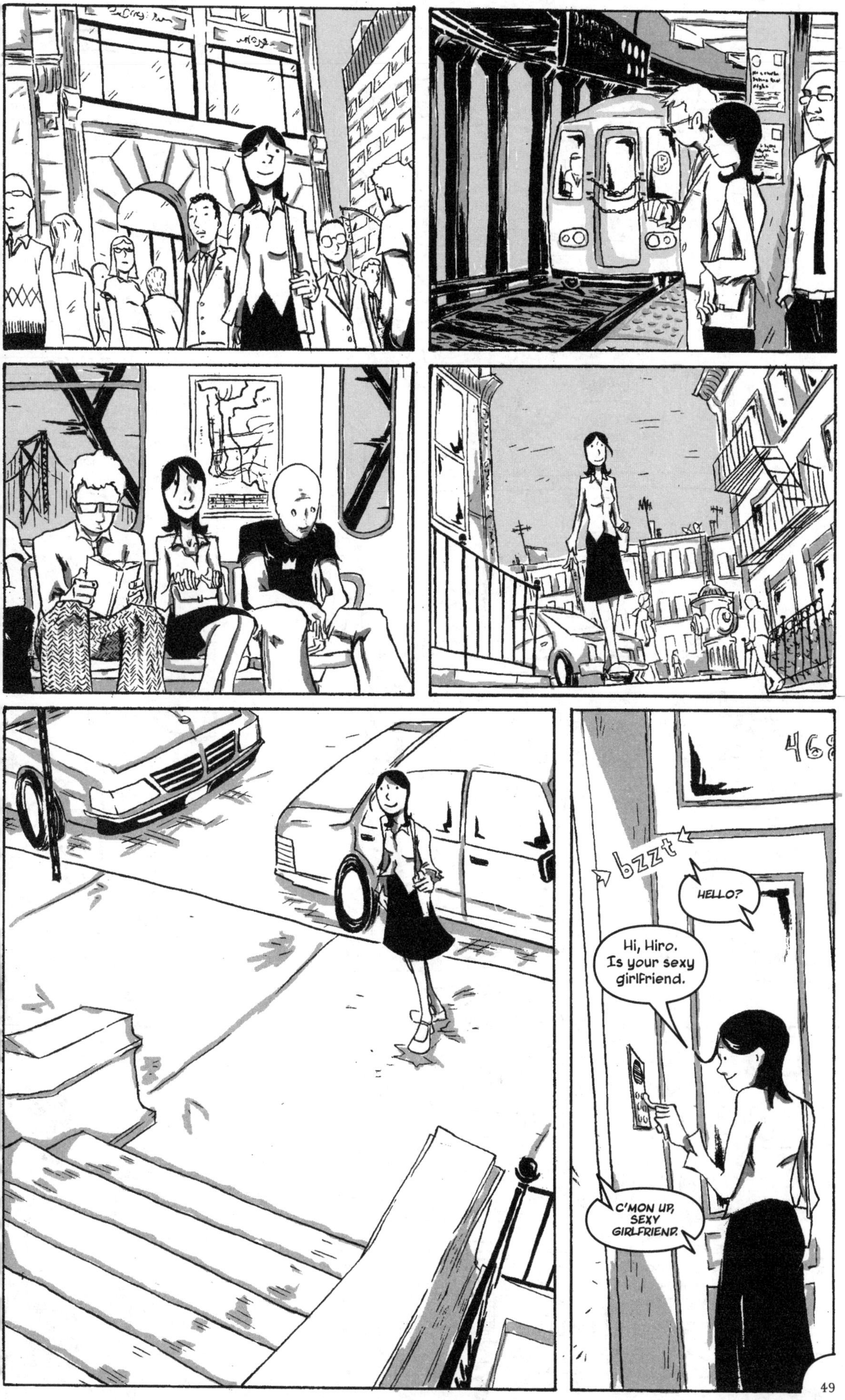
bzzt
HELLO?
Hi, Hiro. Is your sexy girlfriend.
C'MON UP, SEXY GIRLFRIEND.

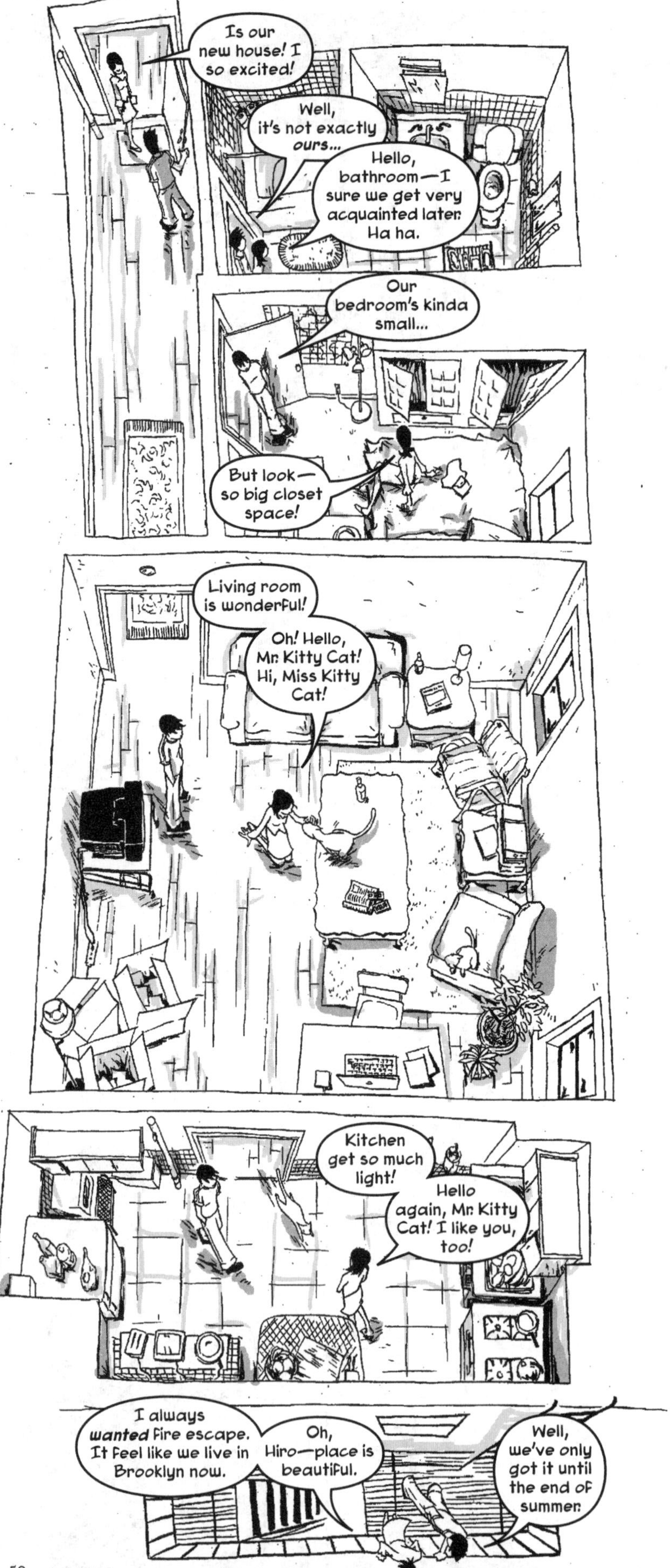
Is our new house! I so excited!
Well, it's not exactly ours...
Hello, bathroom—I sure we get very acquainted later. Ha ha.
Our bedroom's kinda small...
But look—so big closet space!
Living room is wonderful!
Oh! Hello, Mr. Kitty Cat! Hi, Miss Kitty Cat!
Kitchen get so much light!
Hello again, Mr. Kitty Cat! I like you, too!
I always *wanted* fire escape. It feel like we live in Brooklyn now.
Oh, Hiro—place is beautiful.
Well, we've only got it until the end of summer.

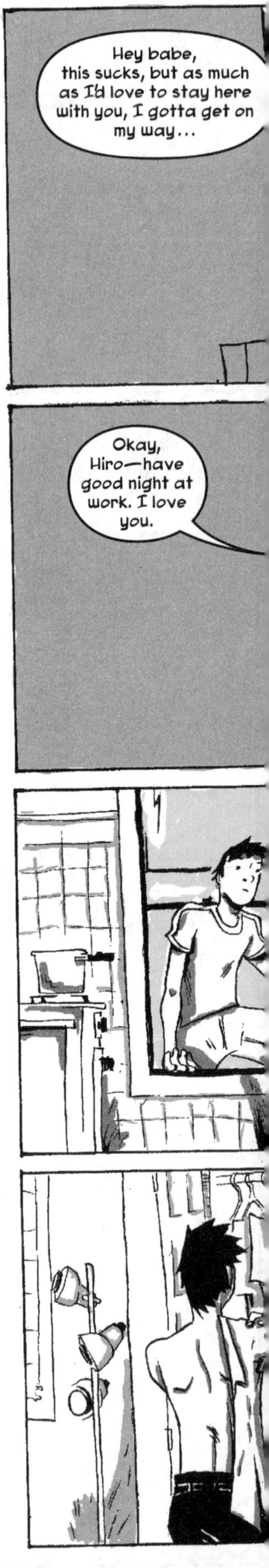
Hey babe, this sucks, but as much as I'd love to stay here with you, I gotta get on my way...
Okay, Hiro—have good night at work. I love you.

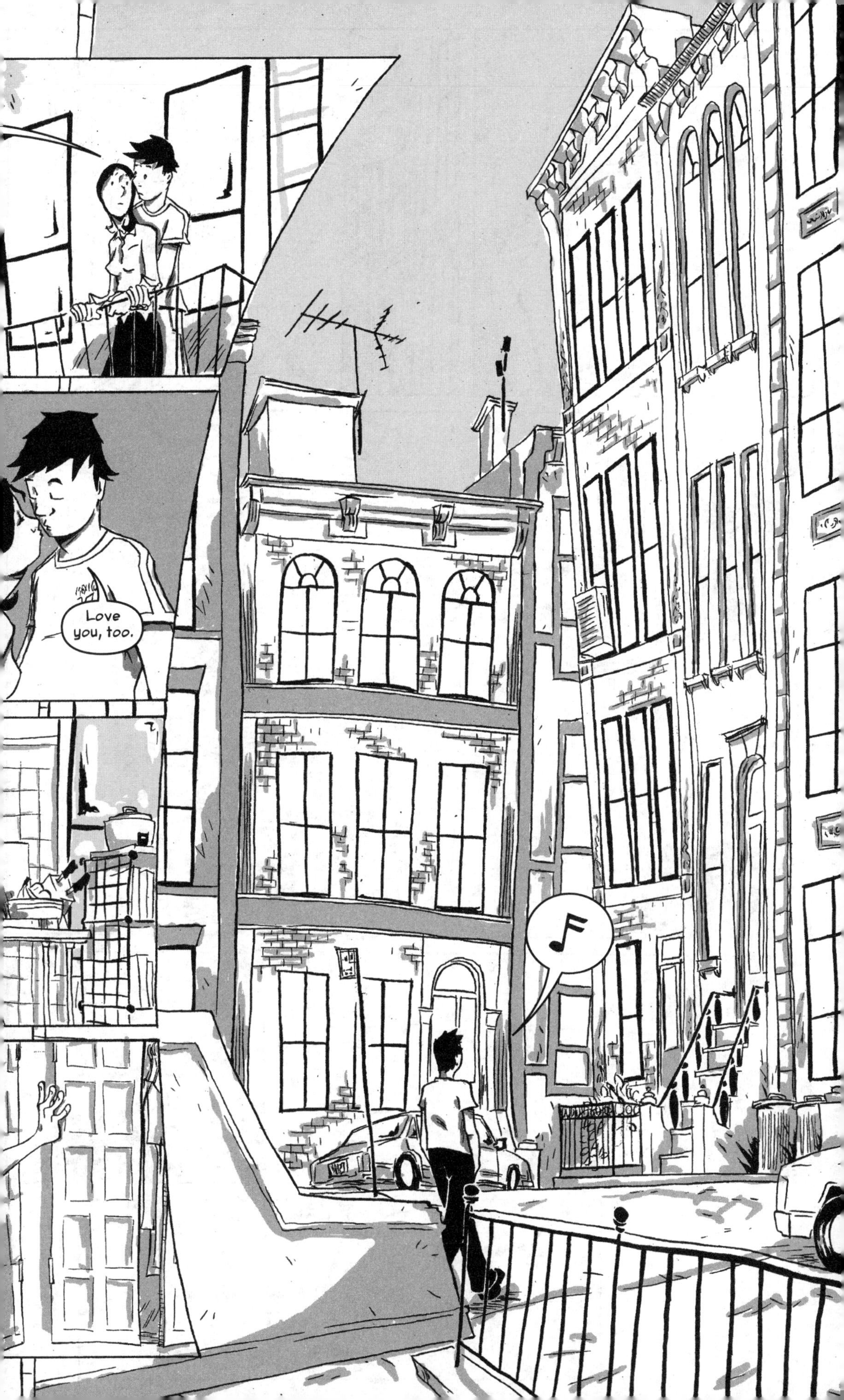
Love you, too.

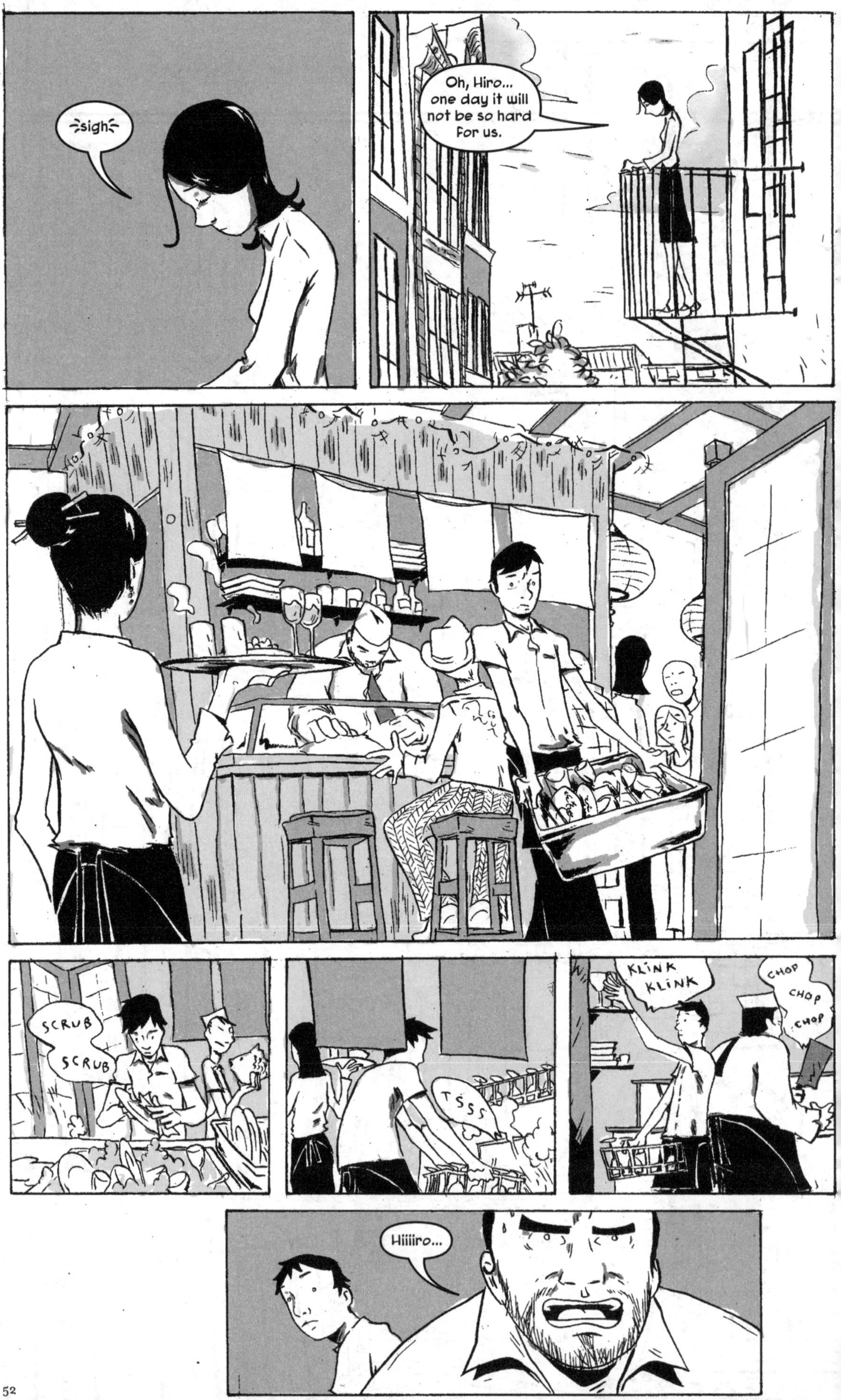
sigh
Oh, Hiro... one day it will not be so hard for us.
SCRUB SCRUB
TSSS
KLINK KLINK
CHOP CHOP CHOP
Hiiiiro...

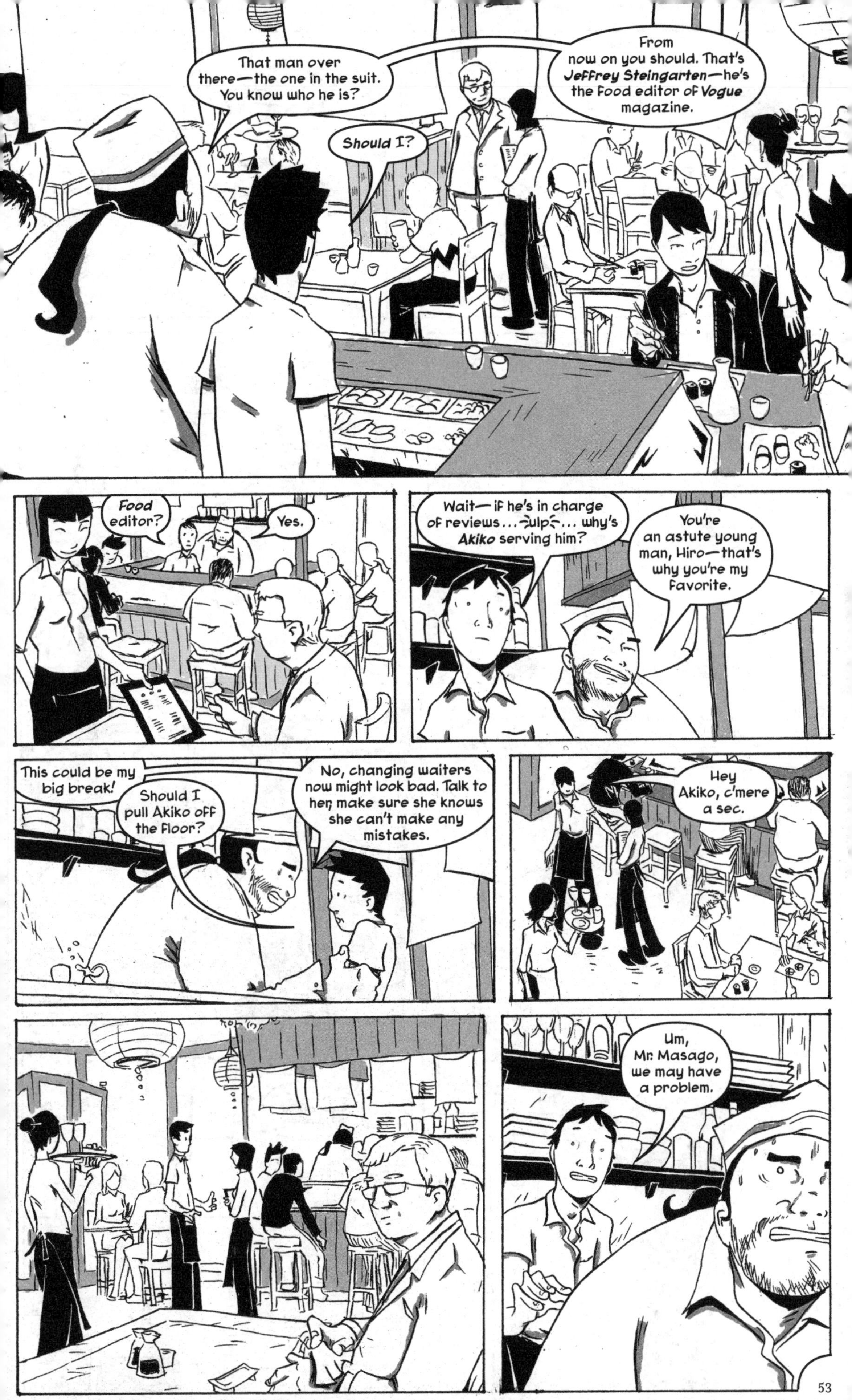
That man over there—the one in the suit. You know who he is?
Should I?
From now on you should. That's Jeffrey Steingarten—he's the food editor of Vogue magazine.
Food editor?
Yes.
Wait—if he's in charge of reviews... gulp... why's Akiko serving him?
You're an astute young man, Hiro—that's why you're my favorite.
This could be my big break!
Should I pull Akiko off the floor?
No, changing waiters now might look bad. Talk to her, make sure she knows she can't make any mistakes.
Hey Akiko, c'mere a sec.
Um, Mr. Masago, we may have a problem.

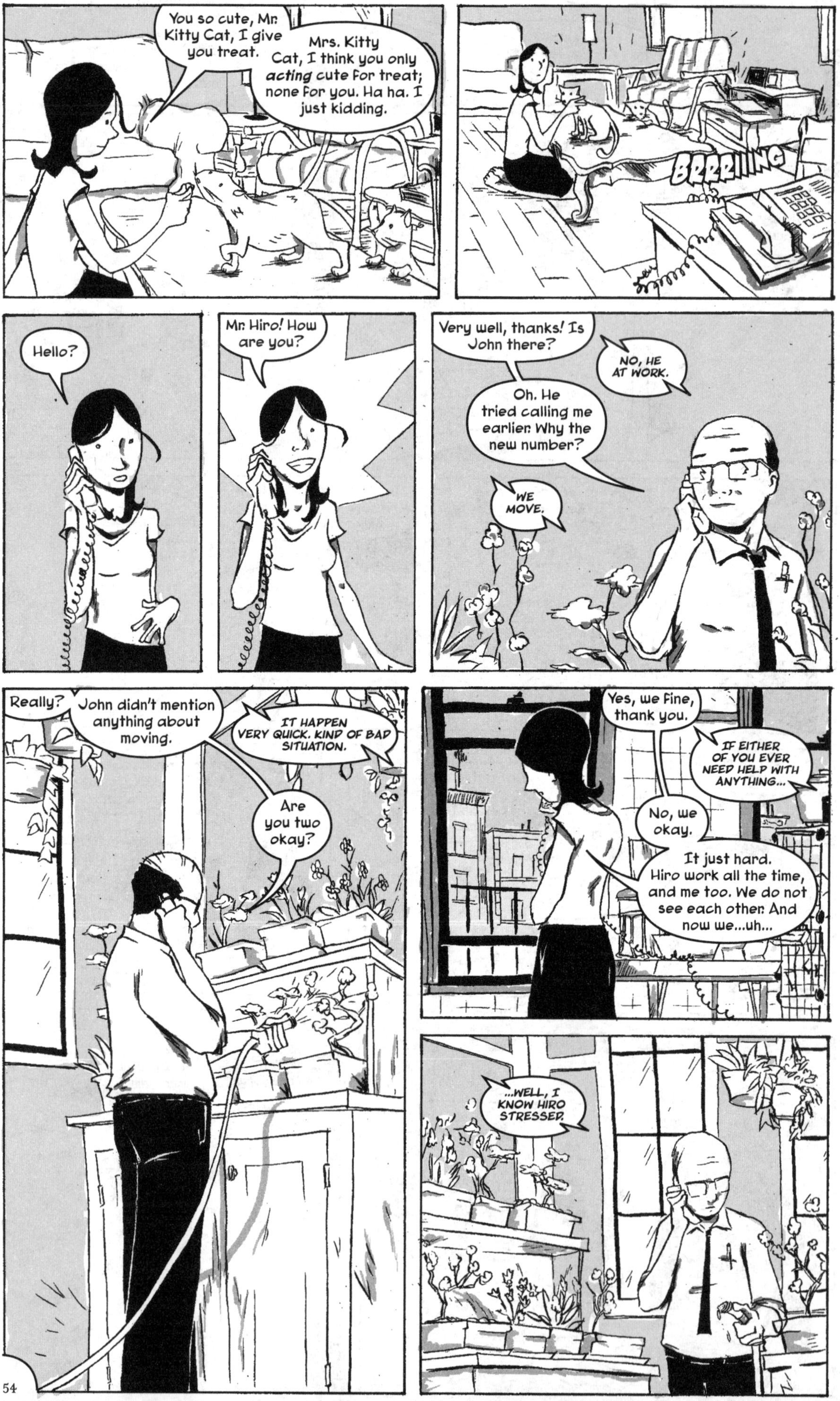
You so cute, Mr. Kitty Cat, I give you treat.
Mrs. Kitty Cat, I think you only *acting* cute for treat; none for you. Ha ha. I just kidding.
BRRRIIING
Hello?
Mr. Hiro! How are you?
Very well, thanks! Is John there?
NO, HE AT WORK.
Oh. He tried calling me earlier. Why the new number?
WE MOVE.
Really?
John didn't mention anything about moving.
IT HAPPEN VERY QUICK. KIND OF BAD SITUATION.
Are you two okay?
Yes, we fine, thank you.
IF EITHER OF YOU EVER NEED HELP WITH ANYTHING...
No, we okay.
It just hard. Hiro work all the time, and me too. We do not see each other. And now we...uh...
...WELL, I KNOW HIRO STRESSED.

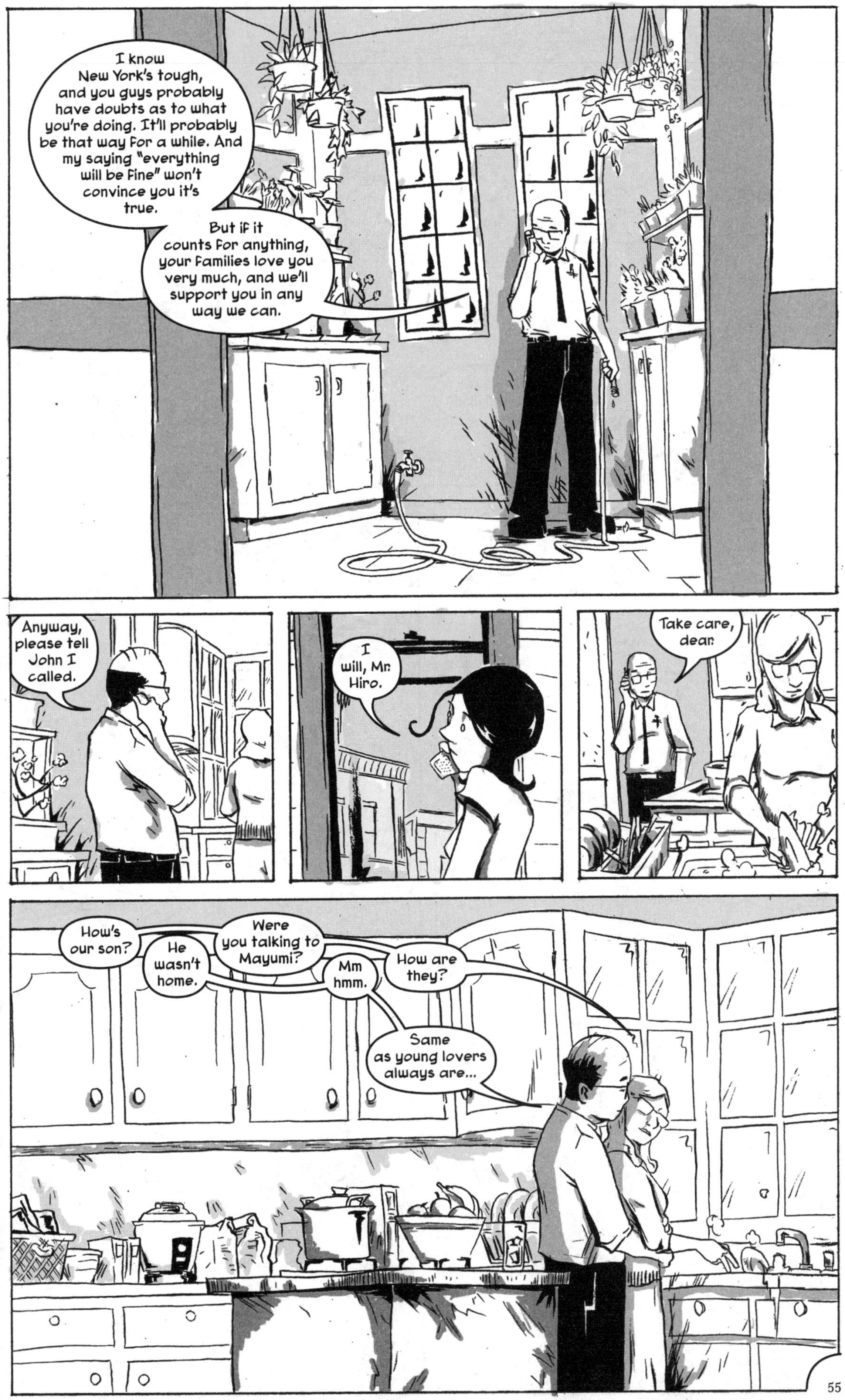
I know New York's tough, and you guys probably have doubts as to what you're doing. It'll probably be that way for a while. And my saying "everything will be fine" won't convince you it's true.
But if it counts for anything, your families love you very much, and we'll support you in any way we can.
Anyway, please tell John I called.
I will, Mr. Hiro.
Take care, dear.
How's our son?
He wasn't home.
Were you talking to Mayumi?
Mm hmm.
How are they?
Same as young lovers always are...

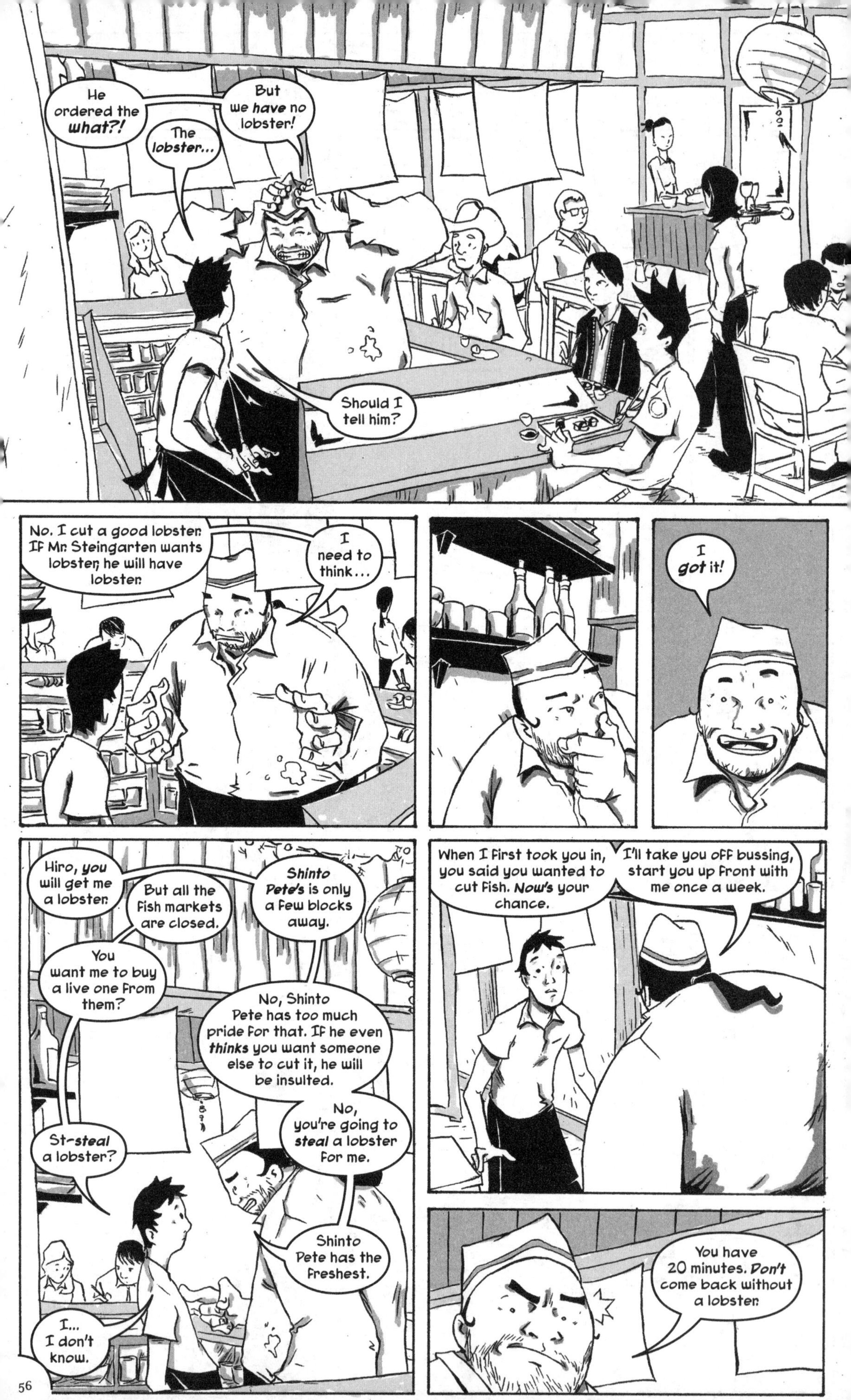
He ordered the *what?!*
The *lobster*...
But we *have* no lobster!
Should I tell him?
No. I cut a good lobster. If Mr. Steingarten wants lobster, he will have lobster.
I need to think...
I *got* it!
Hiro, *you* will get me a lobster.
But all the fish markets are closed.
Shinto Pete's is only a few blocks away.
You want me to buy a live one from them?
No, Shinto Pete has too much pride for that. If he even *thinks* you want someone else to cut it, he will be insulted.
St-*steal* a lobster?
No, you're going to *steal* a lobster for me.
Shinto Pete has the freshest.
I... I don't know.
When I first took you in, you said you wanted to cut fish. *Now's* your chance.
I'll take you off bussing, start you up front with me once a week.
You have 20 minutes. *Don't* come back without a lobster.

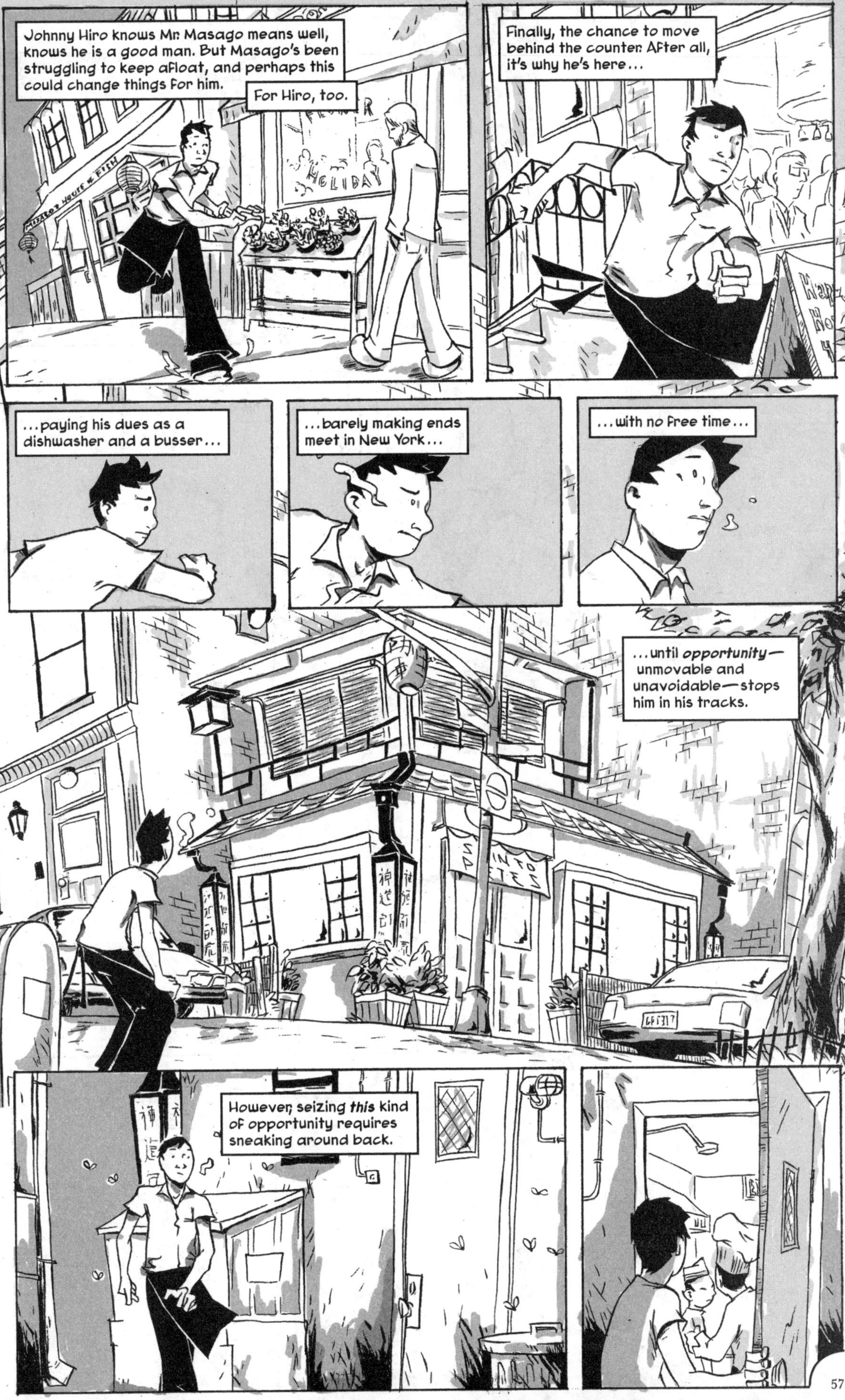
Johnny Hiro knows Mr. Masago means well, knows he is a good man. But Masago's been struggling to keep afloat, and perhaps this could change things for him.
For Hiro, too.
HOLIDAY
Finally, the chance to move behind the counter. After all, it's why he's here...
...paying his dues as a dishwasher and a busser...
...barely making ends meet in New York...
...with no free time...
...until *opportunity*—unmovable and unavoidable—stops him in his tracks.
However, seizing *this* kind of opportunity requires sneaking around back.

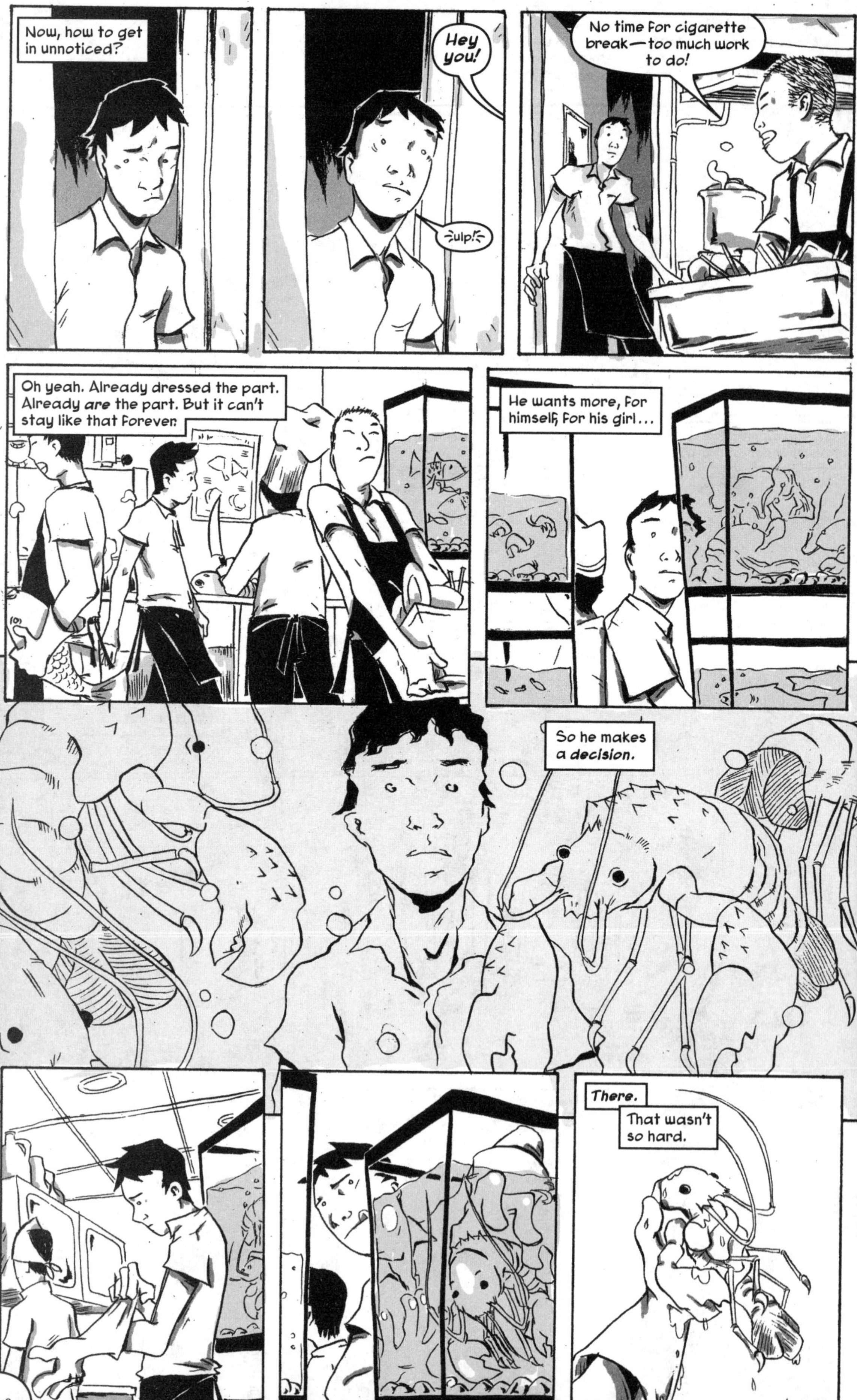
Now, how to get in unnoticed?
Hey you!
ulp!
No time for cigarette break—too much work to do!
Oh yeah. Already dressed the part. Already *are* the part. But it can't stay like that forever.
He wants more, for himself, for his girl...
So he makes a *decision*.
There.
That wasn't so hard.

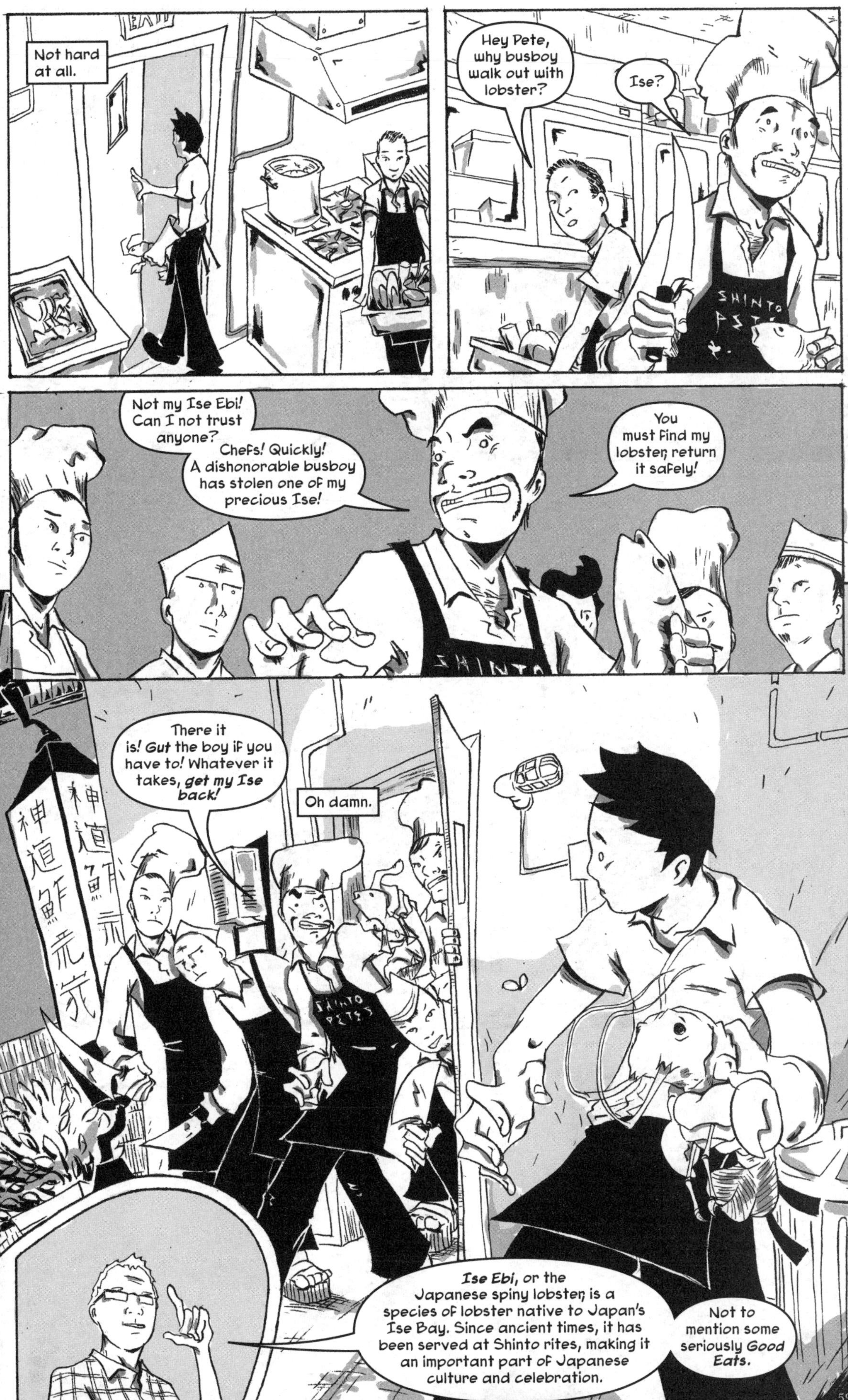
Not hard at all.
Hey Pete, why busboy walk out with lobster?
Ise?
Not my Ise Ebi! Can I not trust anyone?
Chefs! Quickly! A dishonorable busboy has stolen one of my precious Ise!
You must find my lobster, return it safely!
There it is! Gut the boy if you have to! Whatever it takes, get my Ise back!
Oh damn.
Ise Ebi, or the Japanese spiny lobster, is a species of lobster native to Japan's Ise Bay. Since ancient times, it has been served at Shinto rites, making it an important part of Japanese culture and celebration.
Not to mention some seriously Good Eats.

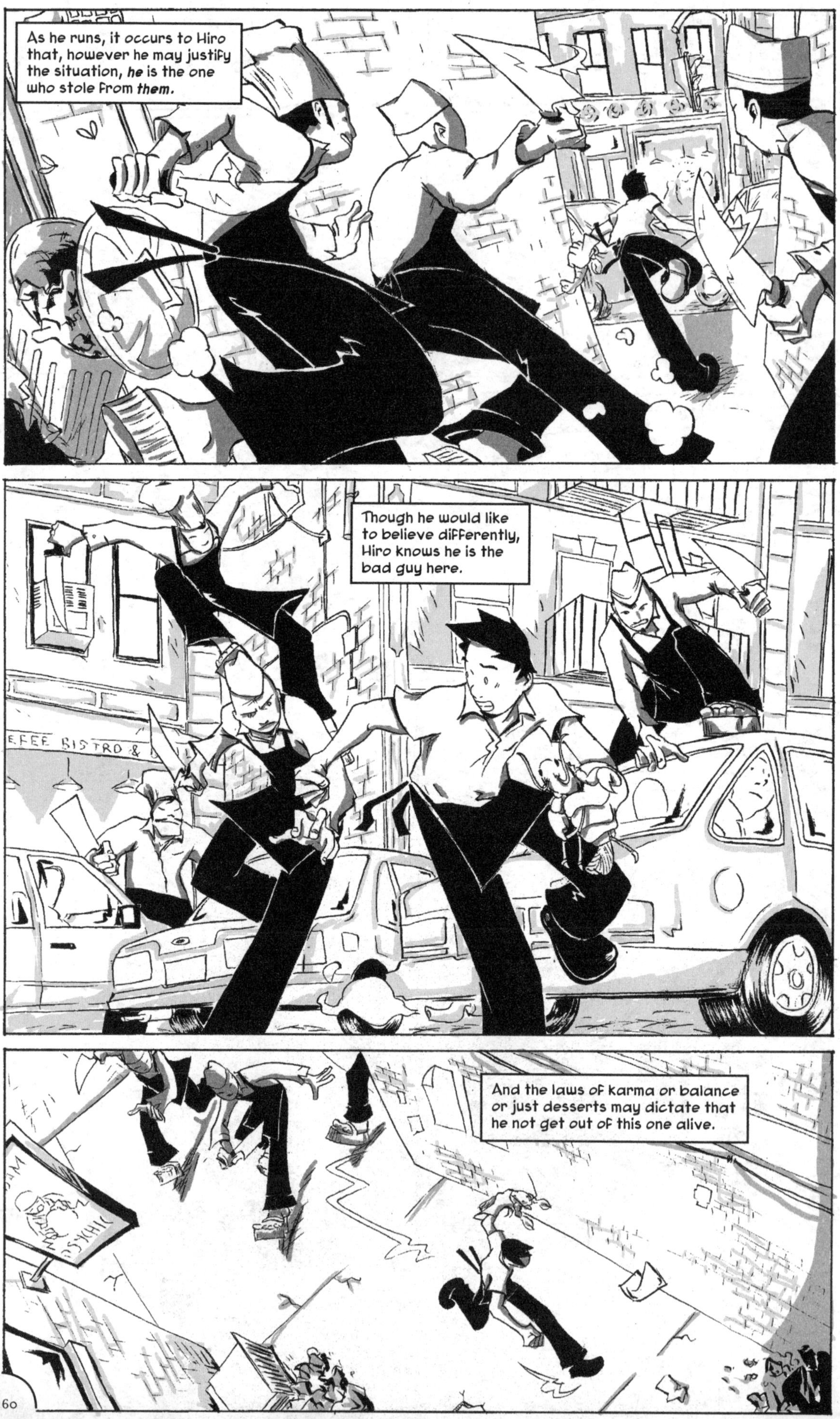
As he runs, it occurs to Hiro that, however he may justify the situation, *he* is the one who stole from *them.*
Though he would like to believe differently, Hiro knows he is the bad guy here.
And the laws of karma or balance or just desserts may dictate that he not get out of this one alive.

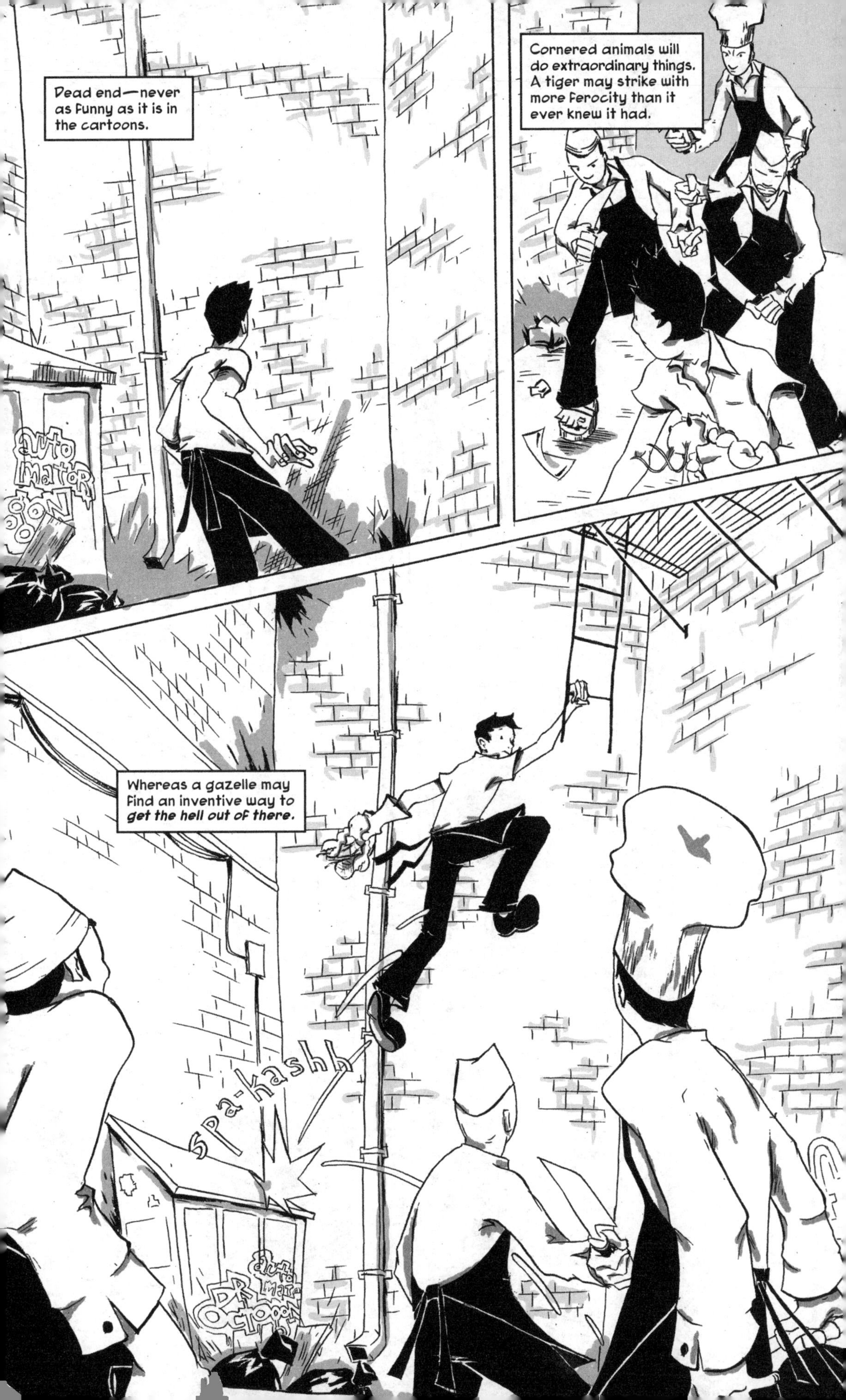
Dead end—never as funny as it is in the cartoons.
Cornered animals will do extraordinary things. A tiger may strike with more ferocity than it ever knew it had.
Whereas a gazelle may find an inventive way to *get the hell out of there.*
spa-kashh

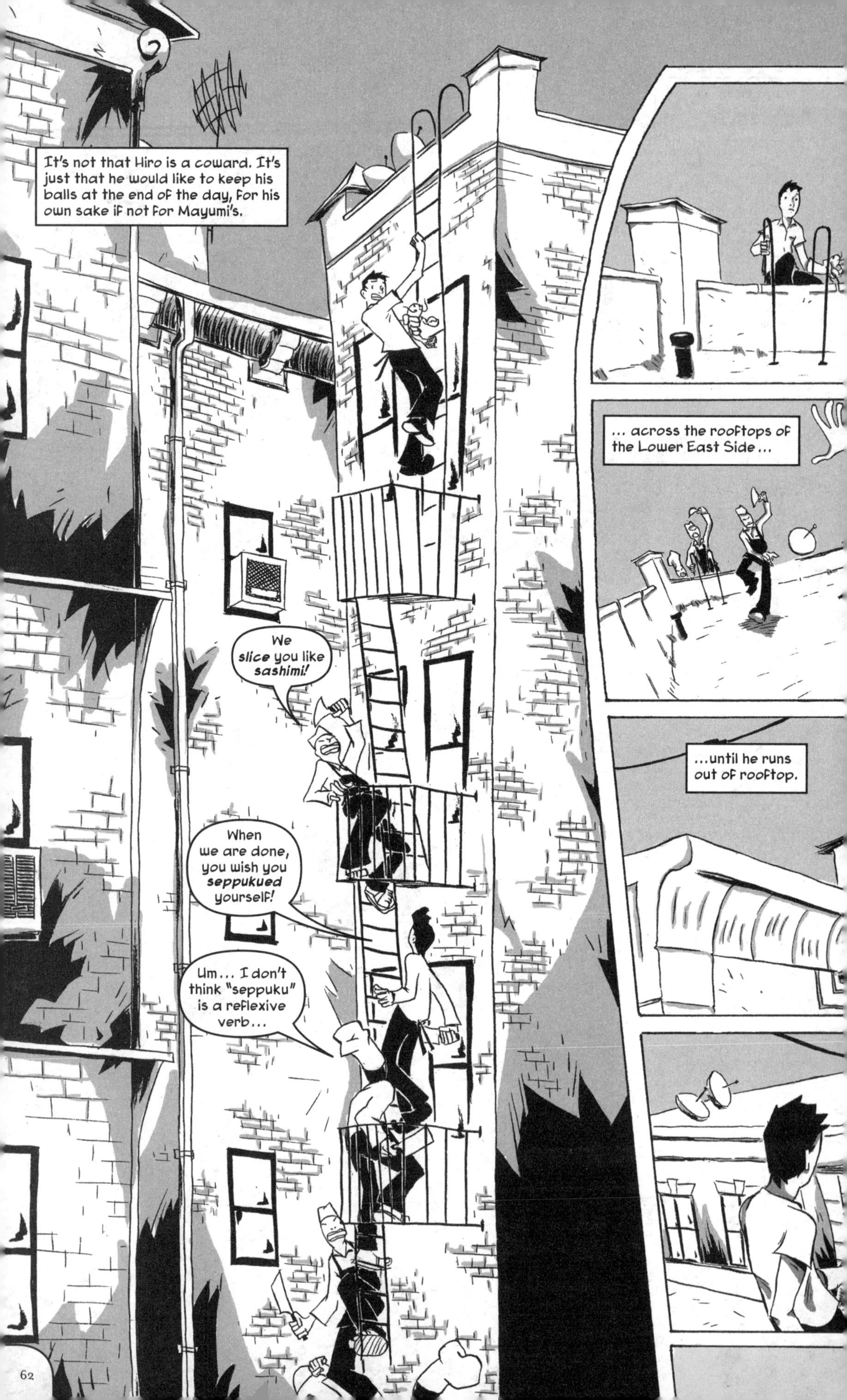
It's not that Hiro is a coward. It's just that he would like to keep his balls at the end of the day, for his own sake if not for Mayumi's.
We slice you like sashimi!
When we are done, you wish you seppukued yourself!
Um... I don't think "seppuku" is a reflexive verb...
... across the rooftops of the Lower East Side...
...until he runs out of rooftop.

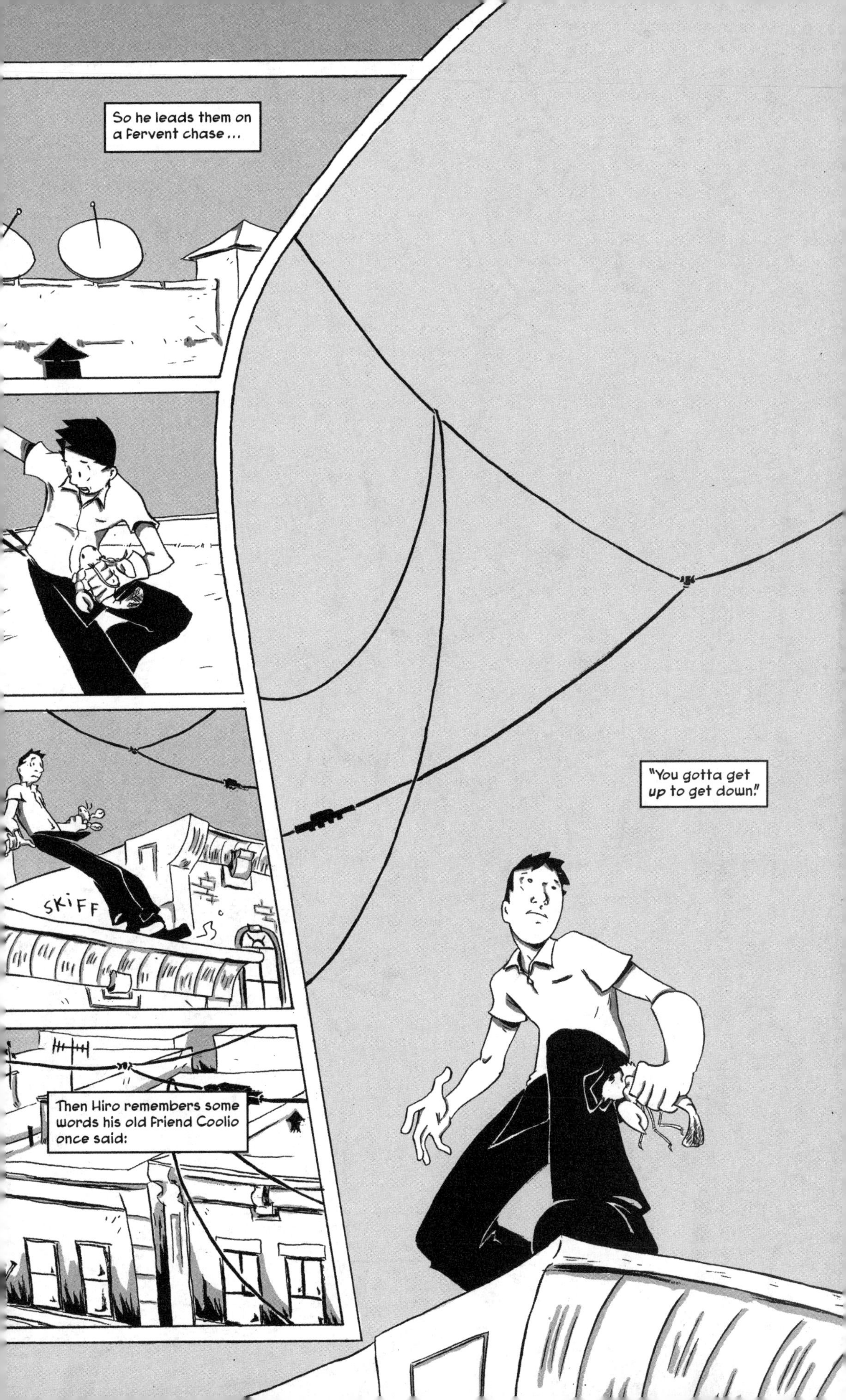
So he leads them on a fervent chase...
SKiFF
Then Hiro remembers some words his old friend Coolio once said:
"You gotta get up to get down."

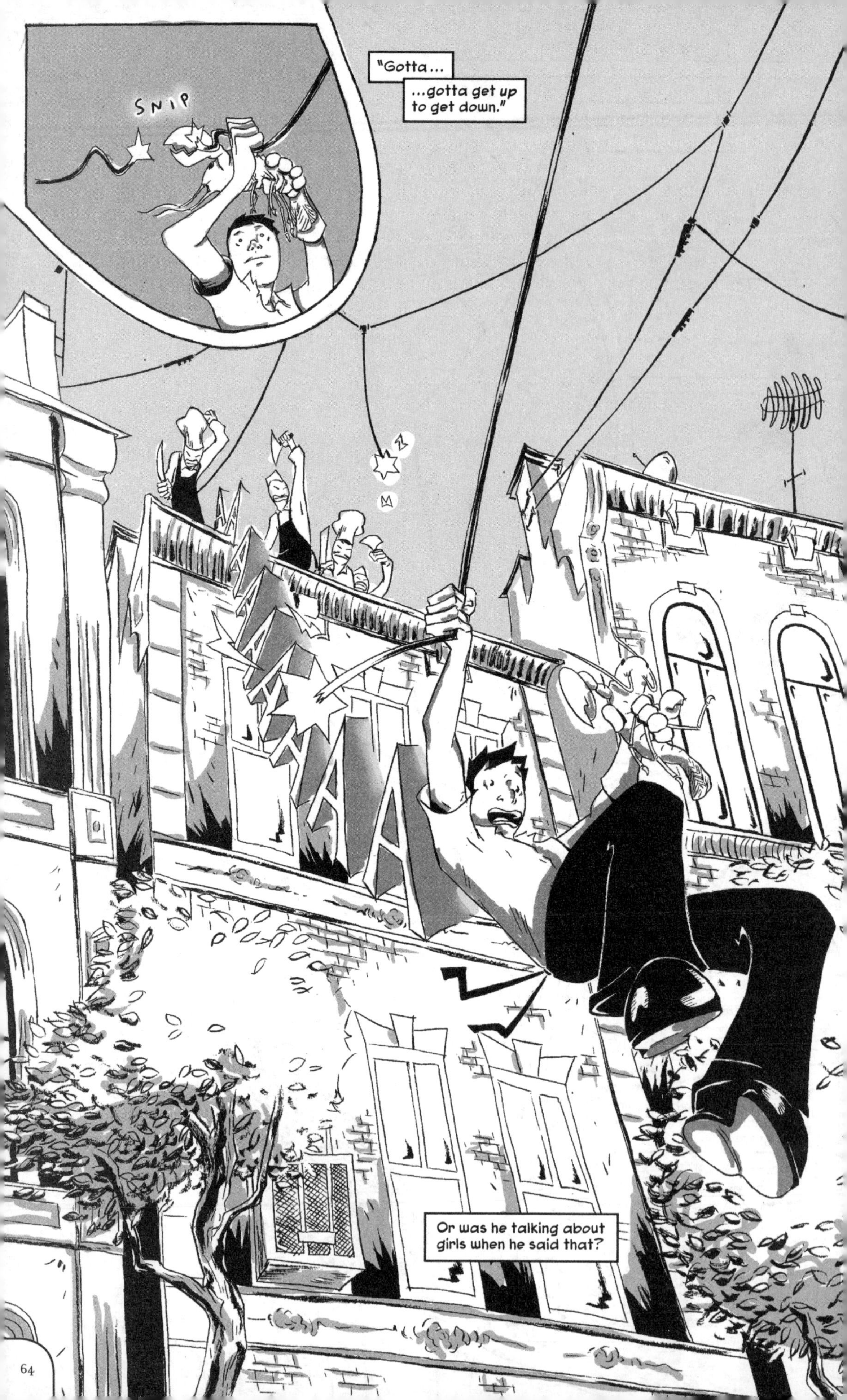
"Gotta...
...gotta get up to get down."
SNIP
Or was he talking about girls when he said that?

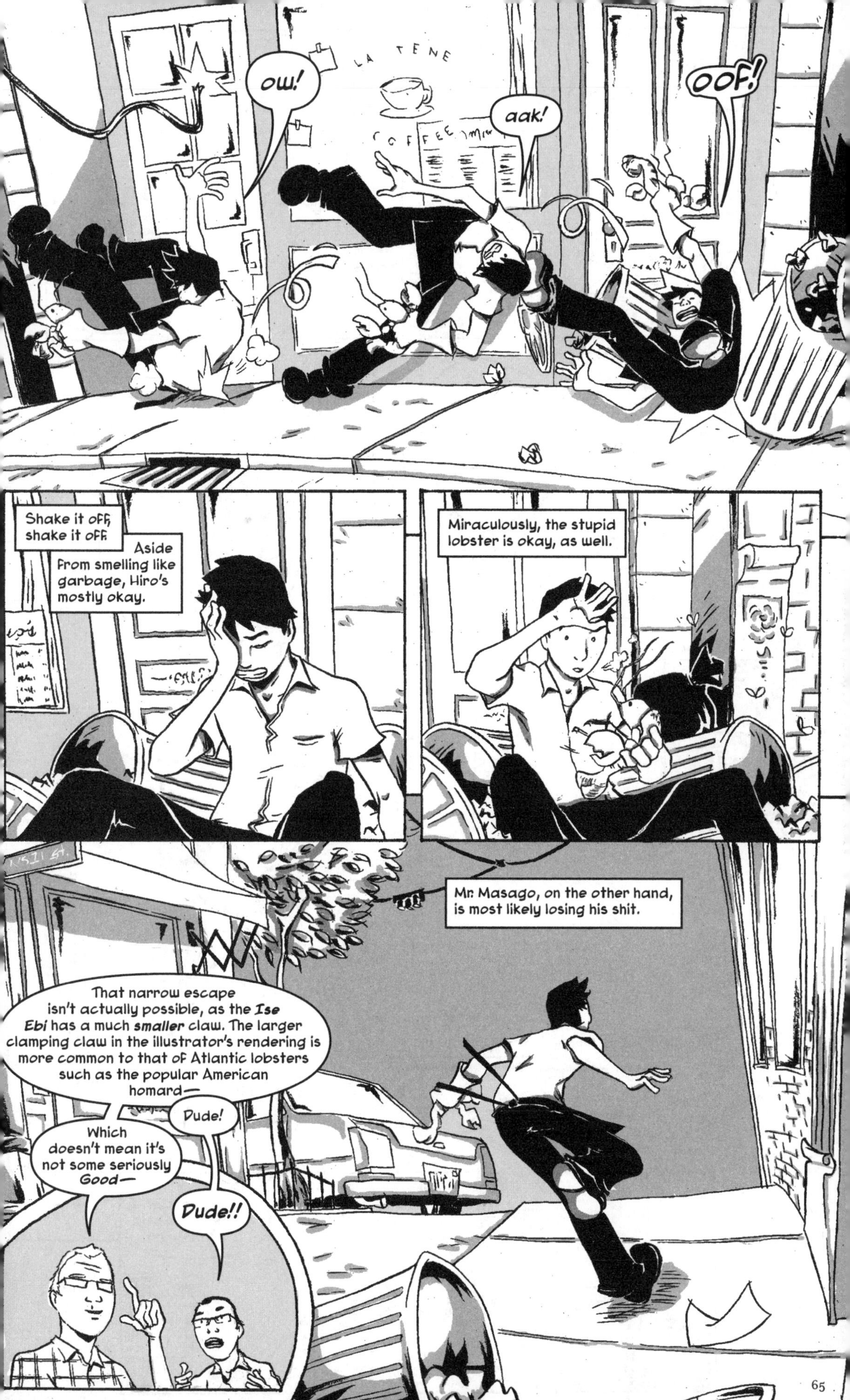
LA TENE
COFFEE
ow!
aak!
OOF!
Shake it off, shake it off.
Aside from smelling like garbage, Hiro's mostly okay.
Miraculously, the stupid lobster is okay, as well.
Mr. Masago, on the other hand, is most likely losing his shit.
That narrow escape isn't actually possible, as the *Ise Ebi* has a much *smaller* claw. The larger clamping claw in the illustrator's rendering is more common to that of Atlantic lobsters such as the popular American homard—
Dude!
Which doesn't mean it's not some seriously *Good*—
Dude!!

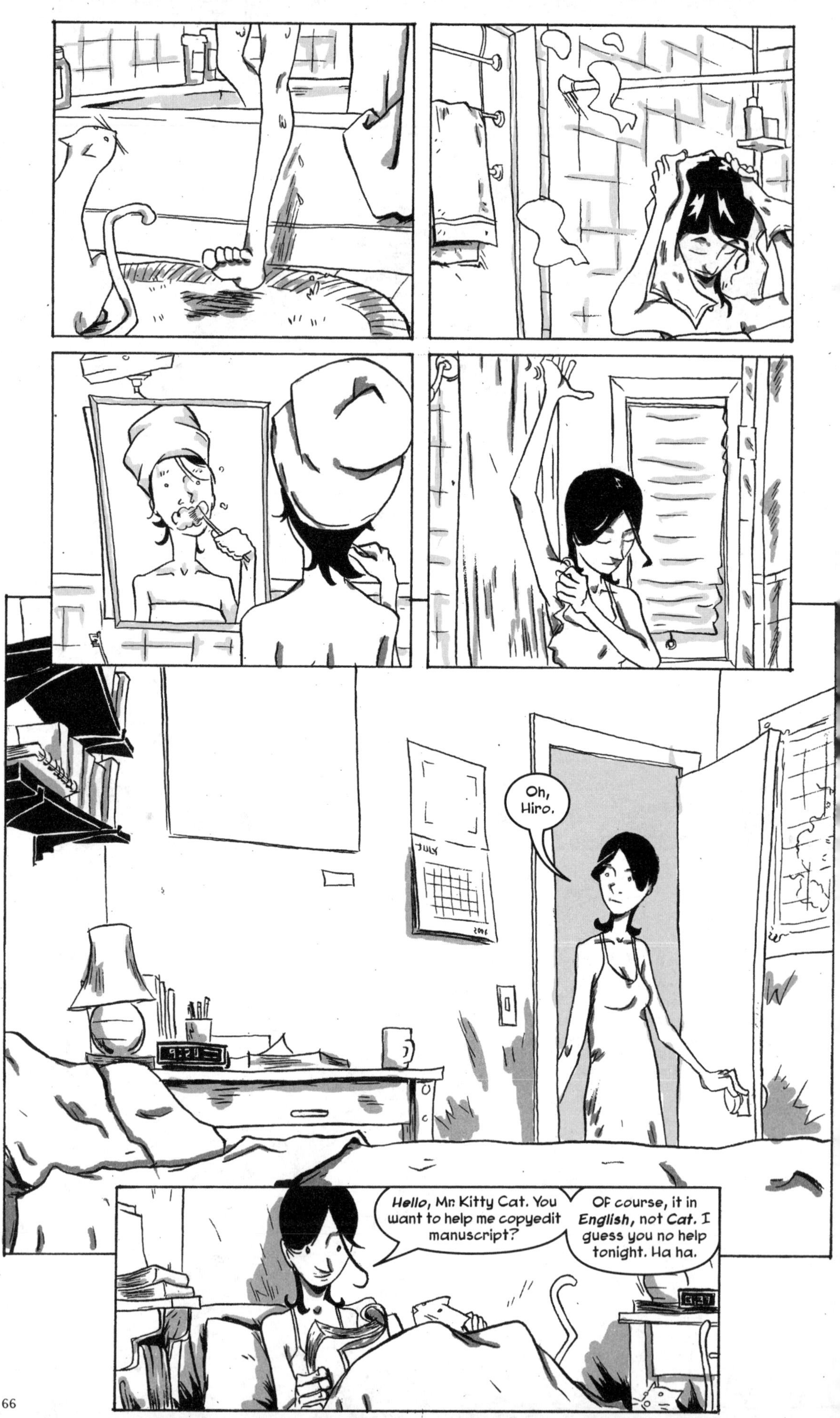
Oh, Hiro.
Hello, Mr. Kitty Cat. You want to help me copyedit manuscript?
Of course, it in English, not Cat. I guess you no help tonight. Ha ha.

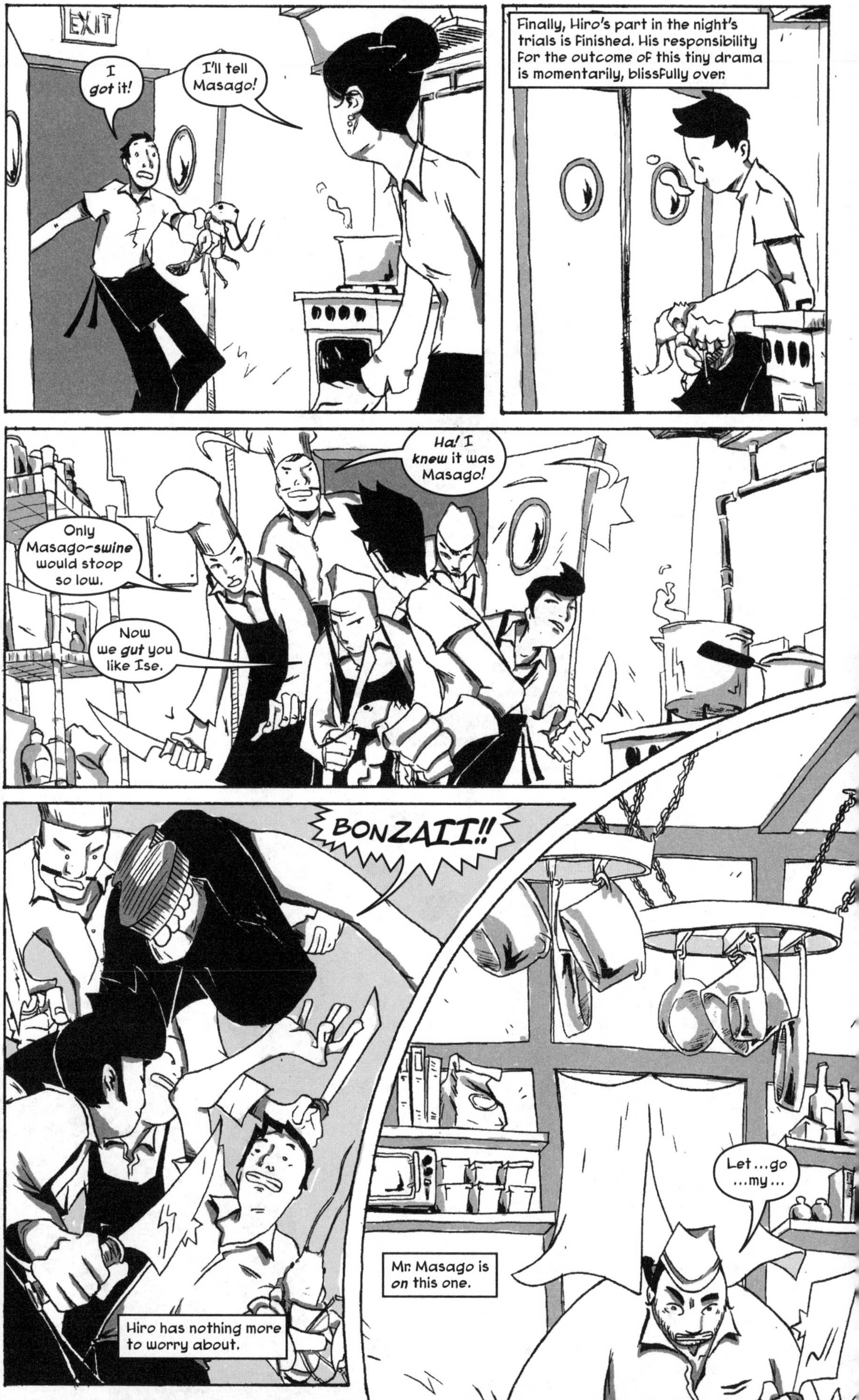
EXIT
I got it!
I'll tell Masago!
Finally, Hiro's part in the night's trials is finished. His responsibility for the outcome of this tiny drama is momentarily, blissfully over.
Ha! I knew it was Masago!
Only Masago-swine would stoop so low.
Now we gut you like Ise.
BONZAII!!
Let...go ...my...
Mr. Masago is on this one.
Hiro has nothing more to worry about.

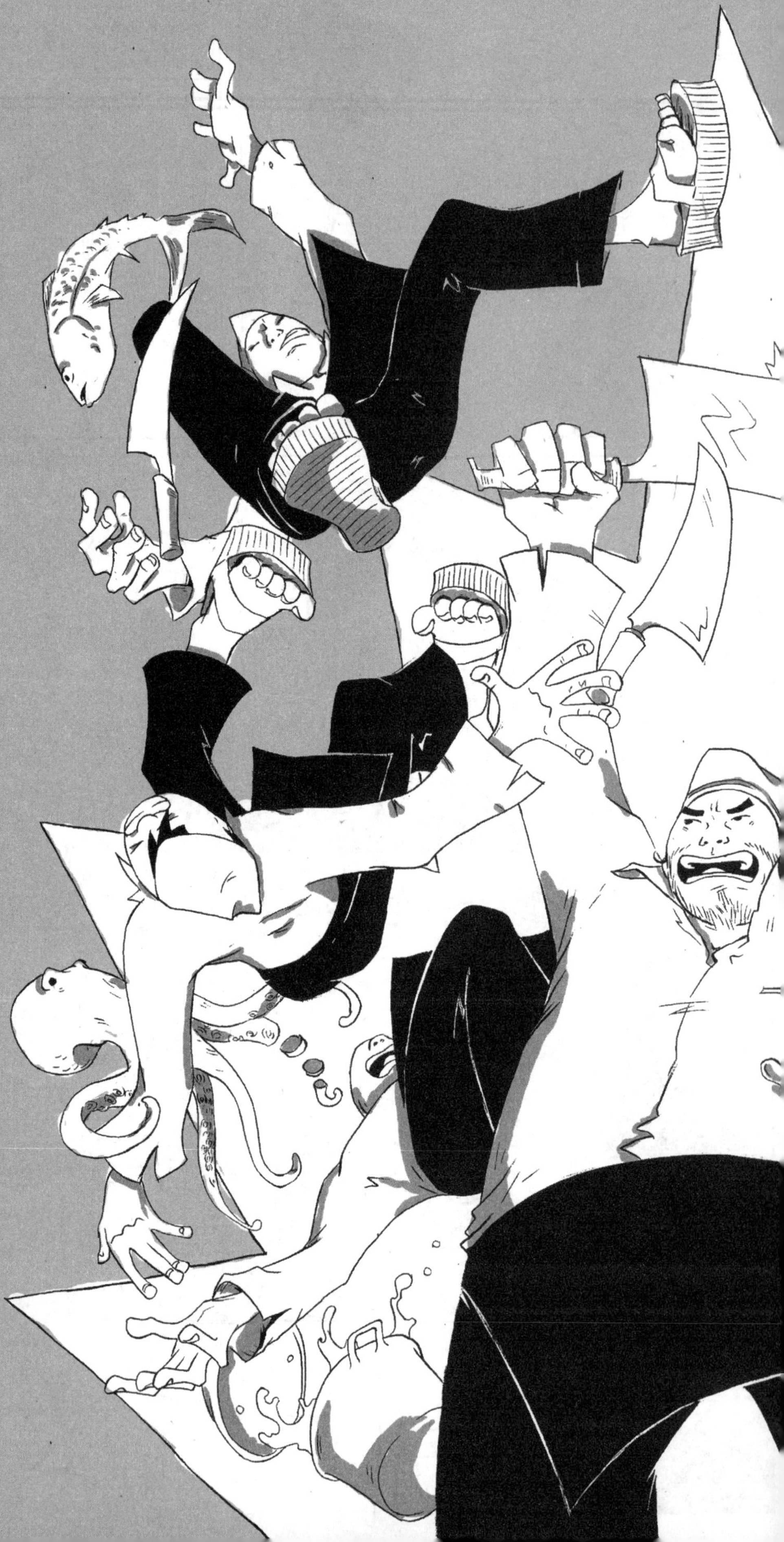

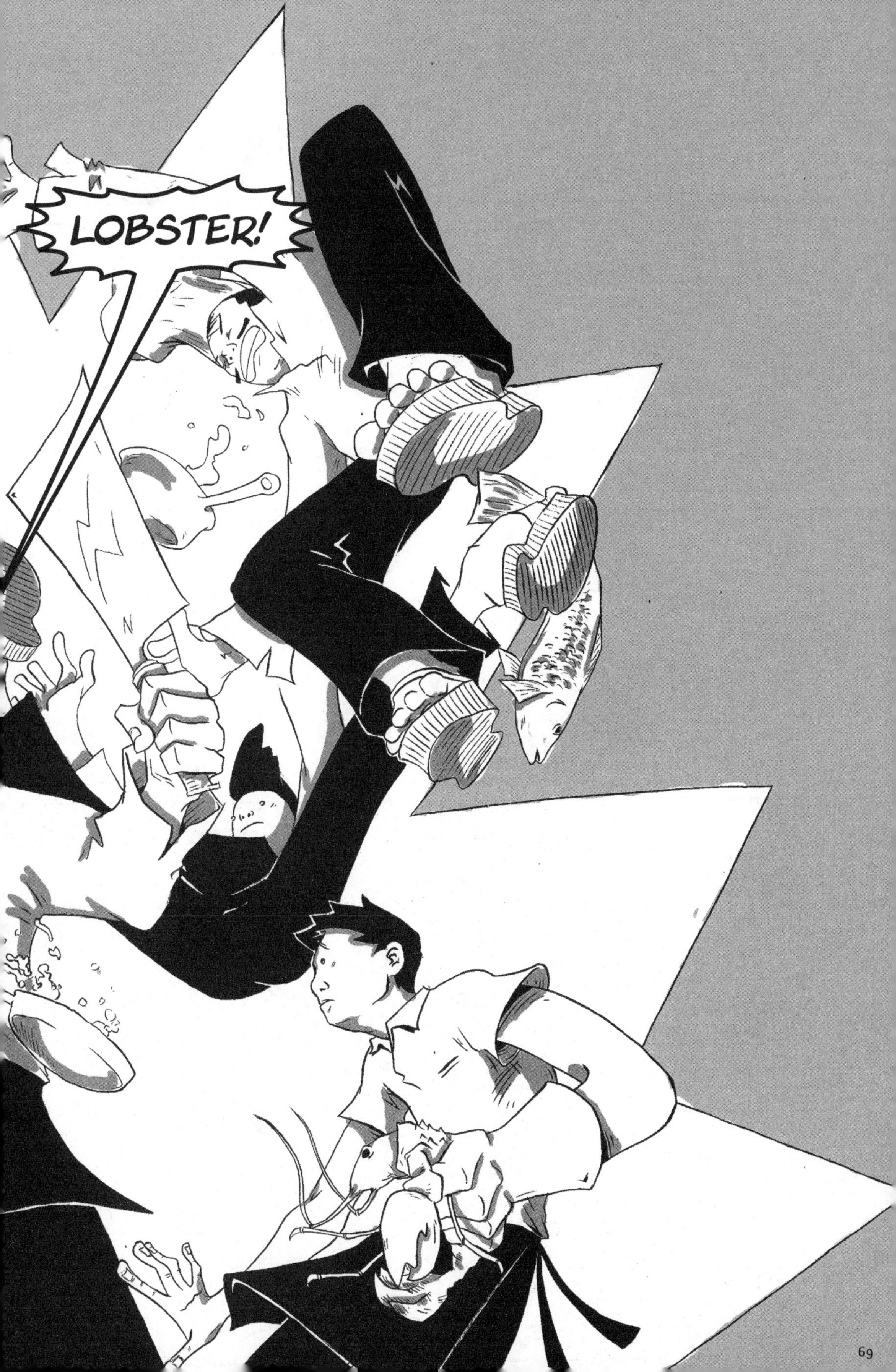
LOBSTER!

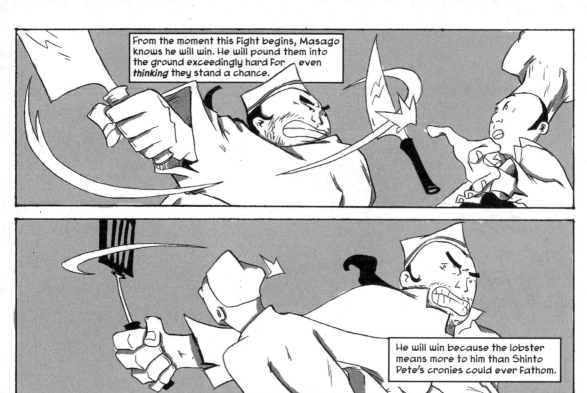

From the moment this fight begins, Masago knows he will win. He will pound them into the ground *exceedingly* hard for even *thinking* they stand a chance.

He will win because the lobster means more to him than Shinto Pete's cronies could ever fathom.

This lobster could garner enough publicity to assuage the financial burdens of the restaurant, perhaps even bring him out of debt.

Perhaps he could have enough money to help his family back in Japan.

He can even pay his staff more. He can pay Hiro more. Hiro—such a good kid, if not a bit on the dim-witted side.

He tries so hard for Masago, they *all* do. They all deserve more than this.

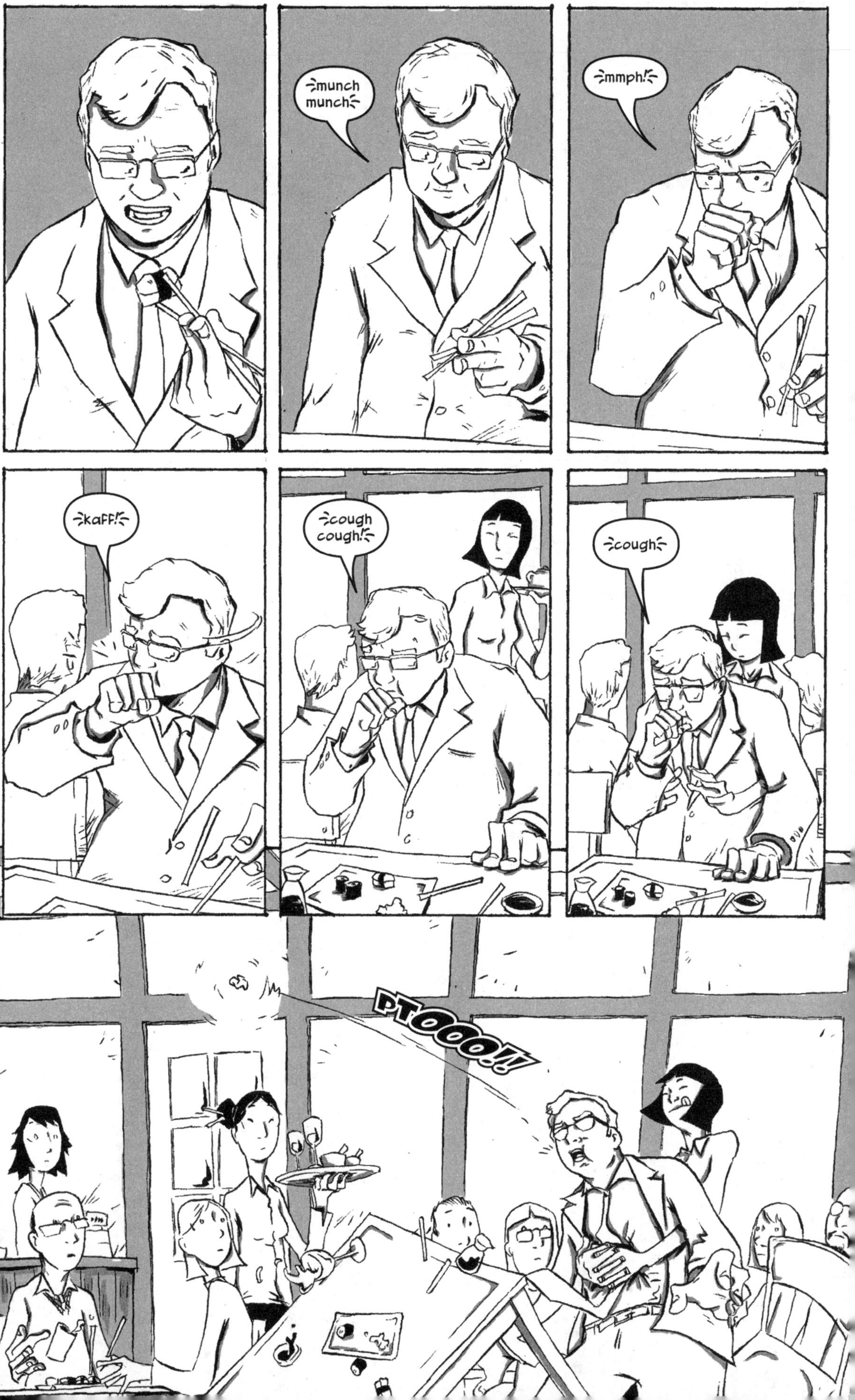
munch munch
mmph!
kaff!
cough cough!
cough
PTOOOO!!

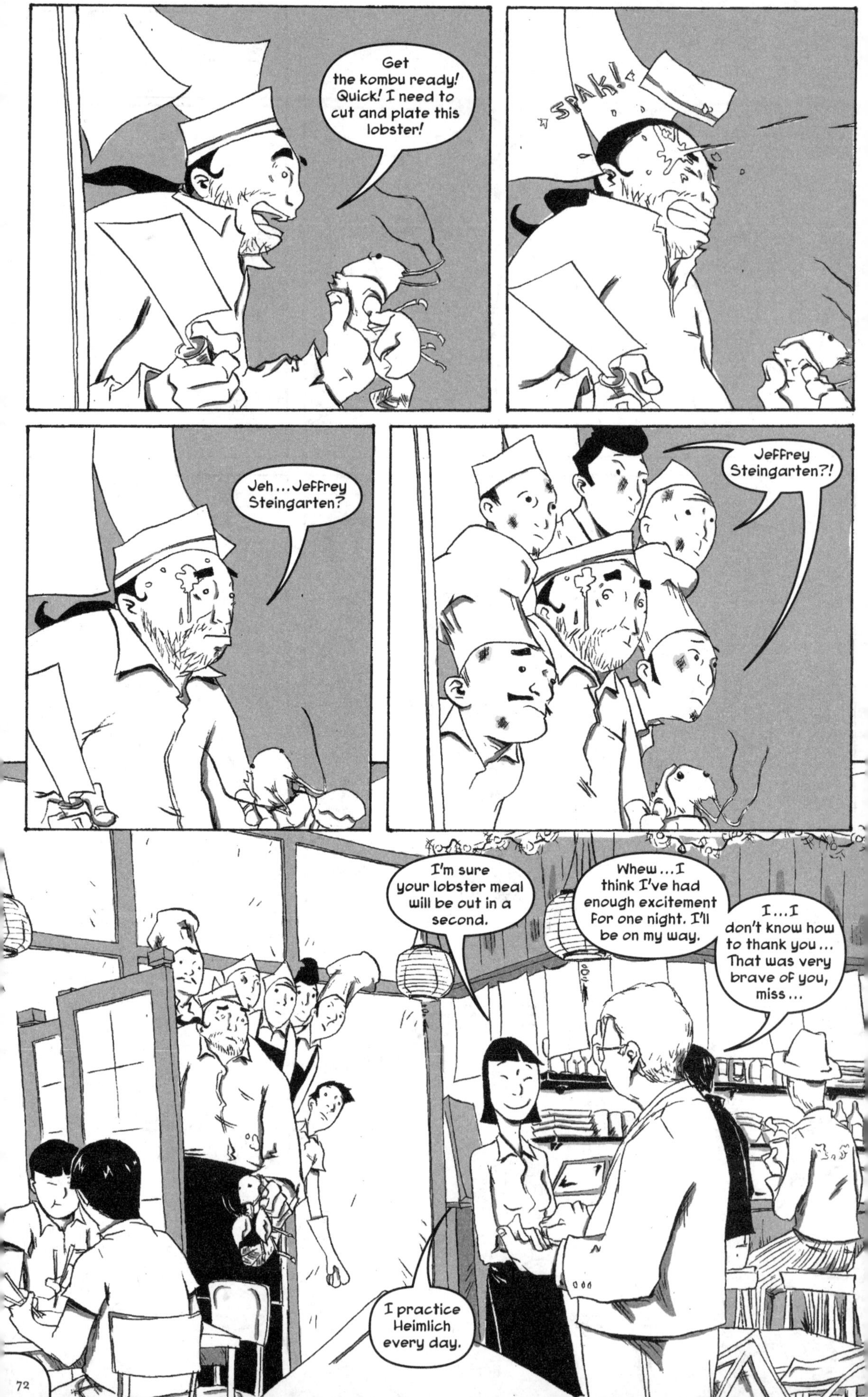
Get the kombu ready! Quick! I need to cut and plate this lobster!
SPAK!
Jeh... Jeffrey Steingarten?
Jeffrey Steingarten?!
I'm sure your lobster meal will be out in a second.
Whew... I think I've had enough excitement for one night. I'll be on my way.
I... I don't know how to thank you... That was very brave of you, miss...
I practice Heimlich every day.

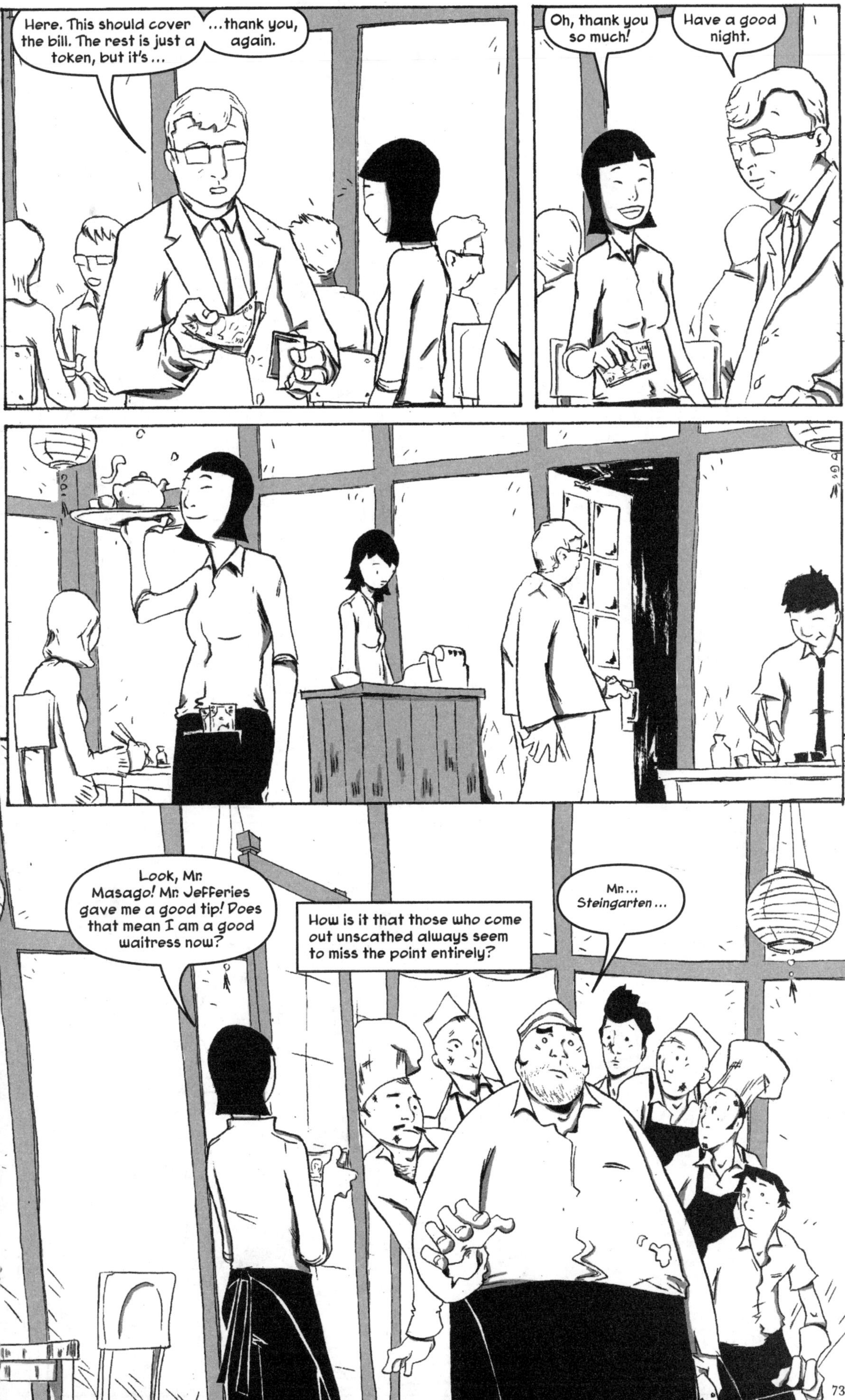
Here. This should cover the bill. The rest is just a token, but it's ...
...thank you, again.
Oh, thank you so much!
Have a good night.
Look, Mr. Masago! Mr. Jefferies gave me a good tip! Does that mean I am a good waitress now?
How is it that those who come out unscathed always seem to miss the point entirely?
Mr. ... Steingarten ...

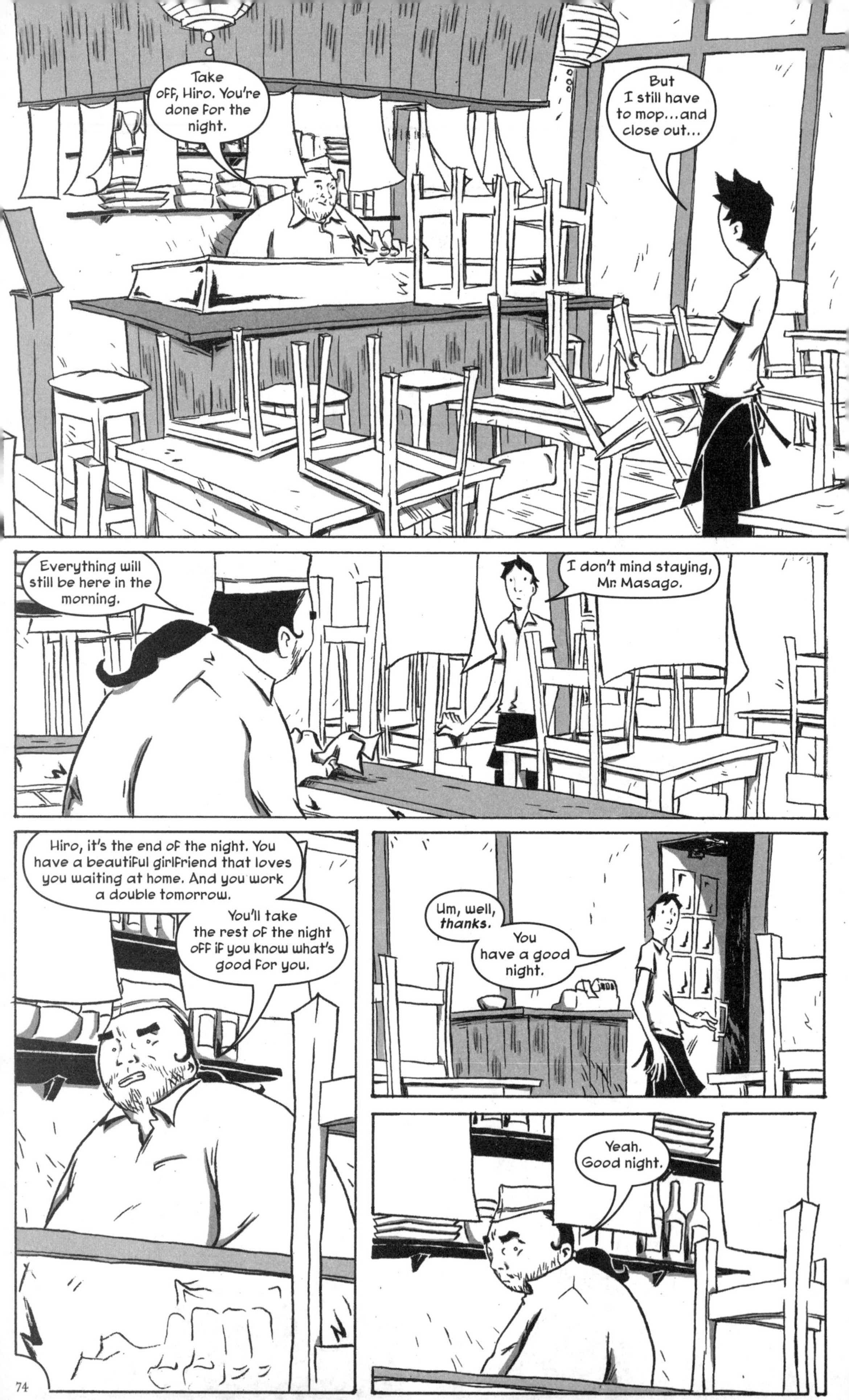
Take off, Hiro. You're done for the night.
But I still have to mop...and close out...
Everything will still be here in the morning.
I don't mind staying, Mr. Masago.
Hiro, it's the end of the night. You have a beautiful girlfriend that loves you waiting at home. And you work a double tomorrow.
You'll take the rest of the night off if you know what's good for you.
Um, well, thanks.
You have a good night.
Yeah. Good night.

Another strange night ends.

And no one came out the better.

John Hiro risked his neck for a busboy's tips tonight.

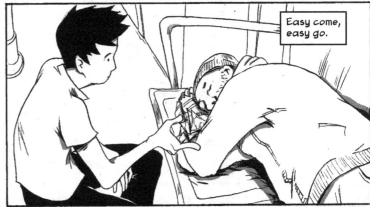

Easy come, easy go.

But there's one other thing: Masago was *right*.

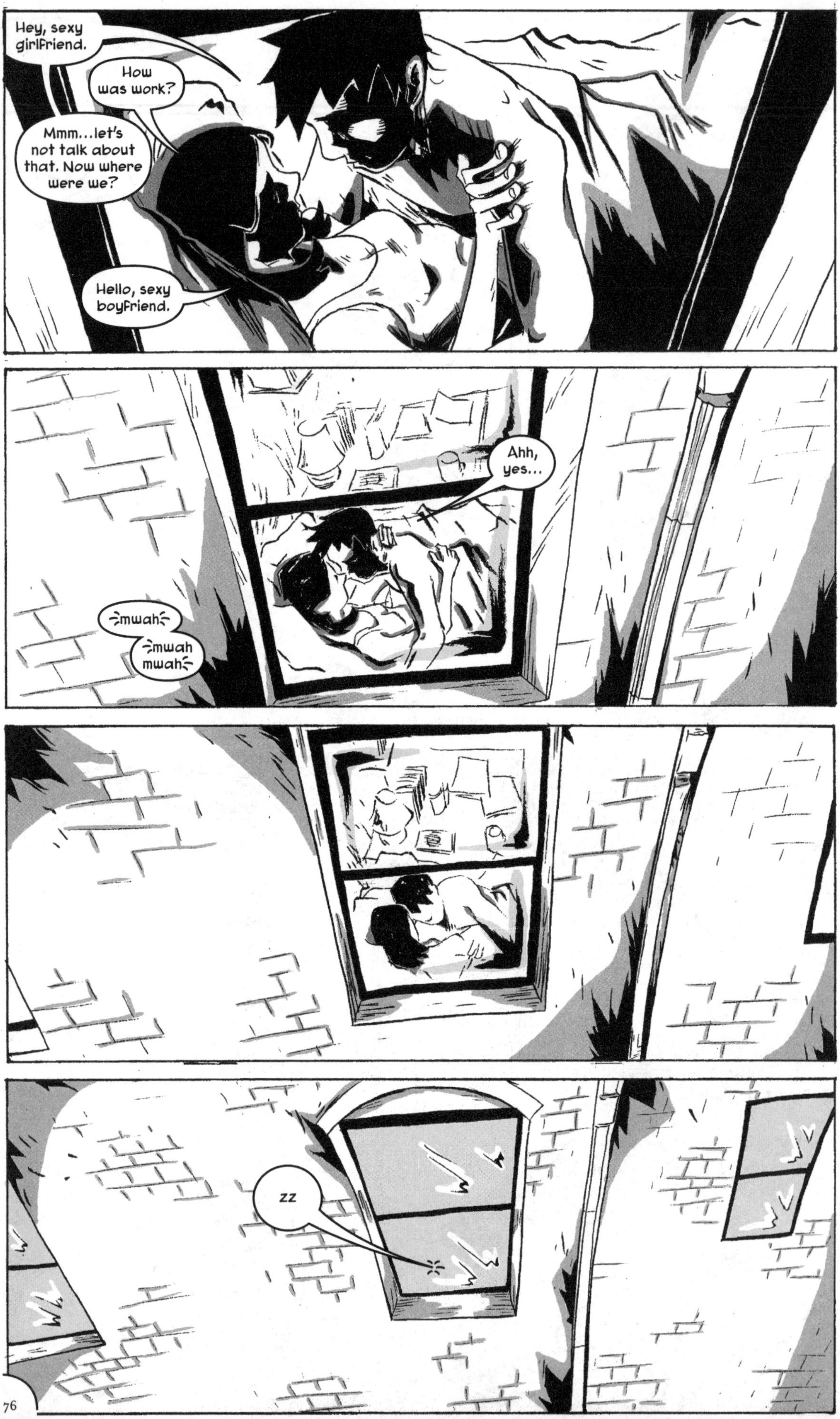
Hey, sexy girlfriend.
How was work?
Mmm...let's not talk about that. Now where were we?
Hello, sexy boyfriend.
Ahh, yes...
mwah
mwah mwah
zz

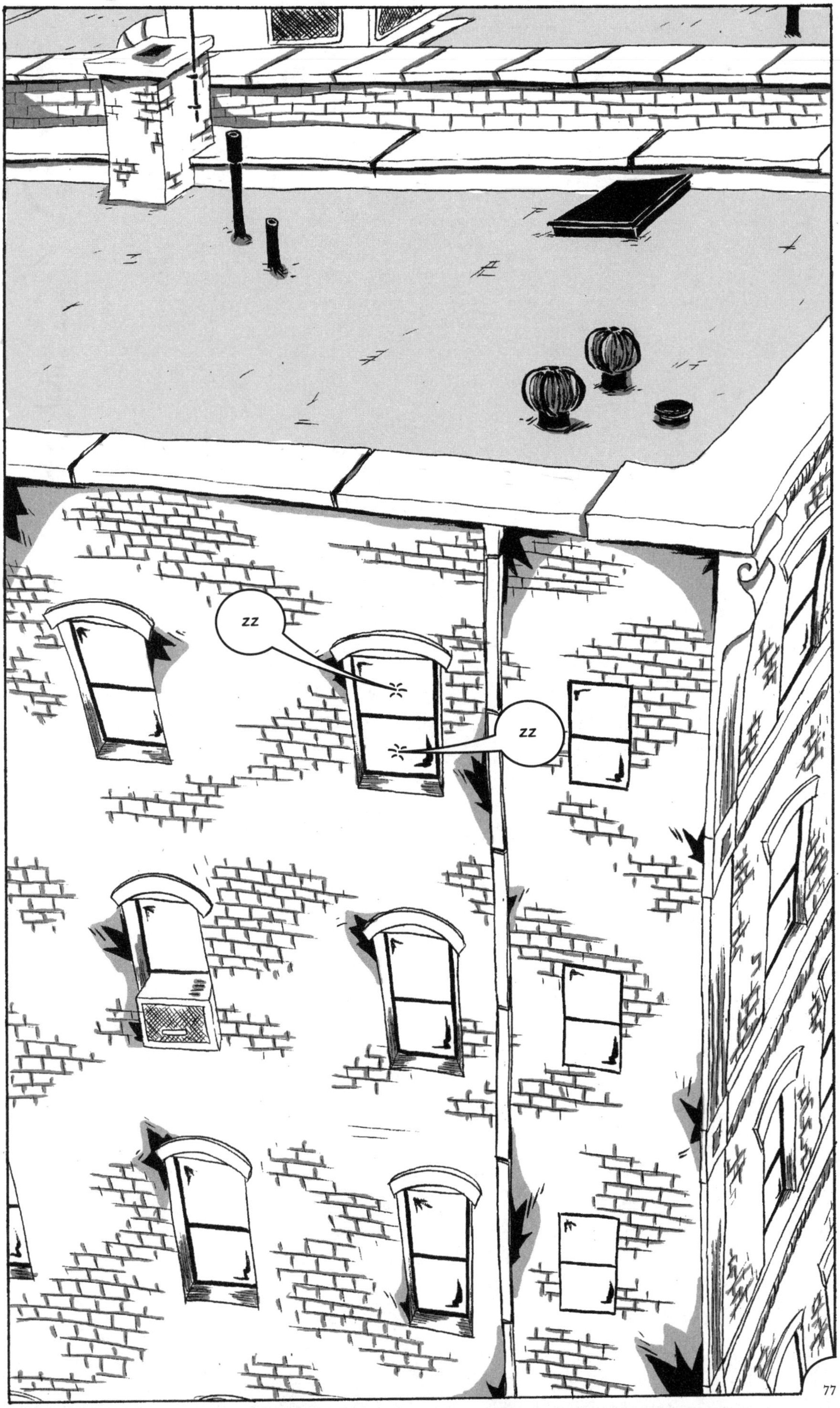
zz
zz

オペラへいきましょう

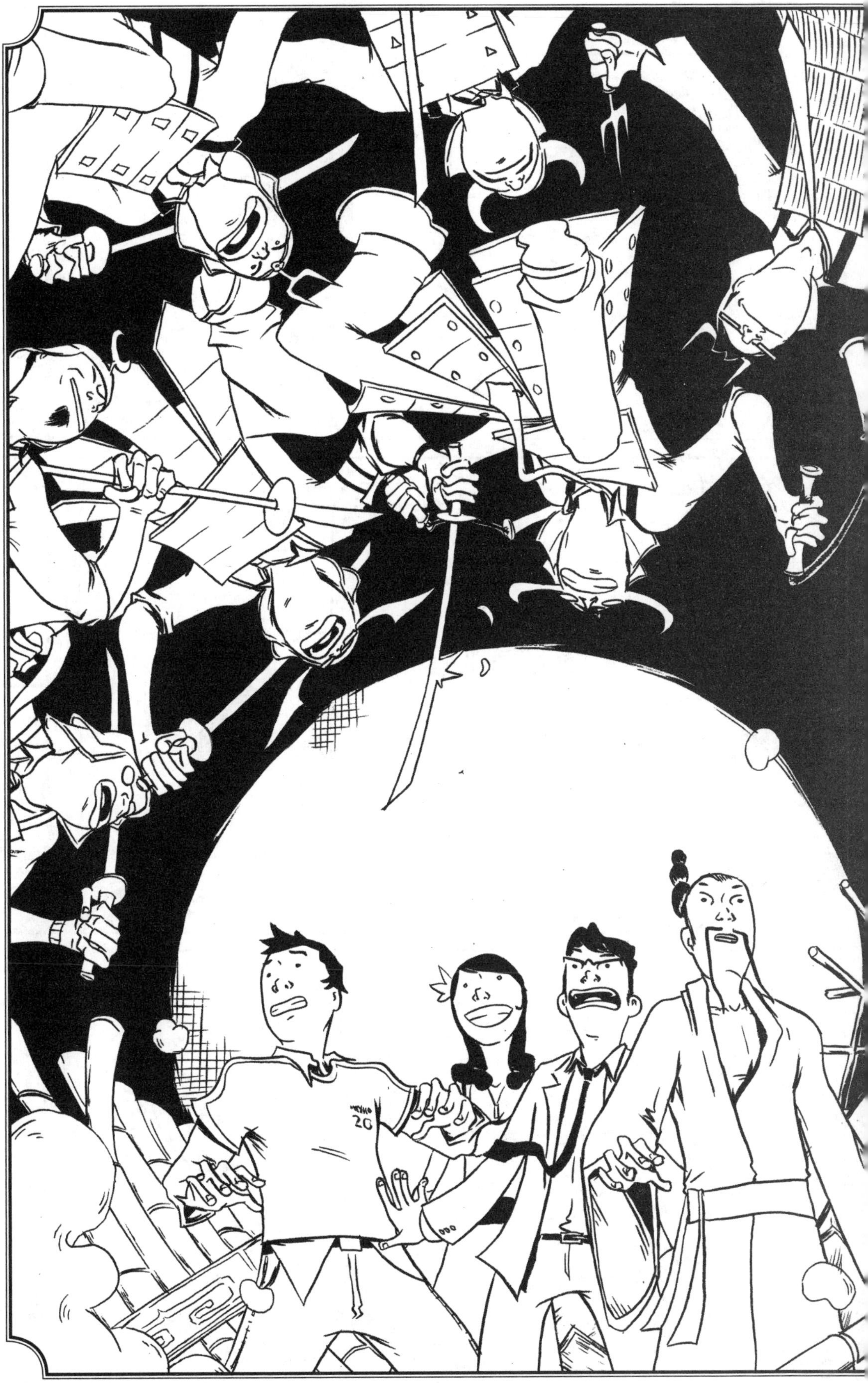
20

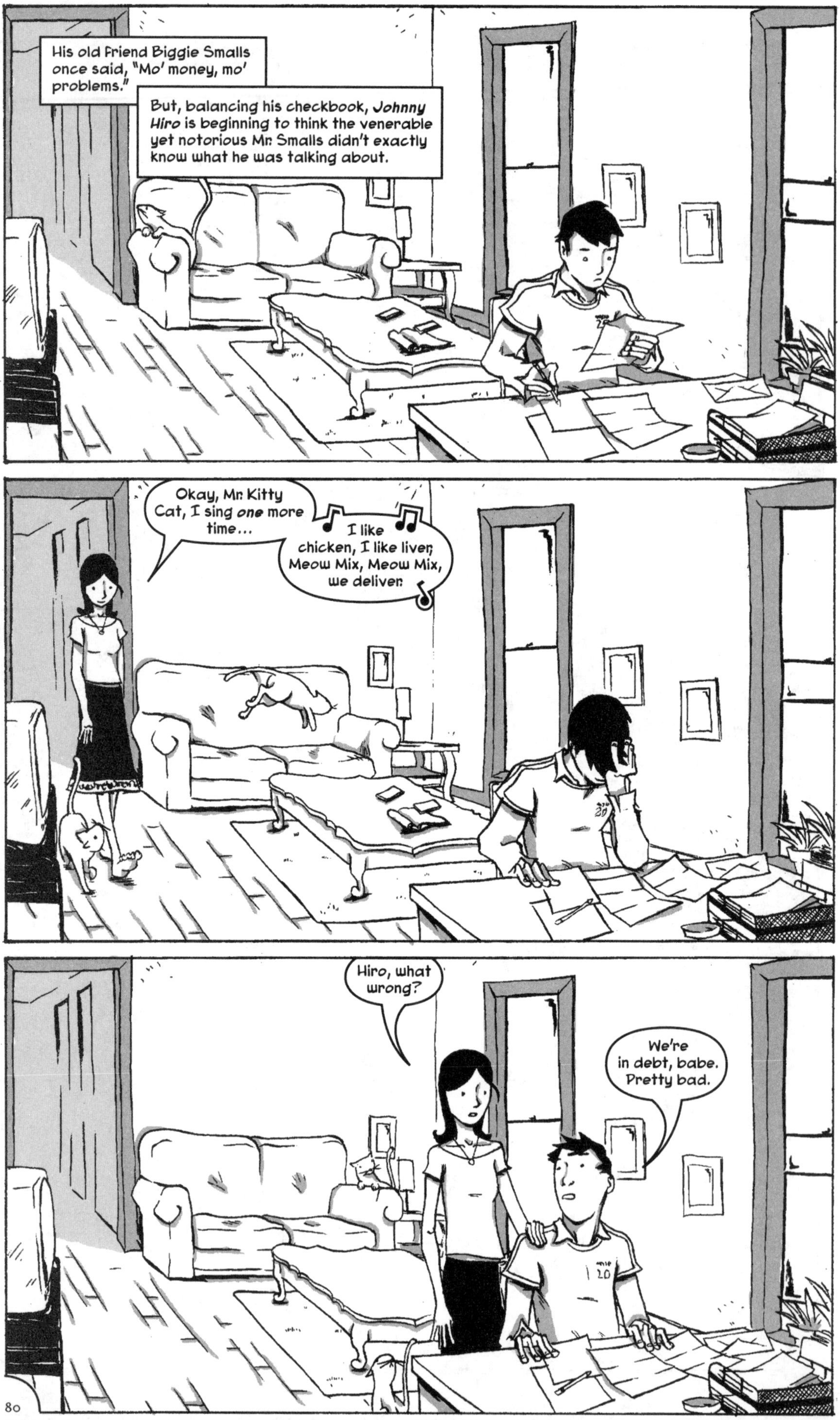
His old friend Biggie Smalls once said, "Mo' money, mo' problems."
But, balancing his checkbook, *Johnny Hiro* is beginning to think the venerable yet notorious Mr. Smalls didn't exactly know what he was talking about.
Okay, Mr. Kitty Cat, I sing *one* more time...
I like chicken, I like liver, Meow Mix, Meow Mix, we deliver.
Hiro, what wrong?
We're in debt, babe. Pretty bad.

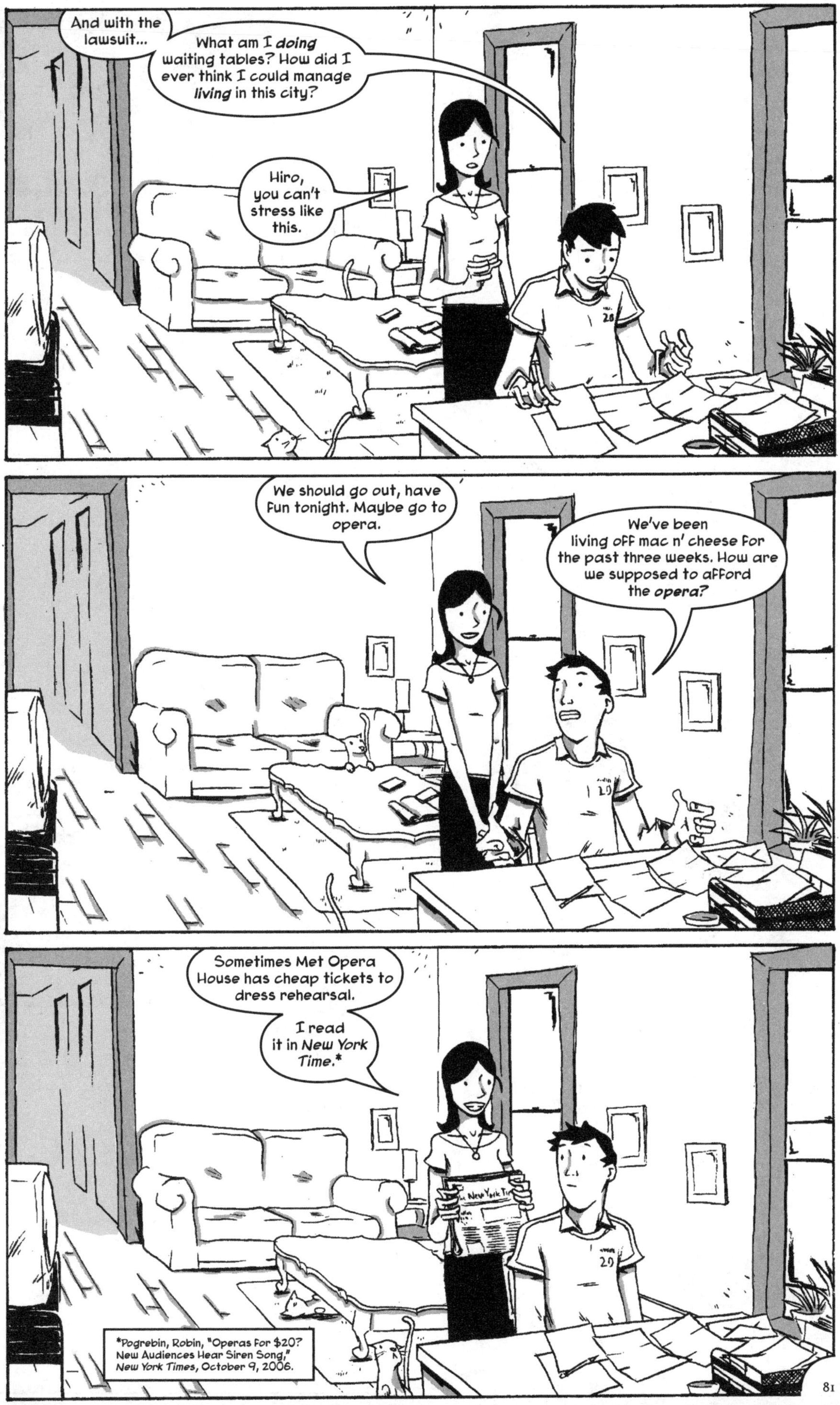
And with the lawsuit...
What am I *doing* waiting tables? How did I ever think I could manage *living* in this city?
Hiro, you can't stress like this.
We should go out, have fun tonight. Maybe go to opera.
We've been living off mac n' cheese for the past three weeks. How are we supposed to afford the *opera?*
Sometimes Met Opera House has cheap tickets to dress rehearsal.
I read it in *New York Time.**
*Pogrebin, Robin, "Operas for $20? New Audiences Hear Siren Song," *New York Times*, October 9, 2006.

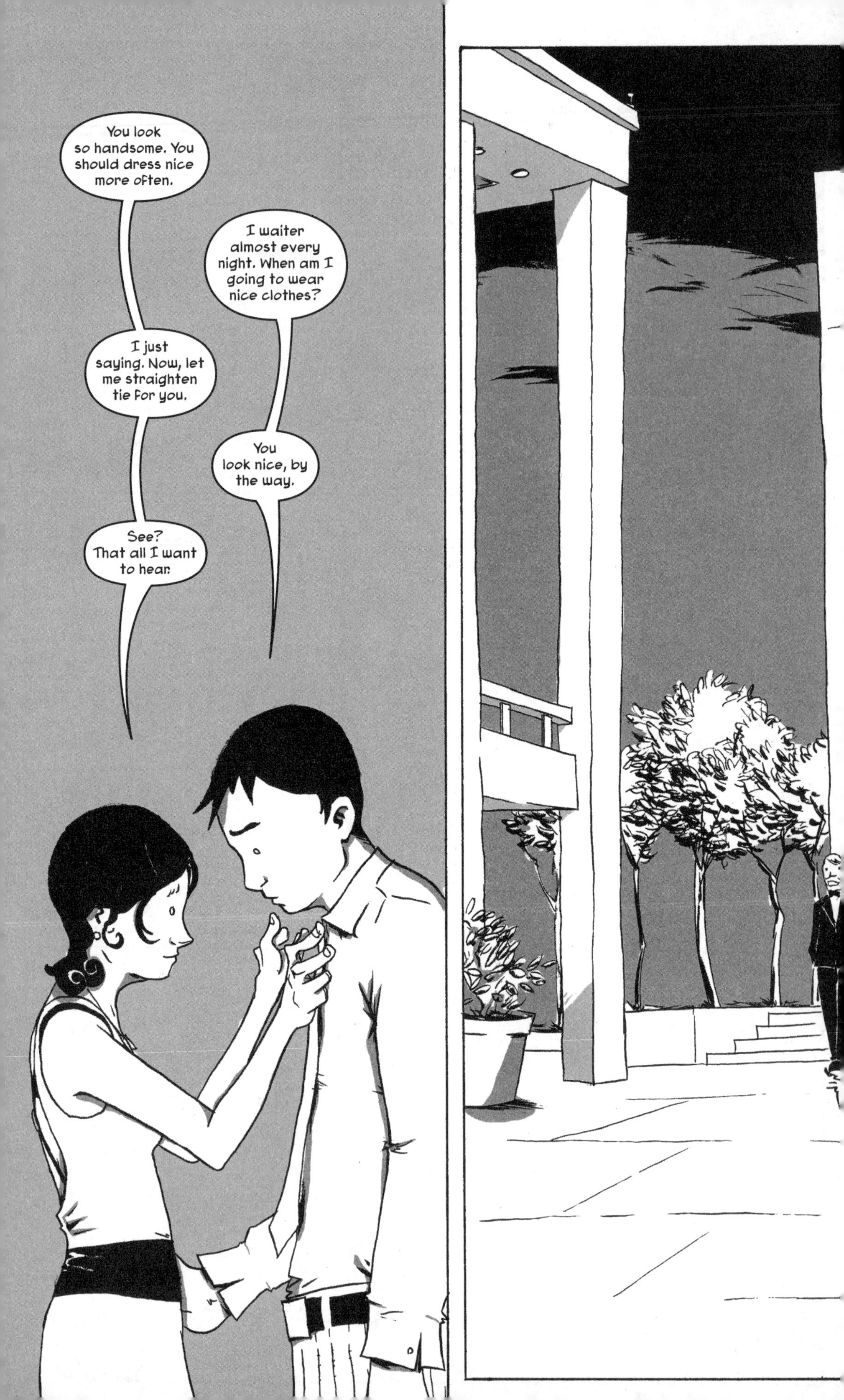
You look so handsome. You should dress nice more often.
I waiter almost every night. When am I going to wear nice clothes?
I just saying. Now, let me straighten tie for you.
You look nice, by the way.
See? That all I want to hear.

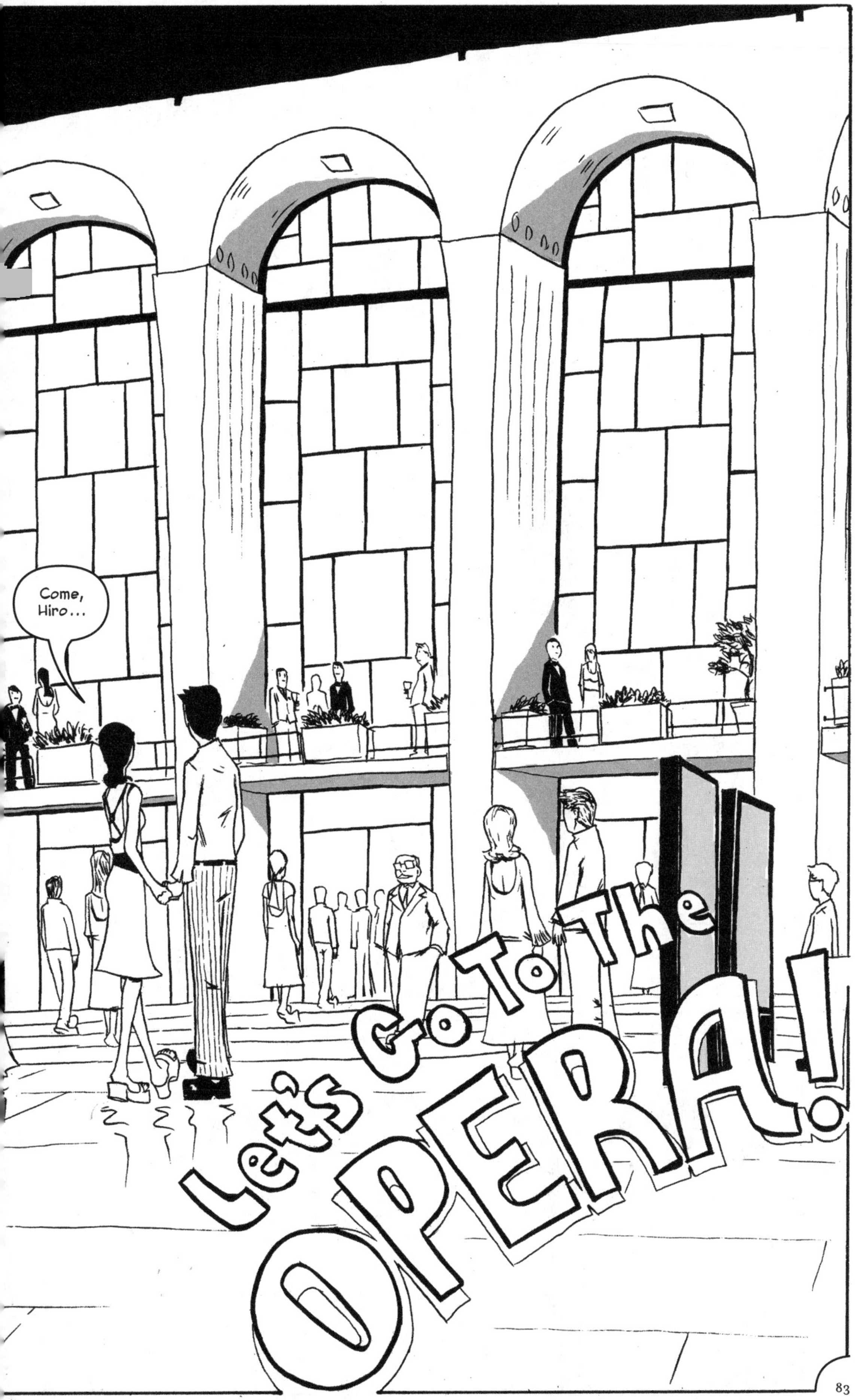
Come, Hiro...
Let's Go To The OPERA!

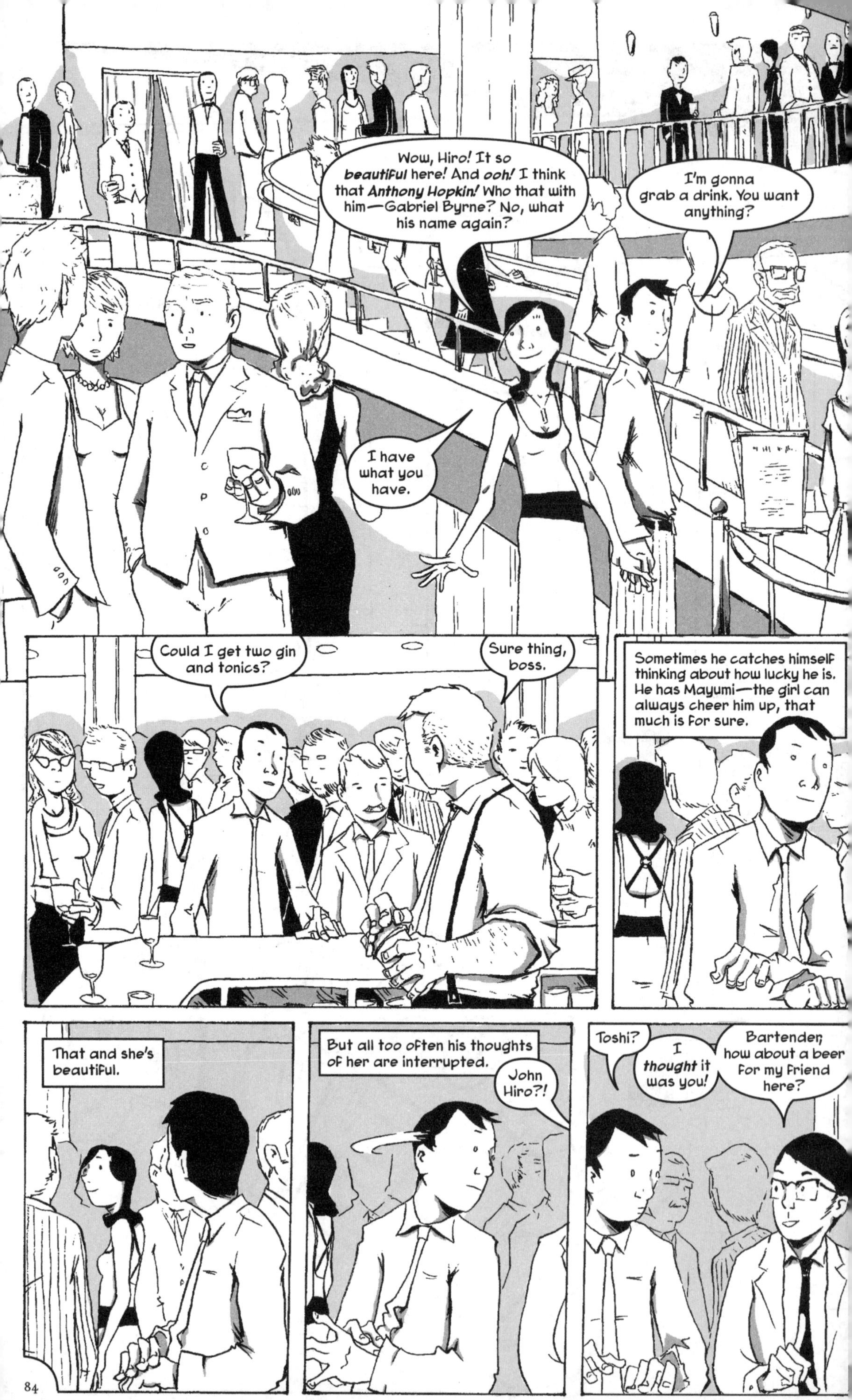
Wow, Hiro! It so *beautiful* here! And *ooh!* I think that *Anthony Hopkin!* Who that with him—Gabriel Byrne? No, what his name again?
I'm gonna grab a drink. You want anything?
I have what you have.
Could I get two gin and tonics?
Sure thing, boss.
Sometimes he catches himself thinking about how lucky he is. He has Mayumi—the girl can always cheer him up, that much is for sure.
That and she's beautiful.
But all too often his thoughts of her are interrupted.
John Hiro?!
Toshi?
I *thought* it was you!
Bartender, how about a beer for my friend here?

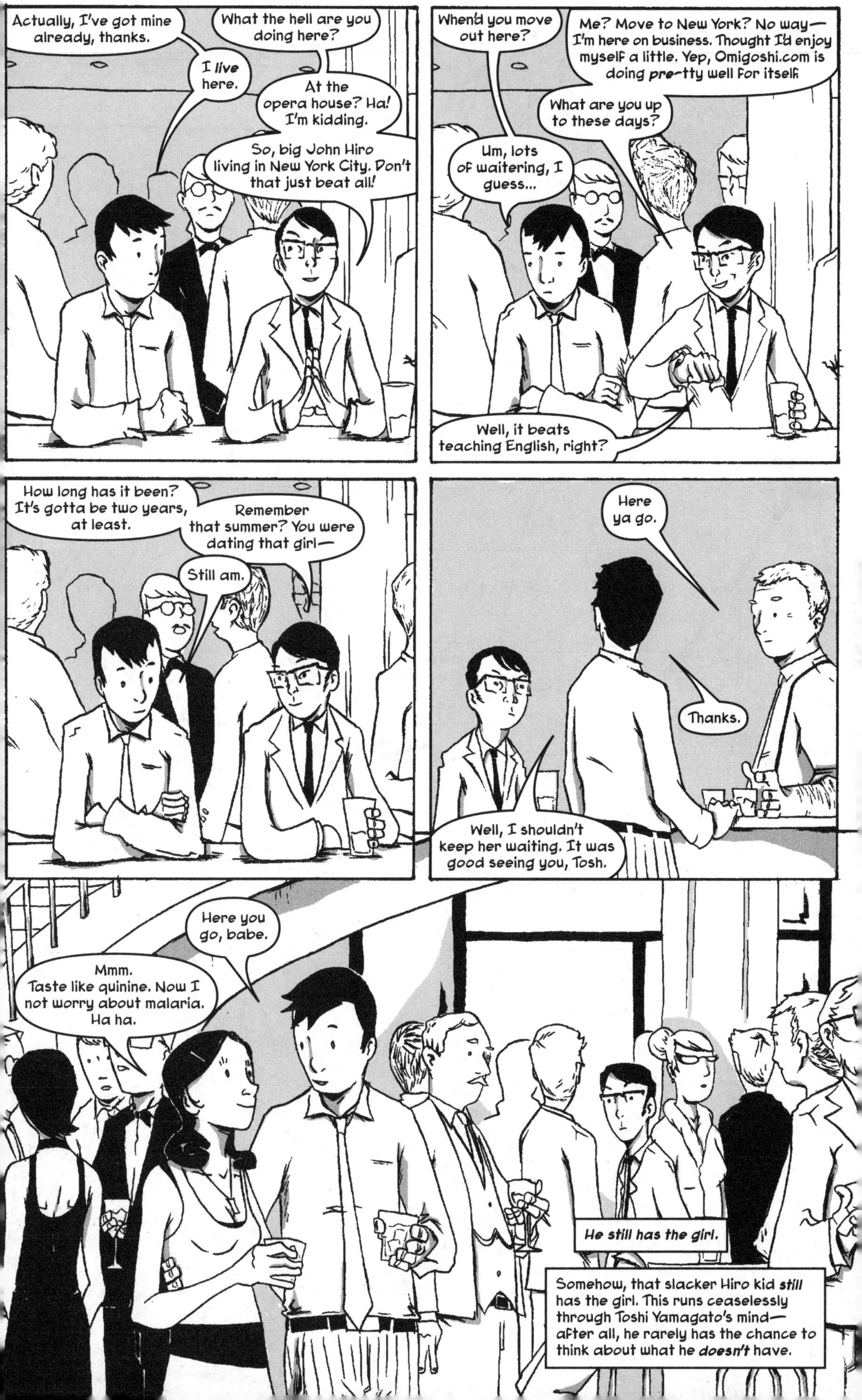
Actually, I've got mine already, thanks.
What the hell are you doing here?
I *live* here.
At the opera house? Ha! I'm kidding.
So, big John Hiro living in New York City. Don't that just beat all!
When'd you move out here?
Me? Move to New York? No way—I'm here on business. Thought I'd enjoy myself a little. Yep, Omigoshi.com is doing *pre*-tty well for itself.
What are you up to these days?
Um, lots of waitering, I guess...
Well, it beats teaching English, right?
How long has it been? It's gotta be two years, at least.
Remember that summer? You were dating that girl—
Still am.
Here ya go.
Thanks.
Well, I shouldn't keep her waiting. It was good seeing you, Tosh.
Here you go, babe.
Mmm. Taste like quinine. Now I not worry about malaria. Ha ha.
He still has the girl.
Somehow, that slacker Hiro kid *still* has the girl. This runs ceaselessly through Toshi Yamagato's mind—after all, he rarely has the chance to think about what he *doesn't* have.

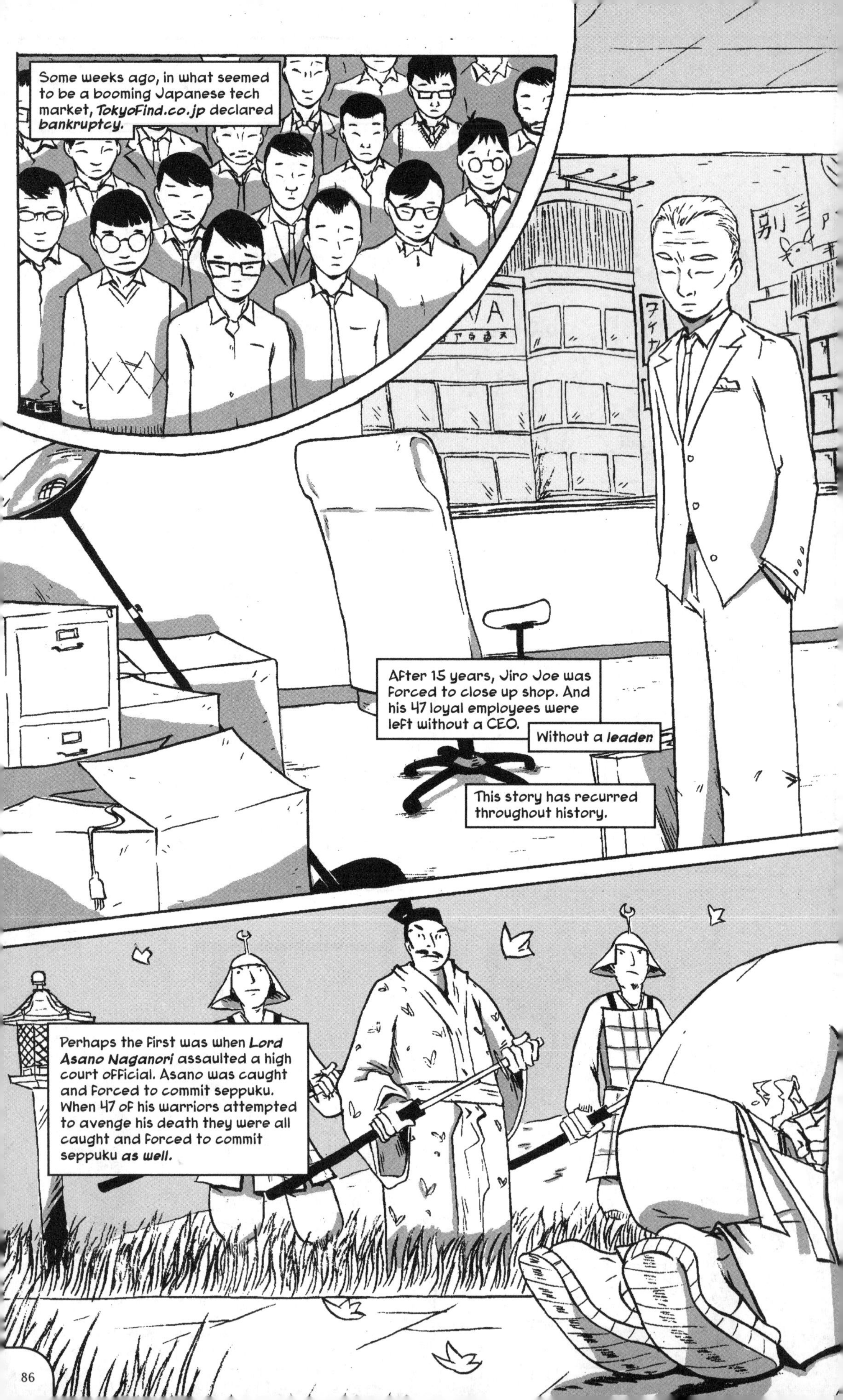
Some weeks ago, in what seemed to be a booming Japanese tech market, *TokyoFind.co.jp* declared ***bankruptcy.***
After 15 years, Jiro Joe was forced to close up shop. And his 47 loyal employees were left without a CEO.
Without a ***leader.***
This story has recurred throughout history.
Perhaps the first was when ***Lord Asano Naganori*** assaulted a high court official. Asano was caught and forced to commit seppuku. When 47 of his warriors attempted to avenge his death they were all caught and forced to commit seppuku ***as well.***

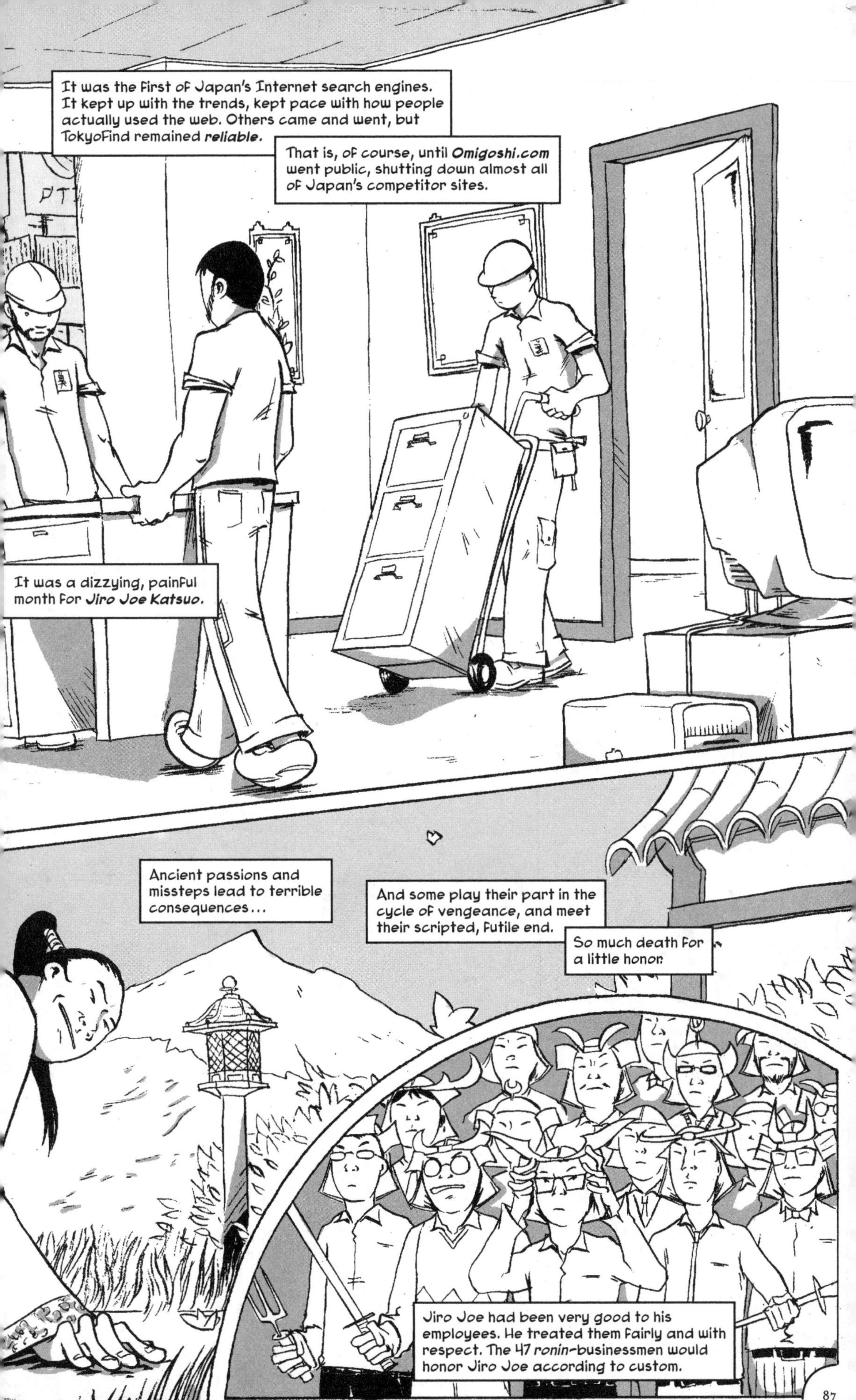
It was the first of Japan's Internet search engines. It kept up with the trends, kept pace with how people actually used the web. Others came and went, but TokyoFind remained *reliable.*
That is, of course, until *Omigoshi.com* went public, shutting down almost all of Japan's competitor sites.
It was a dizzying, painful month for *Jiro Joe Katsuo.*
Ancient passions and missteps lead to terrible consequences...
And some play their part in the cycle of vengeance, and meet their scripted, futile end.
So much death for a little honor.
Jiro Joe had been very good to his employees. He treated them fairly and with respect. The 47 *ronin*-businessmen would honor Jiro Joe according to custom.

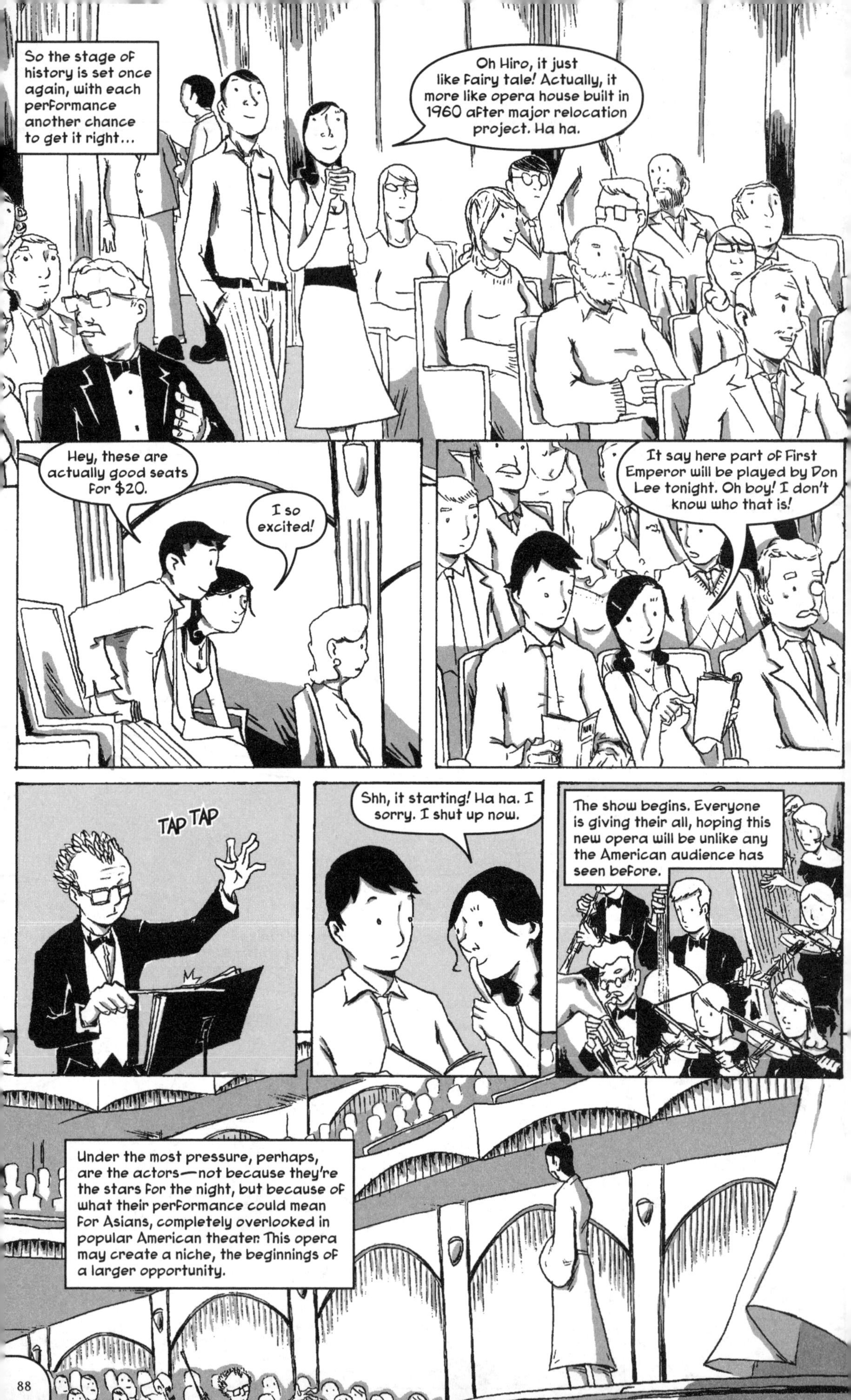

So the stage of history is set once again, with each performance another chance to get it right...
Oh Hiro, it just like fairy tale! Actually, it more like opera house built in 1960 after major relocation project. Ha ha.
Hey, these are actually good seats for $20.
I so excited!
It say here part of First Emperor will be played by Don Lee tonight. Oh boy! I don't know who that is!
TAP TAP
Shh, it starting! Ha ha. I sorry. I shut up now.
The show begins. Everyone is giving their all, hoping this new opera will be unlike any the American audience has seen before.
Under the most pressure, perhaps, are the actors—not because they're the stars for the night, but because of what their performance could mean for Asians, completely overlooked in popular American theater. This opera may create a niche, the beginnings of a larger opportunity.

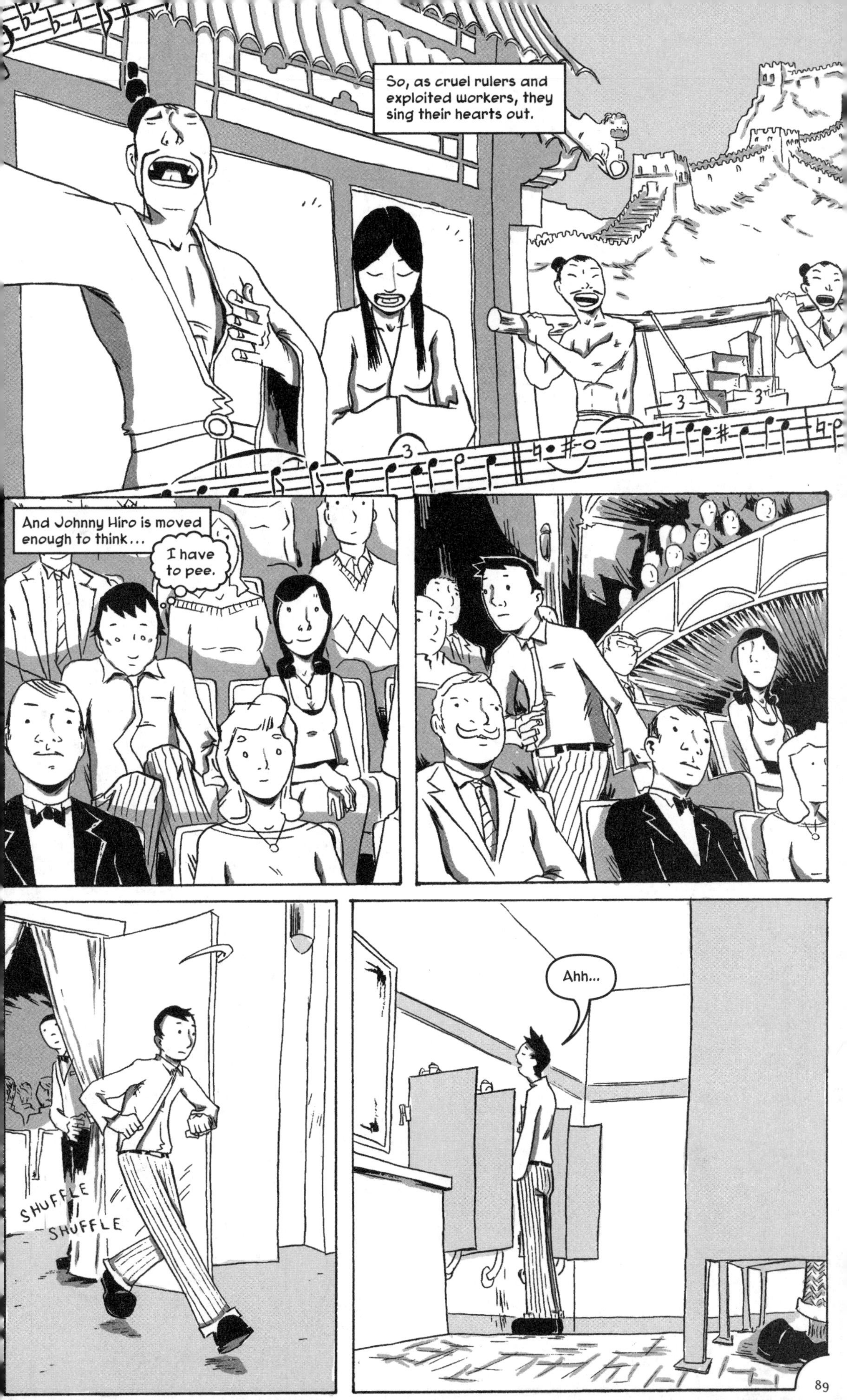
So, as cruel rulers and exploited workers, they sing their hearts out.
And Johnny Hiro is moved enough to think...
I have to pee.
SHUFFLE
SHUFFLE
Ahh...

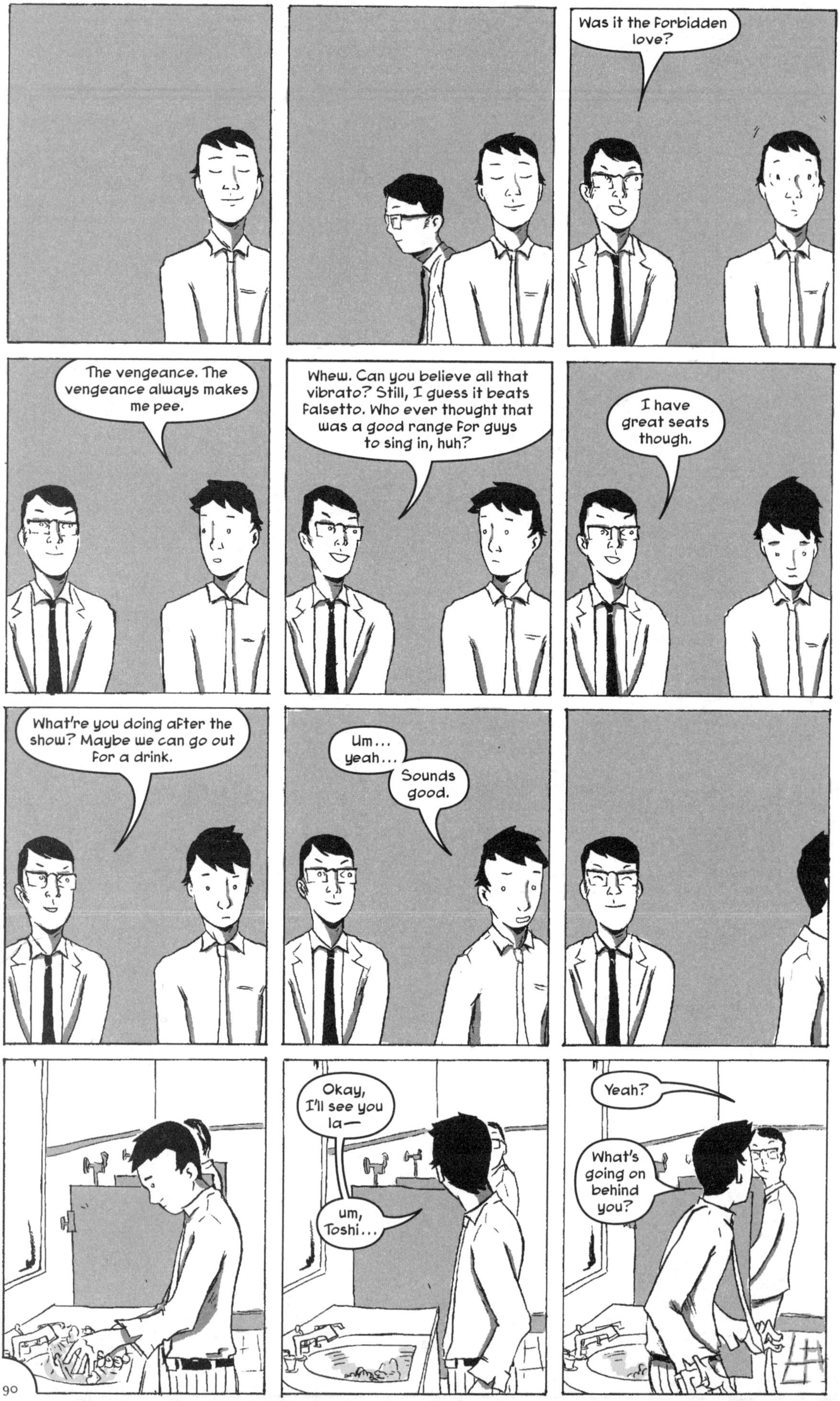
Was it the forbidden love?
The vengeance. The vengeance always makes me pee.
Whew. Can you believe all that vibrato? Still, I guess it beats falsetto. Who ever thought that was a good range for guys to sing in, huh?
I have great seats though.
What're you doing after the show? Maybe we can go out for a drink.
Um... yeah...
Sounds good.
Okay, I'll see you la—
um, Toshi...
Yeah?
What's going on behind you?

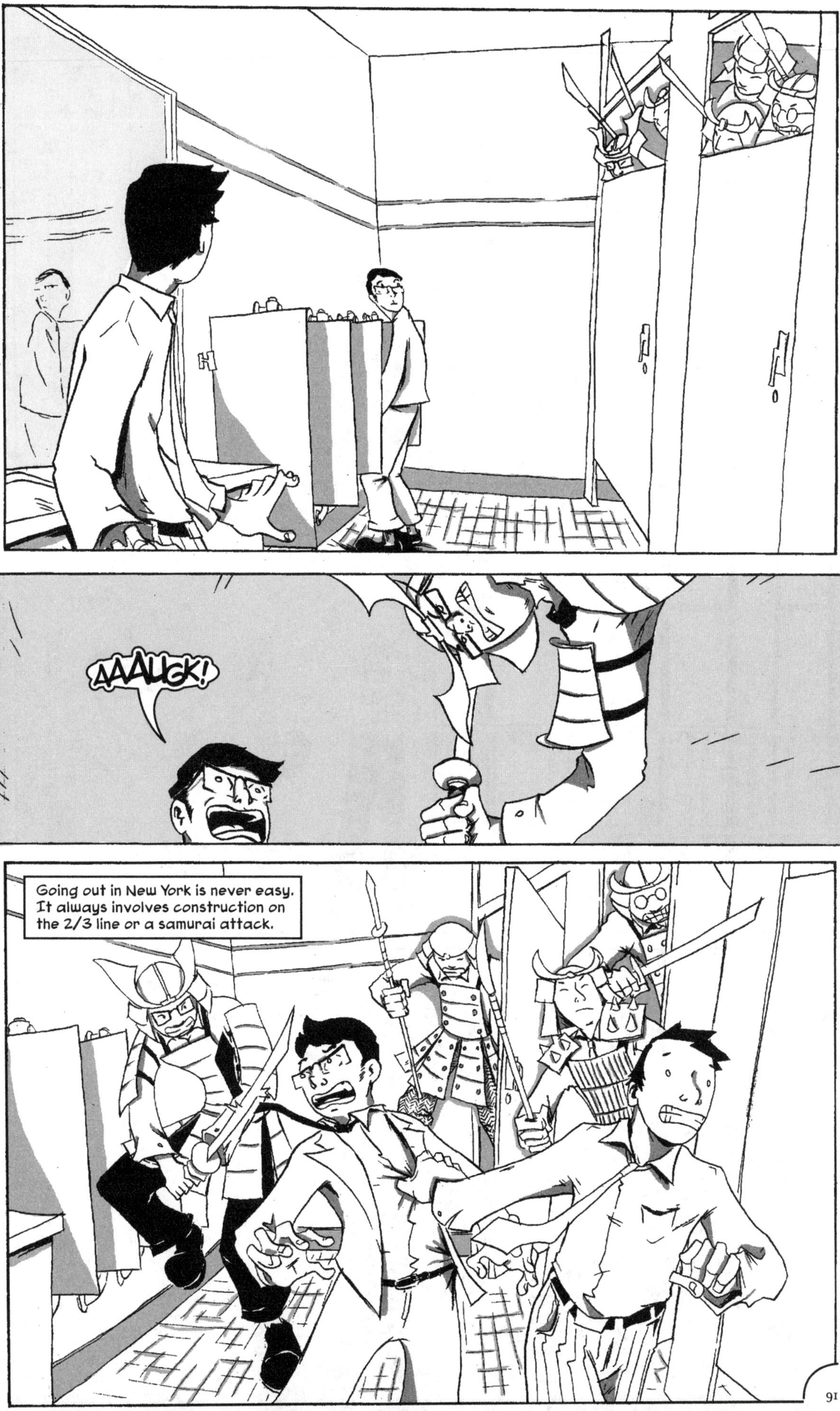
AAAUGK!
Going out in New York is never easy. It always involves construction on the 2/3 line or a samurai attack.

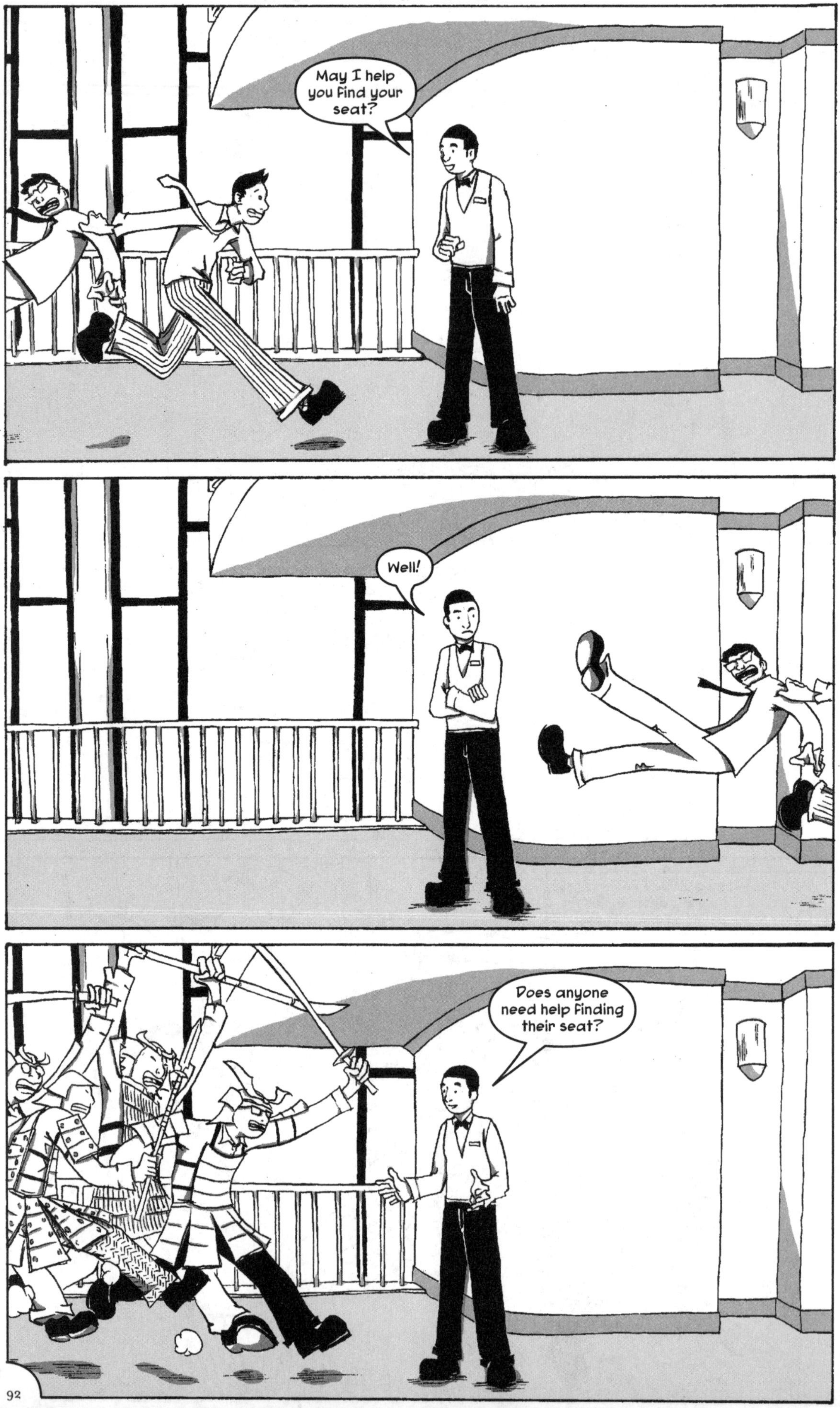
May I help you find your seat?
Well!
Does anyone need help finding their seat?

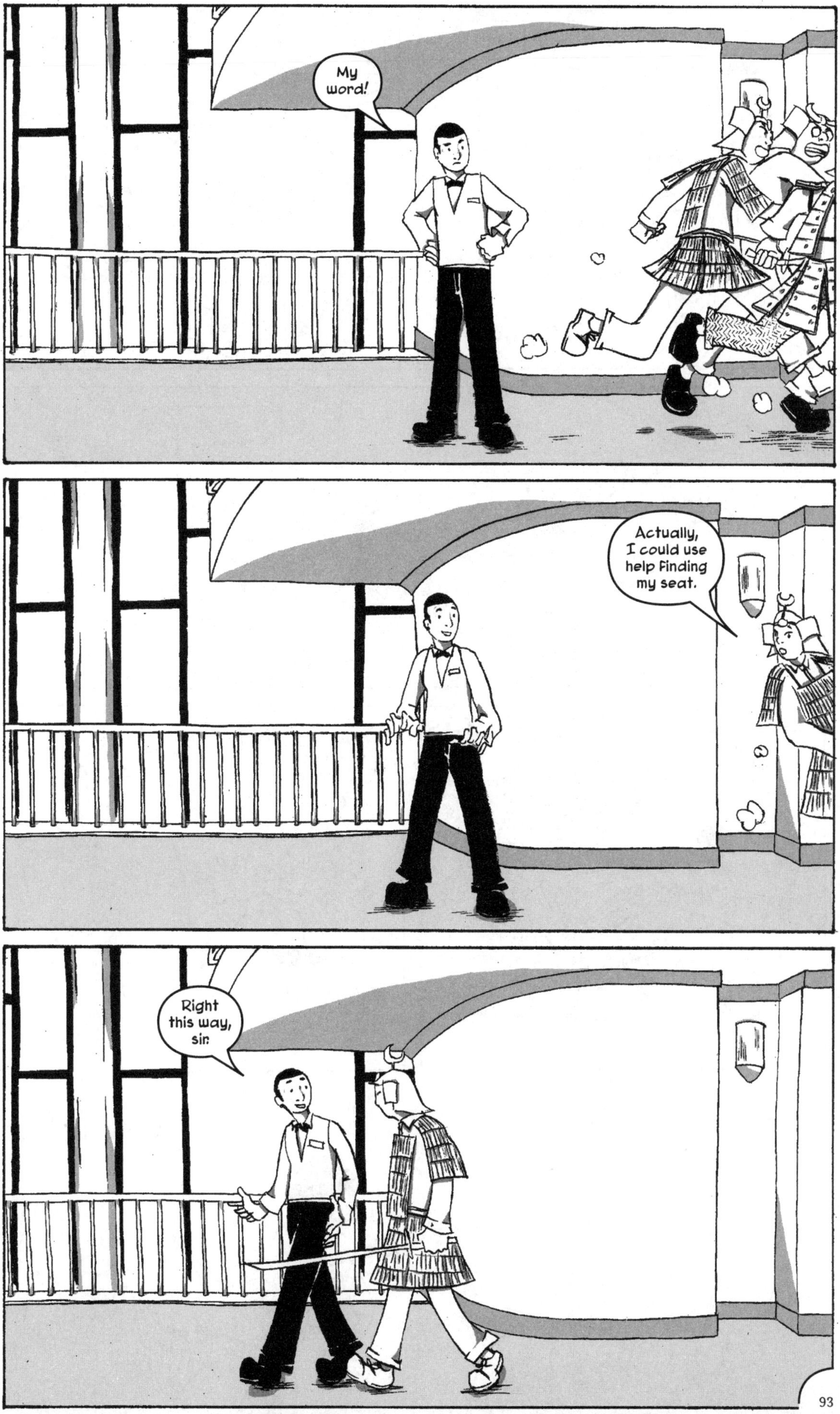
My word!
Actually, I could use help finding my seat.
Right this way, sir.

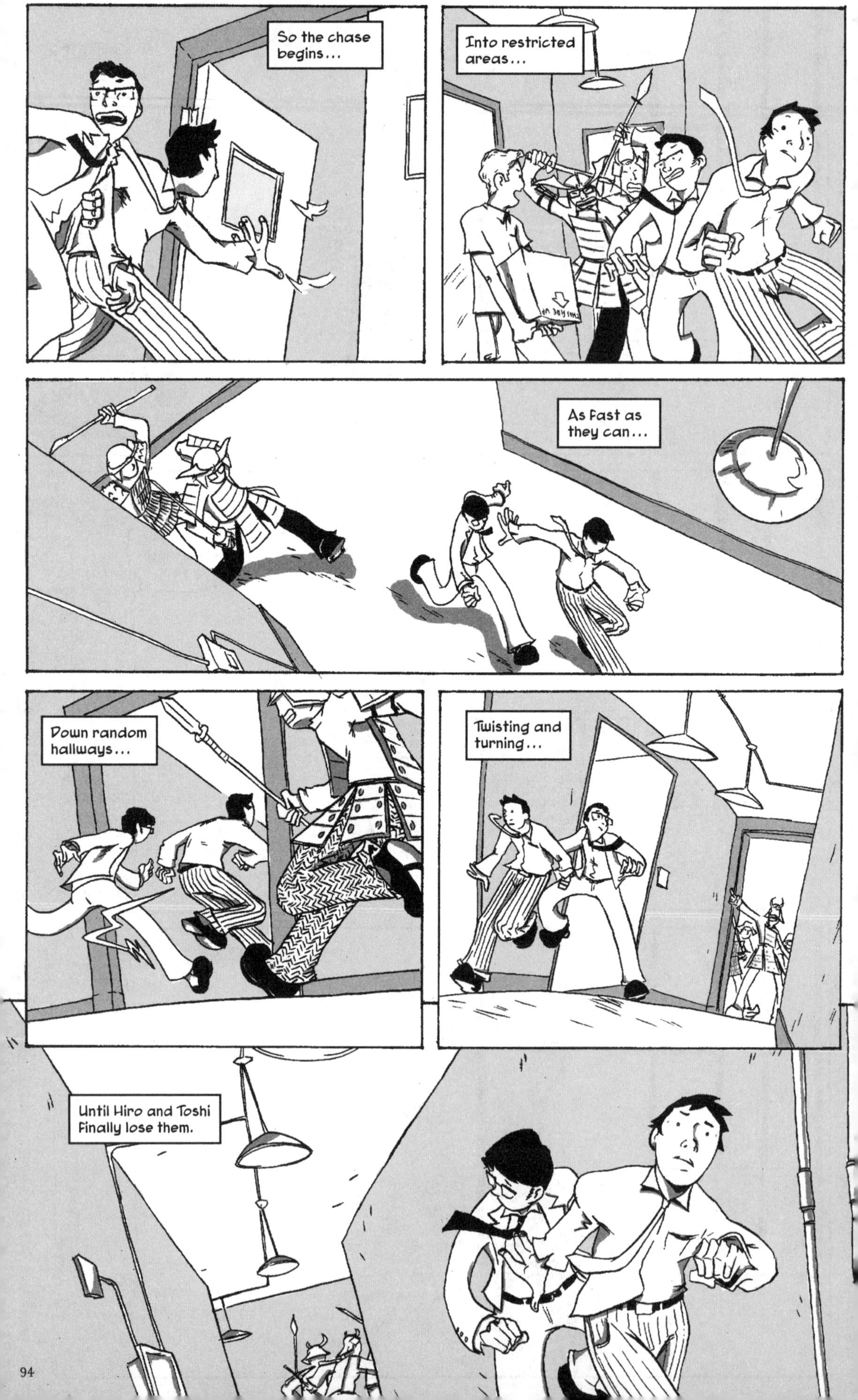
So the chase begins...
Into restricted areas...
As fast as they can...
Down random hallways...
Twisting and turning...
Until Hiro and Toshi finally lose them.

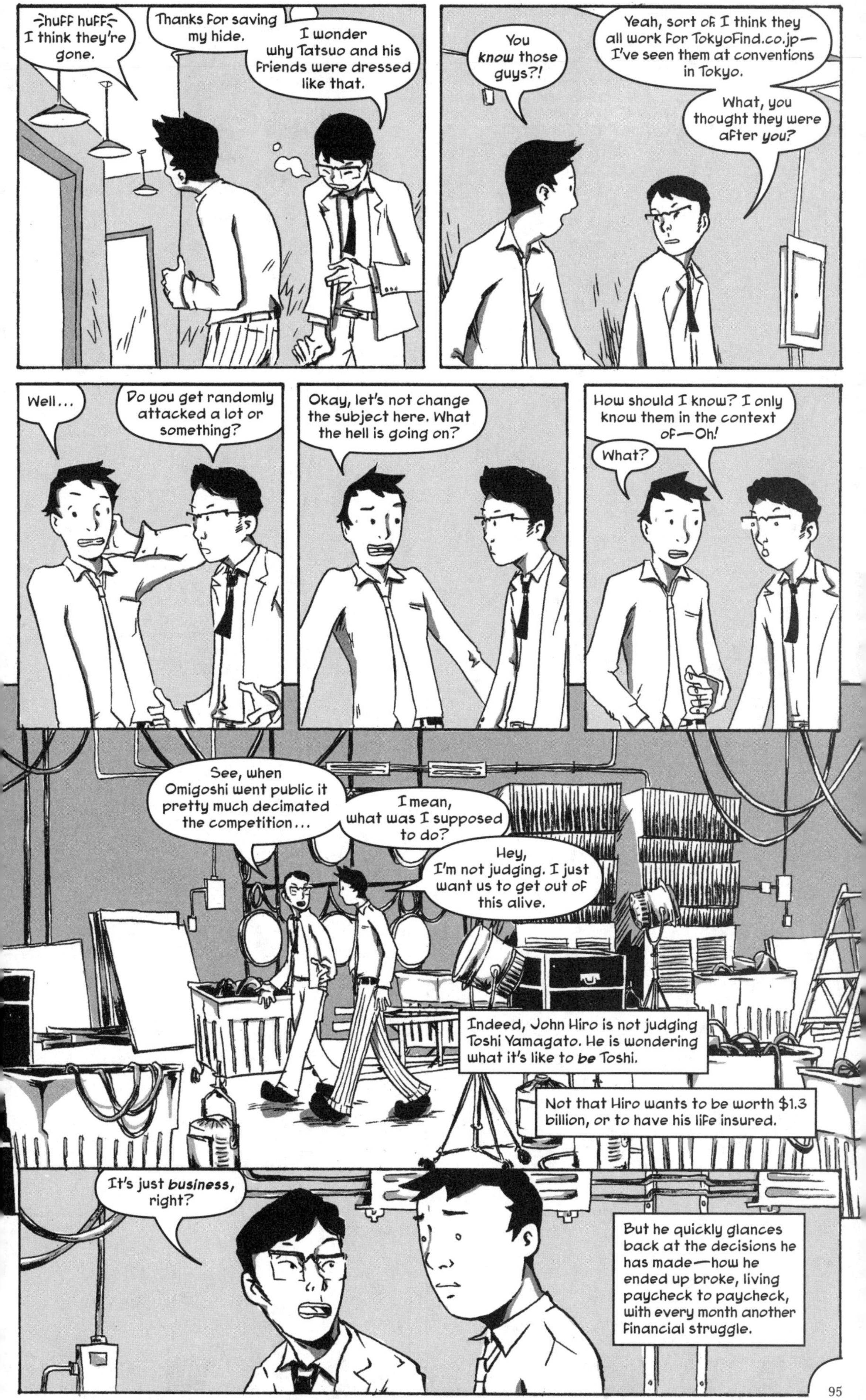

~huff huff~ I think they're gone.
Thanks for saving my hide.
I wonder why Tatsuo and his friends were dressed like that.
You *know* those guys?!
Yeah, sort of. I think they all work for TokyoFind.co.jp— I've seen them at conventions in Tokyo.
What, you thought they were after *you*?
Well...
Do you get randomly attacked a lot or something?
Okay, let's not change the subject here. What the hell is going on?
How should I know? I only know them in the context of—Oh!
What?
See, when Omigoshi went public it pretty much decimated the competition...
I mean, what was I supposed to do?
Hey, I'm not judging. I just want us to get out of this alive.
Indeed, John Hiro is not judging Toshi Yamagato. He is wondering what it's like to *be* Toshi.
Not that Hiro wants to be worth $1.3 billion, or to have his life insured.
It's just *business*, right?
But he quickly glances back at the decisions he has made—how he ended up broke, living paycheck to paycheck, with every month another financial struggle.

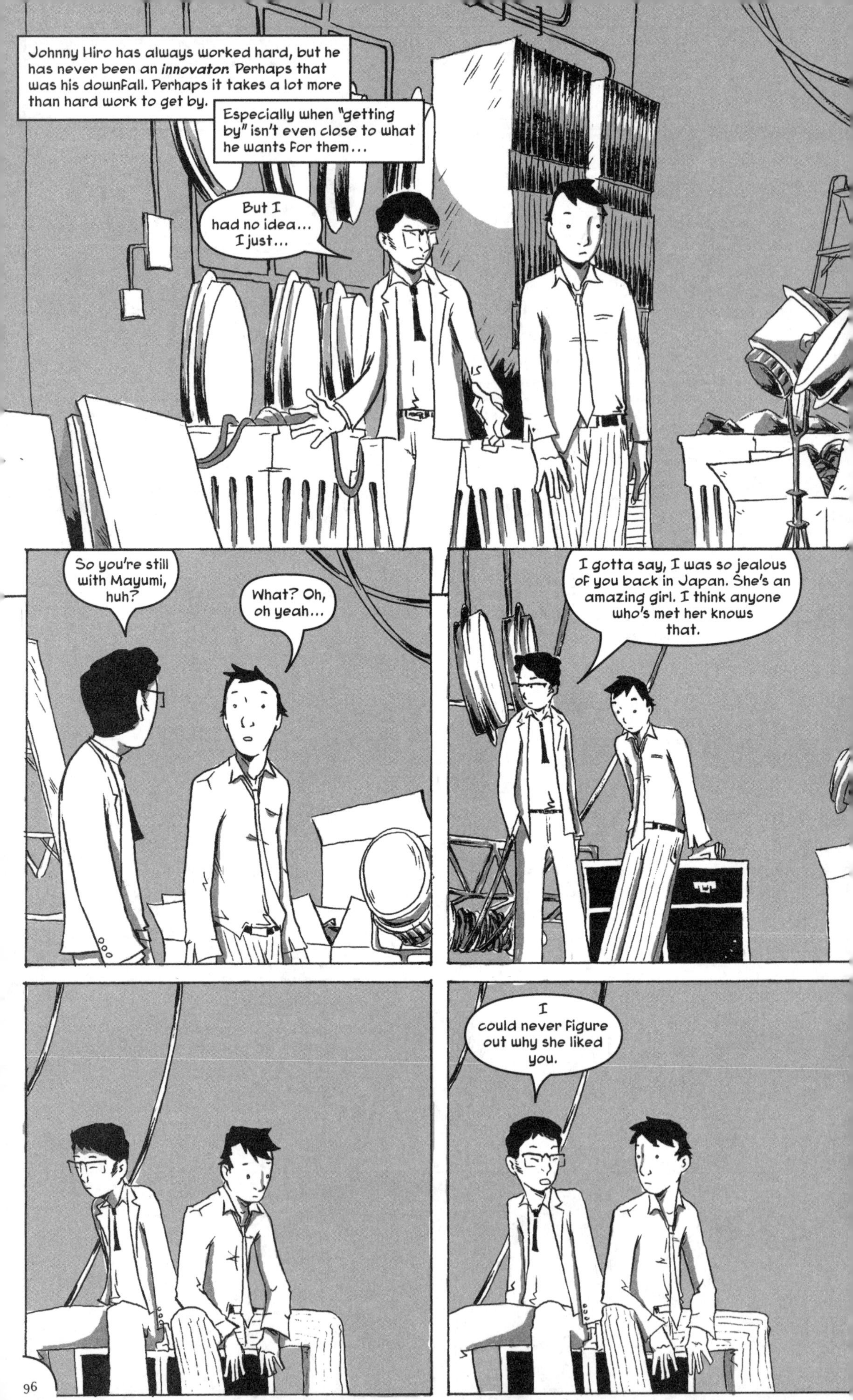

Johnny Hiro has always worked hard, but he has never been an *innovator*. Perhaps that was his downfall. Perhaps it takes a lot more than hard work to get by.
Especially when "getting by" isn't even close to what he wants for them...
But I had no idea... I just...
So you're still with Mayumi, huh?
What? Oh, oh yeah...
I gotta say, I was so jealous of you back in Japan. She's an amazing girl. I think anyone who's met her knows that.
I could never figure out why she liked you.

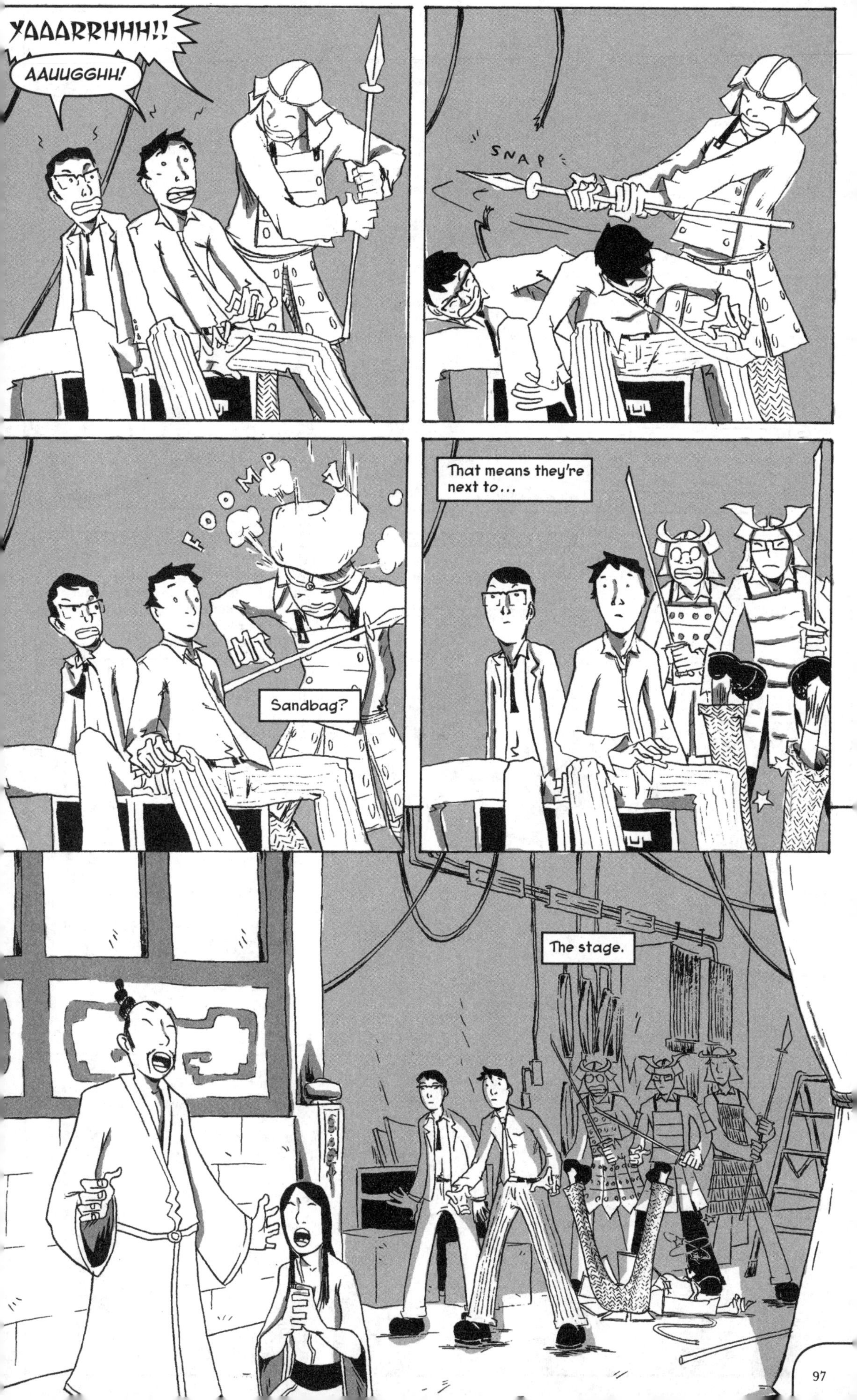
YAAARRHHH!!
AAUUGGHH!
SNAP
FOOMP
Sandbag?
That means they're next to...
The stage.

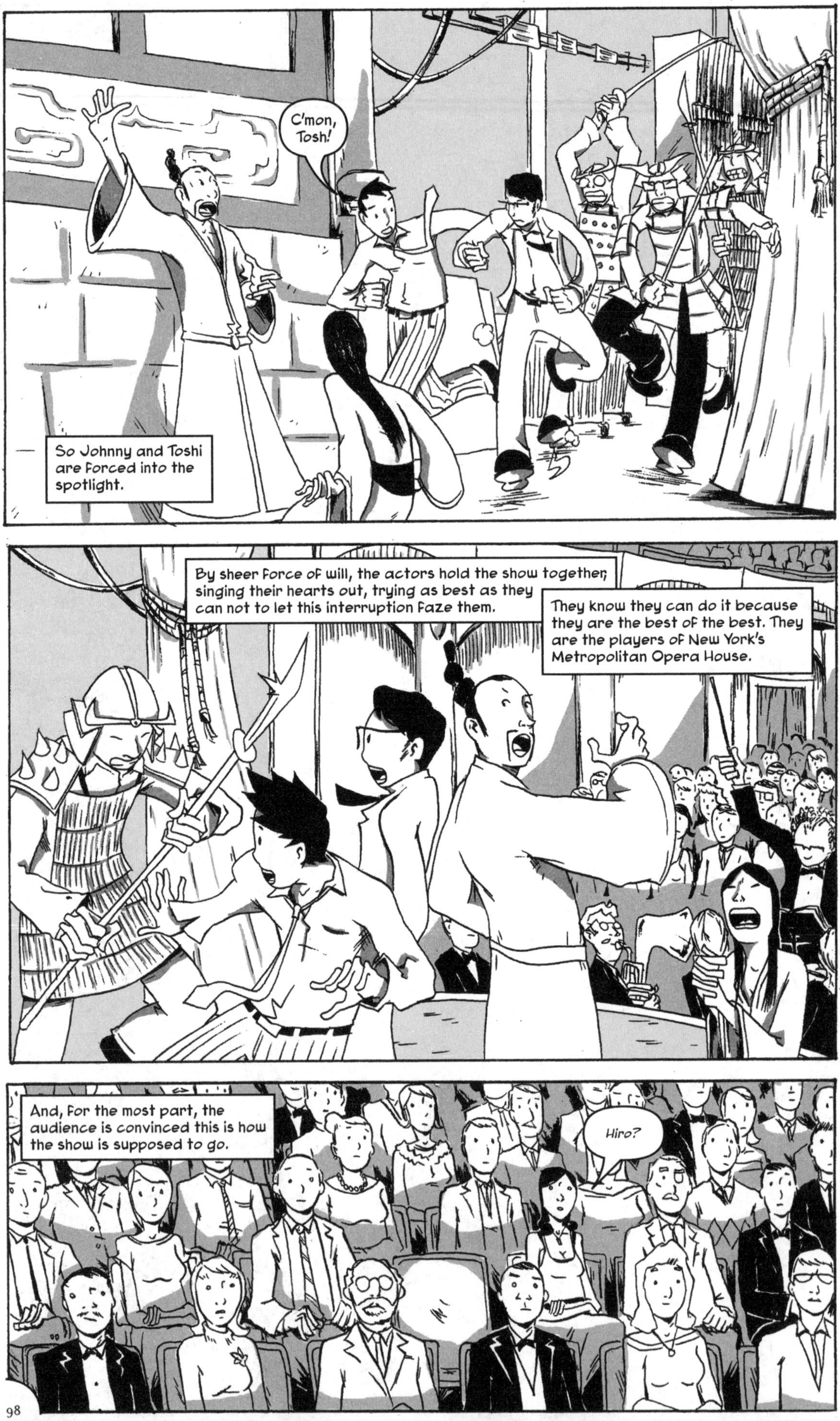

C'mon, Tosh!
So Johnny and Toshi are forced into the spotlight.
By sheer force of will, the actors hold the show together, singing their hearts out, trying as best as they can not to let this interruption faze them.
They know they can do it because they are the best of the best. They are the players of New York's Metropolitan Opera House.
And, for the most part, the audience is convinced this is how the show is supposed to go.
Hiro?

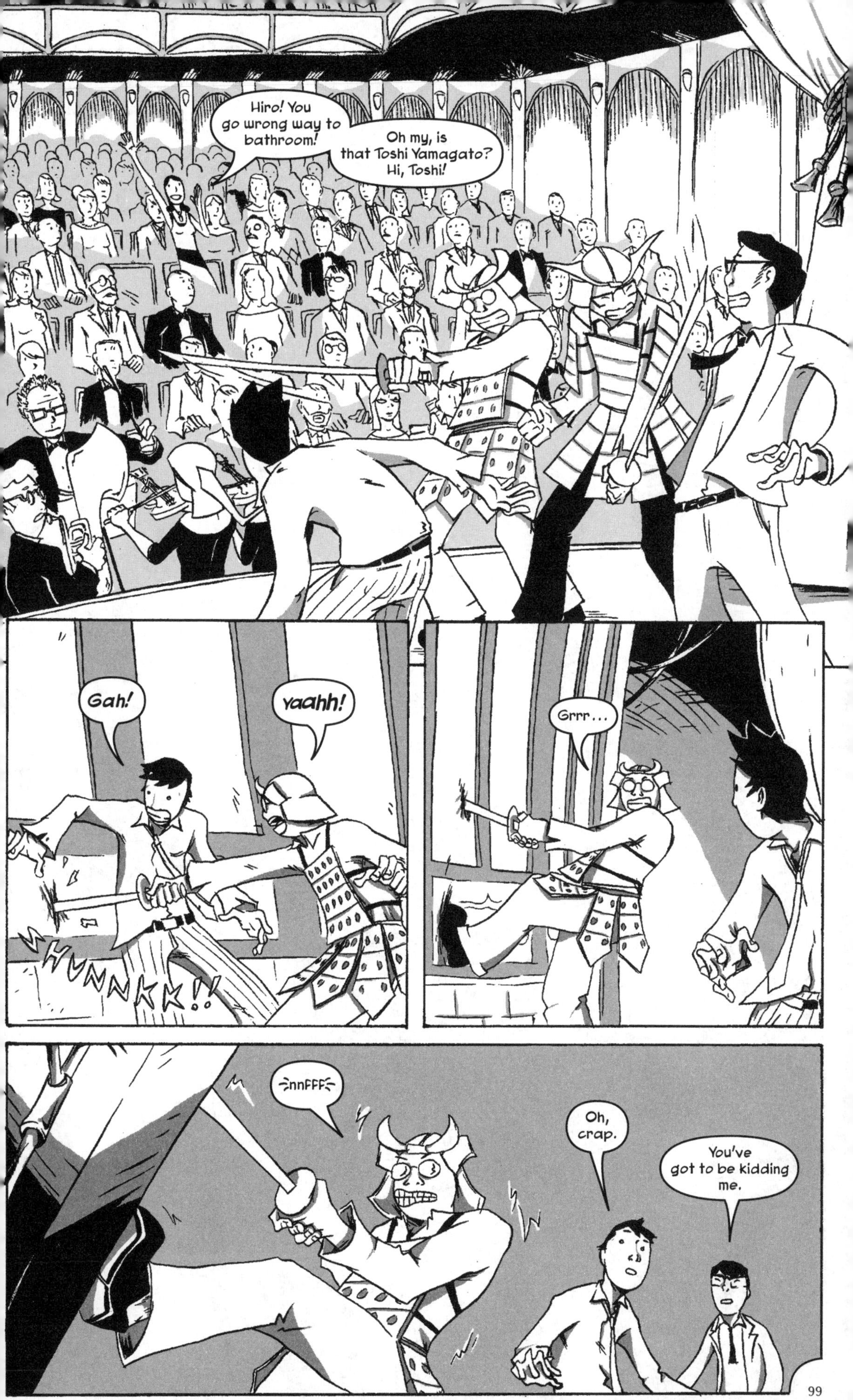

Hiro! You go wrong way to bathroom!
Oh my, is that Toshi Yamagato? Hi, Toshi!
Gah!
yaahh!
SHUNNKK!!
Grrr...
nnFFF
Oh, crap.
You've got to be kidding me.

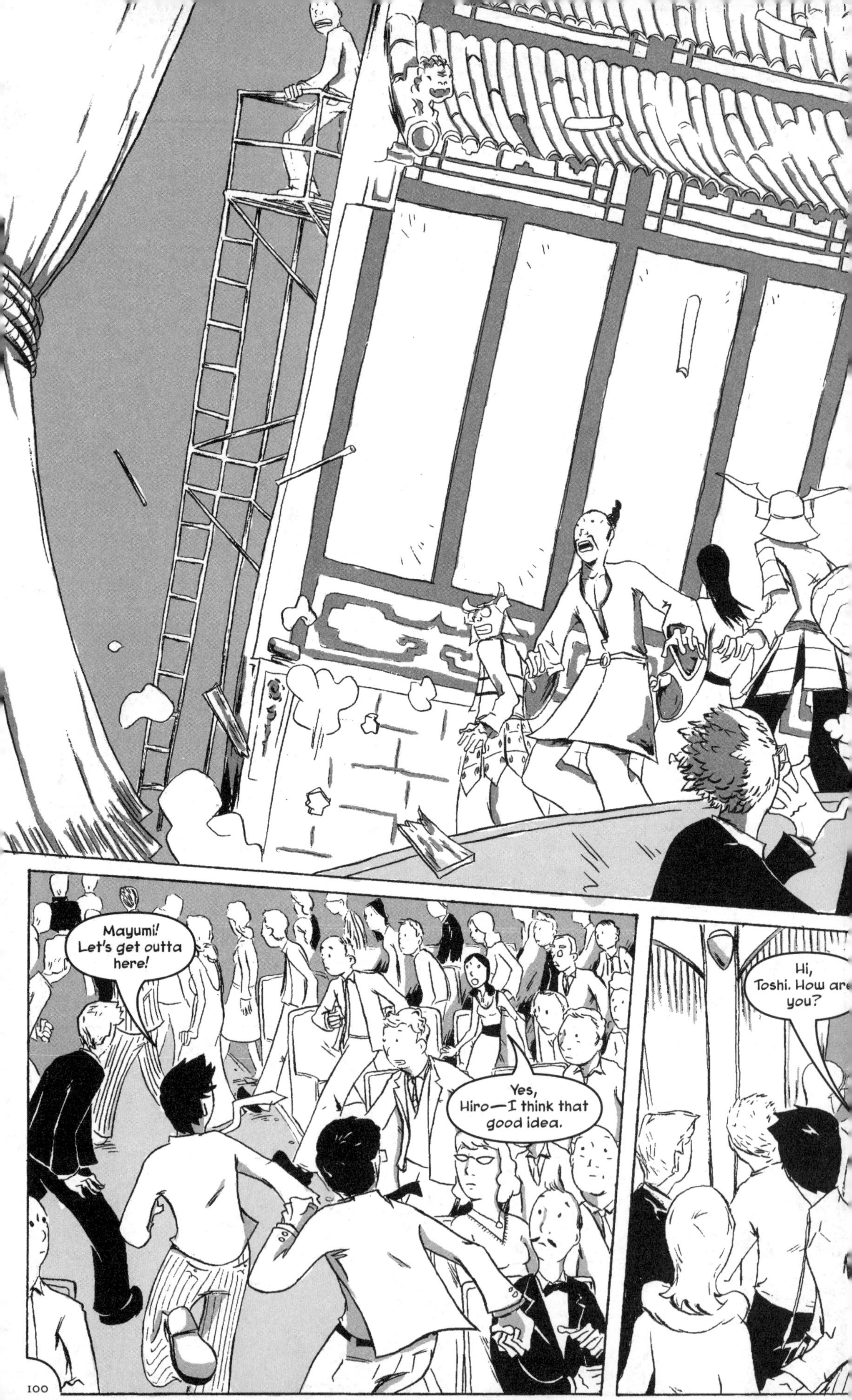
Mayumi! Let's get outta here!
Yes, Hiro—I think that good idea.
Hi, Toshi. How ar
you?

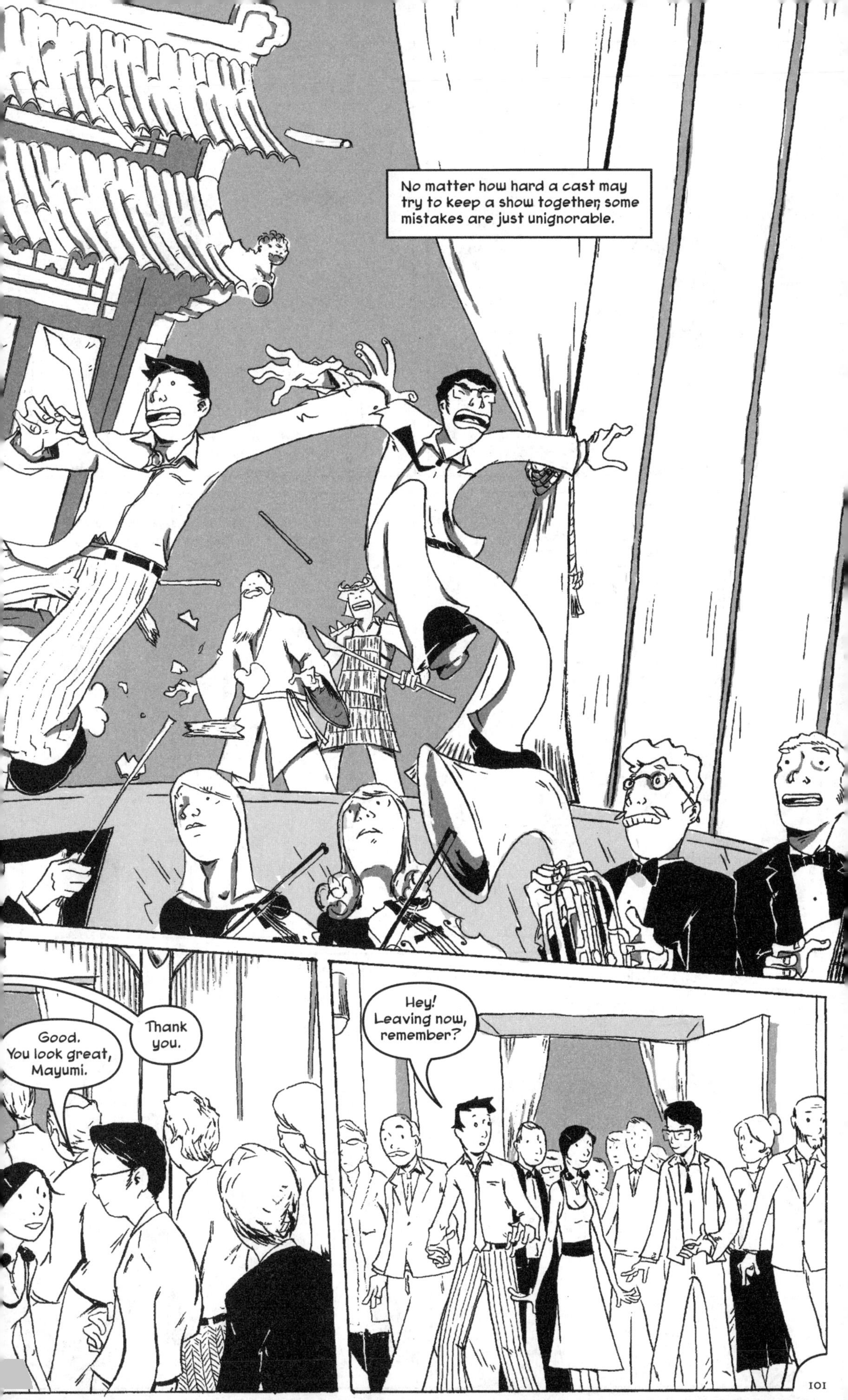
No matter how hard a cast may try to keep a show together, some mistakes are just unignorable.
Good. You look great, Mayumi.
Thank you.
Hey! Leaving now, remember?

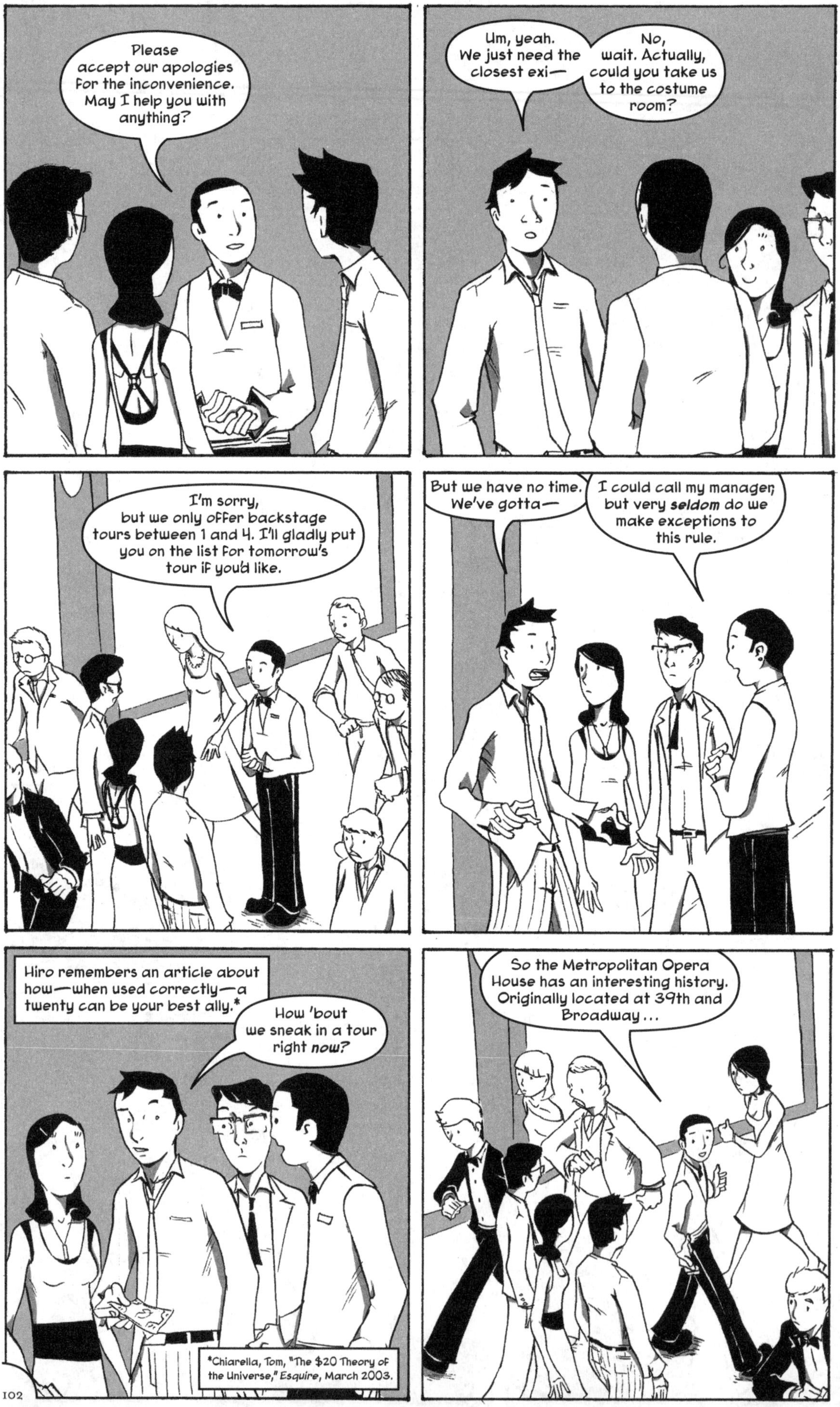
Please accept our apologies for the inconvenience. May I help you with anything?
Um, yeah. We just need the closest exi—
No, wait. Actually, could you take us to the costume room?
I'm sorry, but we only offer backstage tours between 1 and 4. I'll gladly put you on the list for tomorrow's tour if you'd like.
But we have no time. We've gotta—
I could call my manager, but very *seldom* do we make exceptions to this rule.
Hiro remembers an article about how—when used correctly—a twenty can be your best ally.*
How 'bout we sneak in a tour right *now?*
*Chiarella, Tom, "The $20 Theory of the Universe," *Esquire*, March 2003.
So the Metropolitan Opera House has an interesting history. Originally located at 39th and Broadway ...

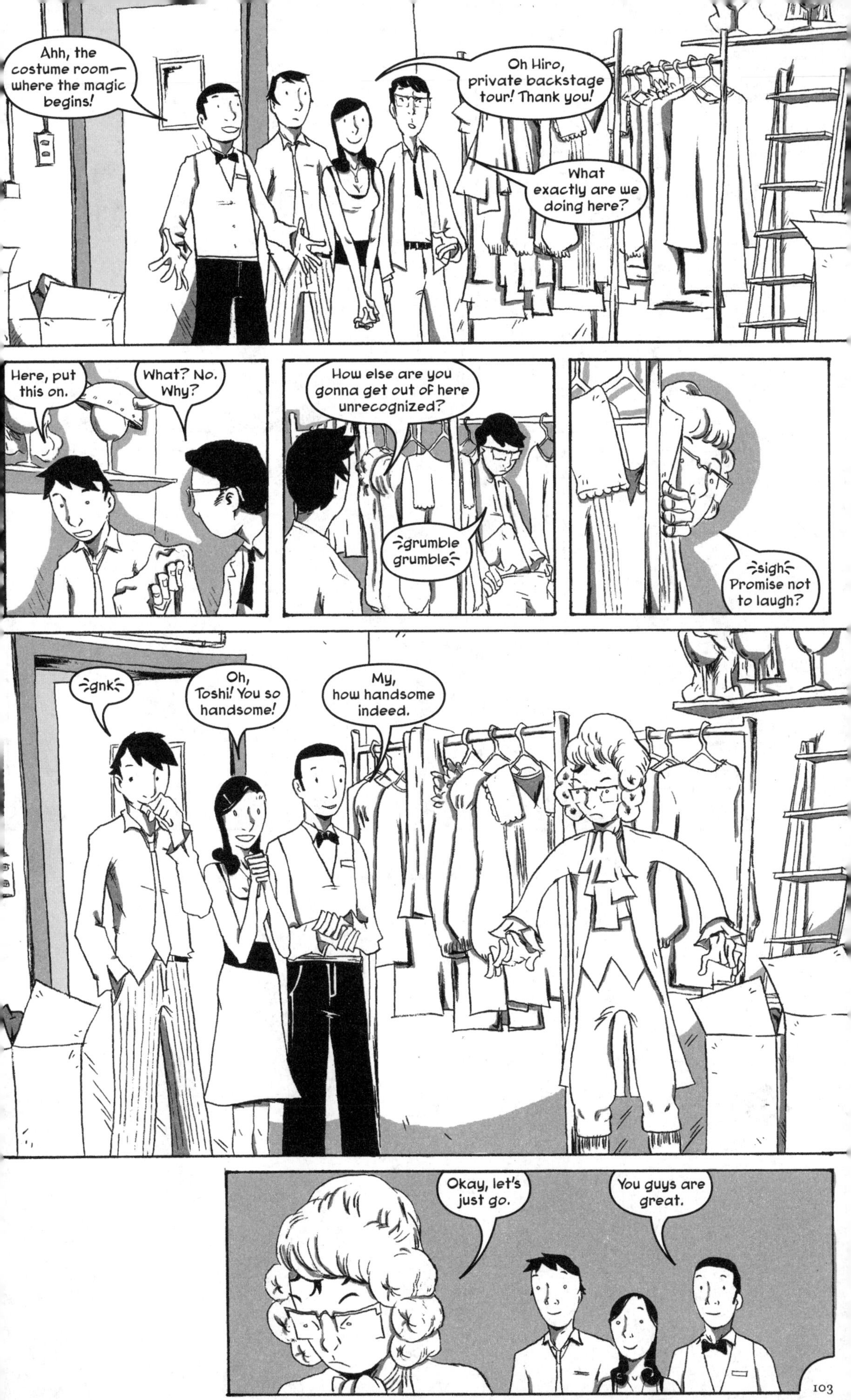
Ahh, the costume room— where the magic begins!
Oh Hiro, private backstage tour! Thank you!
What exactly are we doing here?
Here, put this on.
What? No. Why?
How else are you gonna get out of here unrecognized?
grumble grumble
sigh Promise not to laugh?
gnk
Oh, Toshi! You so handsome!
My, how handsome indeed.
Okay, let's just go.
You guys are great.

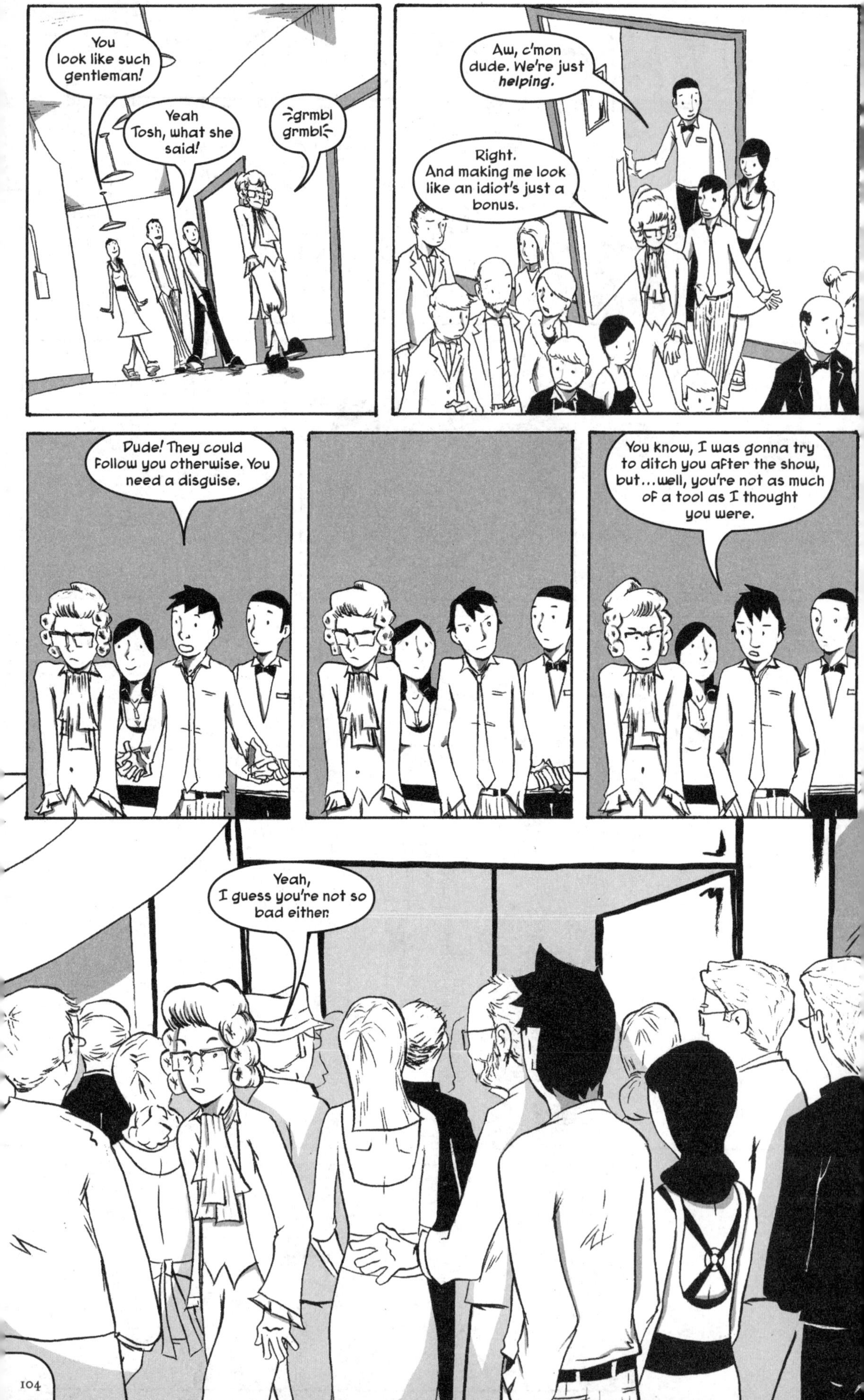
You look like such gentleman!
Yeah Tosh, what she said!
grmbl grmbl
Aw, c'mon dude. We're just *helping*.
Right. And making me look like an idiot's just a bonus.
Dude! They could follow you otherwise. You need a disguise.
You know, I was gonna try to ditch you after the show, but... well, you're not as much of a tool as I thought you were.
Yeah, I guess you're not so bad either.

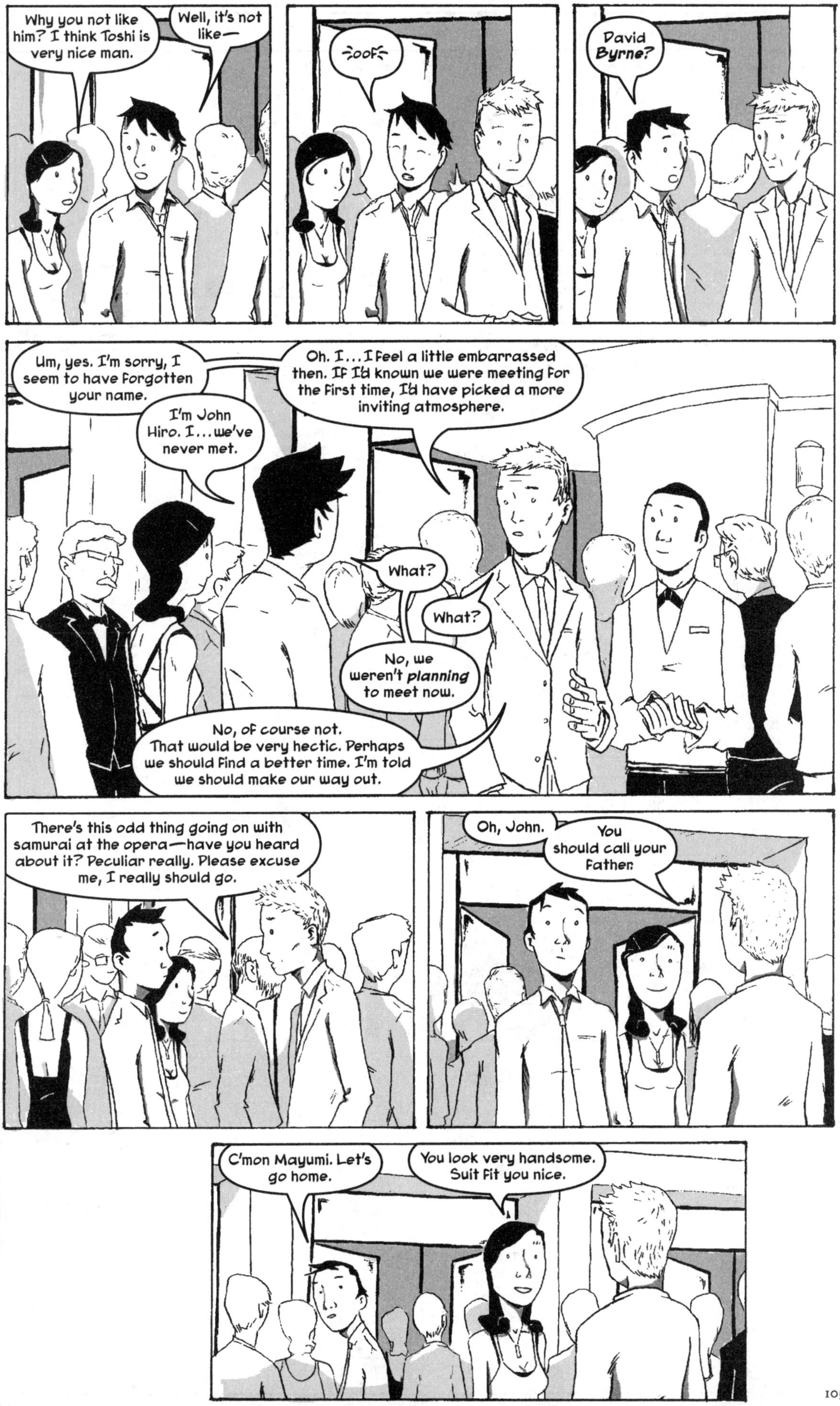
Why you not like him? I think Toshi is very nice man.
Well, it's not like—
ǂoofǂ
David Byrne?
Um, yes. I'm sorry, I seem to have forgotten your name.
I'm John Hiro. I... we've never met.
Oh. I... I feel a little embarrassed then. If I'd known we were meeting for the first time, I'd have picked a more inviting atmosphere.
What?
What?
No, we weren't planning to meet now.
No, of course not. That would be very hectic. Perhaps we should find a better time. I'm told we should make our way out.
There's this odd thing going on with samurai at the opera—have you heard about it? Peculiar really. Please excuse me, I really should go.
Oh, John.
You should call your father.
C'mon Mayumi. Let's go home.
You look very handsome. Suit fit you nice.

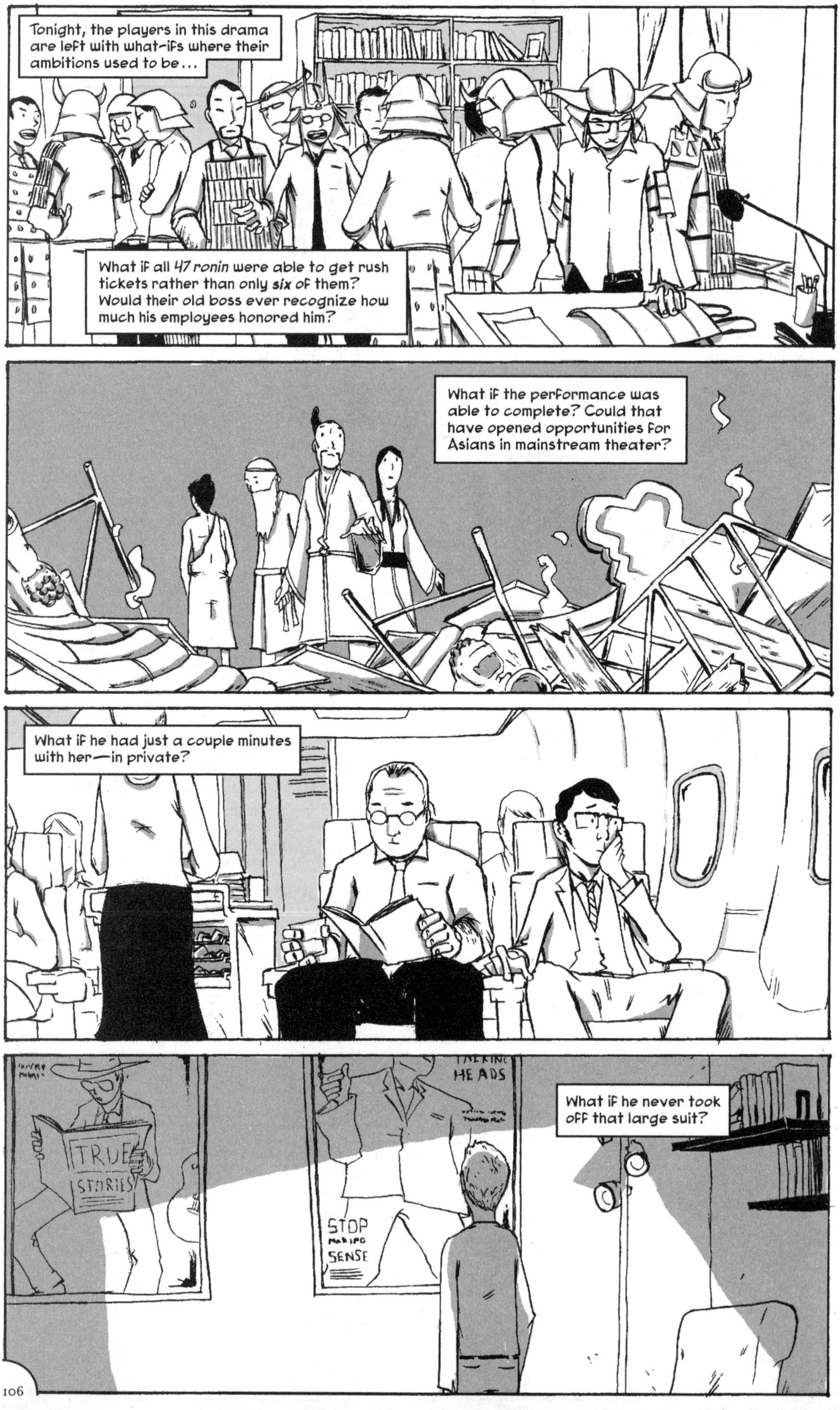
Tonight, the players in this drama are left with what-ifs where their ambitions used to be...
What if all 47 *ronin* were able to get rush tickets rather than only ***six*** of them? Would their old boss ever recognize how much his employees honored him?
What if the performance was able to complete? Could that have opened opportunities for Asians in mainstream theater?
What if he had just a couple minutes with her—in private?
TRUE STORIES
HEADS
STOP
SENSE
What if he never took off that large suit?

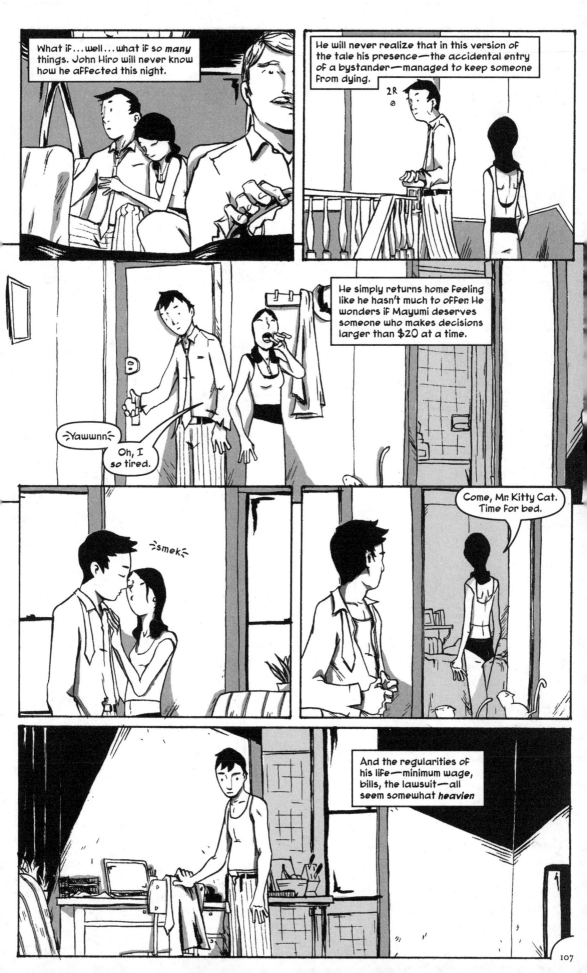

What if...well...what if so *many* things. John Hiro will never know how he affected this night.

He will never realize that in this version of the tale his presence—the accidental entry of a bystander—managed to keep someone from dying.

He simply returns home feeling like he hasn't much to offer. He wonders if Mayumi deserves someone who makes decisions larger than $20 at a time.

÷Yawwnn÷

Oh, I so tired.

÷smek÷

Come, Mr. Kitty Cat. Time for bed.

And the regularities of his life—minimum wage, bills, the lawsuit—all seem somewhat *heavien*

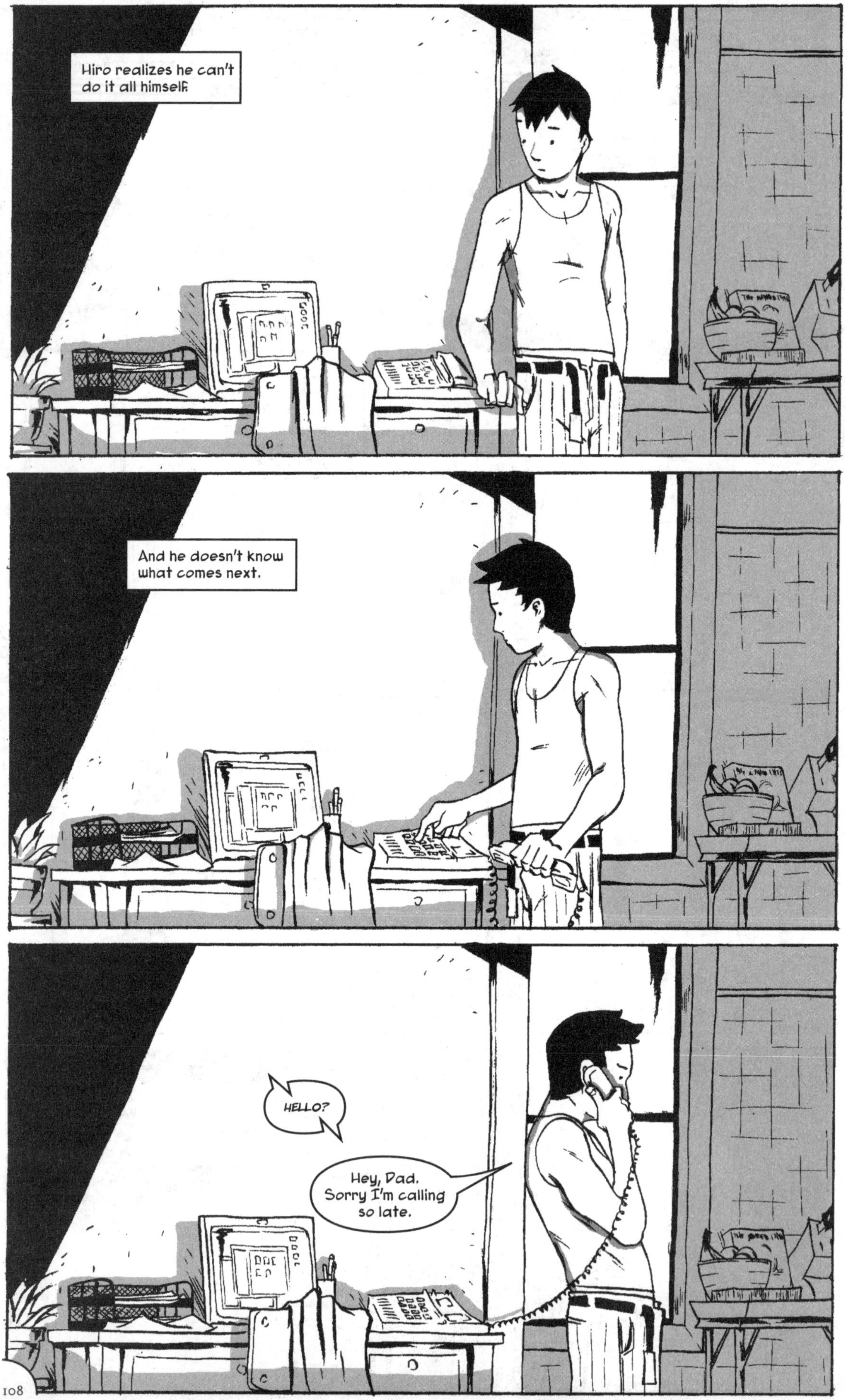
Hiro realizes he can't do it all himself.
And he doesn't know what comes next.
HELLO?
Hey, Dad. Sorry I'm calling so late.

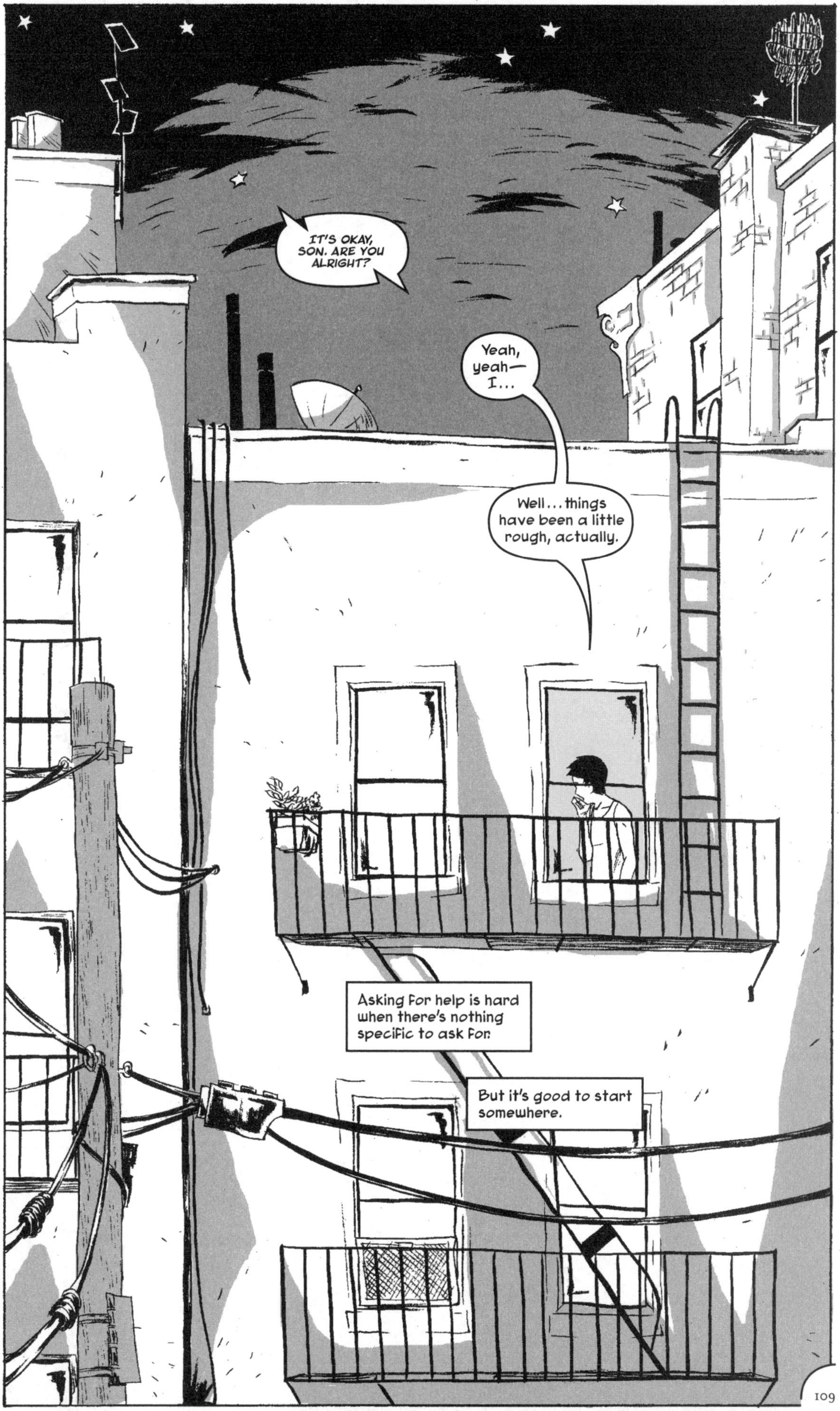
IT'S OKAY, SON. ARE YOU ALRIGHT?
Yeah, yeah— I...
Well... things have been a little rough, actually.
Asking for help is hard when there's nothing specific to ask for.
But it's good to start somewhere.

ぼくのさかなをひらてうち

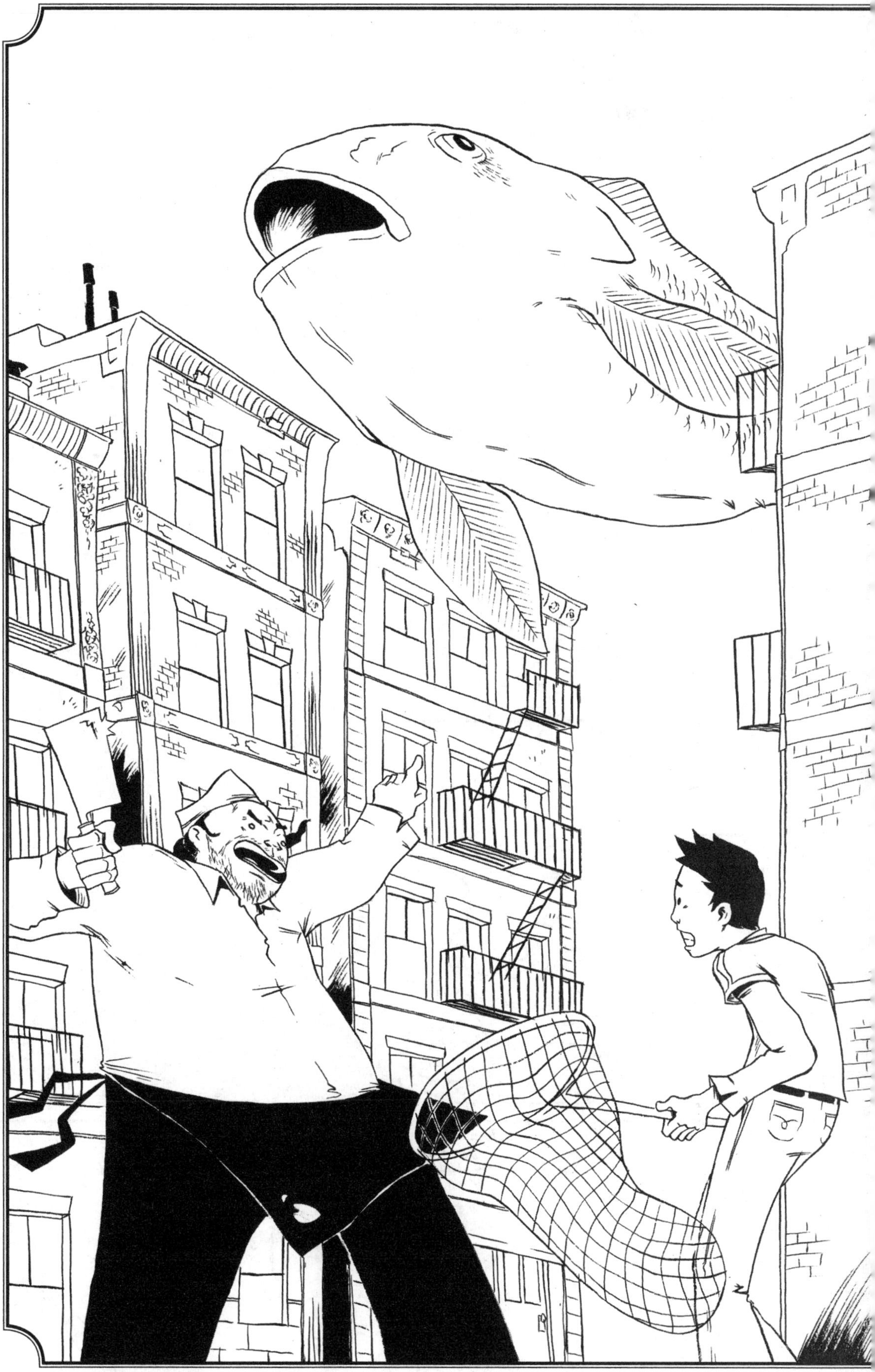

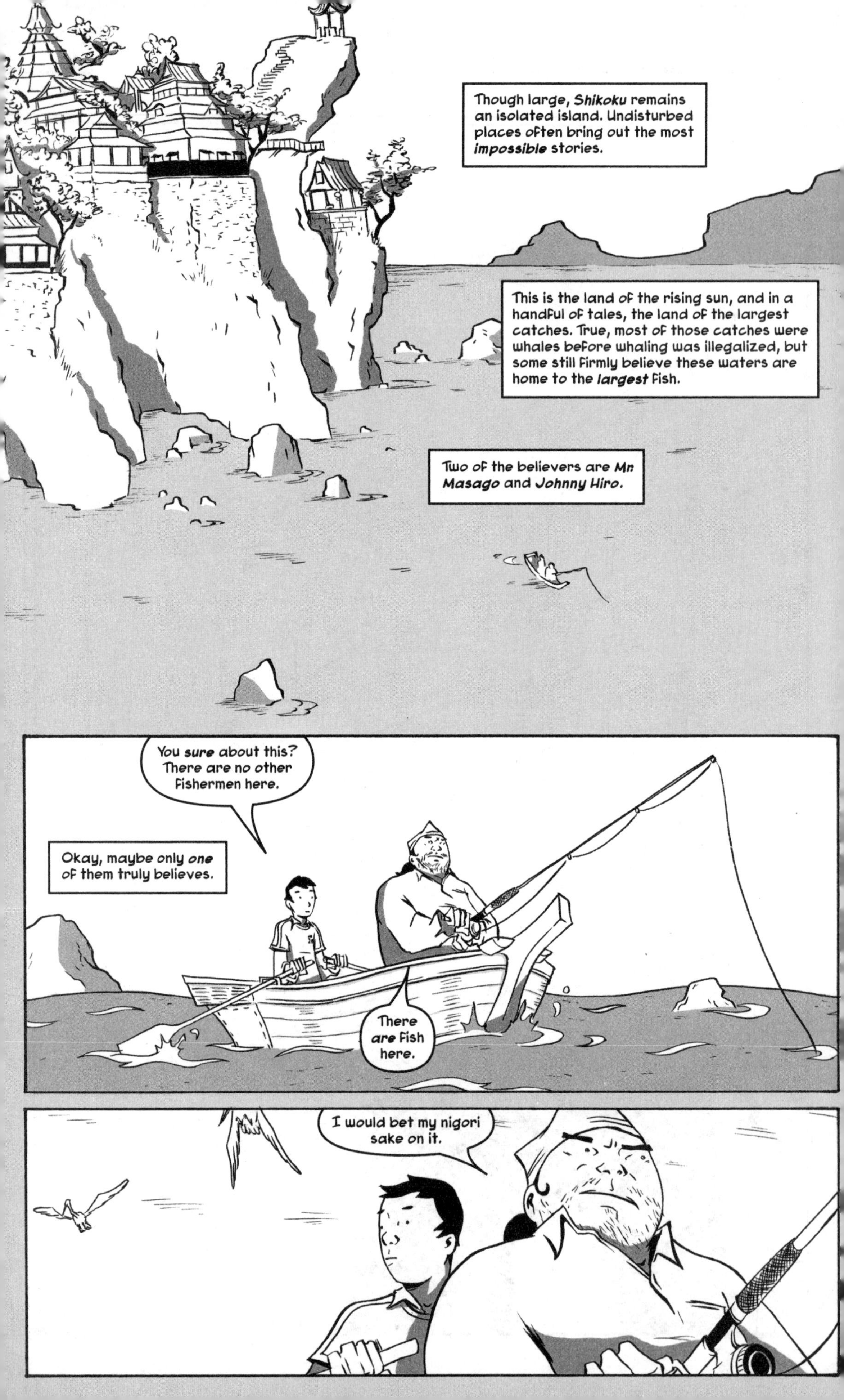
Though large, *Shikoku* remains an isolated island. Undisturbed places often bring out the most *impossible* stories.
This is the land of the rising sun, and in a handful of tales, the land of the largest catches. True, most of those catches were whales before whaling was illegalized, but some still firmly believe these waters are home to the *largest* fish.
Two of the believers are *Mr. Masago* and *Johnny Hiro.*
You *sure* about this? There are no other fishermen here.
Okay, maybe only *one* of them truly believes.
There *are* fish here.
I would bet my nigori sake on it.

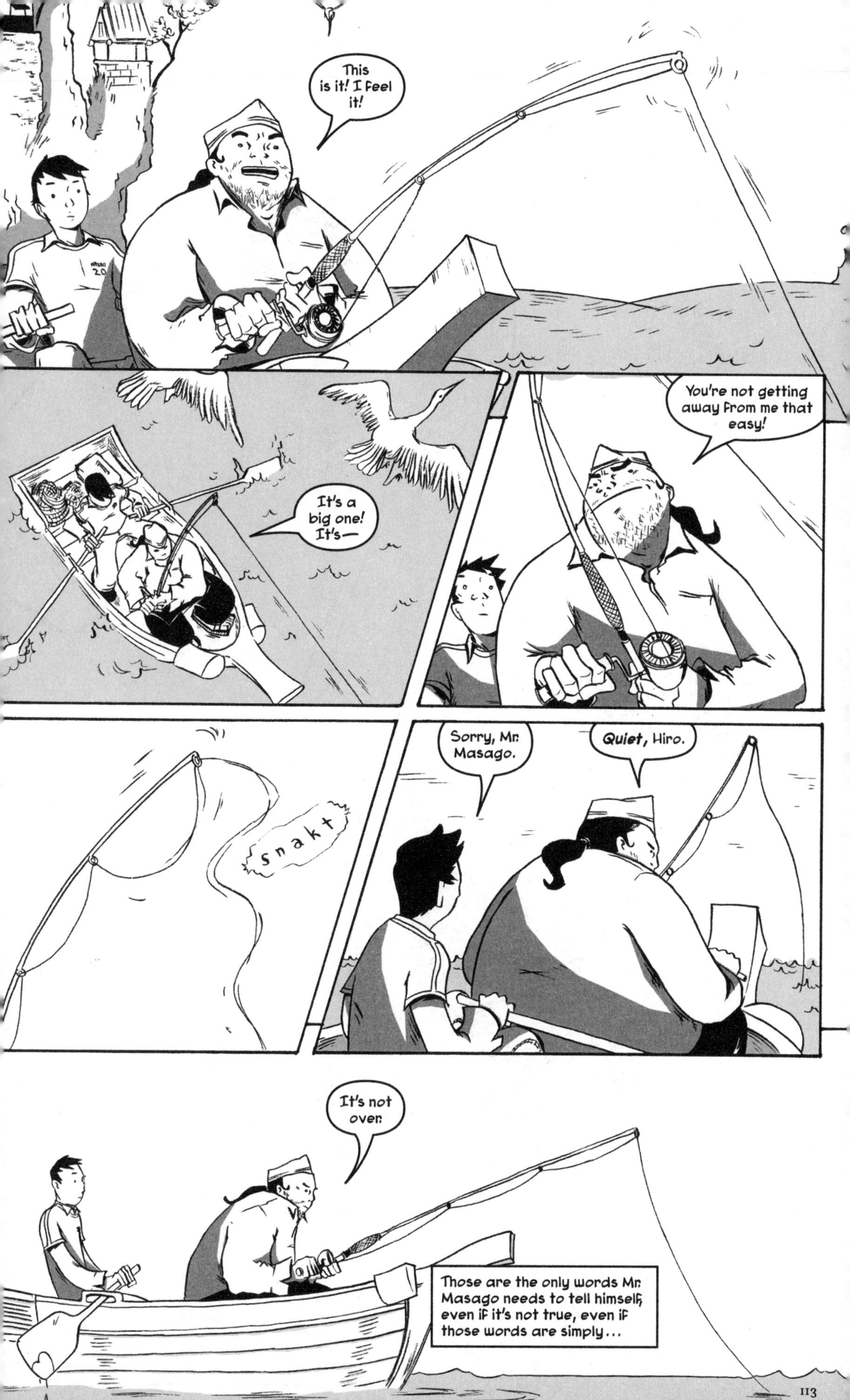
This is it! I feel it!
It's a big one! It's—
You're not getting away from me that easy!
snakt
Sorry, Mr. Masago.
Quiet, Hiro.
It's not over.
Those are the only words Mr. Masago needs to tell himself, even if it's not true, even if those words are simply...

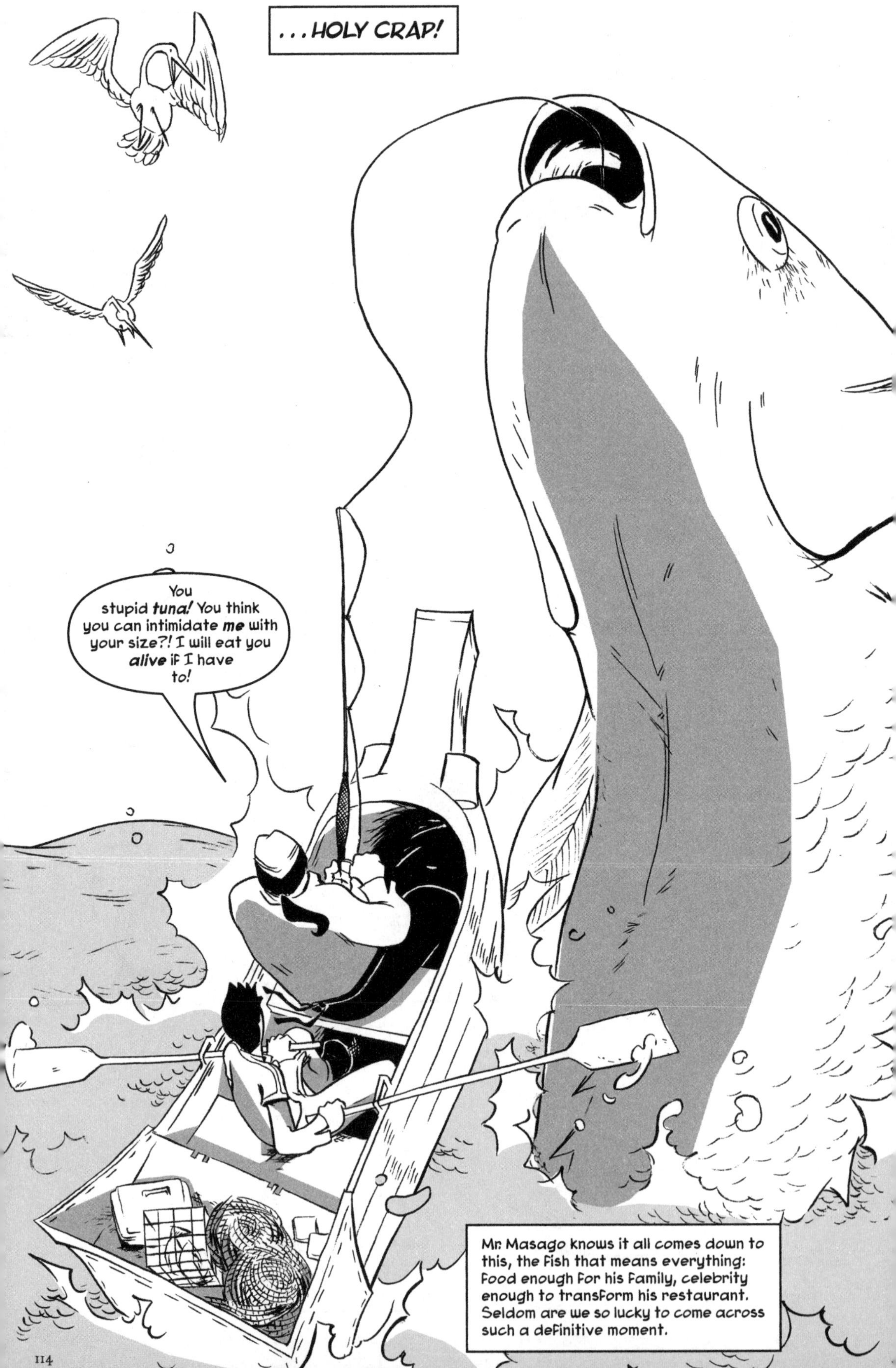

...HOLY CRAP!
You stupid *tuna!* You think you can intimidate *me* with your size?! I will eat you *alive* if I have to!
Mr. Masago knows it all comes down to this, the fish that means everything: food enough for his family, celebrity enough to transform his restaurant. Seldom are we so lucky to come across such a definitive moment.

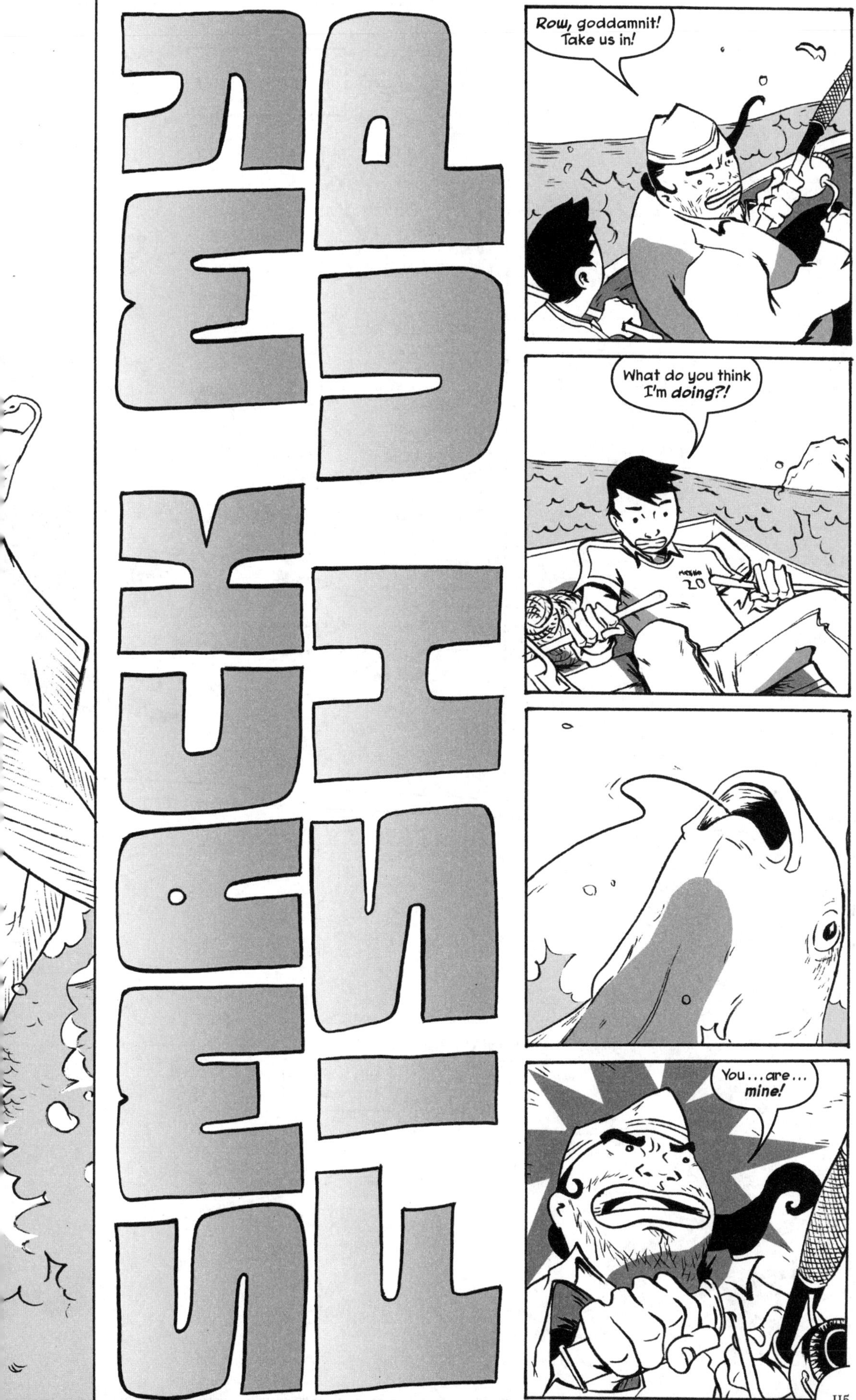
SMACK MY
FISH UP
Row, goddamnit! Take us in!
What do you think I'm doing?!
You...are... mine!

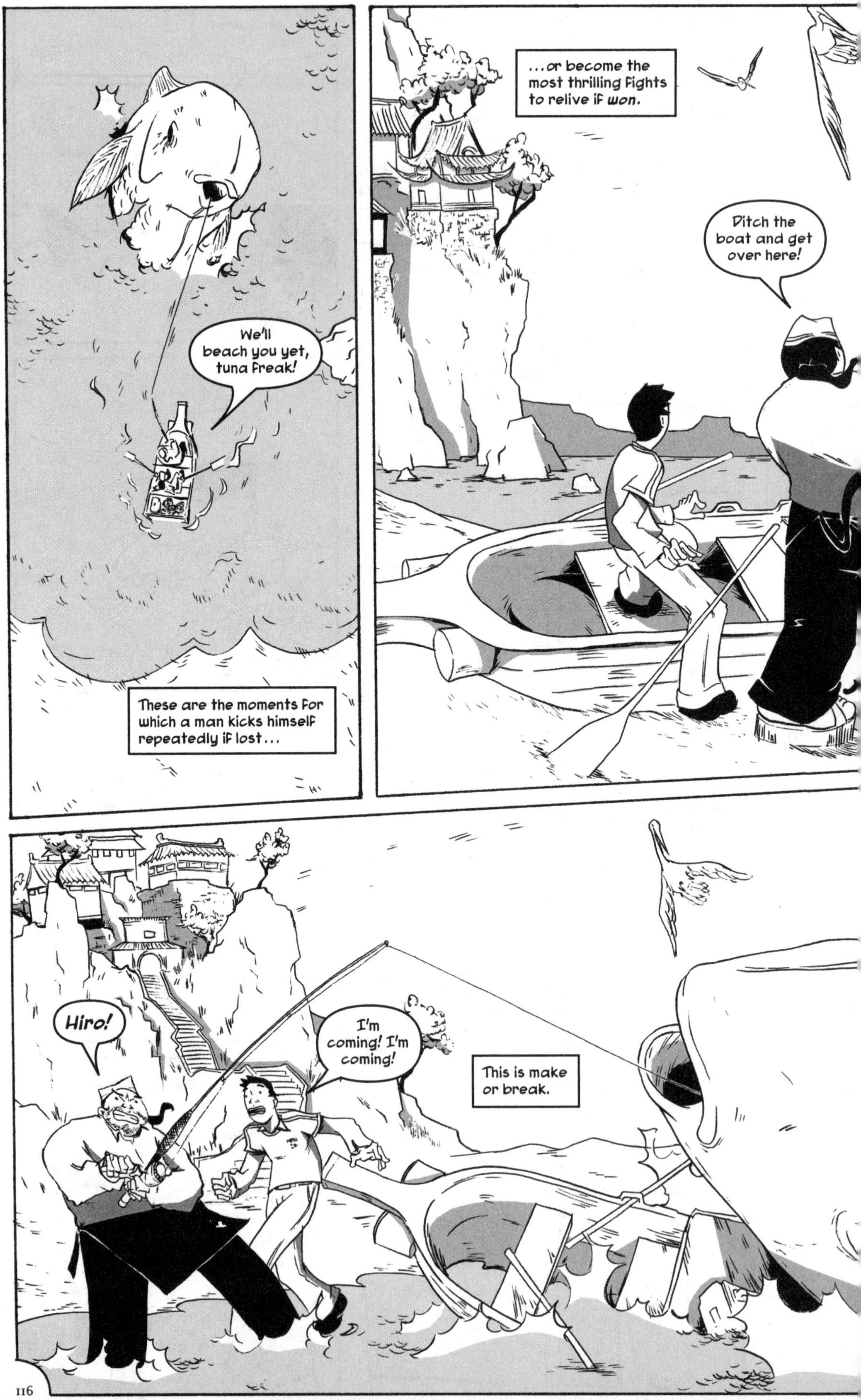
We'll beach you yet, tuna freak!
These are the moments for which a man kicks himself repeatedly if lost...
...or become the most thrilling fights to relive if won.
Ditch the boat and get over here!
Hiro!
I'm coming! I'm coming!
This is make or break.

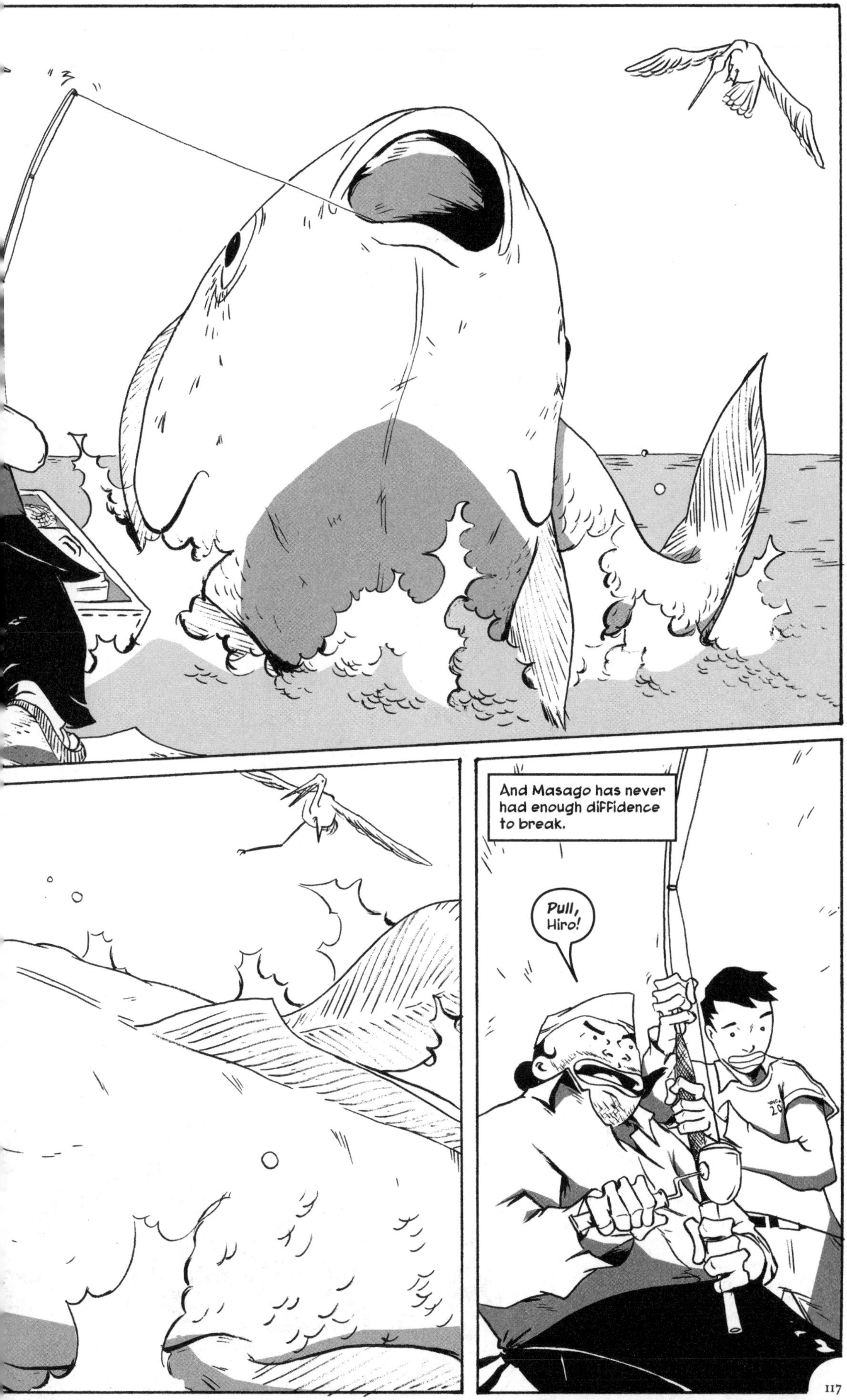
And Masago has never had enough diffidence to break.
Pull, Hiro!

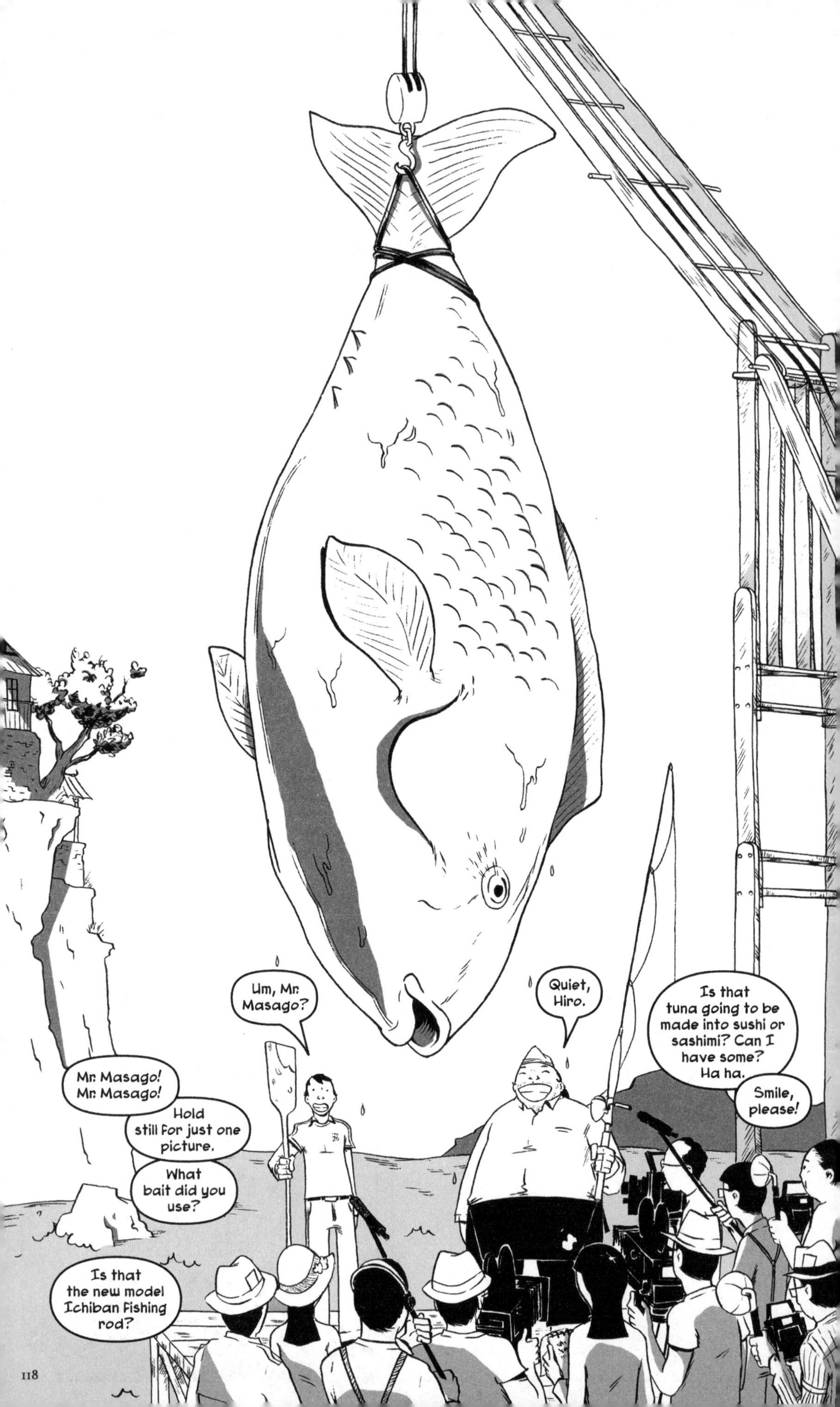
Um, Mr. Masago?
Quiet, Hiro.
Is that tuna going to be made into sushi or sashimi? Can I have some? Ha ha.
Smile, please!
Mr. Masago! Mr. Masago!
Hold still for just one picture.
What bait did you use?
Is that the new model Ichiban fishing rod?

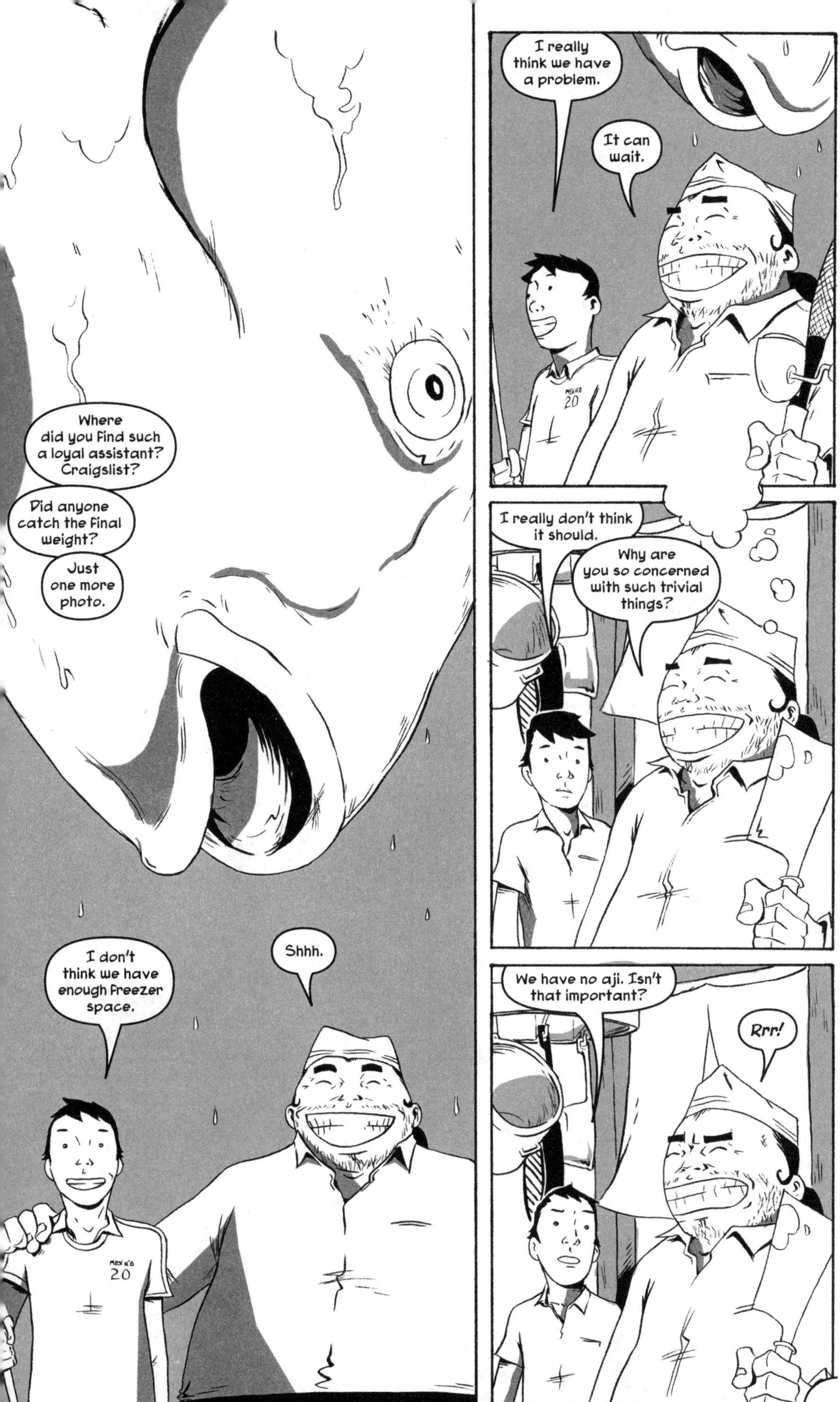
Where did you find such a loyal assistant? Craigslist?
Did anyone catch the final weight?
Just one more photo.
I don't think we have enough freezer space.
Shhh.
I really think we have a problem.
It can wait.
MEXICO 20
I really don't think it should.
Why are you so concerned with such trivial things?
We have no aji. Isn't that important?
Rrr!

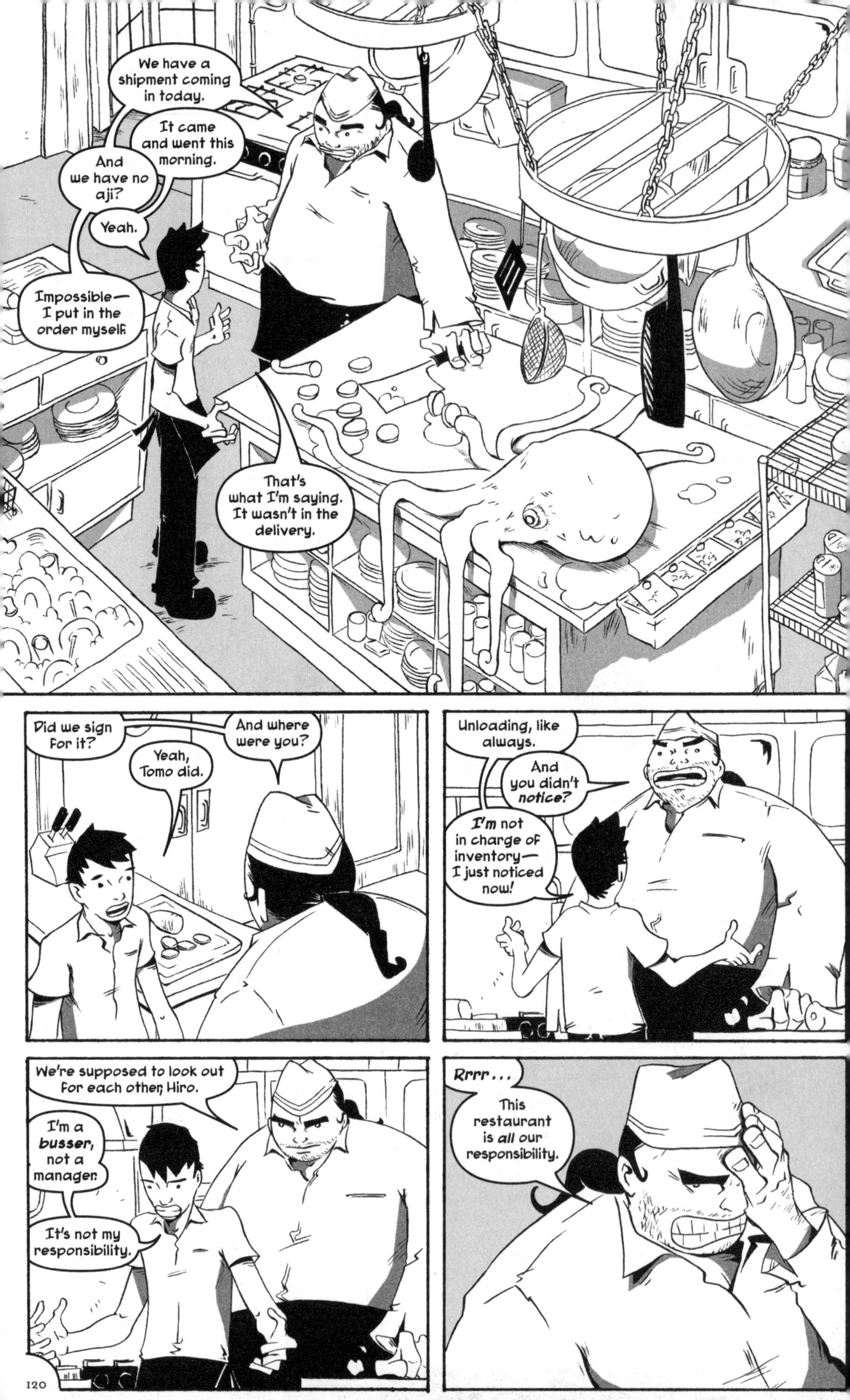
We have a shipment coming in today.
It came and went this morning.
And we have no aji?
Yeah.
Impossible— I put in the order myself.
That's what I'm saying. It wasn't in the delivery.
Did we sign for it?
Yeah, Tomo did.
And where were you?
Unloading, like always.
And you didn't *notice?*
I'm not in charge of inventory— I just noticed now!
We're supposed to look out for each other, Hiro.
I'm a **busser,** not a manager.
It's not my responsibility.
Rrrr . . .
This restaurant is *all* our responsibility.

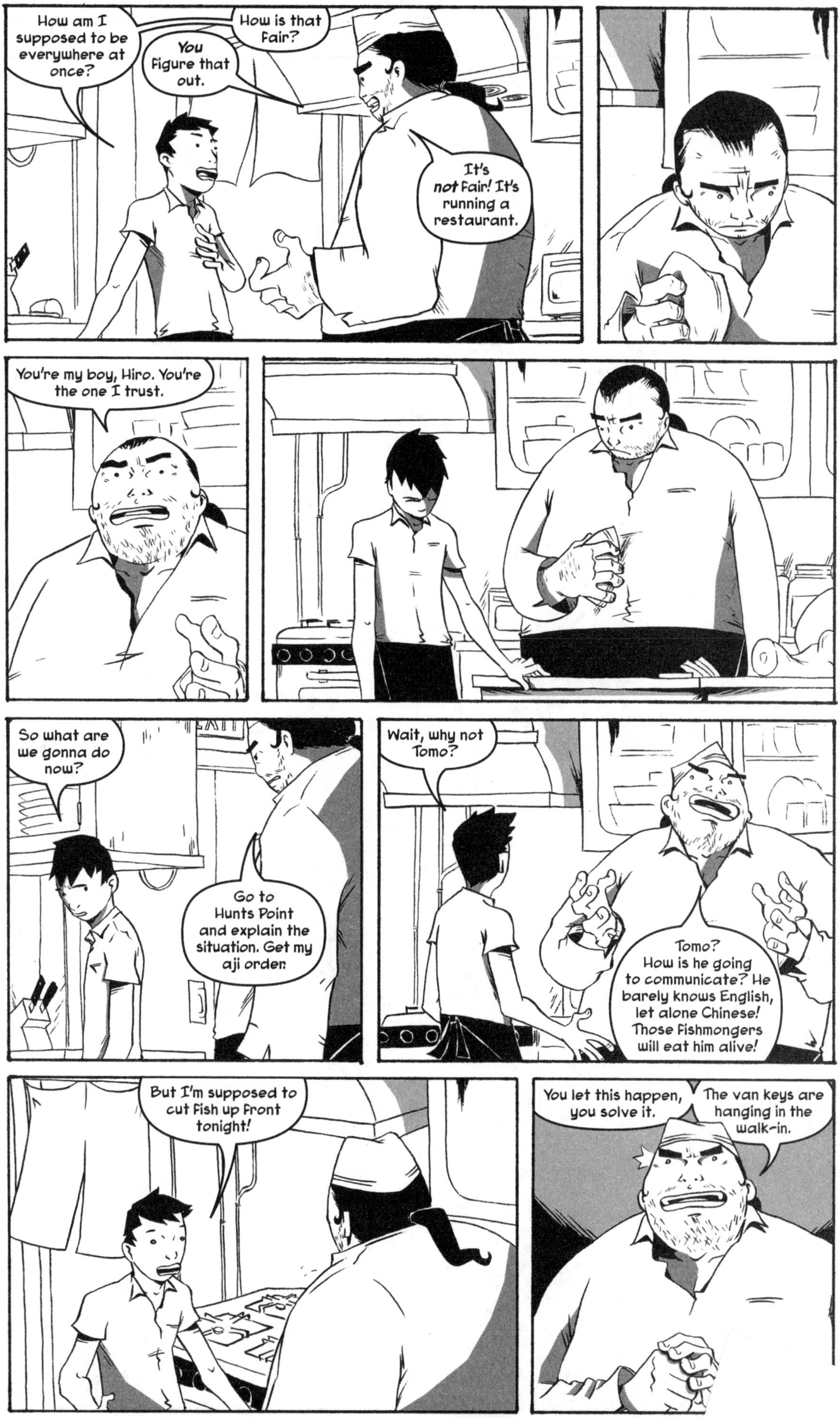
How am I supposed to be everywhere at once?
How is that fair?
You figure that out.
It's not fair! It's running a restaurant.
You're my boy, Hiro. You're the one I trust.
So what are we gonna do now?
Go to Hunts Point and explain the situation. Get my aji order.
Wait, why not Tomo?
Tomo? How is he going to communicate? He barely knows English, let alone Chinese! Those fishmongers will eat him alive!
But I'm supposed to cut fish up front tonight!
You let this happen, you solve it.
The van keys are hanging in the walk-in.

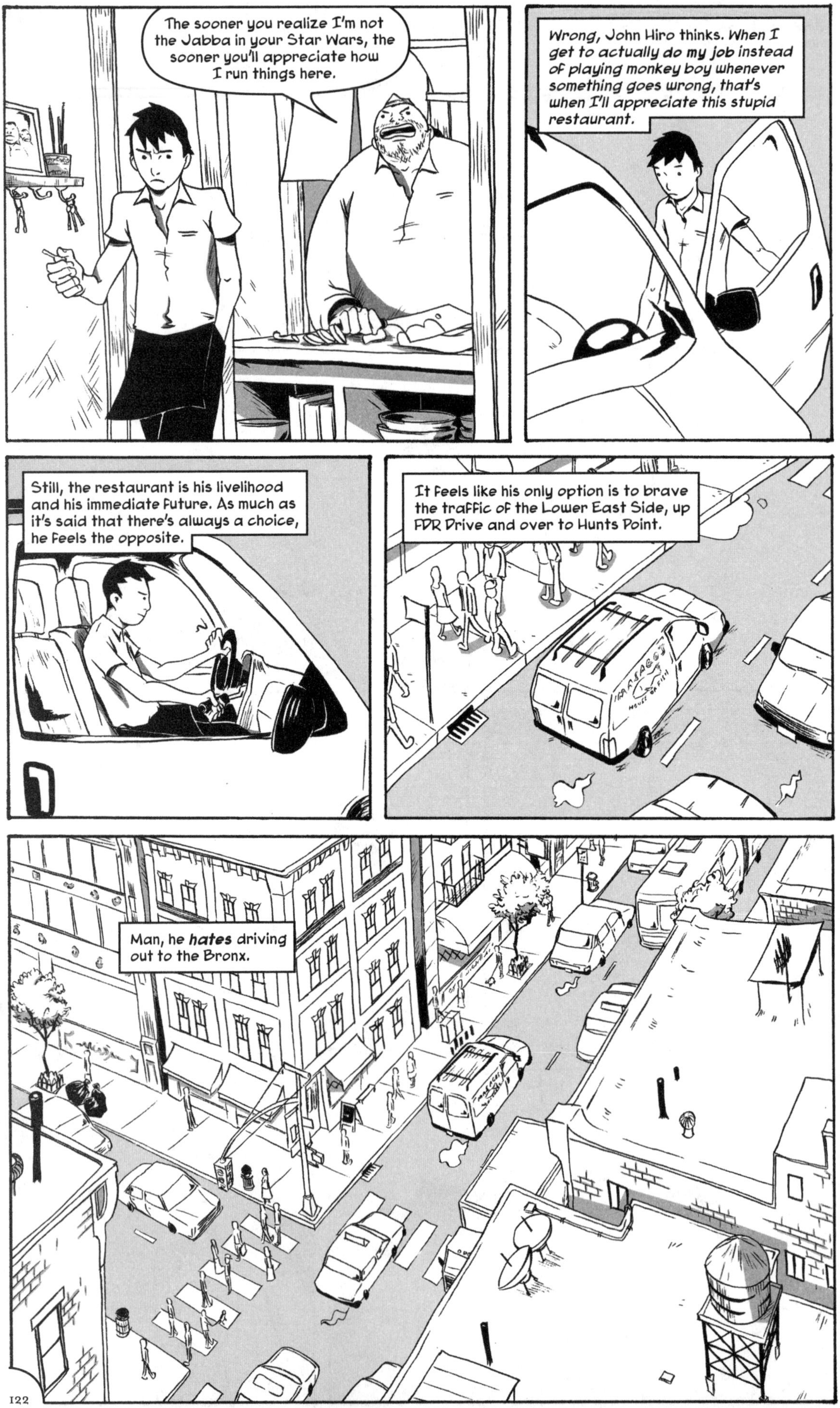
The sooner you realize I'm not the Jabba in your Star Wars, the sooner you'll appreciate how I run things here.
Wrong, John Hiro thinks. When I get to actually do my job instead of playing monkey boy whenever something goes wrong, that's when I'll appreciate this stupid restaurant.
Still, the restaurant is his livelihood and his immediate future. As much as it's said that there's always a choice, he feels the opposite.
It feels like his only option is to brave the traffic of the Lower East Side, up FDR Drive and over to Hunts Point.
Man, he *hates* driving out to the Bronx.

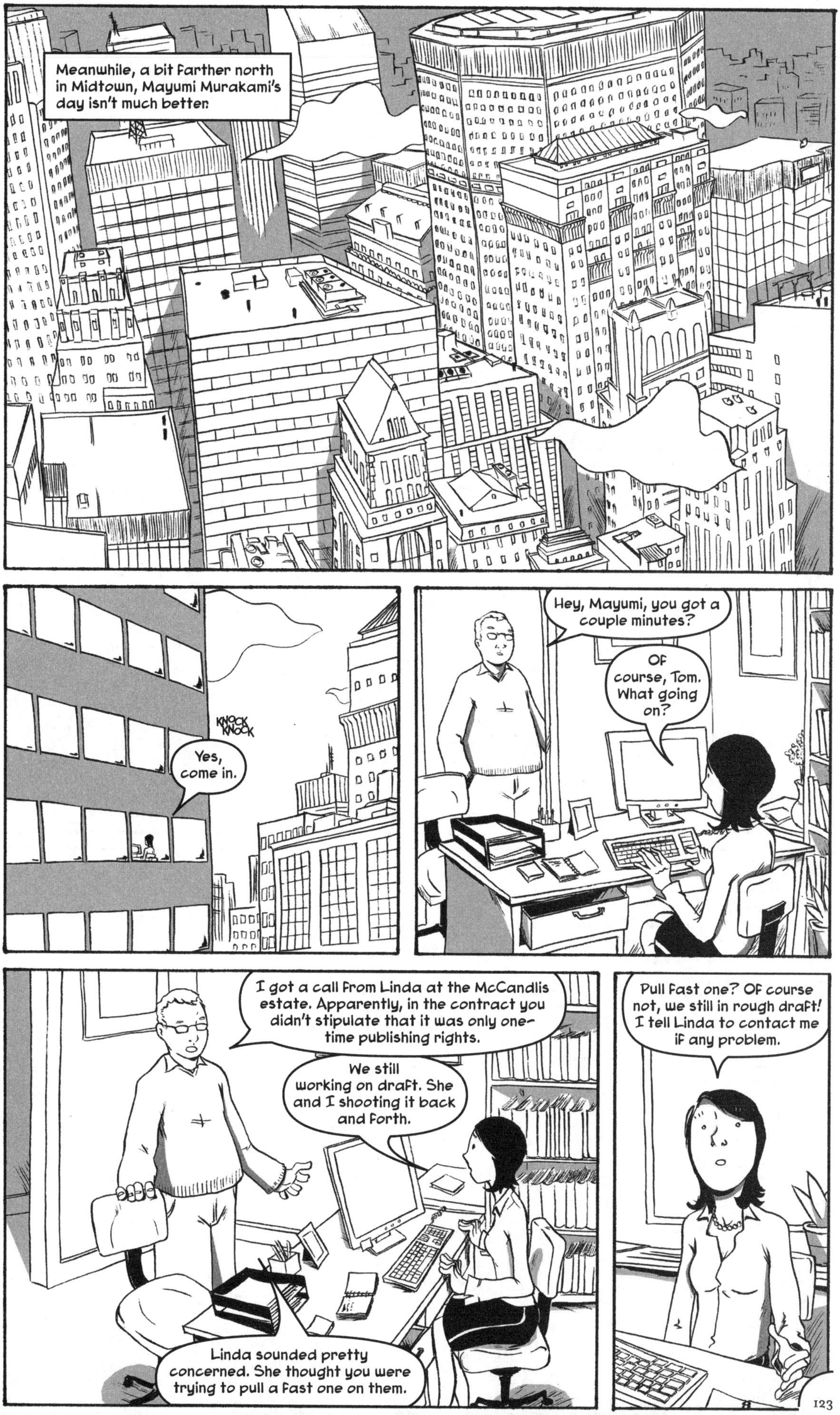
Meanwhile, a bit farther north in Midtown, Mayumi Murakami's day isn't much better.
KNOCK KNOCK
Yes, come in.
Hey, Mayumi, you got a couple minutes?
Of course, Tom. What going on?
I got a call from Linda at the McCandlis estate. Apparently, in the contract you didn't stipulate that it was only one-time publishing rights.
We still working on draft. She and I shooting it back and forth.
Linda sounded pretty concerned. She thought you were trying to pull a fast one on them.
Pull fast one? Of course not, we still in rough draft! I tell Linda to contact me if any problem.

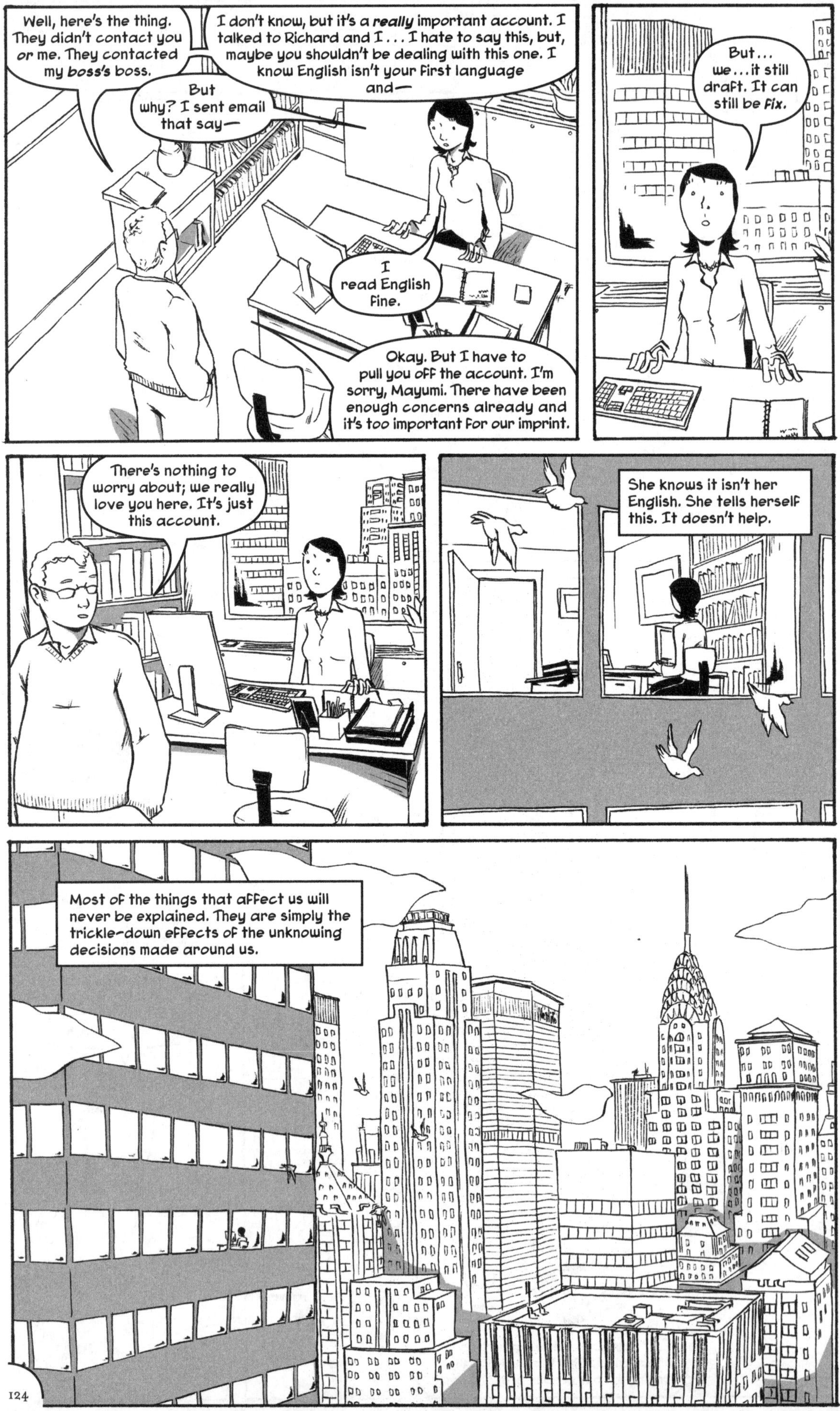
Well, here's the thing. They didn't contact you or me. They contacted my *boss's* boss.
But why? I sent email that say—
I don't know, but it's a ***really*** important account. I talked to Richard and I . . . I hate to say this, but, maybe you shouldn't be dealing with this one. I know English isn't your first language and—
I read English fine.
Okay. But I have to pull you off the account. I'm sorry, Mayumi. There have been enough concerns already and it's too important for our imprint.
But . . . we . . . it still draft. It can still be *fix*.
There's nothing to worry about; we really love you here. It's just this account.
She knows it isn't her English. She tells herself this. It doesn't help.
Most of the things that affect us will never be explained. They are simply the trickle-down effects of the unknowing decisions made around us.

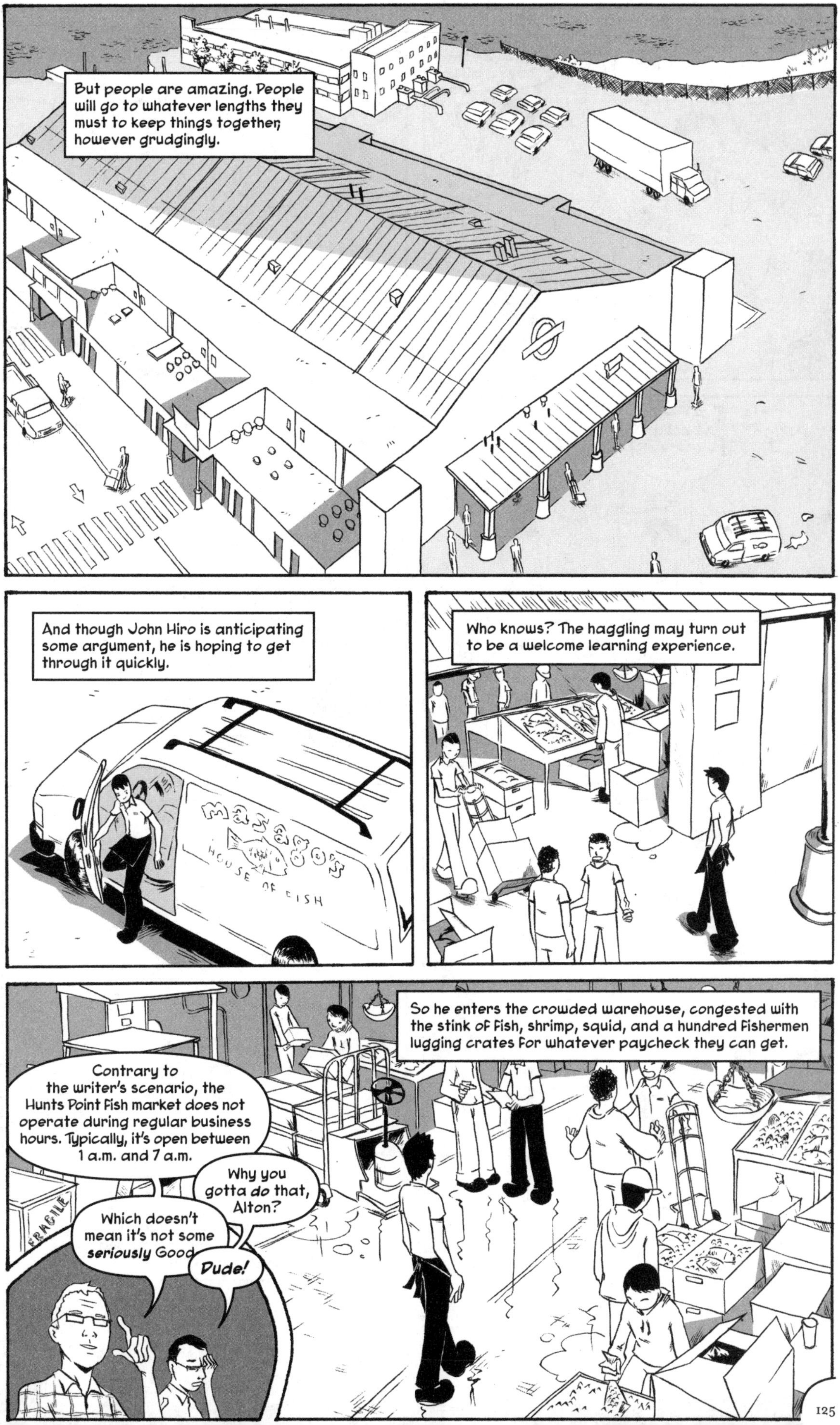

But people are amazing. People will go to whatever lengths they must to keep things together, however grudgingly.
And though John Hiro is anticipating some argument, he is hoping to get through it quickly.
HOUSE OF FISH
Who knows? The haggling may turn out to be a welcome learning experience.
So he enters the crowded warehouse, congested with the stink of fish, shrimp, squid, and a hundred fishermen lugging crates for whatever paycheck they can get.
Contrary to the writer's scenario, the Hunts Point fish market does not operate during regular business hours. Typically, it's open between 1 a.m. and 7 a.m.
Why you gotta *do* that, Alton?
Which doesn't mean it's not some *seriously* Good
Dude!
FRAGILE

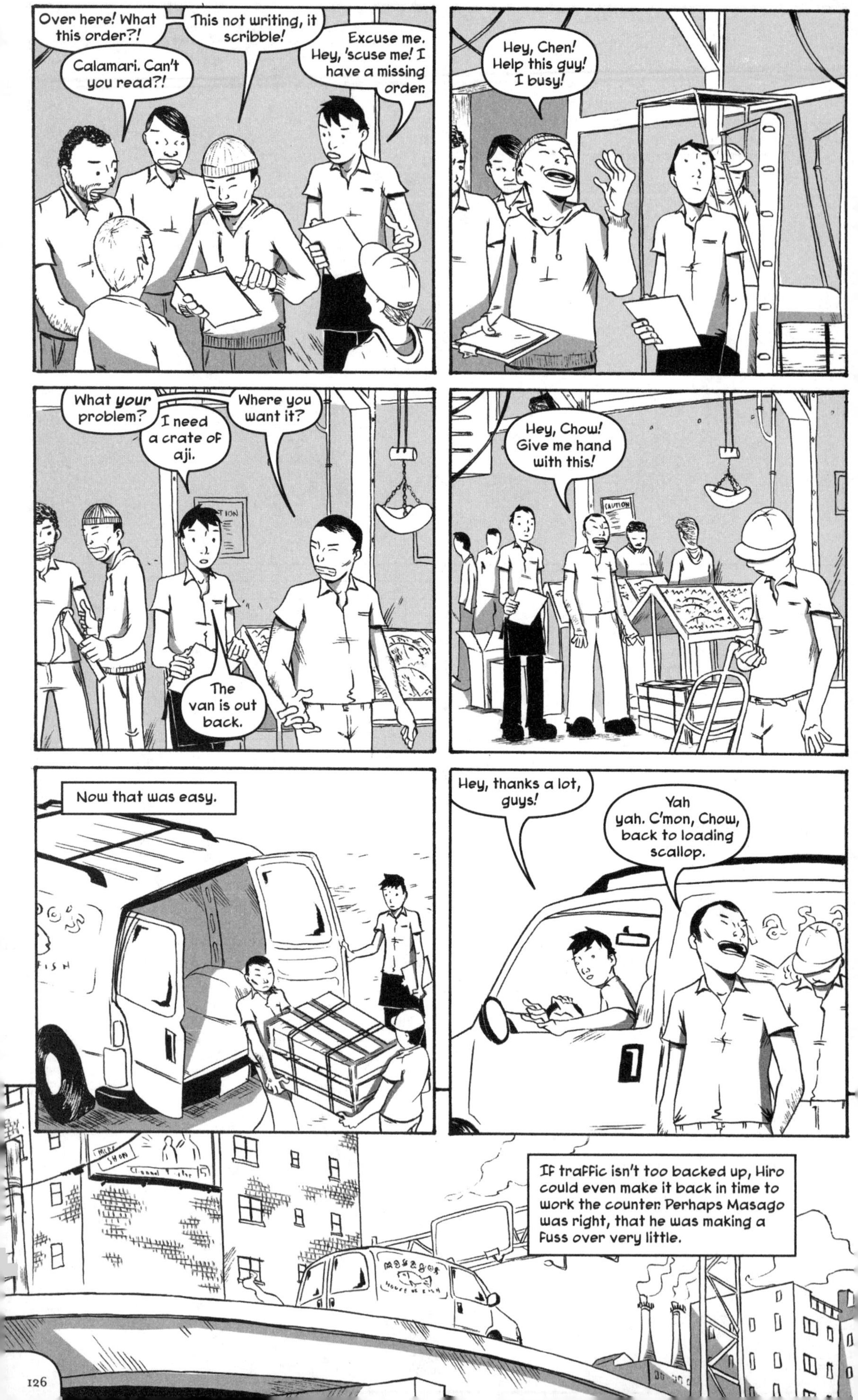

Over here! What this order?!
Calamari. Can't you read?!
This not writing, it scribble!
Excuse me. Hey, 'scuse me! I have a missing order.
Hey, Chen! Help this guy! I busy!
What *your* problem?
I need a crate of aji.
Where you want it?
The van is out back.
Hey, Chow! Give me hand with this!
Now that was easy.
Hey, thanks a lot, guys!
Yah yah. C'mon, Chow, back to loading scallop.
If traffic isn't too backed up, Hiro could even make it back in time to work the counter. Perhaps Masago was right, that he was making a fuss over very little.

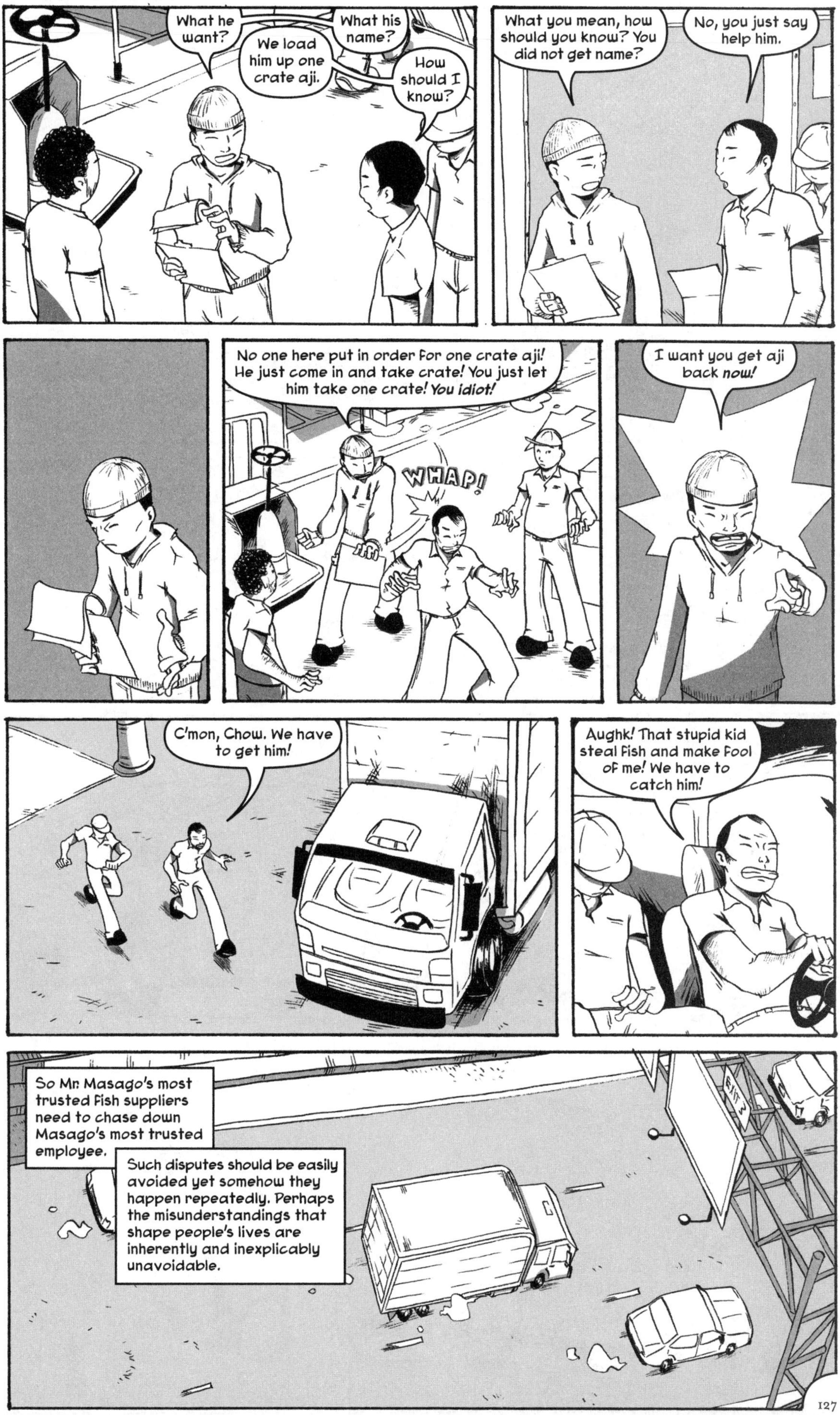
What he want?
What his name?
We load him up one crate aji.
How should I know?
What you mean, how should you know? You did not get name?
No, you just say help him.
No one here put in order for one crate aji! He just come in and take crate! You just let him take one crate! You idiot!
WHAP!
I want you get aji back now!
C'mon, Chow. We have to get him!
Aughk! That stupid kid steal fish and make fool of me! We have to catch him!
So Mr. Masago's most trusted fish suppliers need to chase down Masago's most trusted employee.
Such disputes should be easily avoided yet somehow they happen repeatedly. Perhaps the misunderstandings that shape people's lives are inherently and inexplicably unavoidable.
EXIT 3

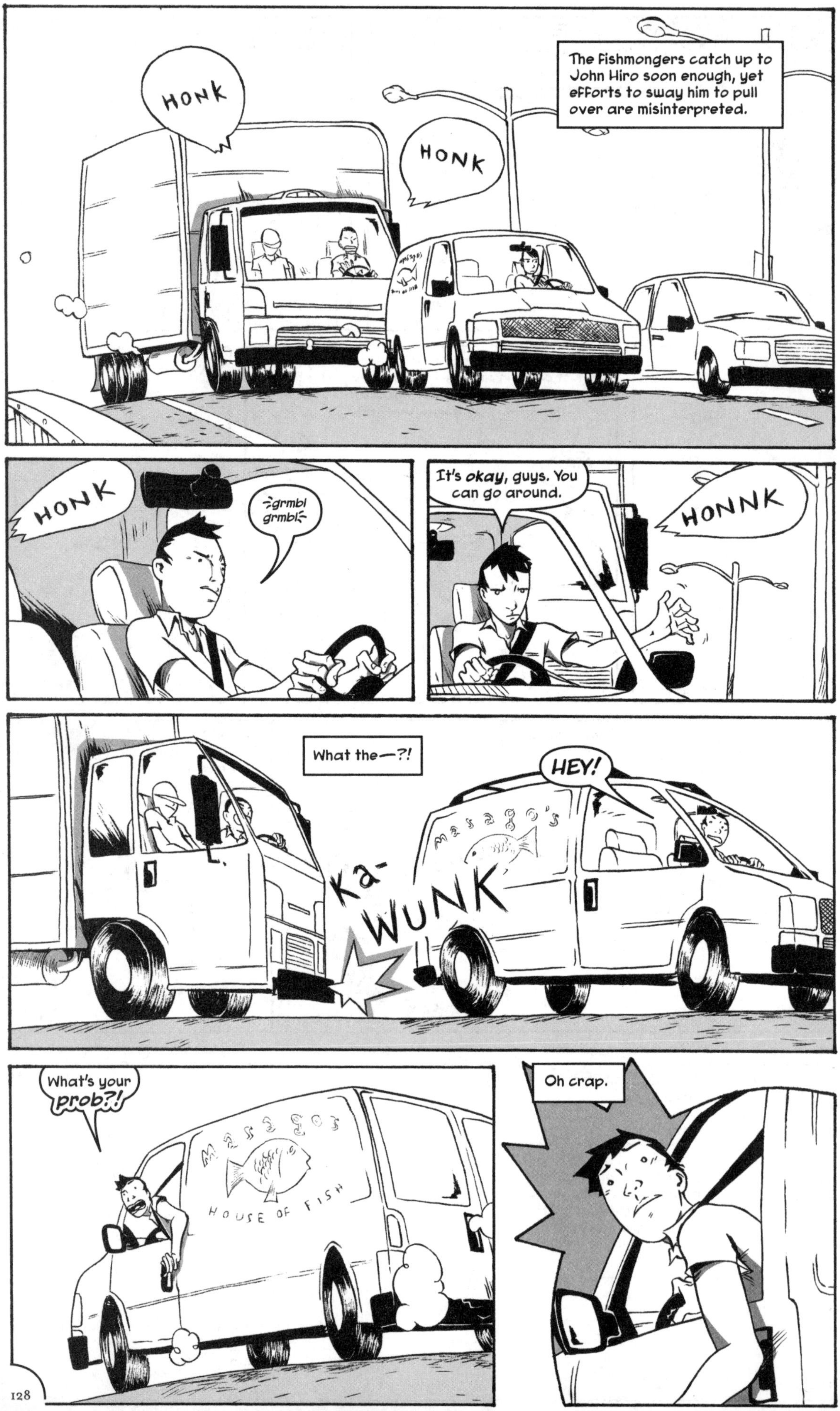
The Fishmongers catch up to John Hiro soon enough, yet efforts to sway him to pull over are misinterpreted.
HONK
HONK
HONK
grmbl grmbl
It's okay, guys. You can go around.
HONNK
What the—?!
HEY!
Ka-WUNK
What's your prob?!
HOUSE OF FISH
Oh crap.

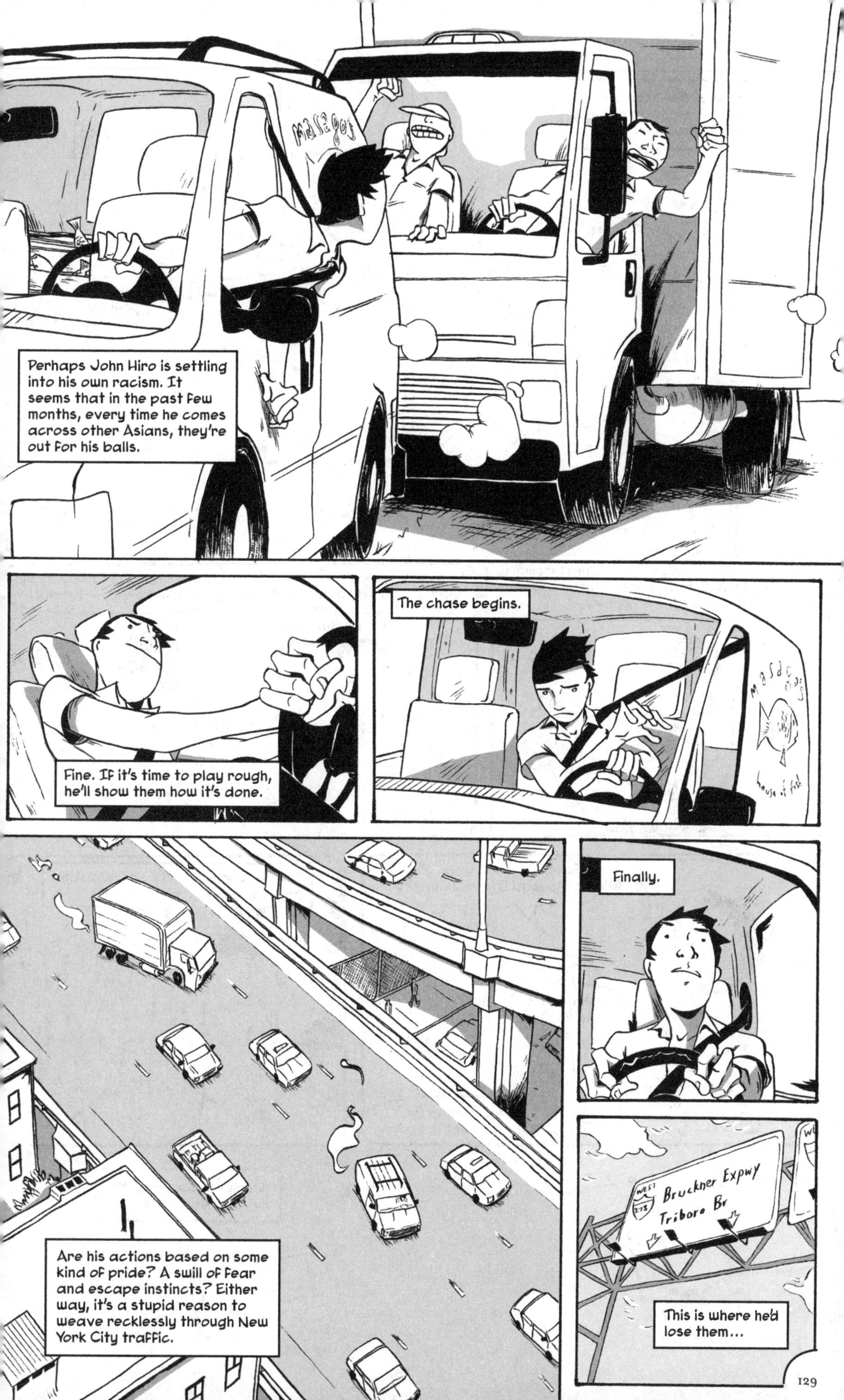
Perhaps John Hiro is settling into his own racism. It seems that in the past few months, every time he comes across other Asians, they're out for his balls.
Fine. If it's time to play rough, he'll show them how it's done.
The chase begins.
house of fish
Are his actions based on some kind of pride? A swill of fear and escape instincts? Either way, it's a stupid reason to weave recklessly through New York City traffic.
Finally.
WEST
278
Bruckner Expwy
Triboro Br
This is where he'd lose them...

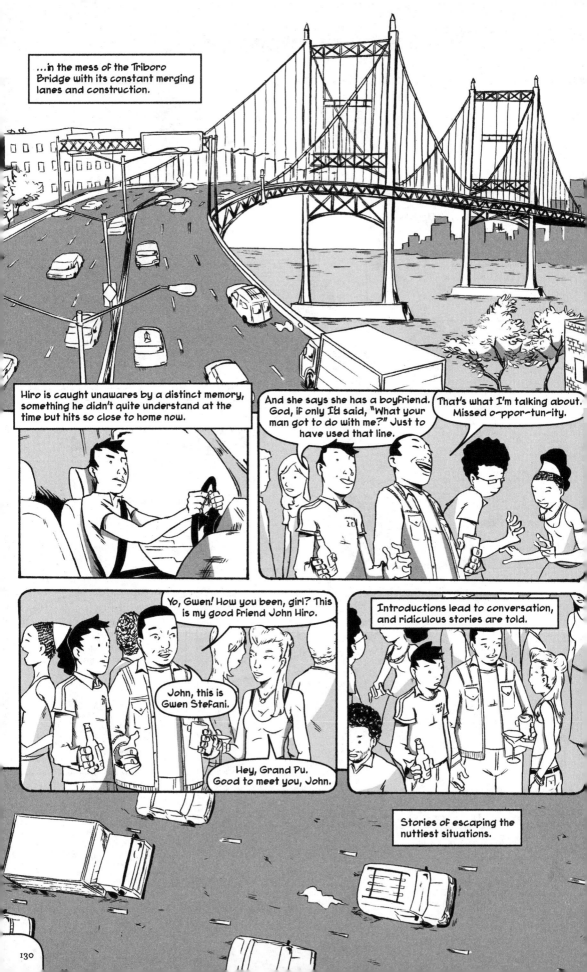

...in the mess of the Triboro Bridge with its constant merging lanes and construction.

Hiro is caught unawares by a distinct memory, something he didn't quite understand at the time but hits so close to home now.

And she says she has a boyfriend. God, if only I'd said, "What your man got to do with me?" Just to have used that line.

That's what I'm talking about. Missed o-ppor-tun-ity.

Yo, Gwen! How you been, girl? This is my good friend John Hiro.

John, this is Gwen Stefani.

Hey, Grand Pu. Good to meet you, John.

Introductions lead to conversation, and ridiculous stories are told.

Stories of escaping the nuttiest situations.

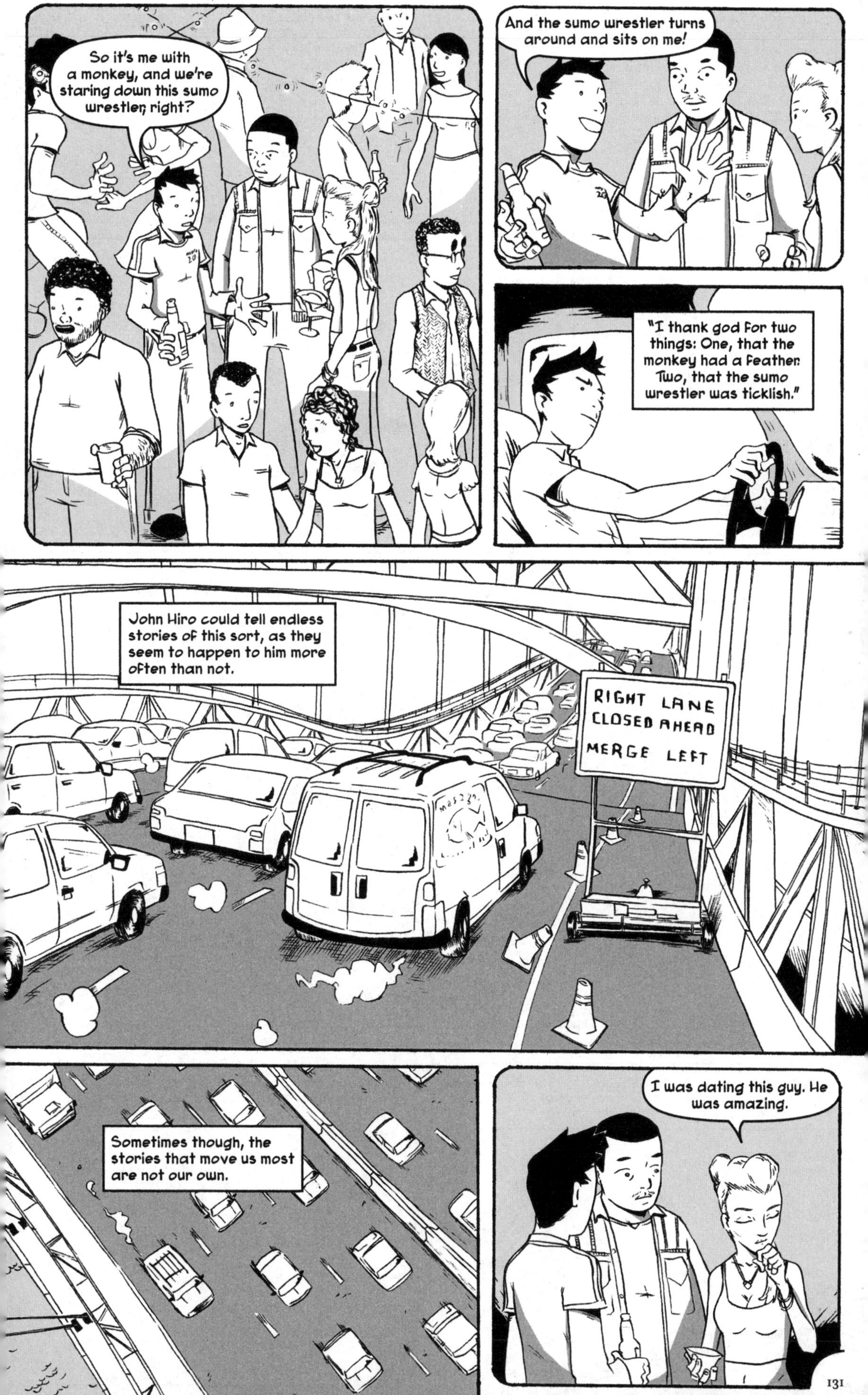
So it's me with a monkey, and we're staring down this sumo wrestler, right?
And the sumo wrestler turns around and sits on me!
"I thank god for two things: One, that the monkey had a feather. Two, that the sumo wrestler was ticklish."
John Hiro could tell endless stories of this sort, as they seem to happen to him more often than not.
RIGHT LANE CLOSED AHEAD MERGE LEFT
Sometimes though, the stories that move us most are not our own.
I was dating this guy. He was amazing.

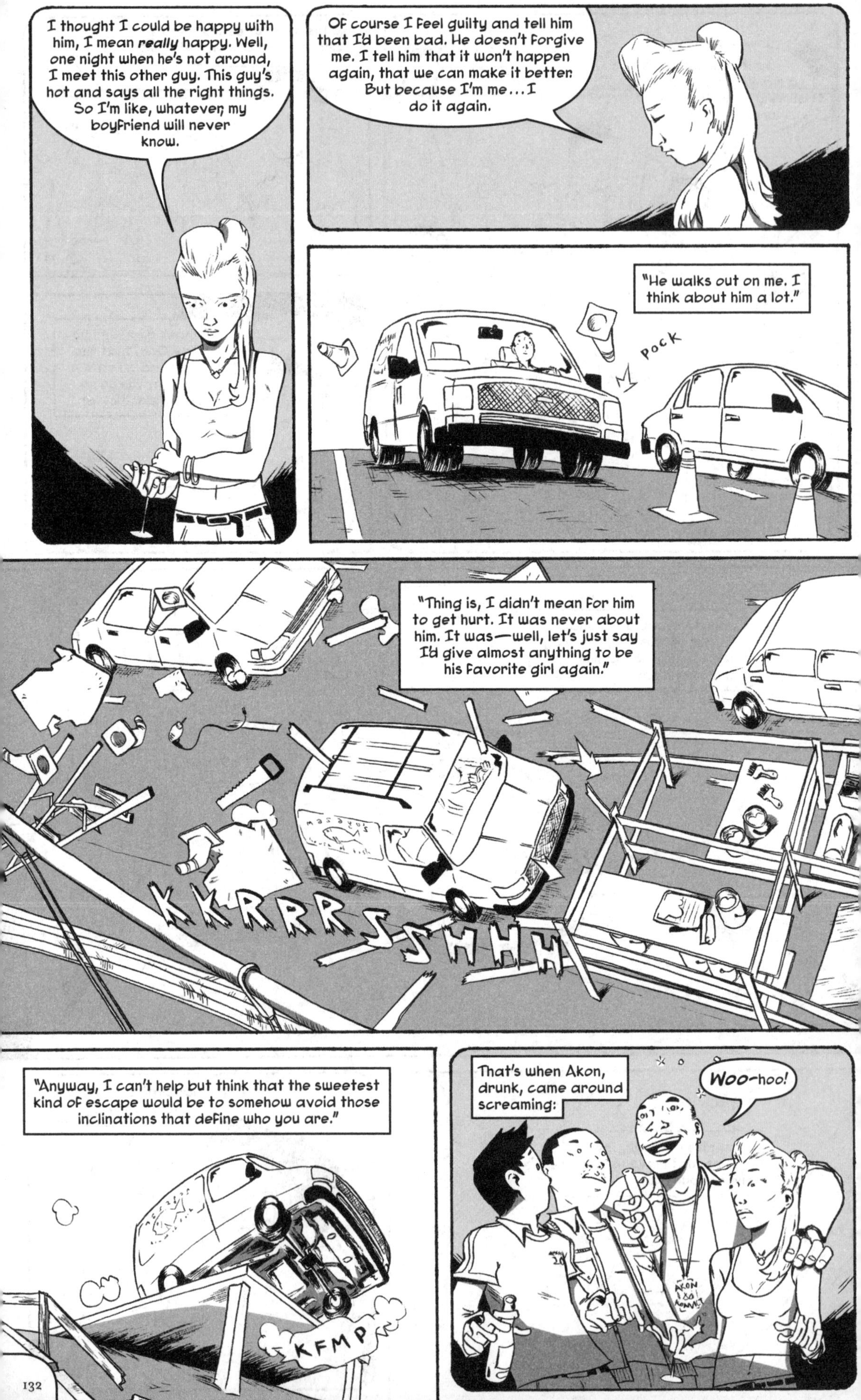
I thought I could be happy with him, I mean **really** happy. Well, one night when he's not around, I meet this other guy. This guy's hot and says all the right things. So I'm like, whatever, my boyfriend will never know.
Of course I feel guilty and tell him that I'd been bad. He doesn't forgive me. I tell him that it won't happen again, that we can make it better. But because I'm me . . . I do it again.
"He walks out on me. I think about him a lot."
POCK
"Thing is, I didn't mean for him to get hurt. It was never about him. It was—well, let's just say I'd give almost anything to be his favorite girl again."
KKRRRSSHHH
"Anyway, I can't help but think that the sweetest kind of escape would be to somehow avoid those inclinations that define who you are."
KFMP
That's when Akon, drunk, came around screaming:
Woo-hoo!

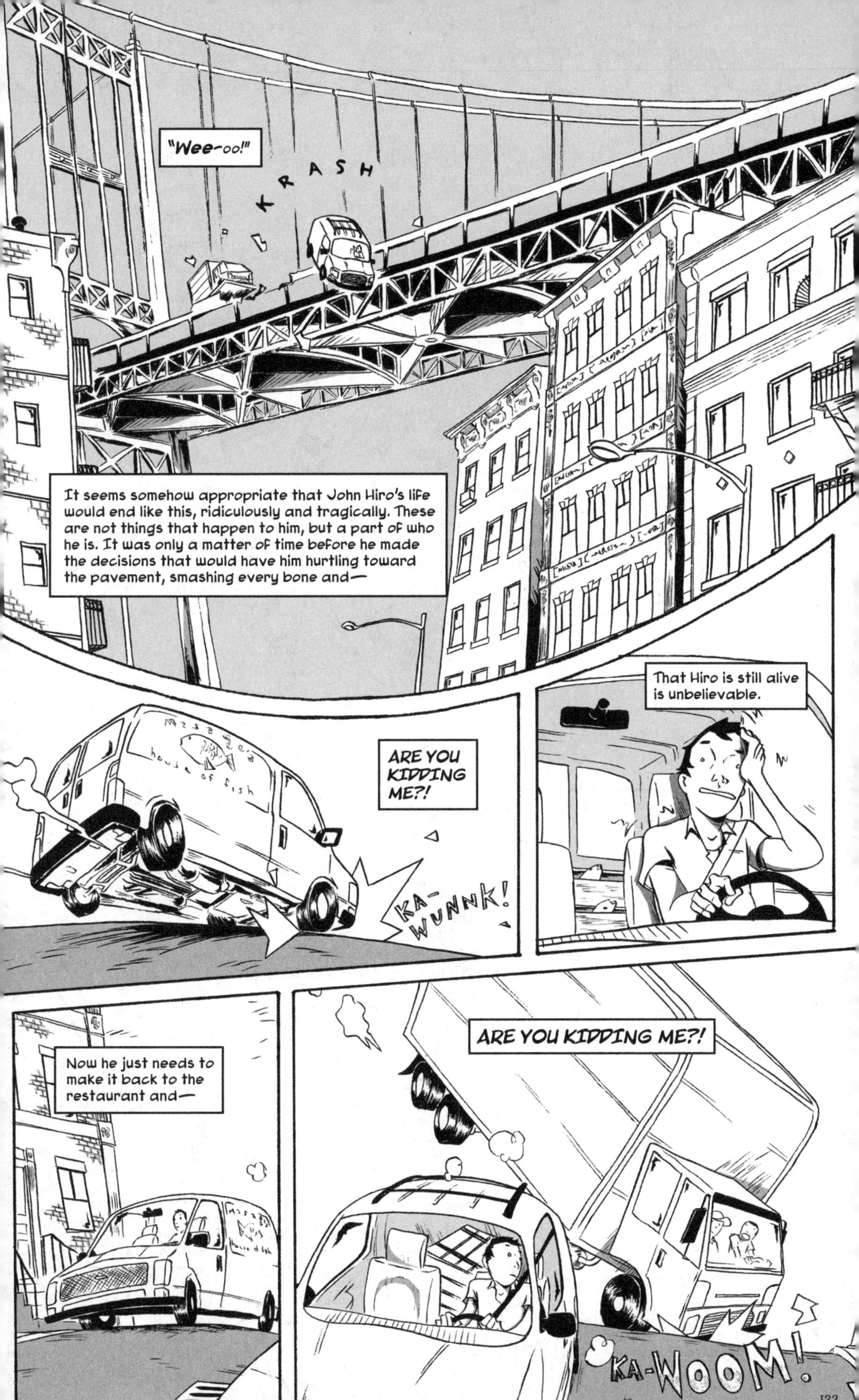

"Wee-oo!"
KRASH
It seems somehow appropriate that John Hiro's life would end like this, ridiculously and tragically. These are not things that happen to him, but a part of who he is. It was only a matter of time before he made the decisions that would have him hurtling toward the pavement, smashing every bone and—
ARE YOU KIDDING ME?!
KA-WUNNK!
That Hiro is still alive is unbelievable.
Now he just needs to make it back to the restaurant and—
ARE YOU KIDDING ME?!
KA-WOOM!

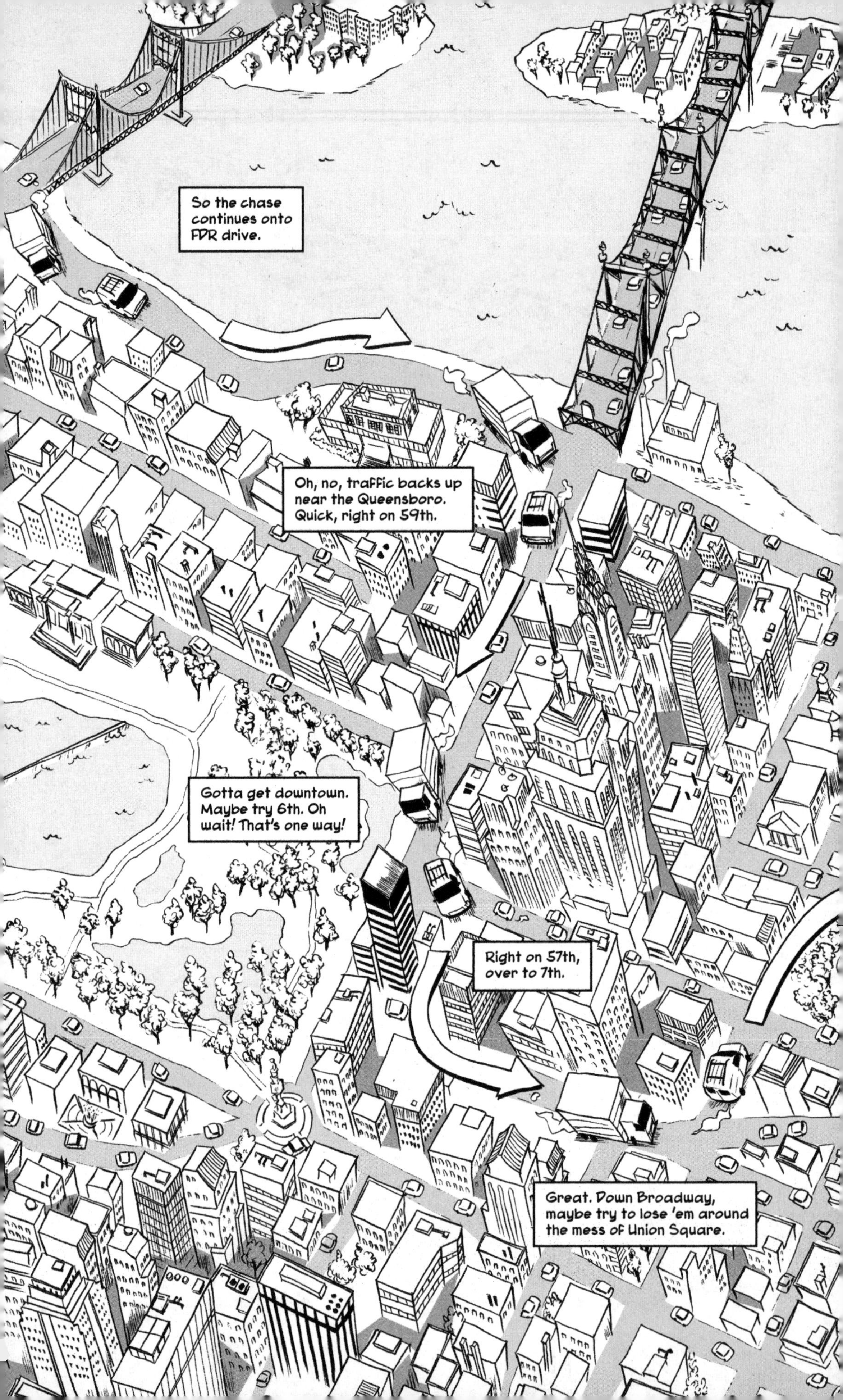
So the chase continues onto FDR drive.
Oh, no, traffic backs up near the Queensboro. Quick, right on 59th.
Gotta get downtown. Maybe try 6th. Oh wait! That's one way!
Right on 57th, over to 7th.
Great. Down Broadway, maybe try to lose 'em around the mess of Union Square.

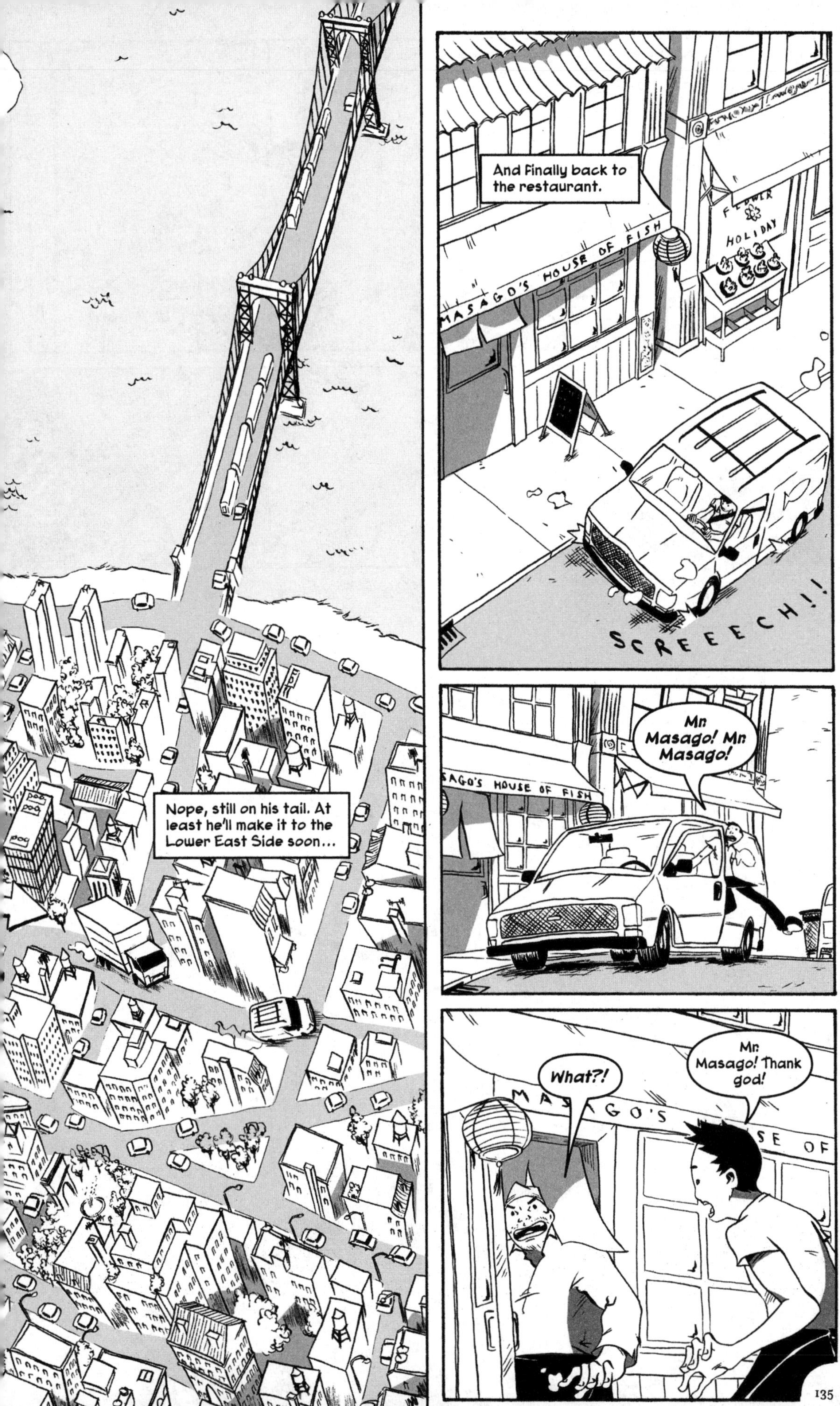
Nope, still on his tail. At least he'll make it to the Lower East Side soon...
And finally back to the restaurant.
MASAGO'S HOUSE OF FISH
FLOWER
HOLIDAY
SCREEECH!!
Mr. Masago! Mr. Masago!
SAGO'S HOUSE OF FISH
Mr. Masago! Thank god!
What?!

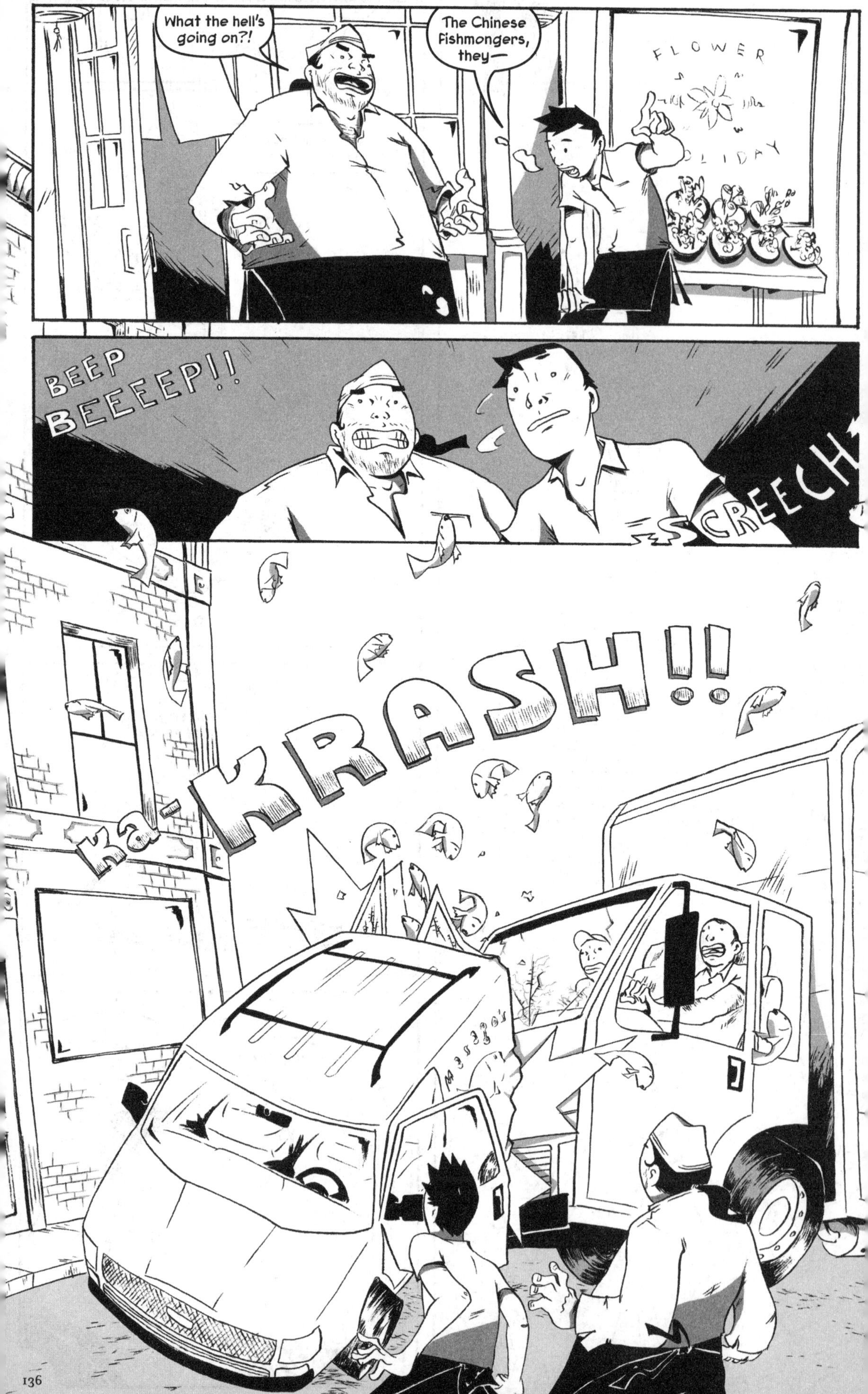
What the hell's going on?!
The Chinese fishmongers, they—
FLOWER
OLIDAY
BEEP BEEEEP!!
SCREECH
Ka-KRASH!!

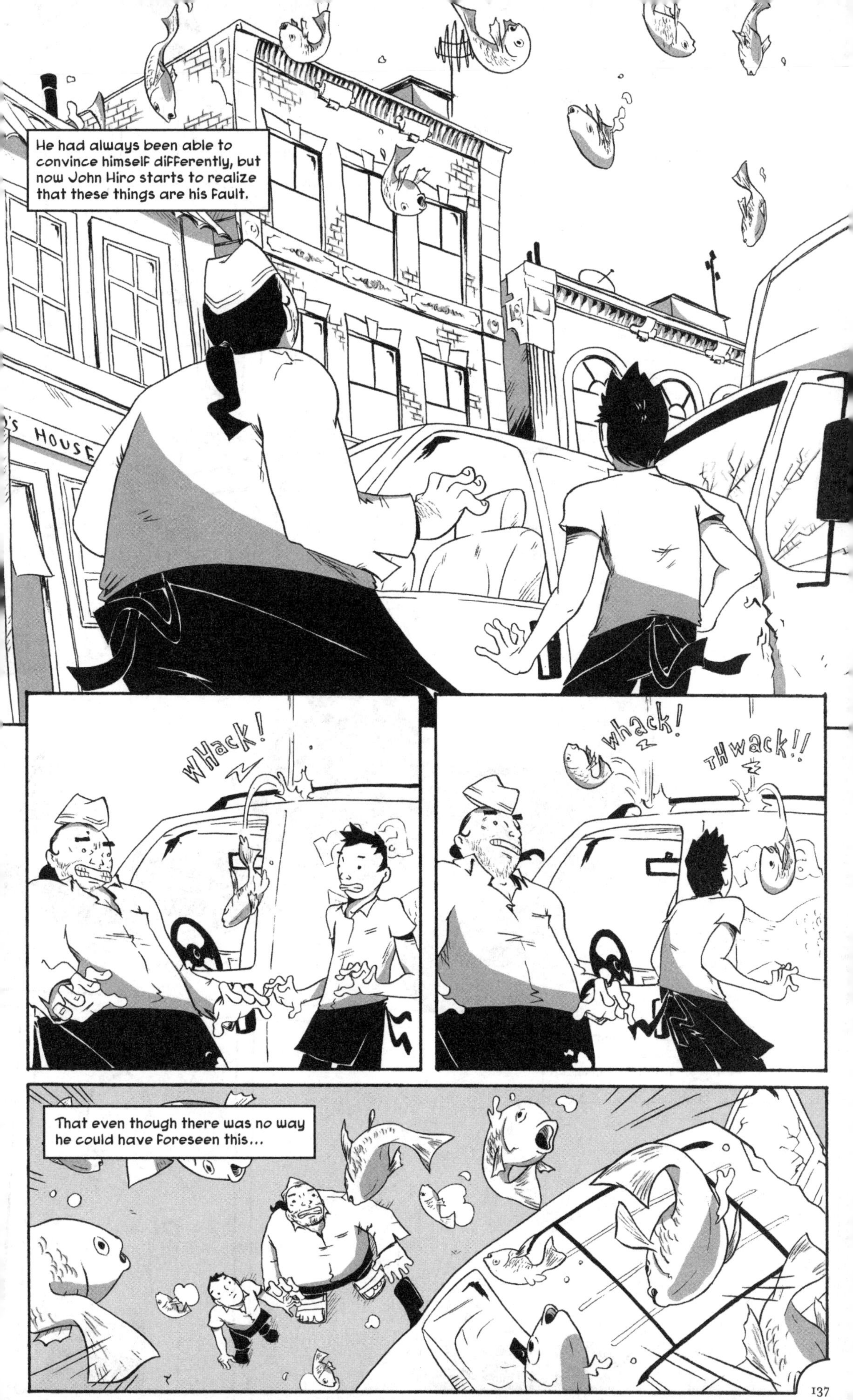
He had always been able to convince himself differently, but now John Hiro starts to realize that these things are his fault.
'S HOUSE
WHACK!
whack!
THWACK!!
That even though there was no way he could have foreseen this...

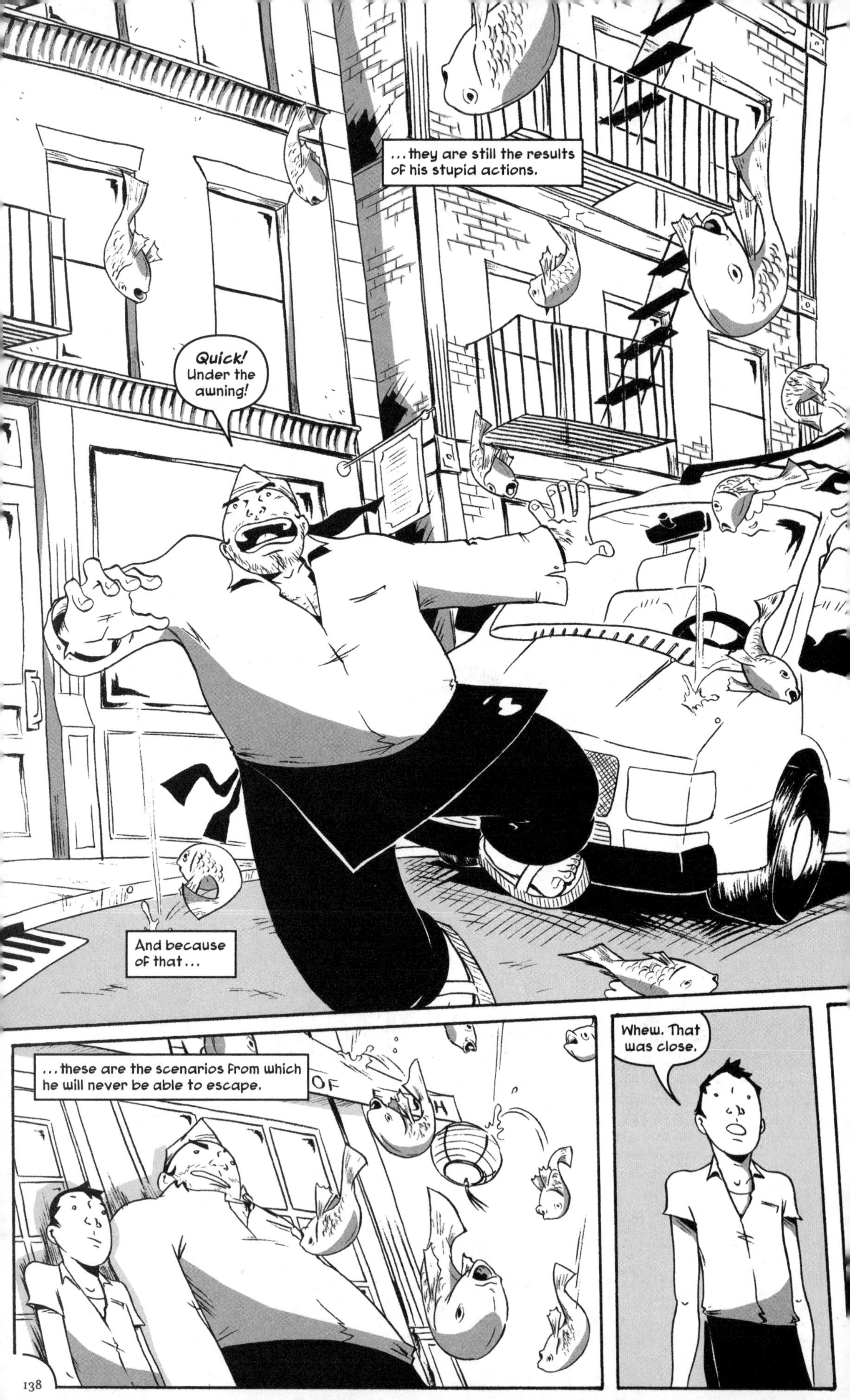
...they are still the results of his stupid actions.
Quick! Under the awning!
And because of that...
...these are the scenarios from which he will never be able to escape.
Whew. That was close.

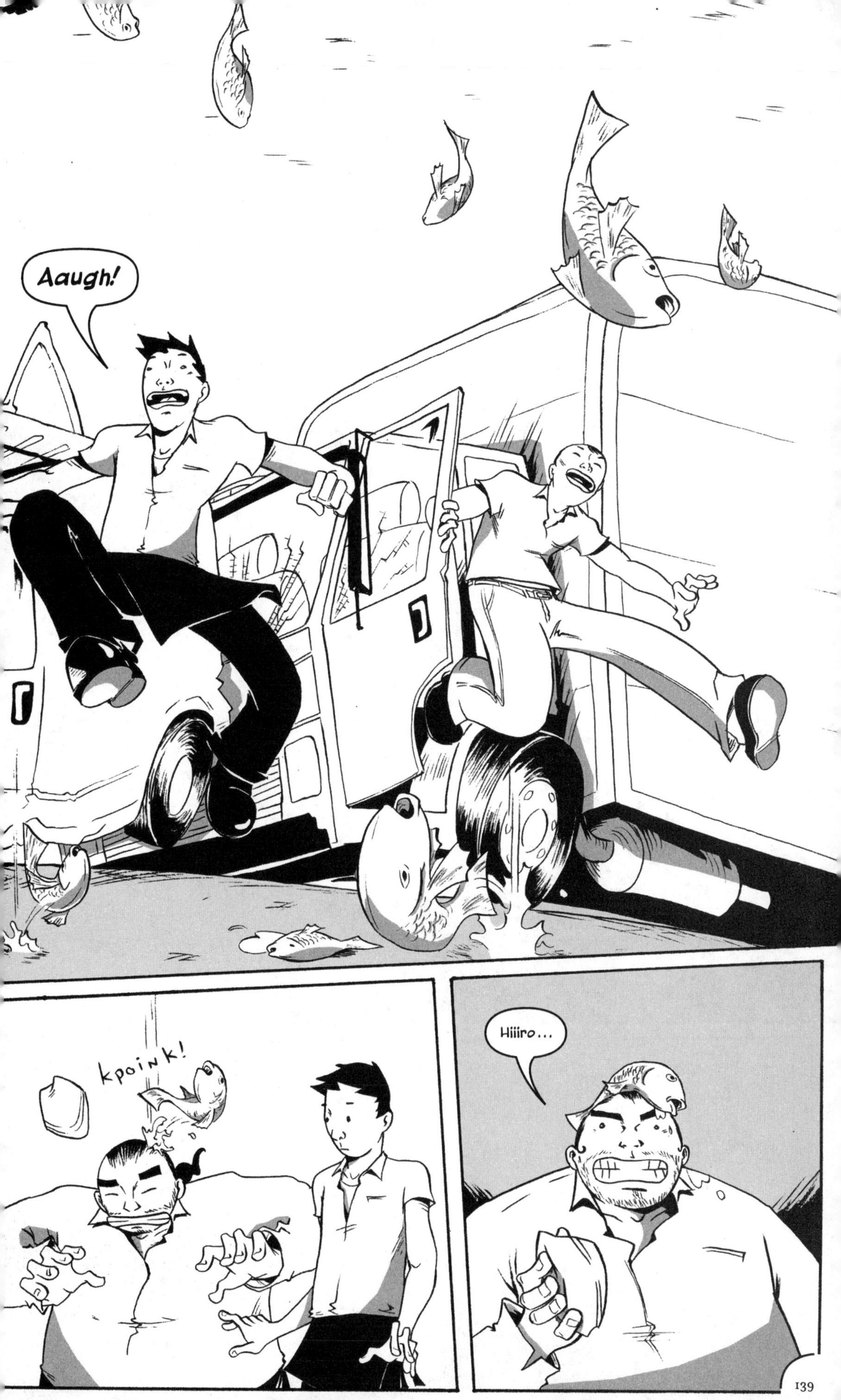
Aaugh!
kpoink!
Hiiiro...

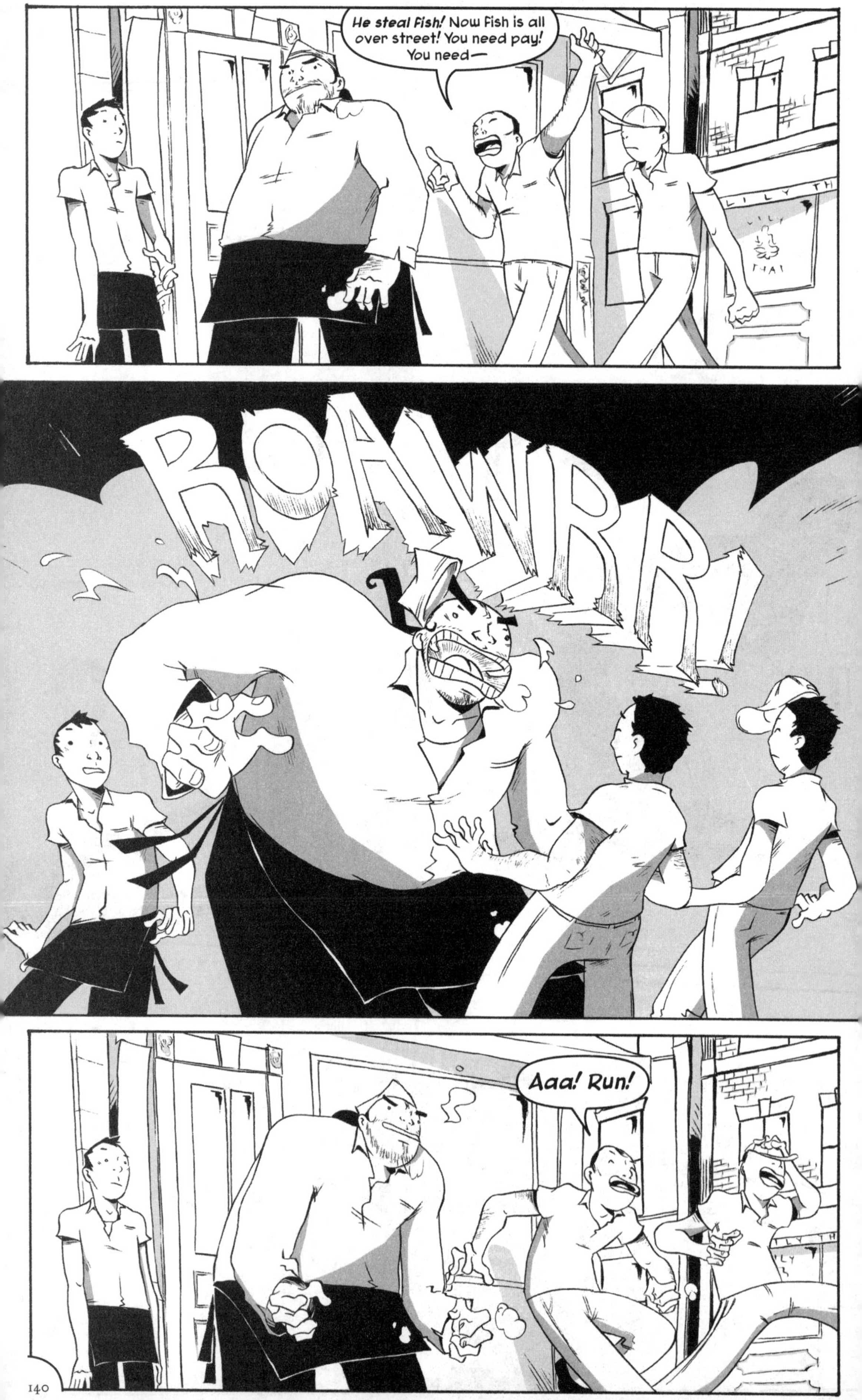
He steal fish! Now fish is all over street! You need pay! You need—
LILY TH
LILY THAI
ROAWRR!
Aaa! Run!

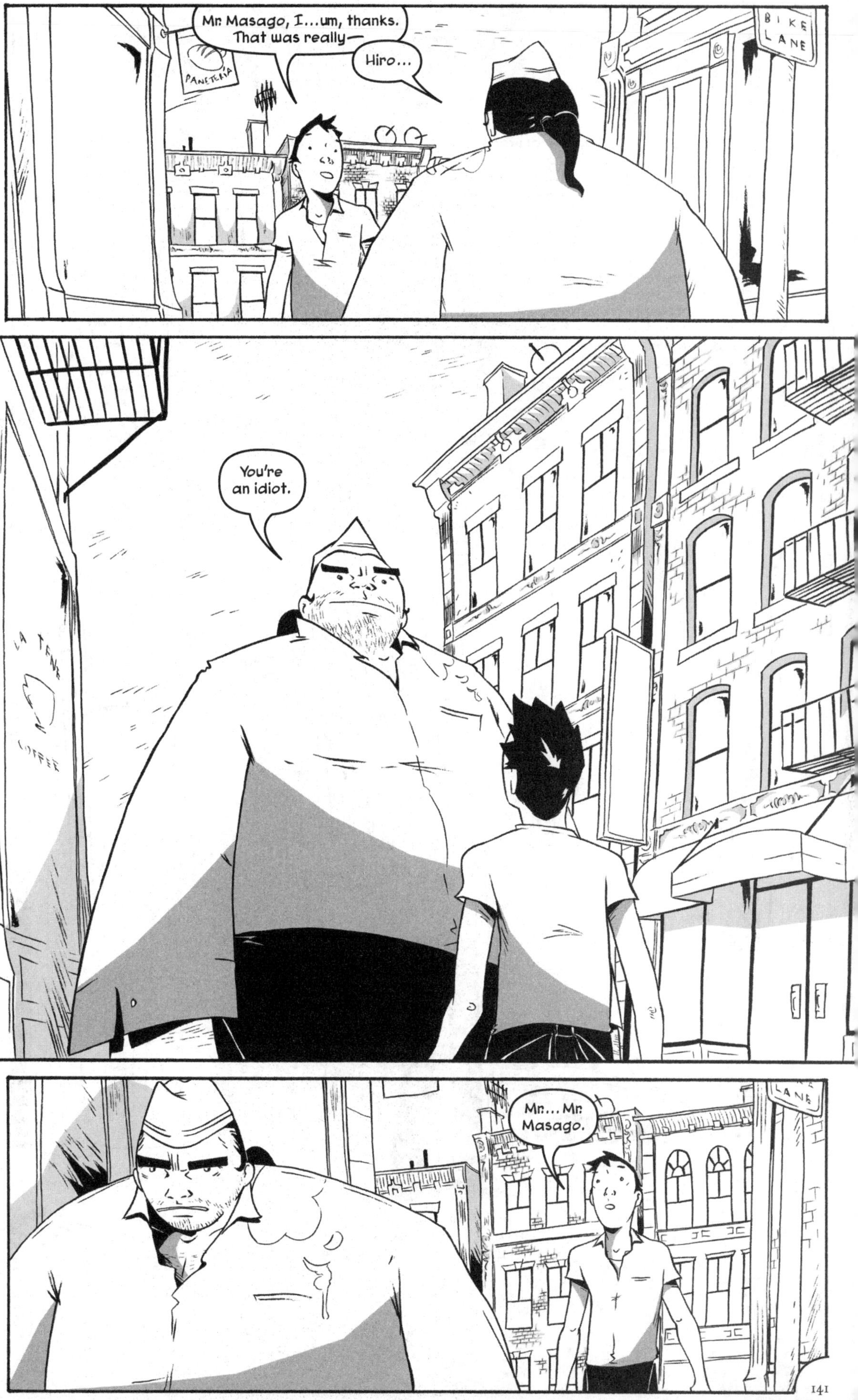
Mr. Masago, I...um, thanks. That was really—
Hiro...
BIKE LANE
You're an idiot.
Mr.... Mr. Masago.

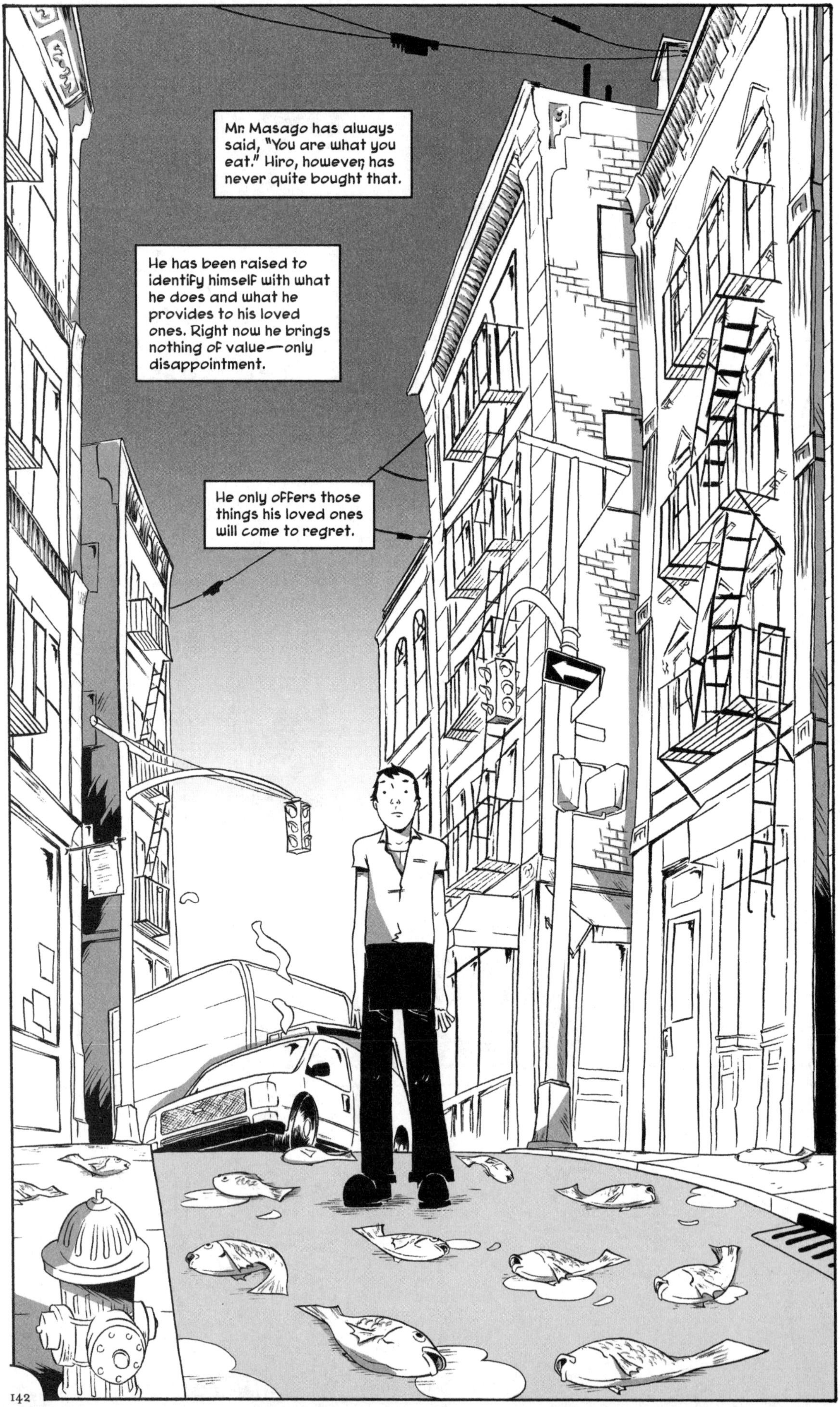
Mr. Masago has always said, "You are what you eat." Hiro, however, has never quite bought that.
He has been raised to identify himself with what he does and what he provides to his loved ones. Right now he brings nothing of value—only disappointment.
He only offers those things his loved ones will come to regret.

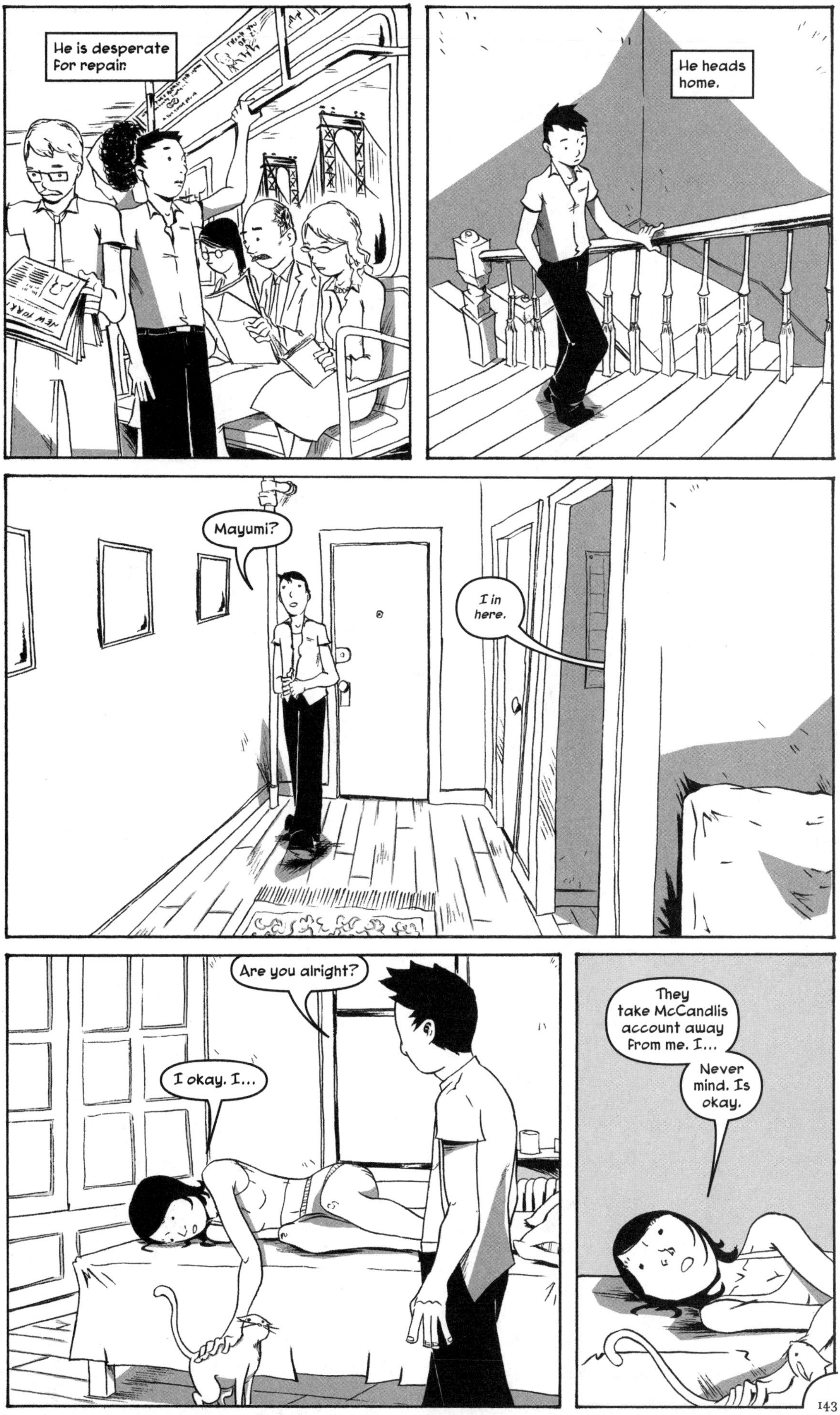
He is desperate for repair.
He heads home.
Mayumi?
I in here.
Are you alright?
I okay. I...
They take McCandlis account away from me. I...
Never mind. Is okay.

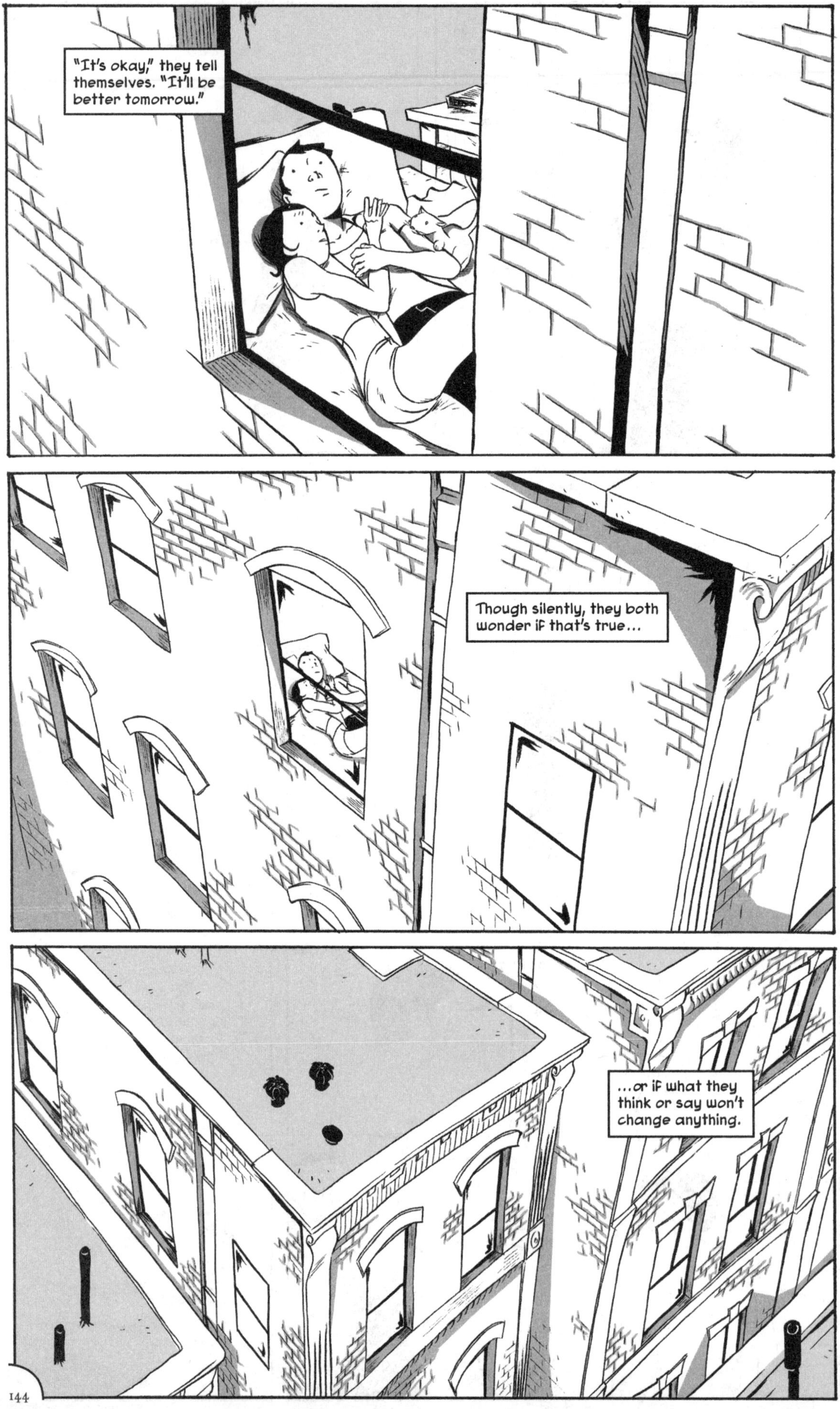
"It's okay," they tell themselves. "It'll be better tomorrow."
Though silently, they both wonder if that's true...
...or if what they think or say won't change anything.

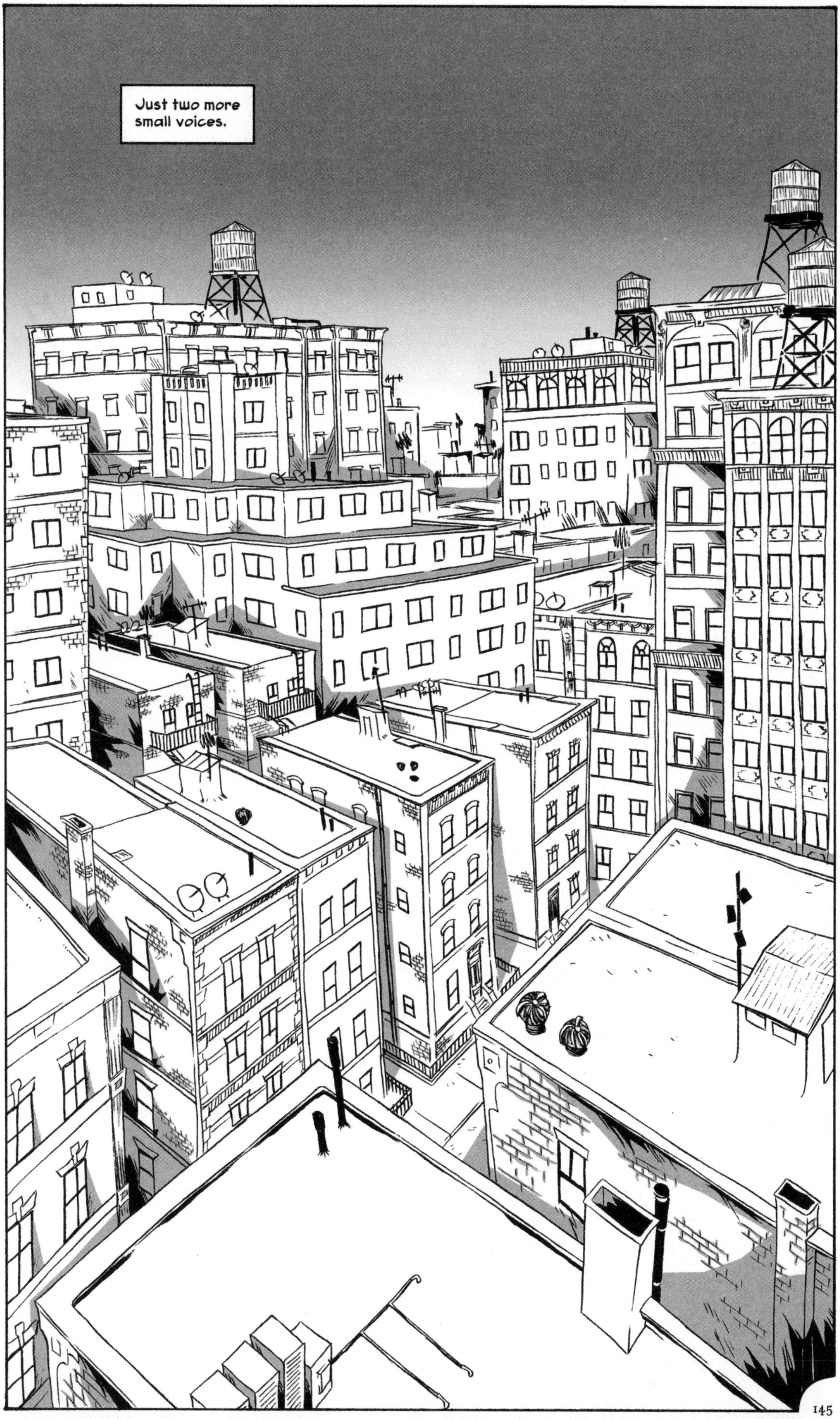
Just two more small voices.

カムバック

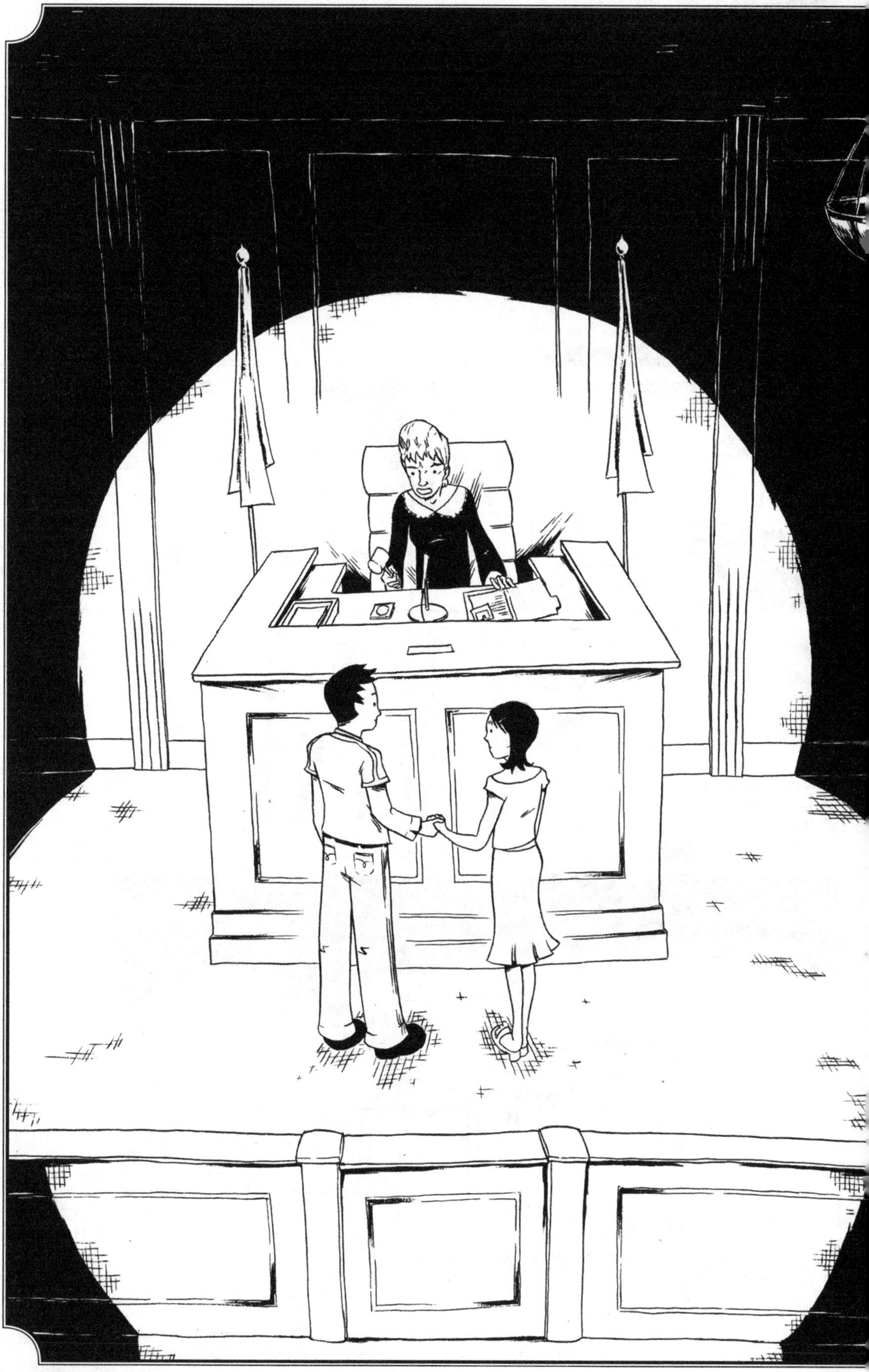

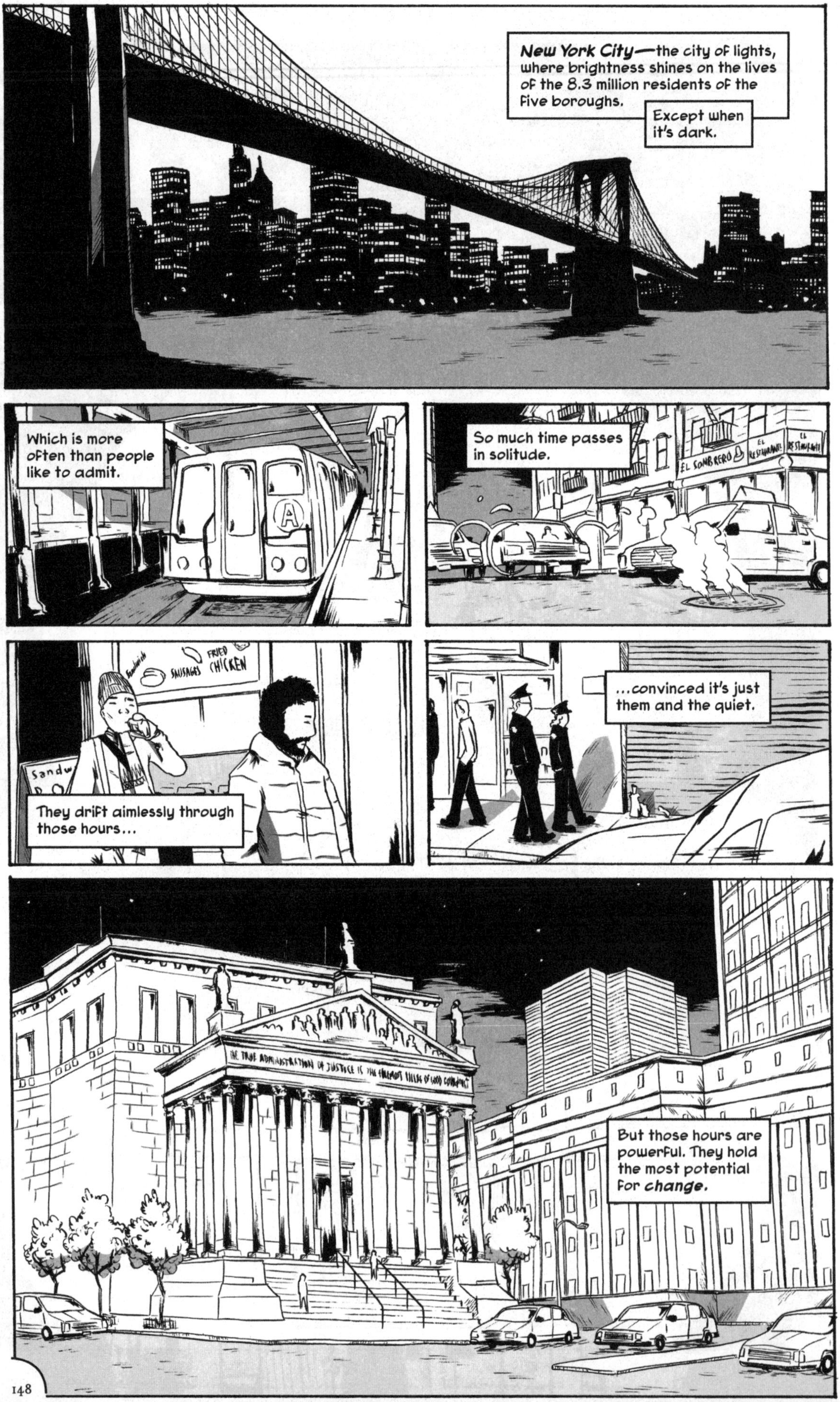
New York City—the city of lights, where brightness shines on the lives of the 8.3 million residents of the five boroughs.
Except when it's dark.
Which is more often than people like to admit.
A
So much time passes in solitude.
EL SOMBRERO
SAUSAGES
FRIED CHICKEN
They drift aimlessly through those hours...
...convinced it's just them and the quiet.
But those hours are powerful. They hold the most potential for *change*.

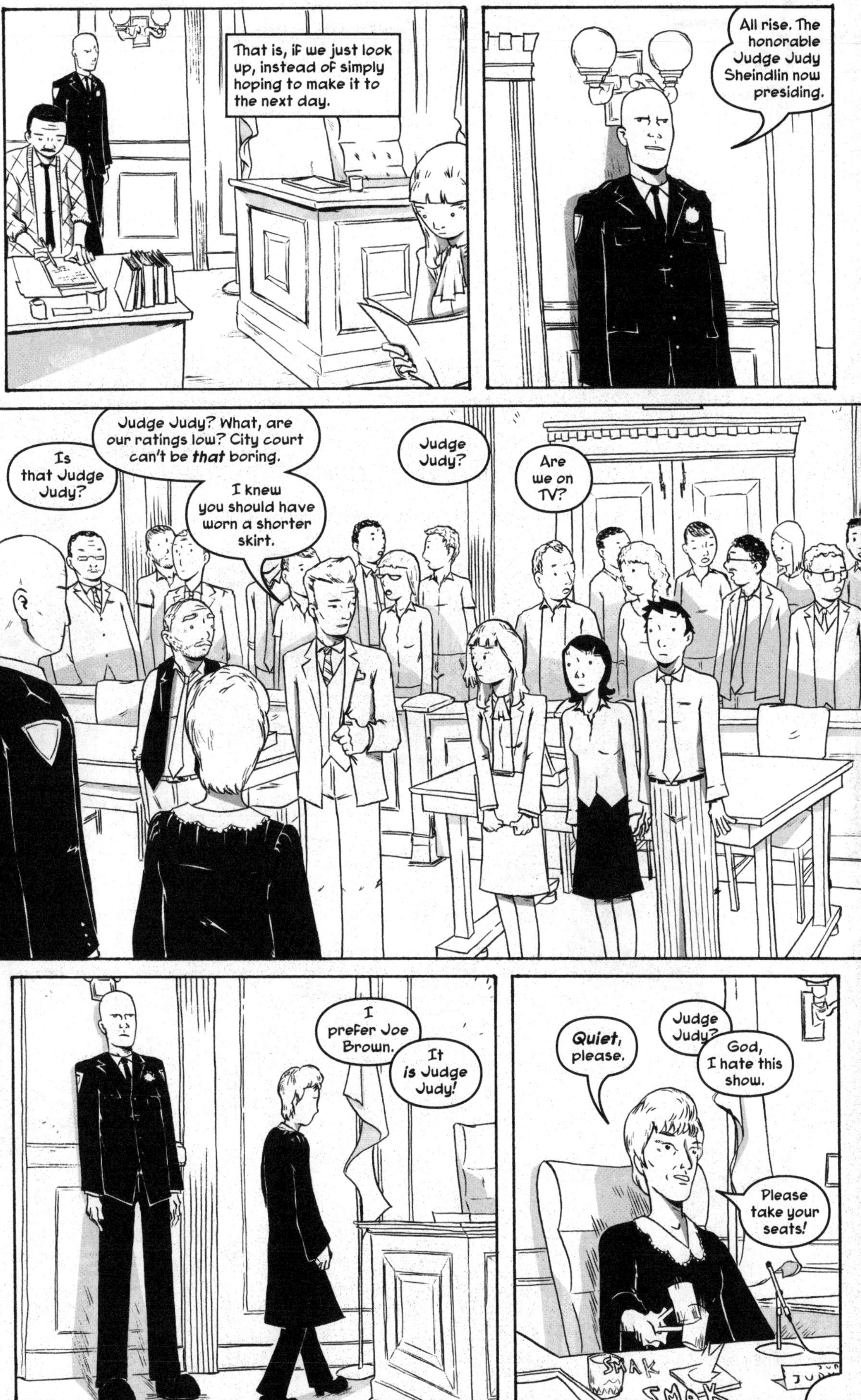
That is, if we just look up, instead of simply hoping to make it to the next day.
All rise. The honorable Judge Judy Sheindlin now presiding.
Is that Judge Judy?
Judge Judy? What, are our ratings low? City court can't be *that* boring.
I knew you should have worn a shorter skirt.
Judge Judy?
Are we on TV?
I prefer Joe Brown.
It *is* Judge Judy!
Quiet, please.
Judge Judy?
God, I hate this show.
Please take your seats!
SMAK
SMAK

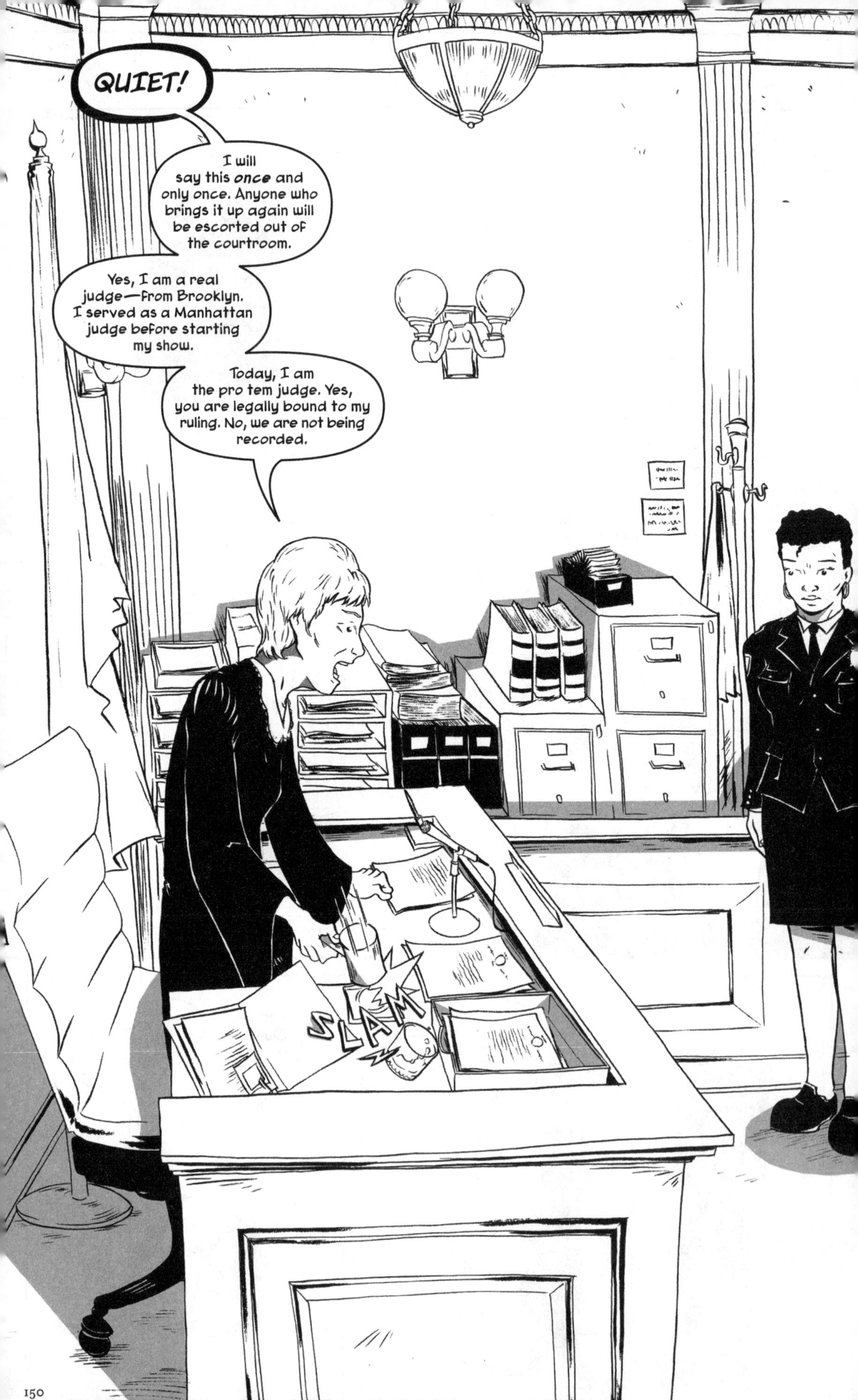
QUIET!
I will say this *once* and only once. Anyone who brings it up again will be escorted out of the courtroom.
Yes, I am a real judge—from Brooklyn. I served as a Manhattan judge before starting my show.
Today, I am the pro tem judge. Yes, you are legally bound to my ruling. No, we are not being recorded.
SLAM

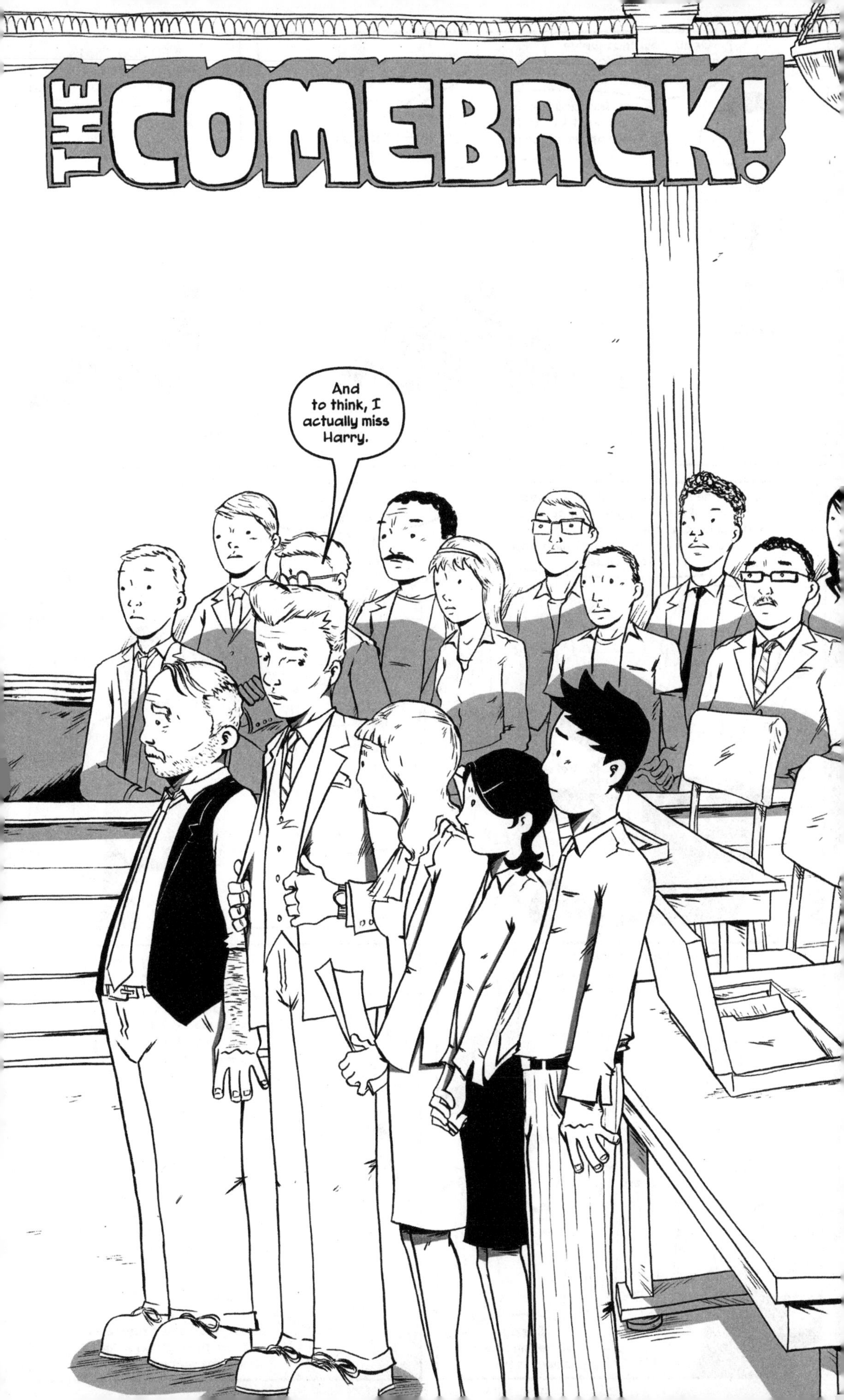
THE COMEBACK!
And to think, I actually miss Harry.

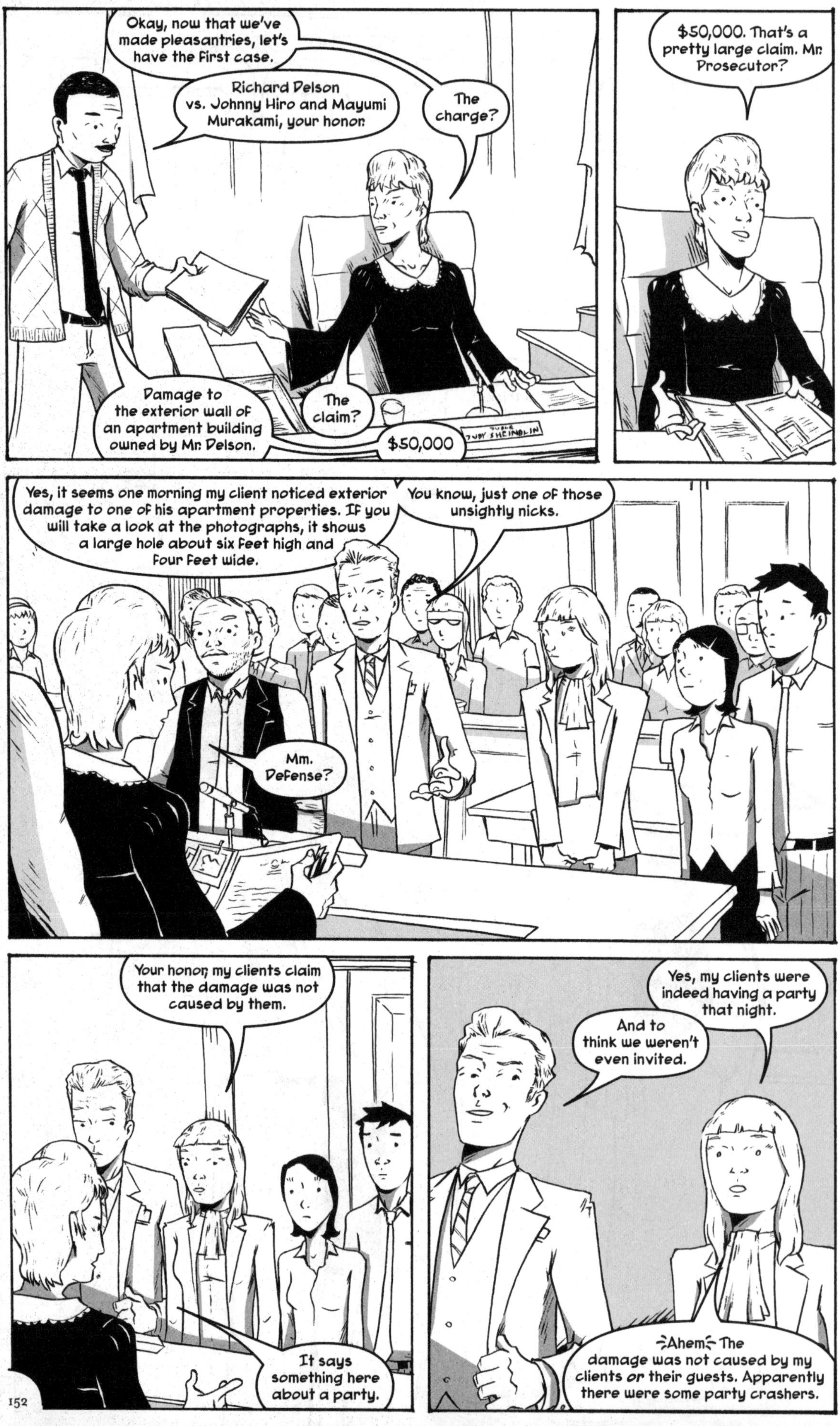
Okay, now that we've made pleasantries, let's have the first case.
Richard Delson vs. Johnny Hiro and Mayumi Murakami, your honor.
The charge?
Damage to the exterior wall of an apartment building owned by Mr. Delson.
The claim?
$50,000
JUDY SHEINDLIN
$50,000. That's a pretty large claim. Mr. Prosecutor?
Yes, it seems one morning my client noticed exterior damage to one of his apartment properties. If you will take a look at the photographs, it shows a large hole about six feet high and four feet wide.
You know, just one of those unsightly nicks.
Mm. Defense?
Your honor, my clients claim that the damage was not caused by them.
It says something here about a party.
Yes, my clients were indeed having a party that night.
And to think we weren't even invited.
Ahem The damage was not caused by my clients *or* their guests. Apparently there were some party crashers.

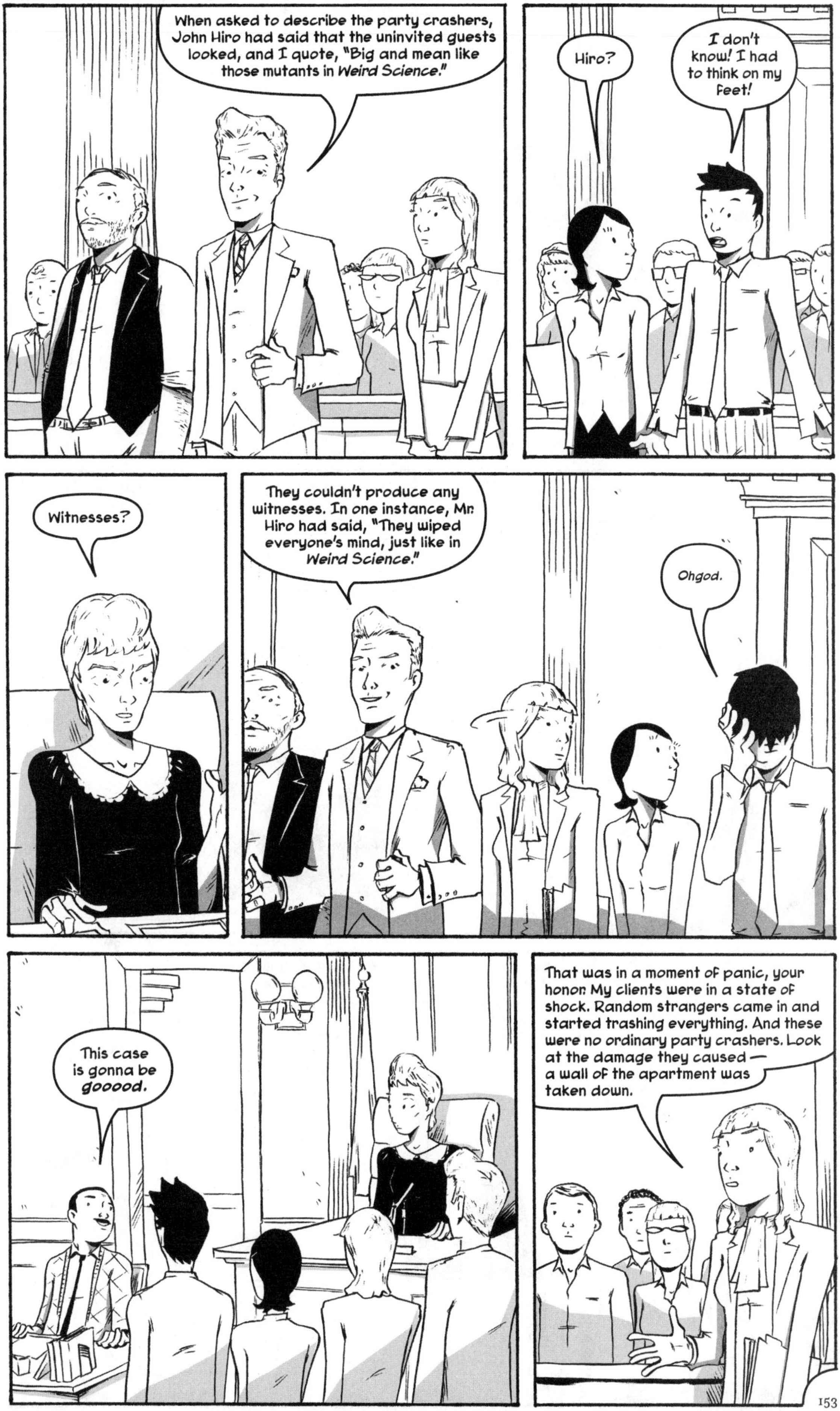
When asked to describe the party crashers, John Hiro had said that the uninvited guests looked, and I quote, "Big and mean like those mutants in *Weird Science*."
Hiro?
I don't know! I had to think on my feet!
Witnesses?
They couldn't produce any witnesses. In one instance, Mr. Hiro had said, "They wiped everyone's mind, just like in *Weird Science*."
Ohgod.
This case is gonna be gooood.
That was in a moment of panic, your honor. My clients were in a state of shock. Random strangers came in and started trashing everything. And these were no ordinary party crashers. Look at the damage they caused— a wall of the apartment was taken down.

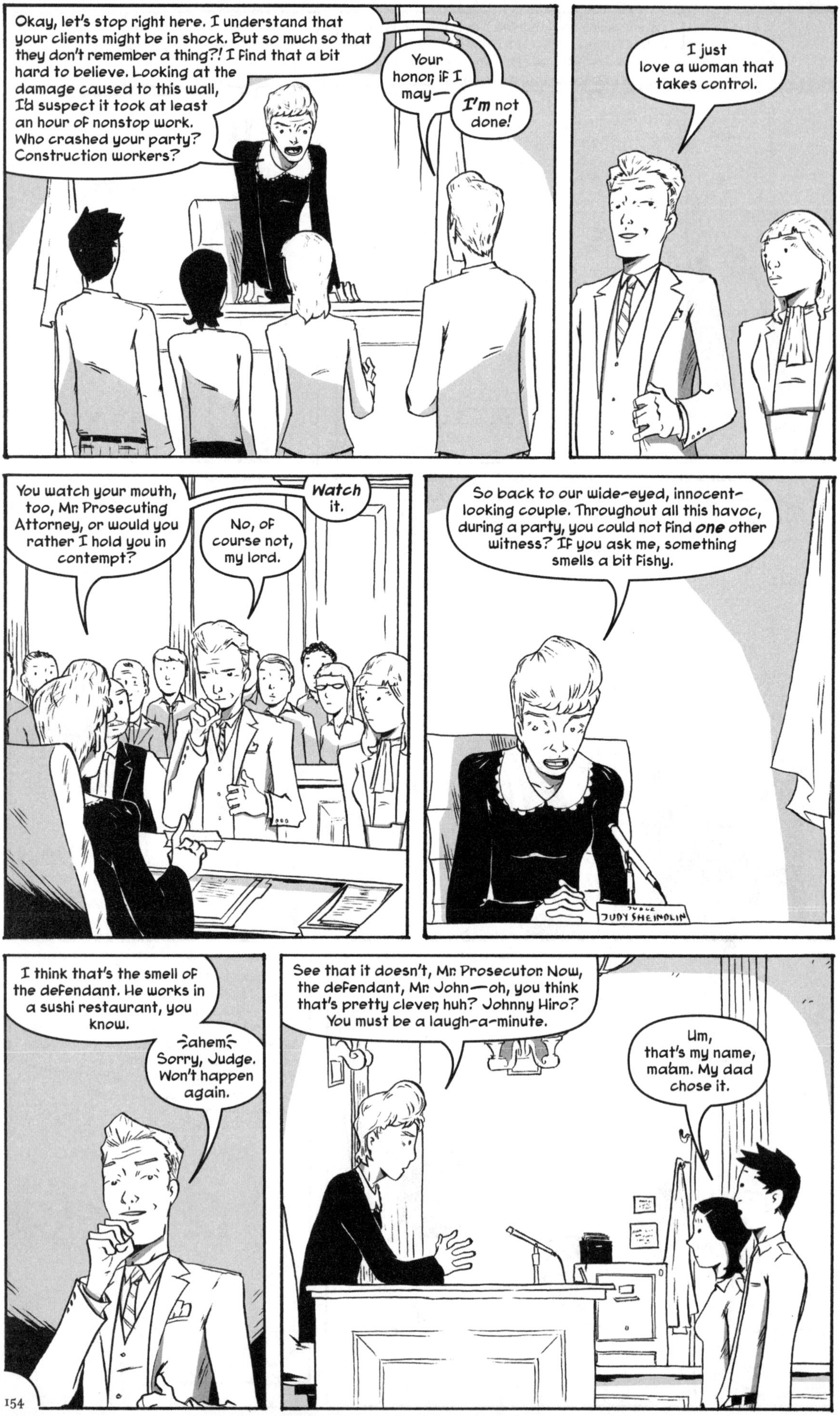

Okay, let's stop right here. I understand that your clients might be in shock. But so much so that they don't remember a thing?! I find that a bit hard to believe. Looking at the damage caused to this wall, I'd suspect it took at least an hour of nonstop work. Who crashed your party? Construction workers?
Your honor, if I may—
I'm not done!
I just love a woman that takes control.
You watch your mouth, too, Mr. Prosecuting Attorney, or would you rather I hold you in contempt?
No, of course not, my lord.
Watch it.
So back to our wide-eyed, innocent-looking couple. Throughout all this havoc, during a party, you could not find one other witness? If you ask me, something smells a bit fishy.
JUDY SHEINDLIN
I think that's the smell of the defendant. He works in a sushi restaurant, you know.
ahem
Sorry, Judge. Won't happen again.
See that it doesn't, Mr. Prosecutor. Now, the defendant, Mr. John—oh, you think that's pretty clever, huh? Johnny Hiro? You must be a laugh-a-minute.
Um, that's my name, ma'am. My dad chose it.

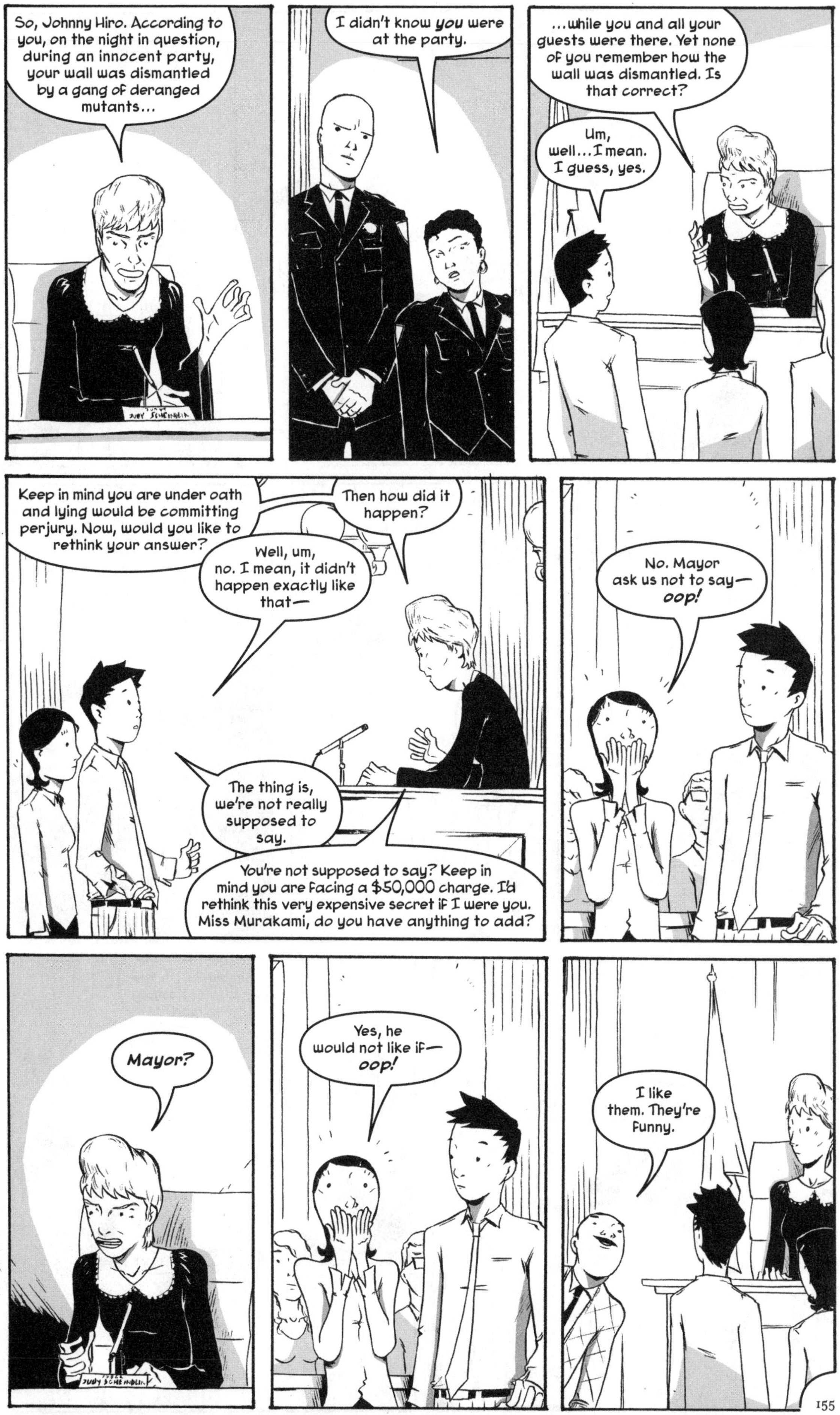

So, Johnny Hiro. According to you, on the night in question, during an innocent party, your wall was dismantled by a gang of deranged mutants...
I didn't know *you* were at the party.
...while you and all your guests were there. Yet none of you remember how the wall was dismantled. Is that correct?
Um, well...I mean. I guess, yes.
Keep in mind you are under oath and lying would be committing perjury. Now, would you like to rethink your answer?
Well, um, no. I mean, it didn't happen exactly like that—
Then how did it happen?
The thing is, we're not really supposed to say.
You're not supposed to say? Keep in mind you are facing a $50,000 charge. I'd rethink this very expensive secret if I were you. Miss Murakami, do you have anything to add?
No. Mayor ask us not to say— *oop!*
Mayor?
Yes, he would not like if— *oop!*
I like them. They're funny.

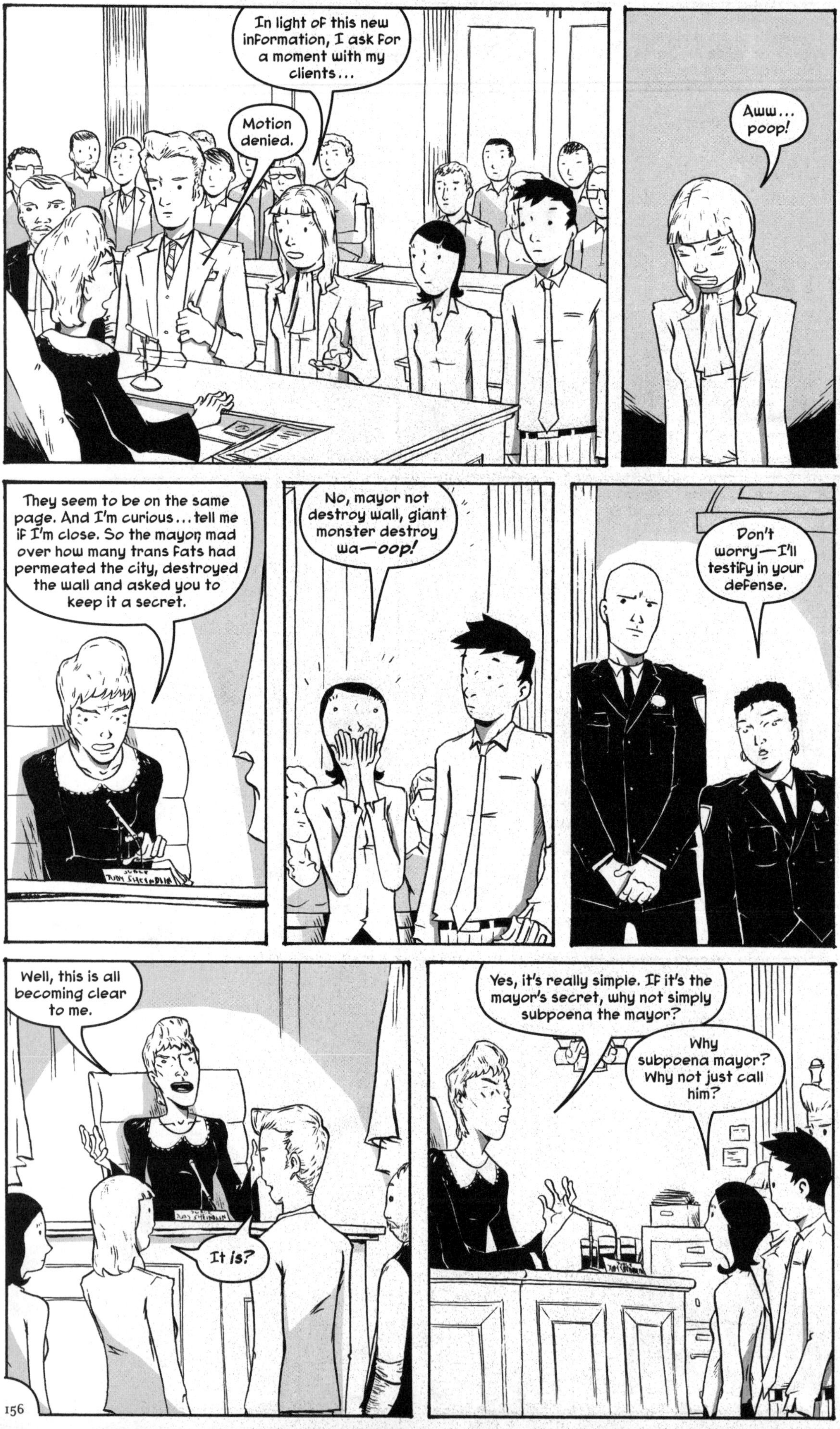
In light of this new information, I ask for a moment with my clients...
Motion denied.
Aww... poop!
They seem to be on the same page. And I'm curious... tell me if I'm close. So the mayor, mad over how many trans fats had permeated the city, destroyed the wall and asked you to keep it a secret.
No, mayor not destroy wall, giant monster destroy wa—oop!
Don't worry—I'll testify in your defense.
Well, this is all becoming clear to me.
It is?
Yes, it's really simple. If it's the mayor's secret, why not simply subpoena the mayor?
Why subpoena mayor? Why not just call him?

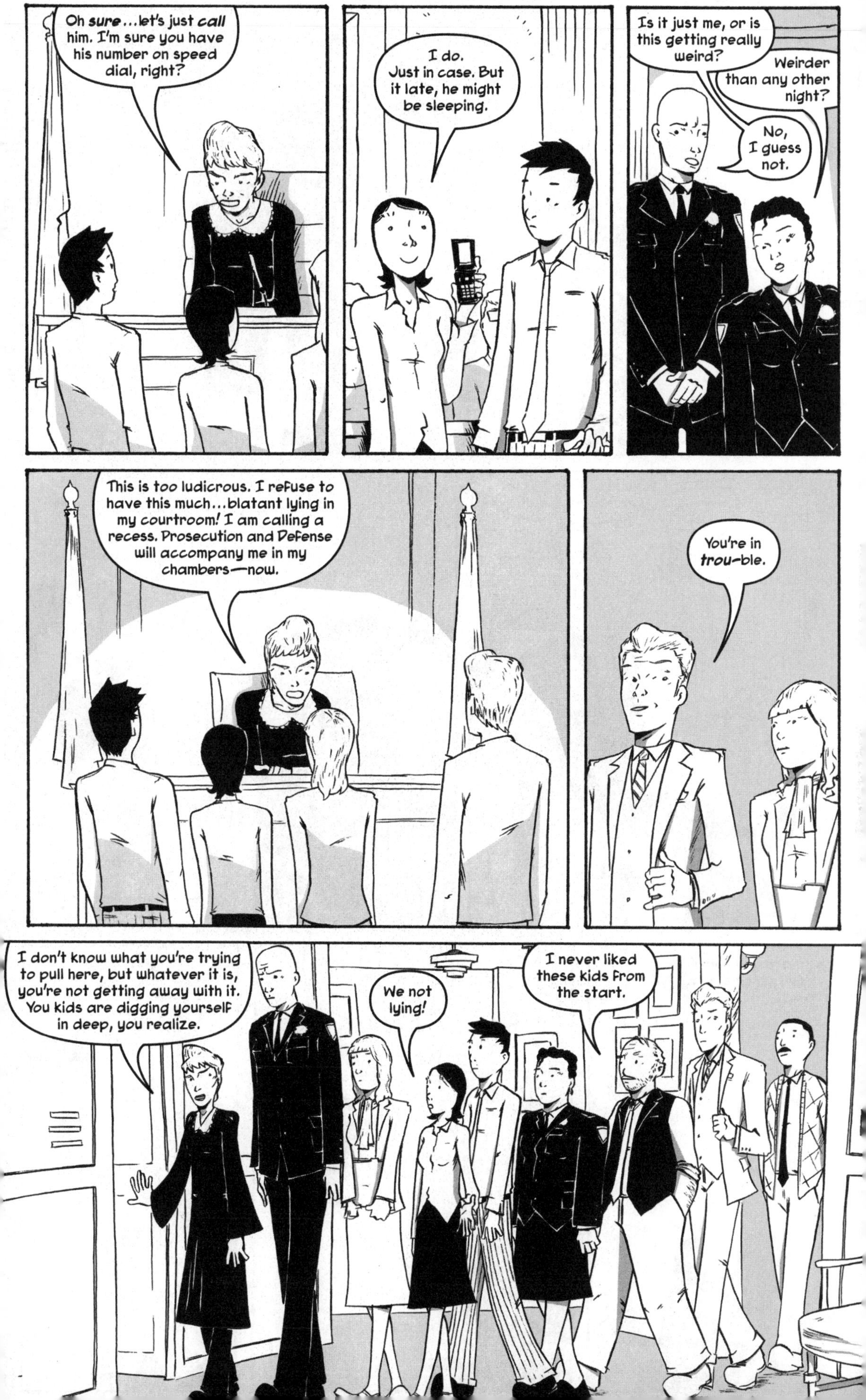
Oh sure…let's just call him. I'm sure you have his number on speed dial, right?
I do. Just in case. But it late, he might be sleeping.
Is it just me, or is this getting really weird?
Weirder than any other night?
No, I guess not.
This is too ludicrous. I refuse to have this much…blatant lying in my courtroom! I am calling a recess. Prosecution and Defense will accompany me in my chambers—now.
You're in trou-ble.
I don't know what you're trying to pull here, but whatever it is, you're not getting away with it. You kids are digging yourself in deep, you realize.
We not lying!
I never liked these kids from the start.

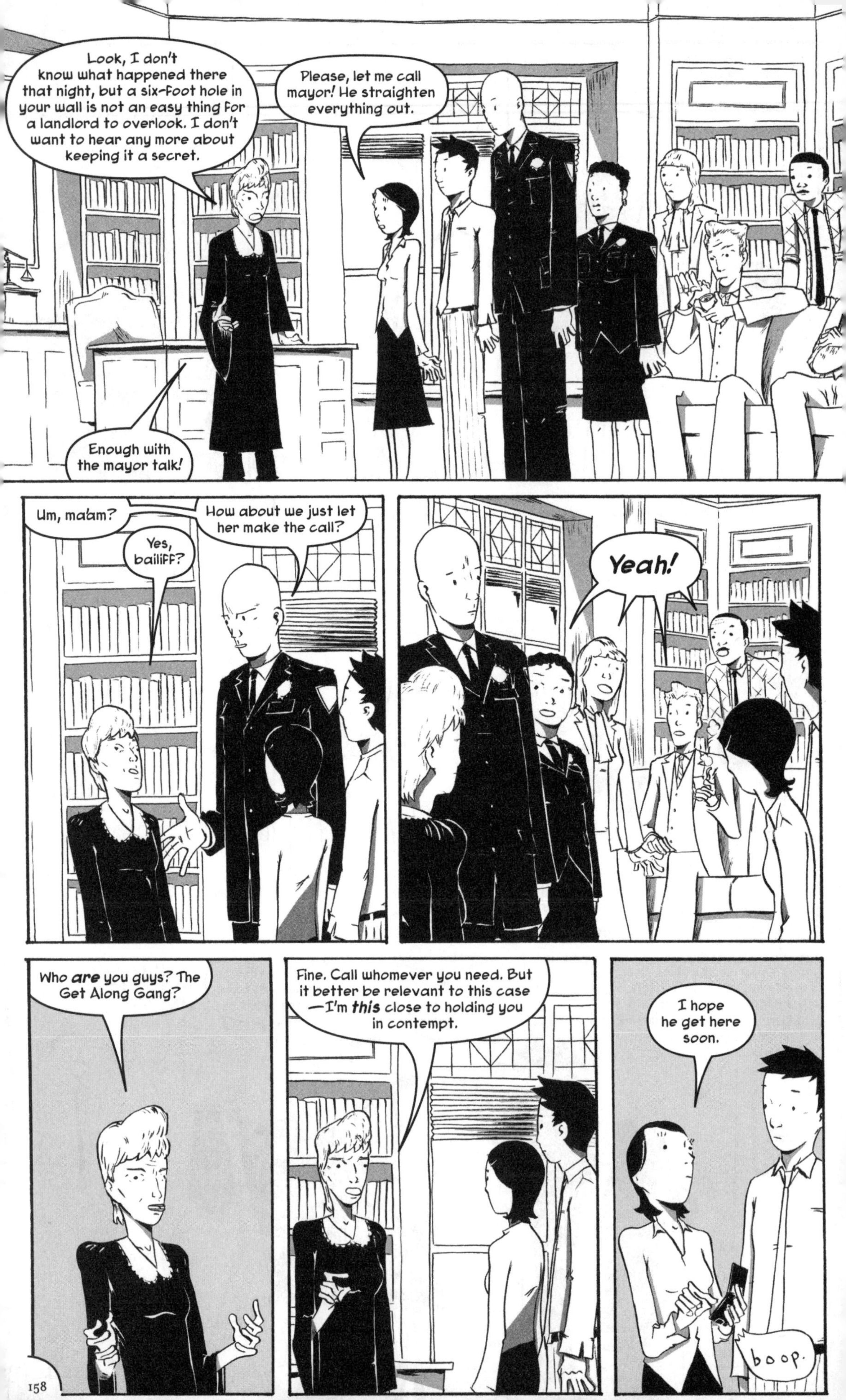
Look, I don't know what happened there that night, but a six-foot hole in your wall is not an easy thing for a landlord to overlook. I don't want to hear any more about keeping it a secret.
Please, let me call mayor! He straighten everything out.
Enough with the mayor talk!
Um, ma'am?
How about we just let her make the call?
Yes, bailiff?
Yeah!
Who are you guys? The Get Along Gang?
Fine. Call whomever you need. But it better be relevant to this case —I'm this close to holding you in contempt.
I hope he get here soon.
boop.

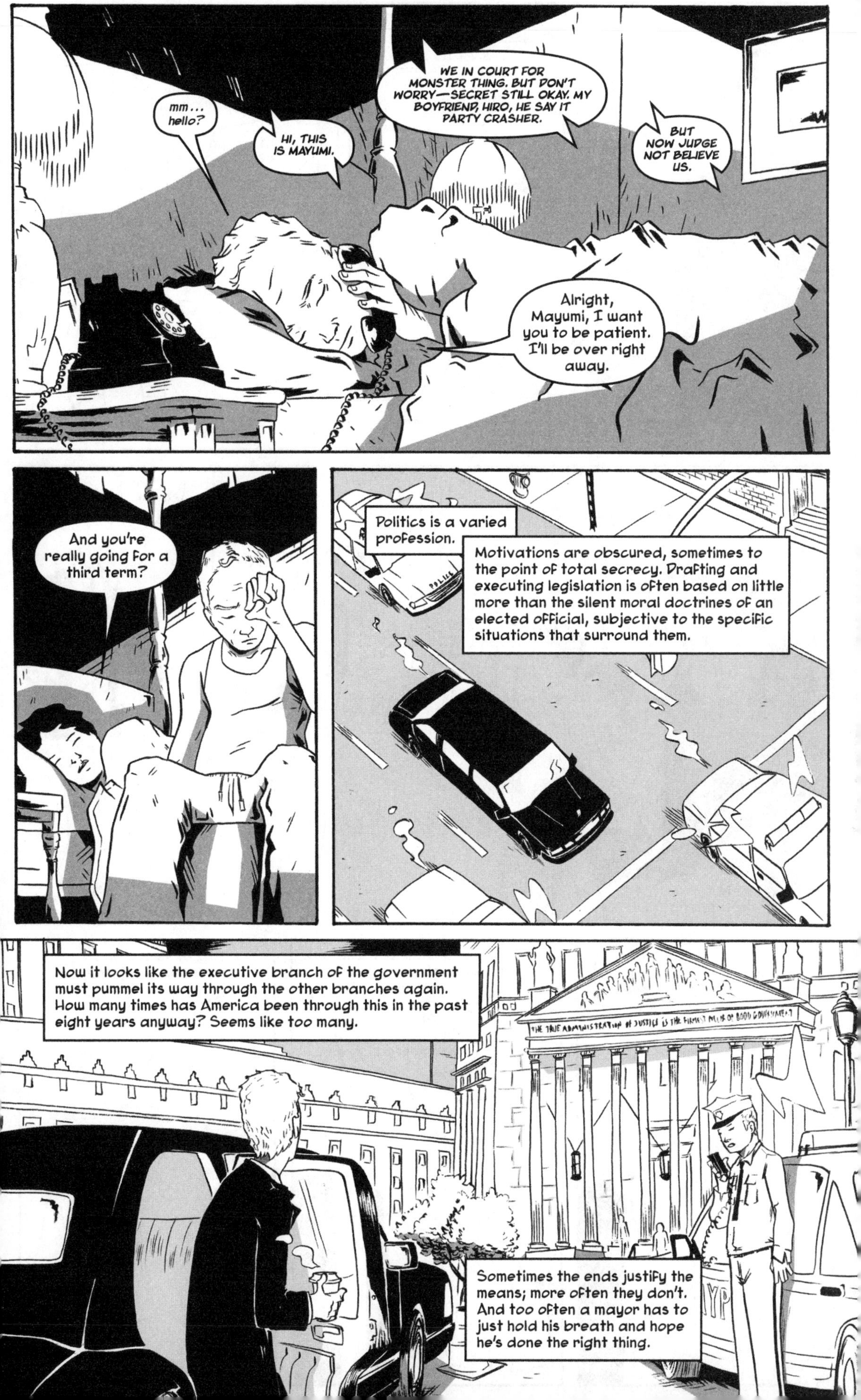
mm... hello?
HI, THIS IS MAYUMI.
WE IN COURT FOR MONSTER THING. BUT DON'T WORRY—SECRET STILL OKAY. MY BOYFRIEND, HIRO, HE SAY IT PARTY CRASHER.
BUT NOW JUDGE NOT BELIEVE US.
Alright, Mayumi, I want you to be patient. I'll be over right away.
And you're really going for a third term?
Politics is a varied profession.
Motivations are obscured, sometimes to the point of total secrecy. Drafting and executing legislation is often based on little more than the silent moral doctrines of an elected official, subjective to the specific situations that surround them.
Now it looks like the executive branch of the government must pummel its way through the other branches again. How many times has America been through this in the past eight years anyway? Seems like too many.
Sometimes the ends justify the means; more often they don't. And too often a mayor has to just hold his breath and hope he's done the right thing.

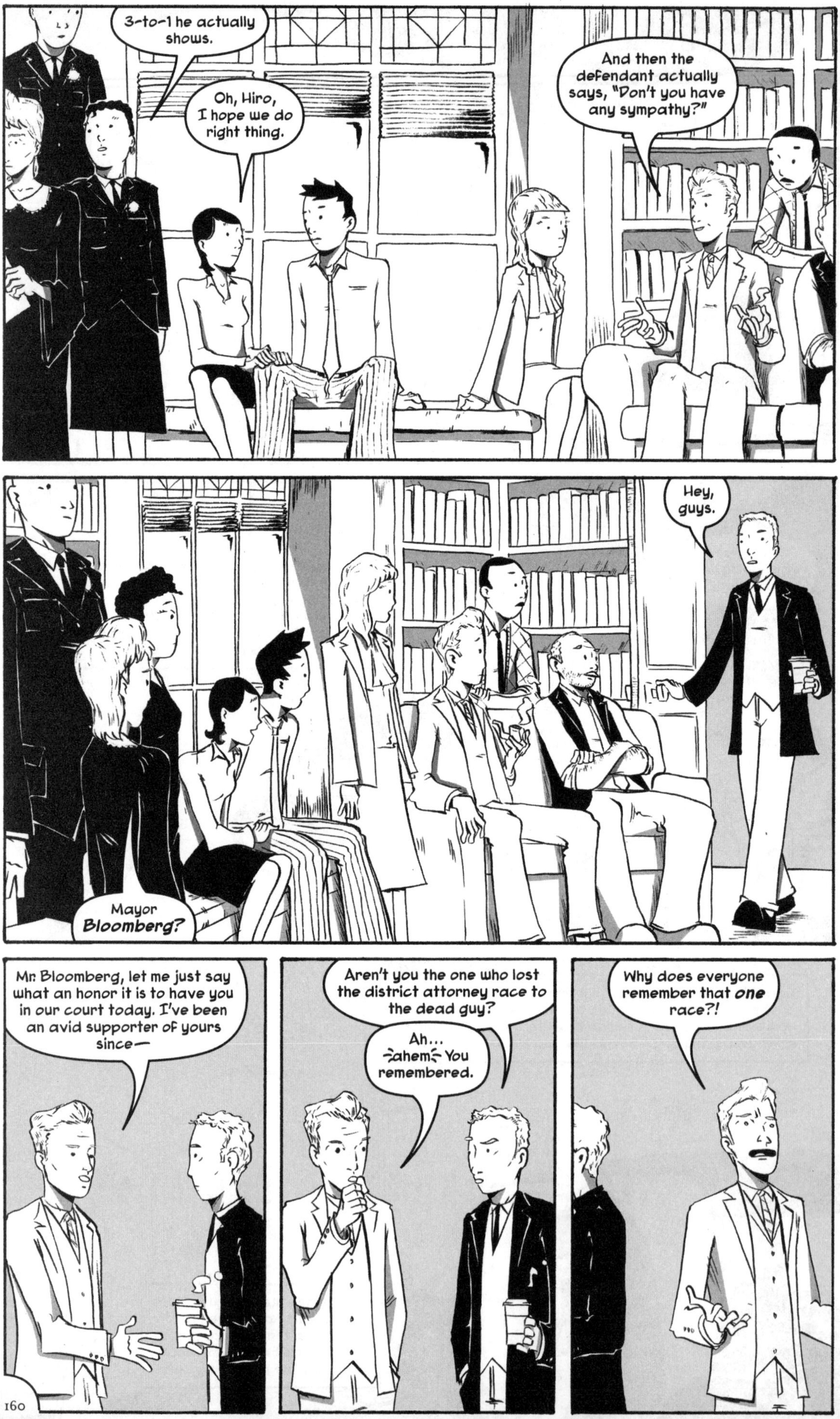
3-to-1 he actually shows.
Oh, Hiro, I hope we do right thing.
And then the defendant actually says, "Don't you have any sympathy?"
Hey, guys.
Mayor **Bloomberg?**
Mr. Bloomberg, let me just say what an honor it is to have you in our court today. I've been an avid supporter of yours since—
Aren't you the one who lost the district attorney race to the dead guy?
Ah... *ahem* You remembered.
Why does everyone remember that *one* race?!

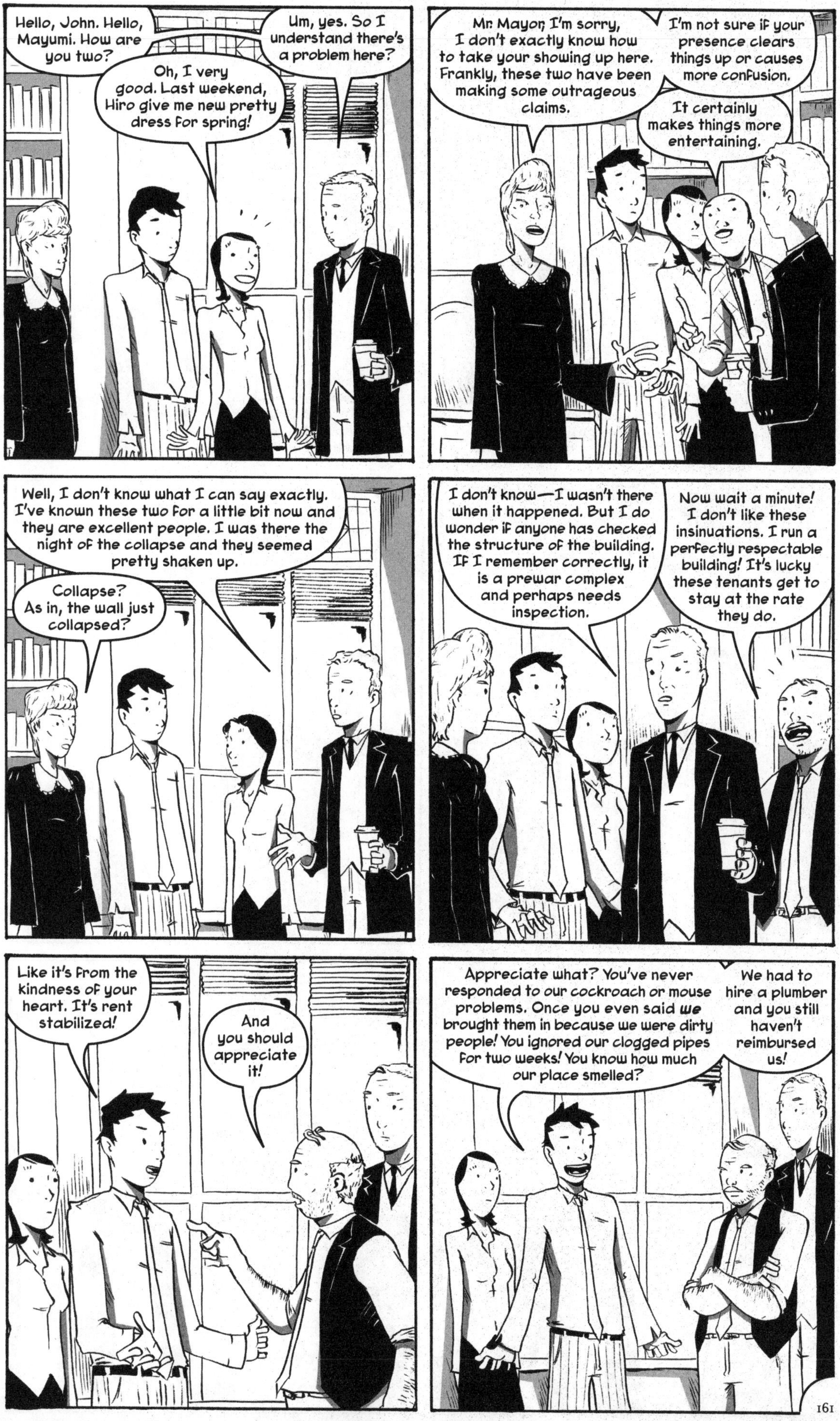
Hello, John. Hello, Mayumi. How are you two?
Oh, I very good. Last weekend, Hiro give me new pretty dress for spring!
Um, yes. So I understand there's a problem here?
Mr. Mayor, I'm sorry, I don't exactly know how to take your showing up here. Frankly, these two have been making some outrageous claims.
I'm not sure if your presence clears things up or causes more confusion.
It certainly makes things more entertaining.
Well, I don't know what I can say exactly. I've known these two for a little bit now and they are excellent people. I was there the night of the collapse and they seemed pretty shaken up.
Collapse? As in, the wall just collapsed?
I don't know—I wasn't there when it happened. But I do wonder if anyone has checked the structure of the building. If I remember correctly, it is a prewar complex and perhaps needs inspection.
Now wait a minute! I don't like these insinuations. I run a perfectly respectable building! It's lucky these tenants get to stay at the rate they do.
Like it's from the kindness of your heart. It's rent stabilized!
And you should appreciate it!
Appreciate what? You've never responded to our cockroach or mouse problems. Once you even said *we* brought them in because we were dirty people! You ignored our clogged pipes for two weeks! You know how much our place smelled?
We had to hire a plumber and you still haven't reimbursed us!

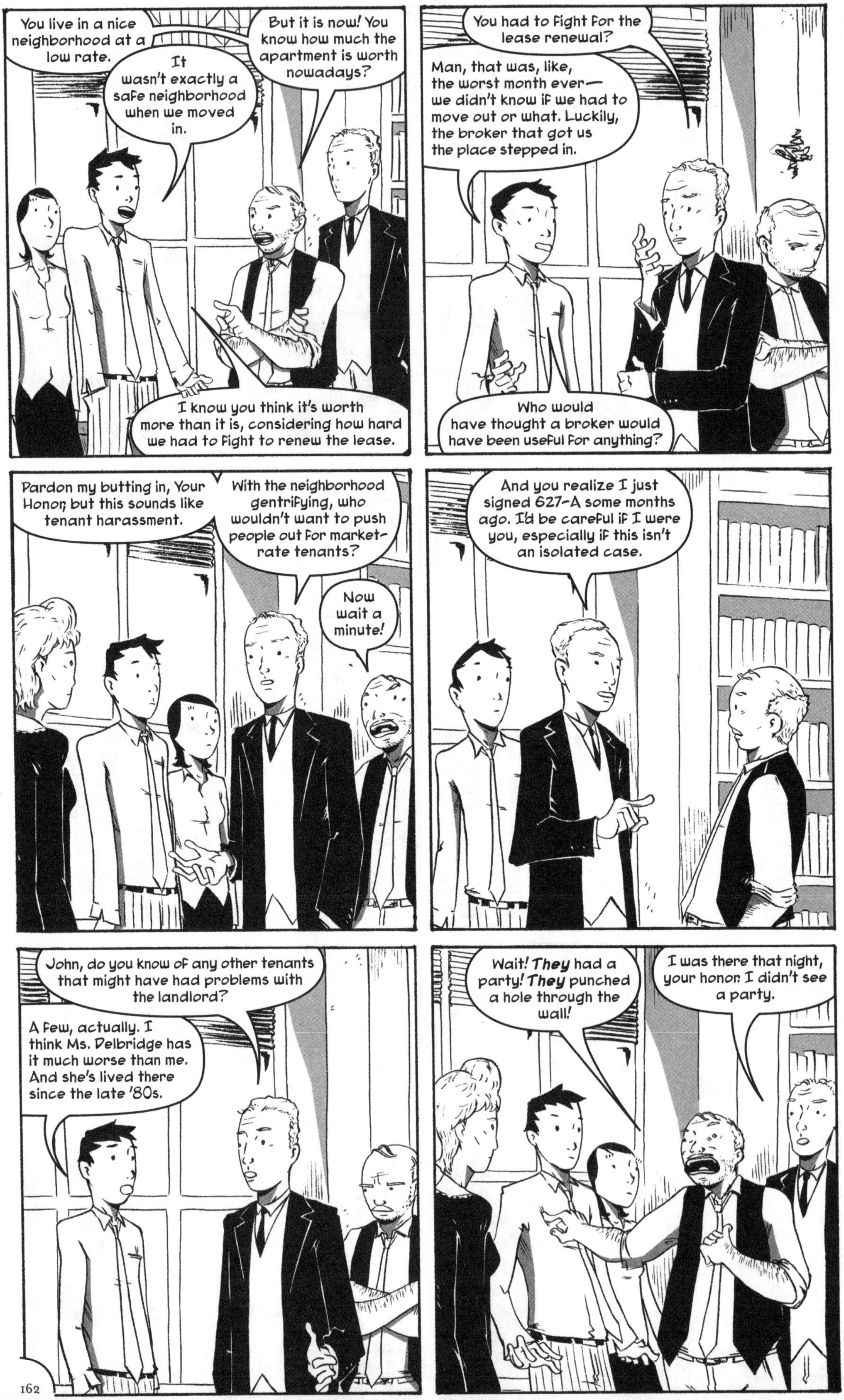
You live in a nice neighborhood at a low rate.
It wasn't exactly a safe neighborhood when we moved in.
But it is now! You know how much the apartment is worth nowadays?
I know you think it's worth more than it is, considering how hard we had to fight to renew the lease.
You had to fight for the lease renewal?
Man, that was, like, the worst month ever— we didn't know if we had to move out or what. Luckily, the broker that got us the place stepped in.
Who would have thought a broker would have been useful for anything?
Pardon my butting in, Your Honor, but this sounds like tenant harassment.
With the neighborhood gentrifying, who wouldn't want to push people out for market-rate tenants?
Now wait a minute!
And you realize I just signed 627-A some months ago. I'd be careful if I were you, especially if this isn't an isolated case.
John, do you know of any other tenants that might have had problems with the landlord?
A few, actually. I think Ms. Delbridge has it much worse than me. And she's lived there since the late '80s.
Wait! *They* had a party! *They* punched a hole through the wall!
I was there that night, your honor. I didn't see a party.

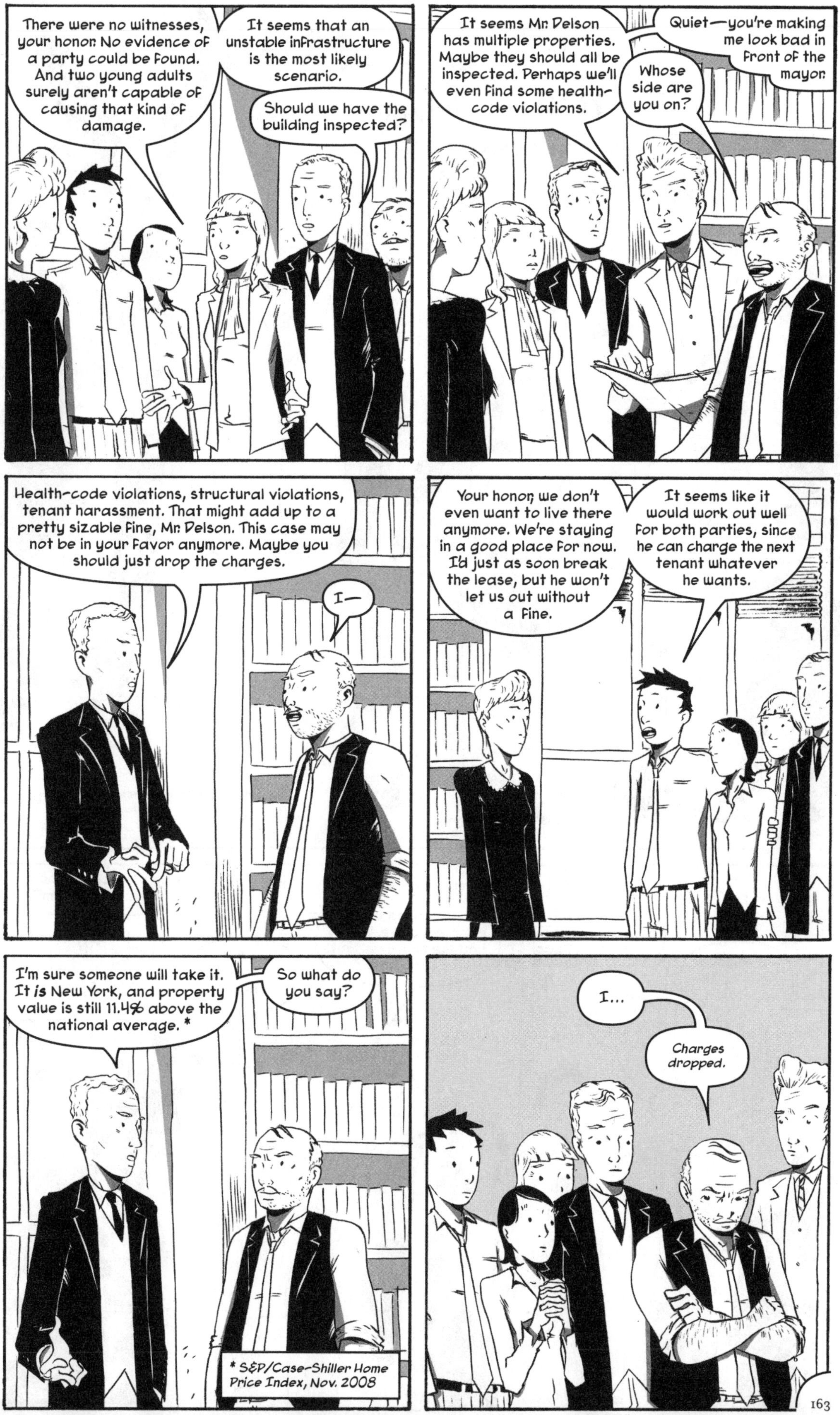
There were no witnesses, your honor. No evidence of a party could be found. And two young adults surely aren't capable of causing that kind of damage.
It seems that an unstable infrastructure is the most likely scenario.
Should we have the building inspected?
It seems Mr. Delson has multiple properties. Maybe they should all be inspected. Perhaps we'll even find some health-code violations.
Quiet—you're making me look bad in front of the mayor.
Whose side are you on?
Health-code violations, structural violations, tenant harassment. That might add up to a pretty sizable fine, Mr. Delson. This case may not be in your favor anymore. Maybe you should just drop the charges.
I—
Your honor, we don't even want to live there anymore. We're staying in a good place for now. I'd just as soon break the lease, but he won't let us out without a fine.
It seems like it would work out well for both parties, since he can charge the next tenant whatever he wants.
I'm sure someone will take it. It *is* New York, and property value is still 11.4% above the national average. *
So what do you say?
* S&P/Case-Shiller Home Price Index, Nov. 2008
I...
Charges dropped.

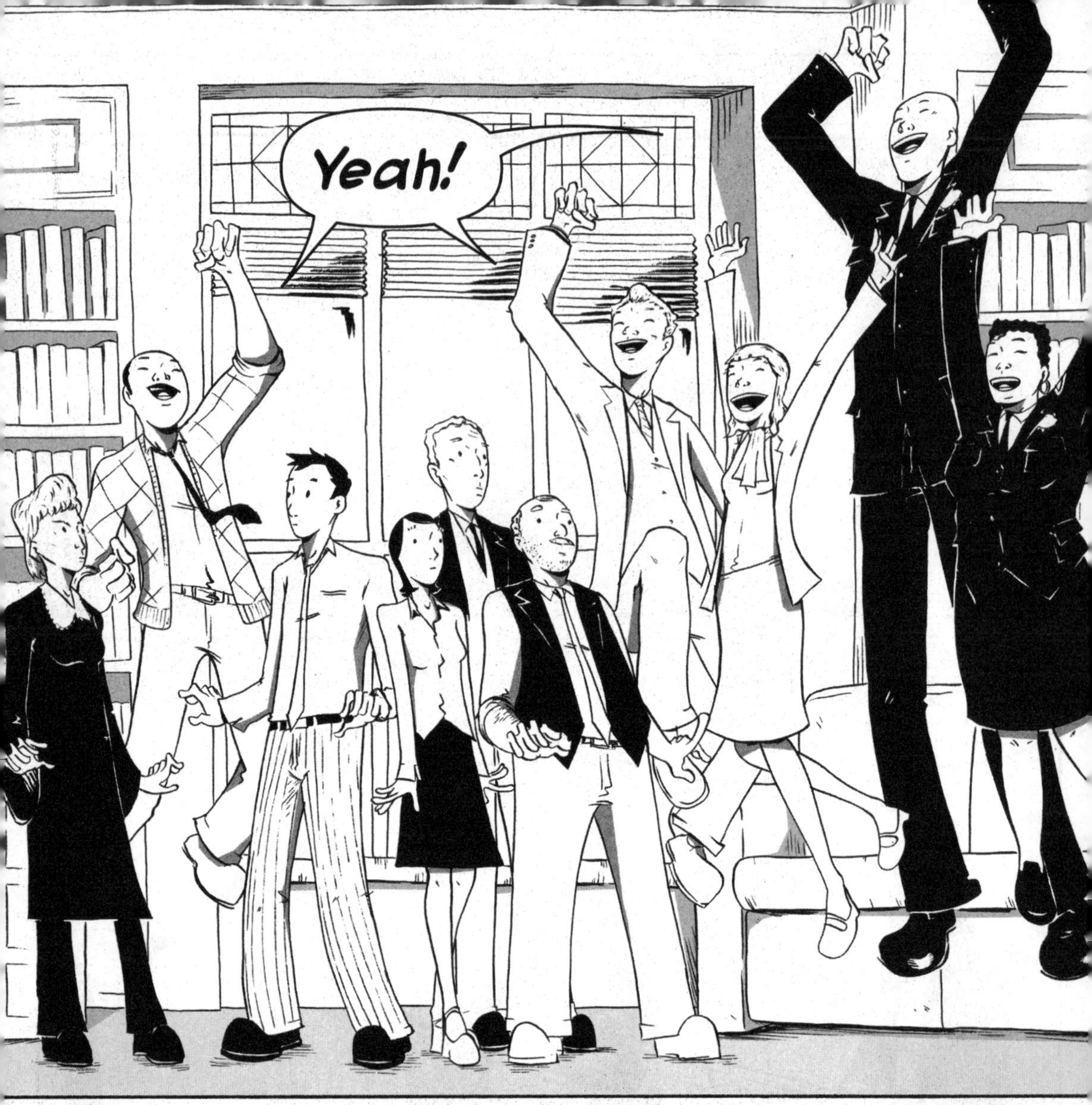
Yeah!

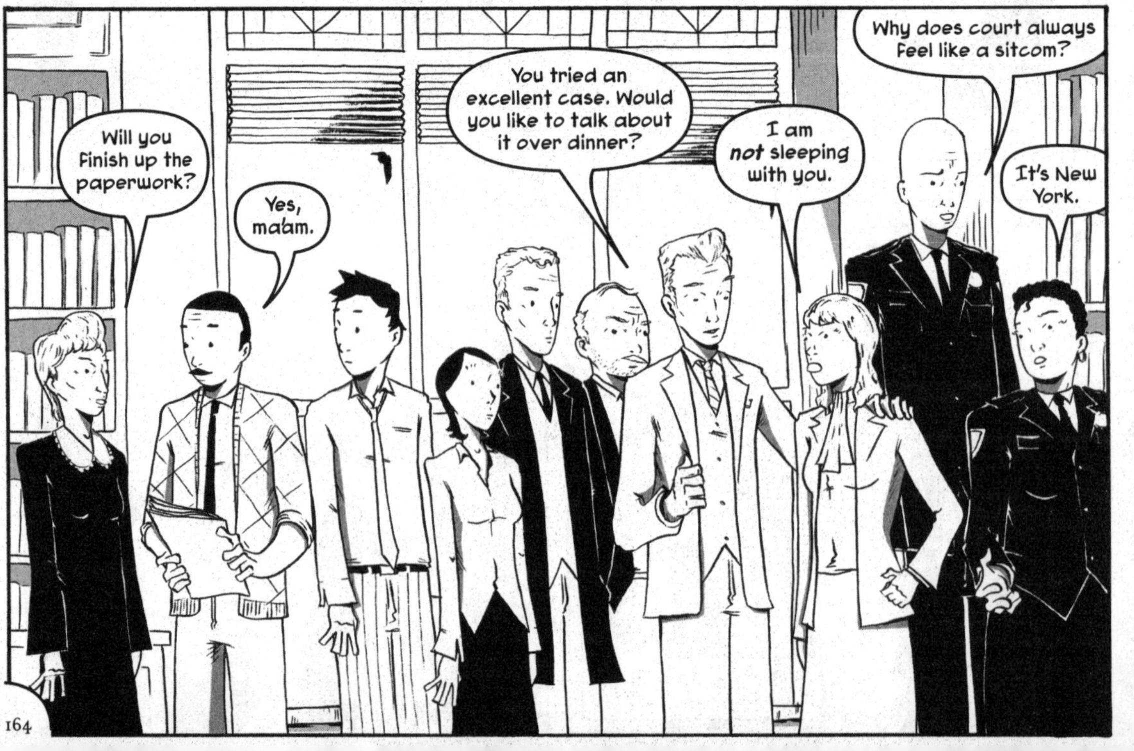
Will you finish up the paperwork?
Yes, ma'am.
You tried an excellent case. Would you like to talk about it over dinner?
I am *not* sleeping with you.
Why does court always feel like a sitcom?
It's New York.

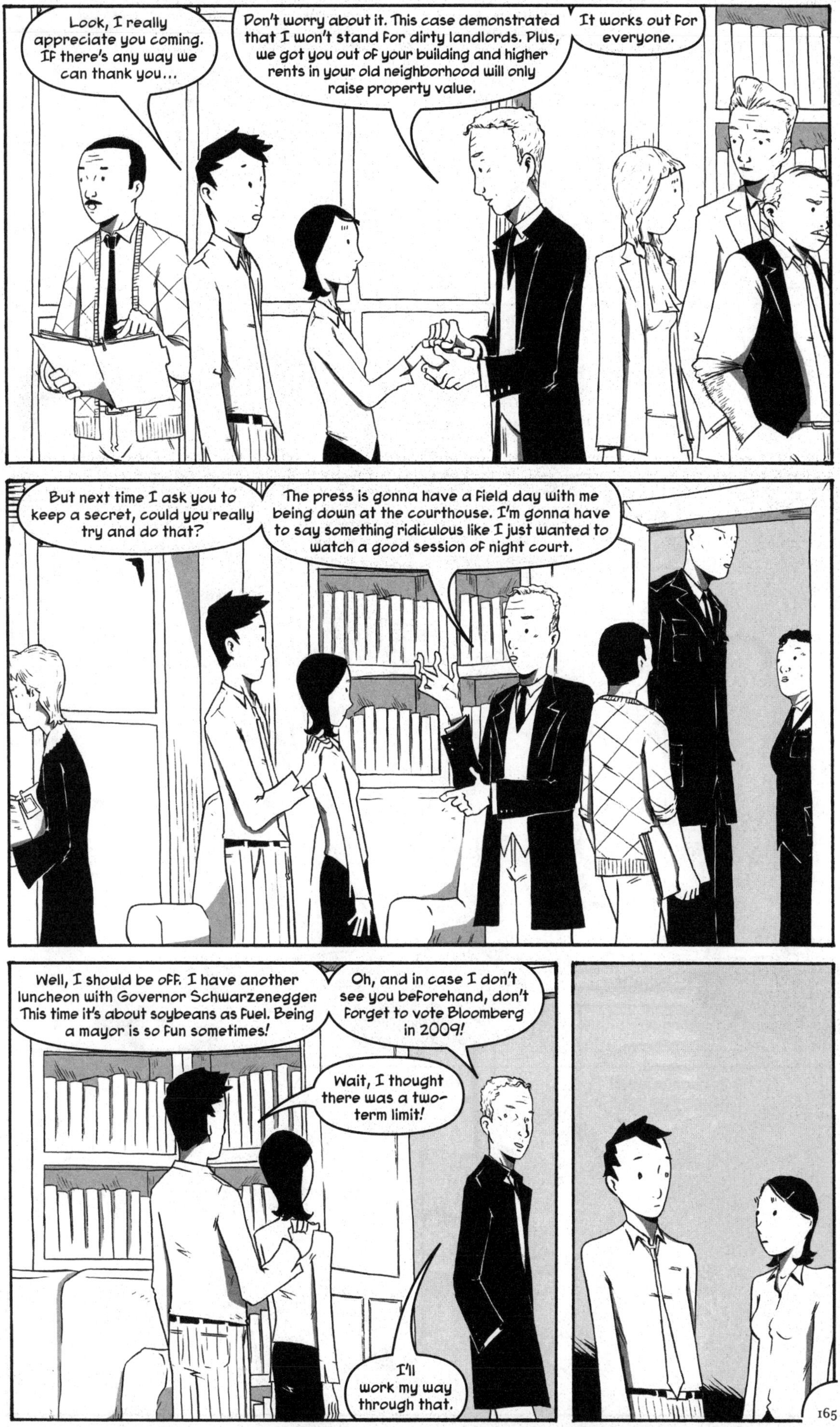

Look, I really appreciate you coming. If there's any way we can thank you...
Don't worry about it. This case demonstrated that I won't stand for dirty landlords. Plus, we got you out of your building and higher rents in your old neighborhood will only raise property value.
It works out for everyone.
But next time I ask you to keep a secret, could you really try and do that?
The press is gonna have a field day with me being down at the courthouse. I'm gonna have to say something ridiculous like I just wanted to watch a good session of night court.
Well, I should be off. I have another luncheon with Governor Schwarzenegger. This time it's about soybeans as fuel. Being a mayor is so fun sometimes!
Oh, and in case I don't see you beforehand, don't forget to vote Bloomberg in 2009!
Wait, I thought there was a two-term limit!
I'll work my way through that.

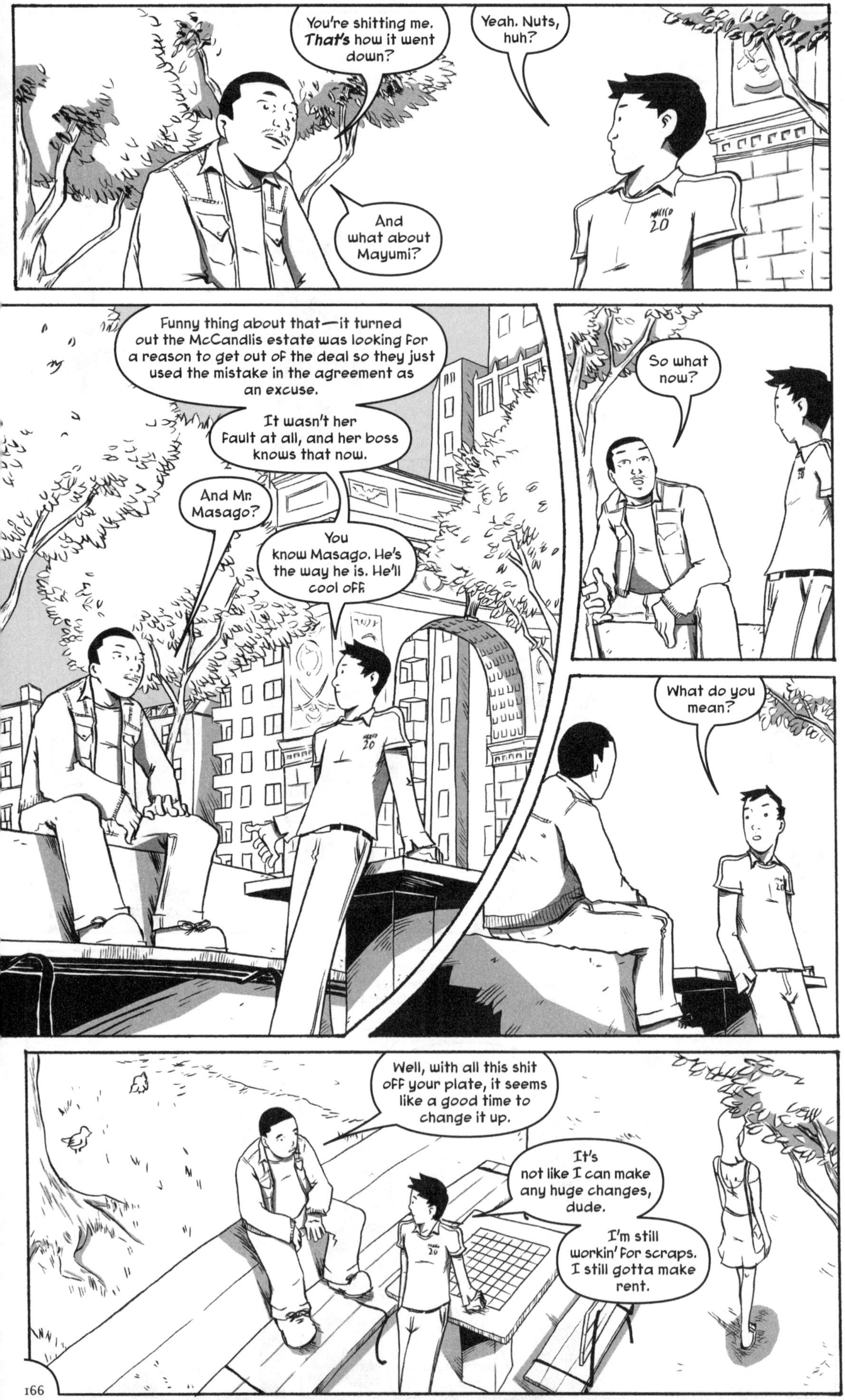
You're shitting me. *That's* how it went down?
Yeah. Nuts, huh?
And what about Mayumi?
Funny thing about that—it turned out the McCandlis estate was looking for a reason to get out of the deal so they just used the mistake in the agreement as an excuse.
It wasn't her fault at all, and her boss knows that now.
And Mr. Masago?
You know Masago. He's the way he is. He'll cool off.
So what now?
What do you mean?
Well, with all this shit off your plate, it seems like a good time to change it up.
It's not like I can make any huge changes, dude.
I'm still workin' for scraps. I still gotta make rent.

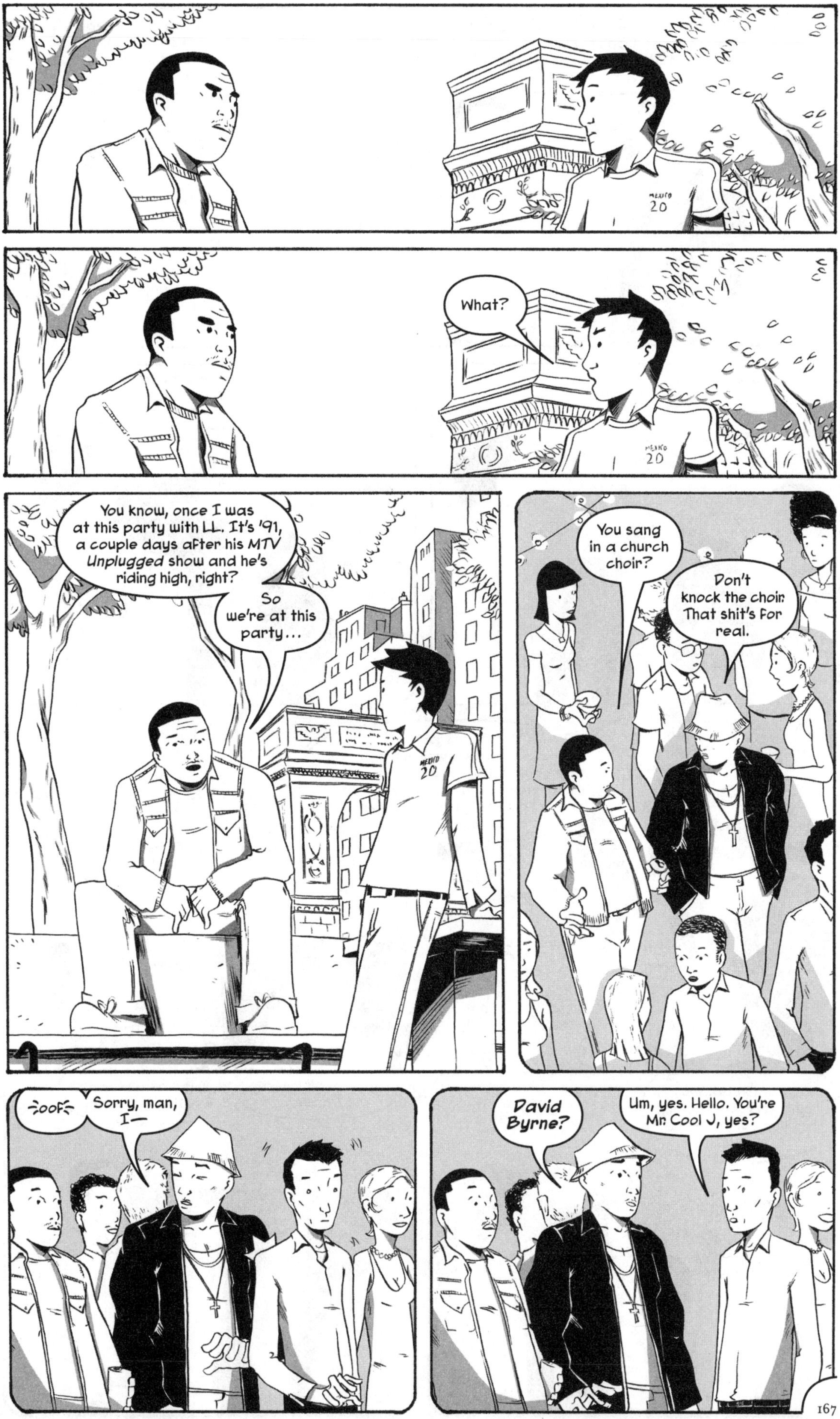
What?
You know, once I was at this party with LL. It's '91, a couple days after his MTV *Unplugged* show and he's riding high, right?
So we're at this party...
MEXICO 20
You sang in a church choir?
Don't knock the choir. That shit's for real.
OOF
Sorry, man, I—
David Byrne?
Um, yes. Hello. You're Mr. Cool J, yes?

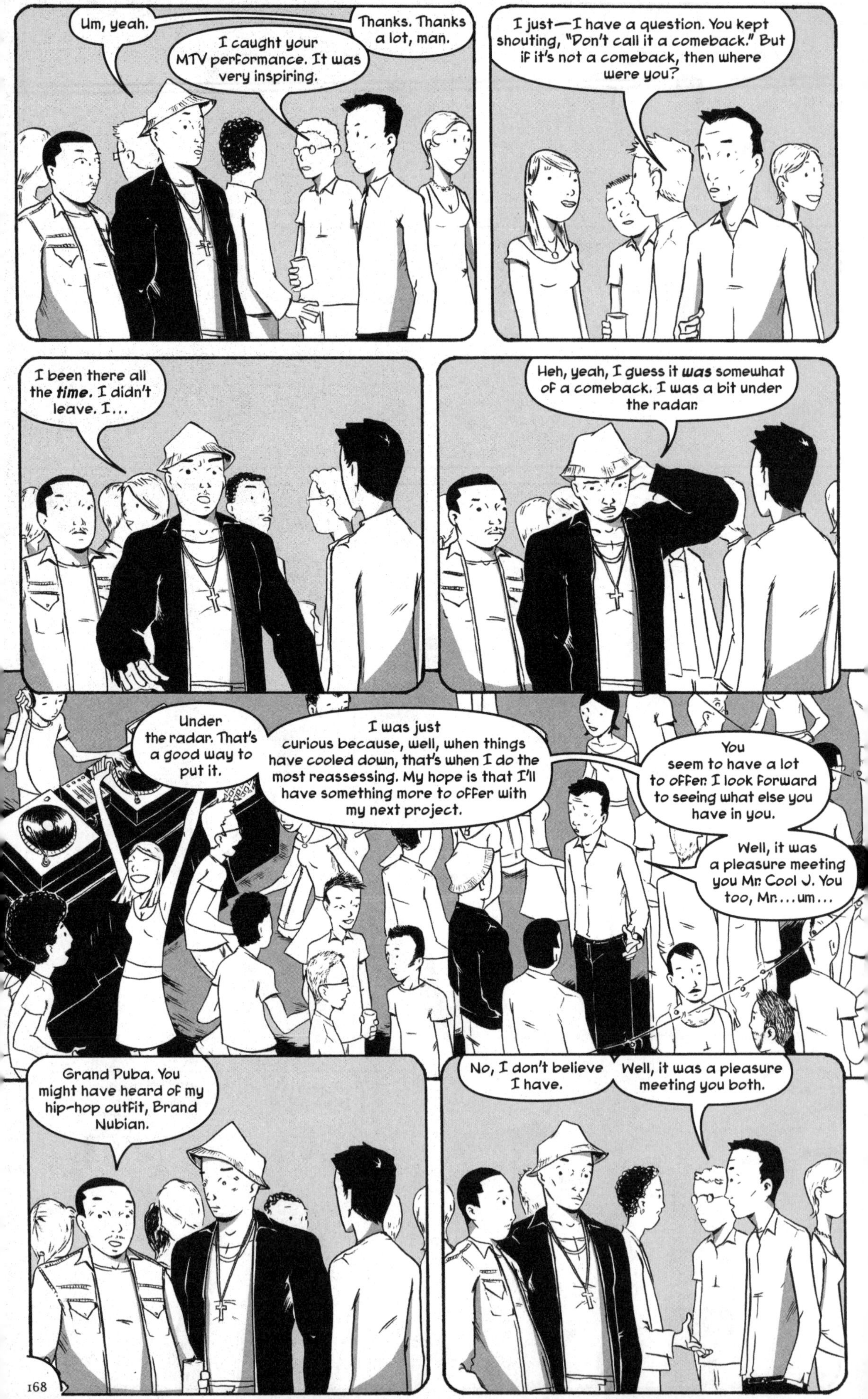
Um, yeah.
Thanks. Thanks a lot, man.
I caught your MTV performance. It was very inspiring.
I just—I have a question. You kept shouting, "Don't call it a comeback." But if it's not a comeback, then where were you?
I been there all the *time.* I didn't leave. I...
Heh, yeah, I guess it *was* somewhat of a comeback. I was a bit under the radar.
Under the radar. That's a good way to put it.
I was just curious because, well, when things have cooled down, that's when I do the most reassessing. My hope is that I'll have something more to offer with my next project.
You seem to have a lot to offer. I look forward to seeing what else you have in you.
Well, it was a pleasure meeting you Mr. Cool J. You too, Mr....um...
Grand Puba. You might have heard of my hip-hop outfit, Brand Nubian.
No, I don't believe I have.
Well, it was a pleasure meeting you both.

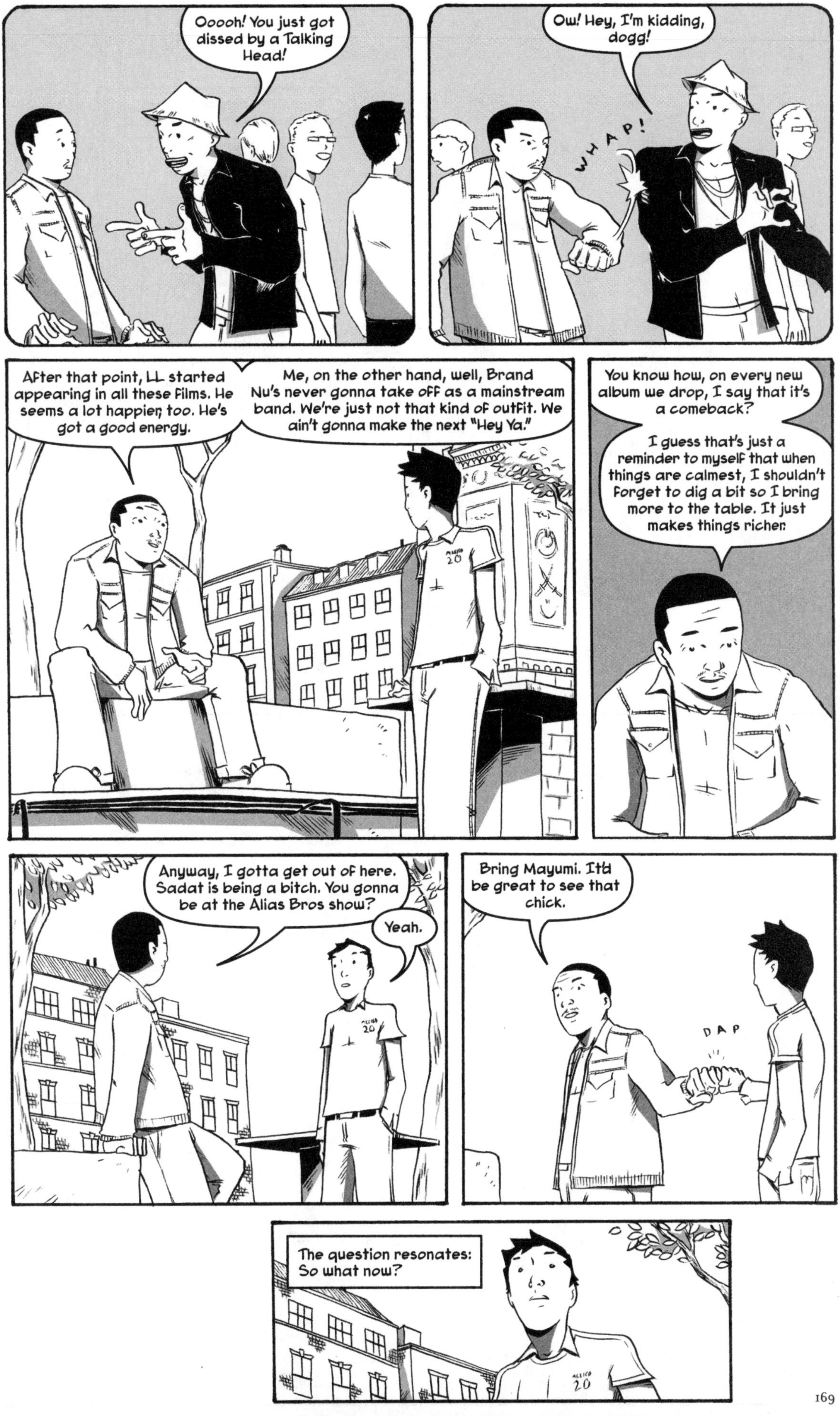
Ooooh! You just got dissed by a Talking Head!
Ow! Hey, I'm kidding, dogg!
WHAP!
After that point, LL started appearing in all these films. He seems a lot happier, too. He's got a good energy.
Me, on the other hand, well, Brand Nu's never gonna take off as a mainstream band. We're just not that kind of outfit. We ain't gonna make the next "Hey Ya."
You know how, on every new album we drop, I say that it's a comeback?
I guess that's just a reminder to myself that when things are calmest, I shouldn't forget to dig a bit so I bring more to the table. It just makes things richer.
Anyway, I gotta get out of here. Sadat is being a bitch. You gonna be at the Alias Bros show?
Yeah.
Bring Mayumi. It'd be great to see that chick.
DAP
The question resonates: So what now?

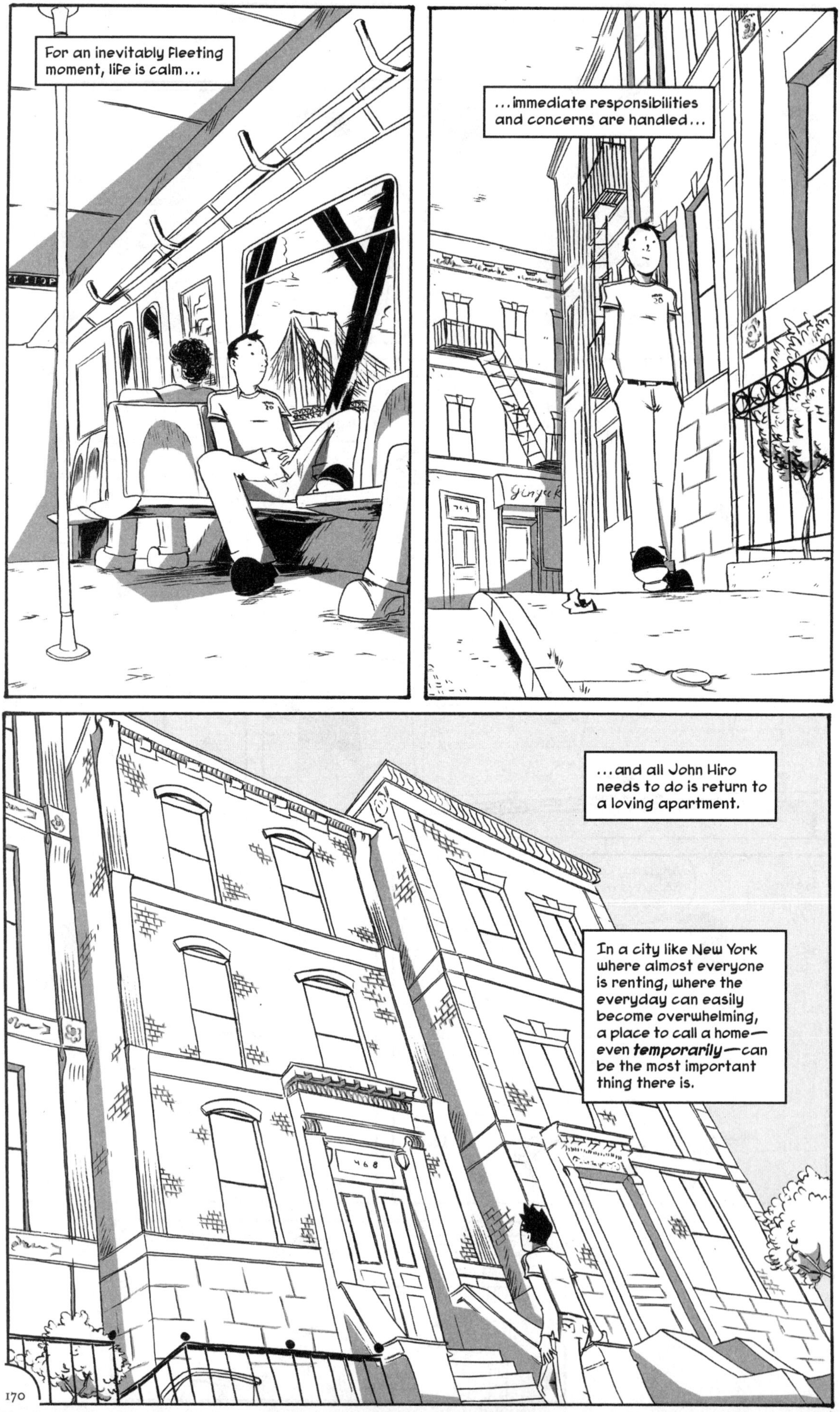
For an inevitably fleeting moment, life is calm...
...immediate responsibilities and concerns are handled...
...and all John Hiro needs to do is return to a loving apartment.
In a city like New York where almost everyone is renting, where the everyday can easily become overwhelming, a place to call a home—even *temporarily*—can be the most important thing there is.

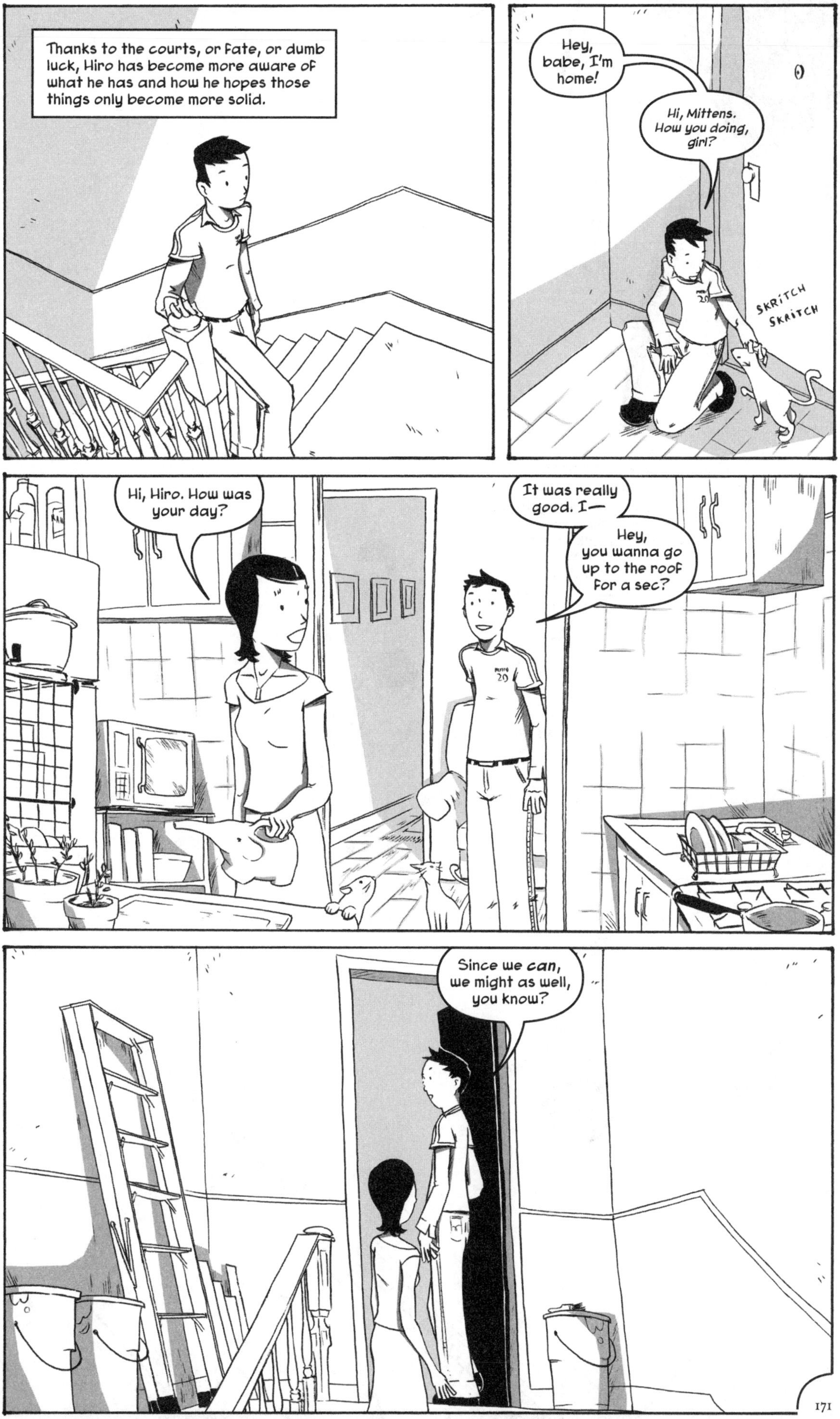

Thanks to the courts, or fate, or dumb luck, Hiro has become more aware of what he has and how he hopes those things only become more solid.
Hey, babe, I'm home!
Hi, Mittens. How you doing, girl?
SKRITCH SKRITCH
Hi, Hiro. How was your day?
It was really good. I—
Hey, you wanna go up to the roof for a sec?
Since we can, we might as well, you know?

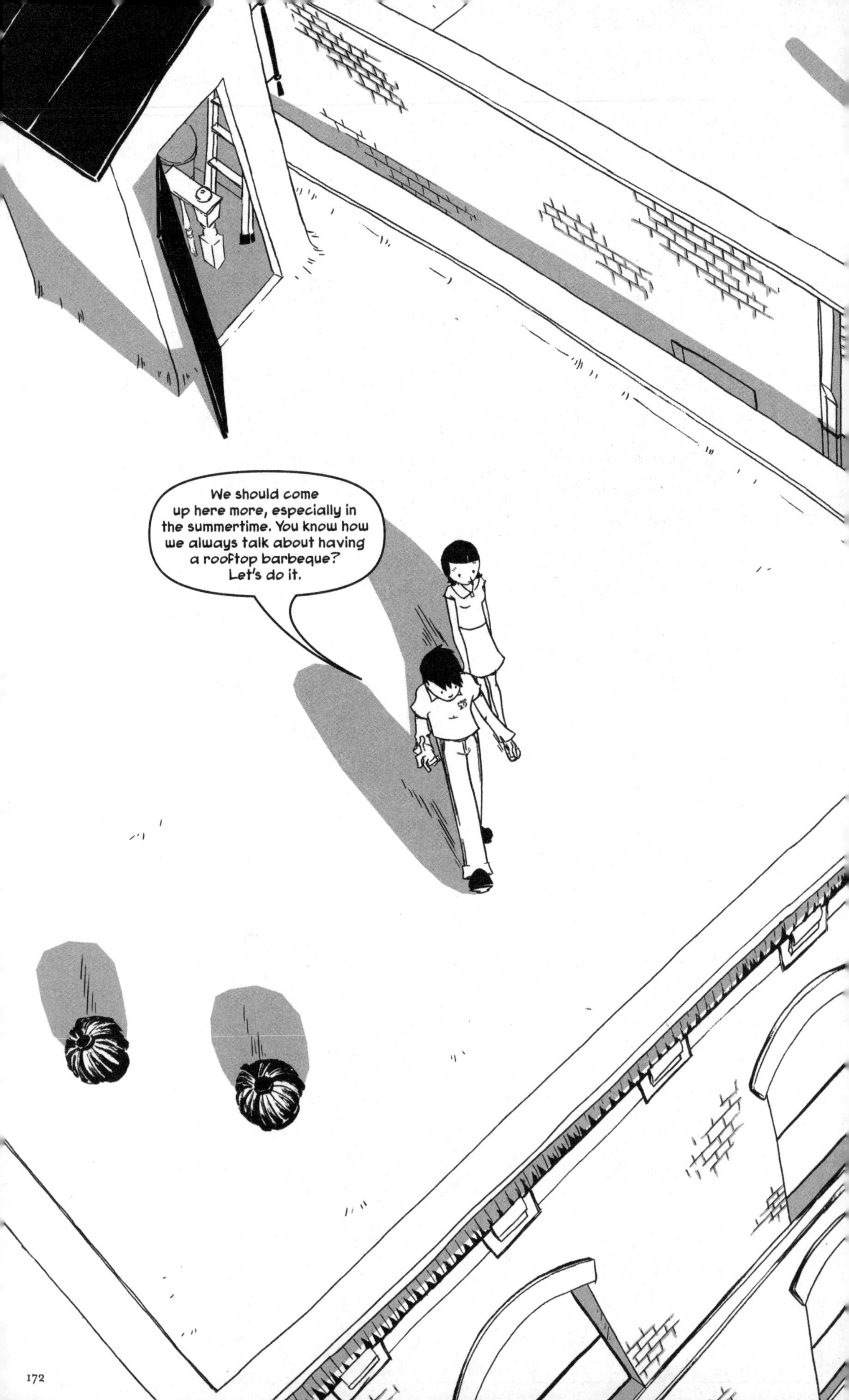
We should come up here more, especially in the summertime. You know how we always talk about having a rooftop barbeque? Let's do it.

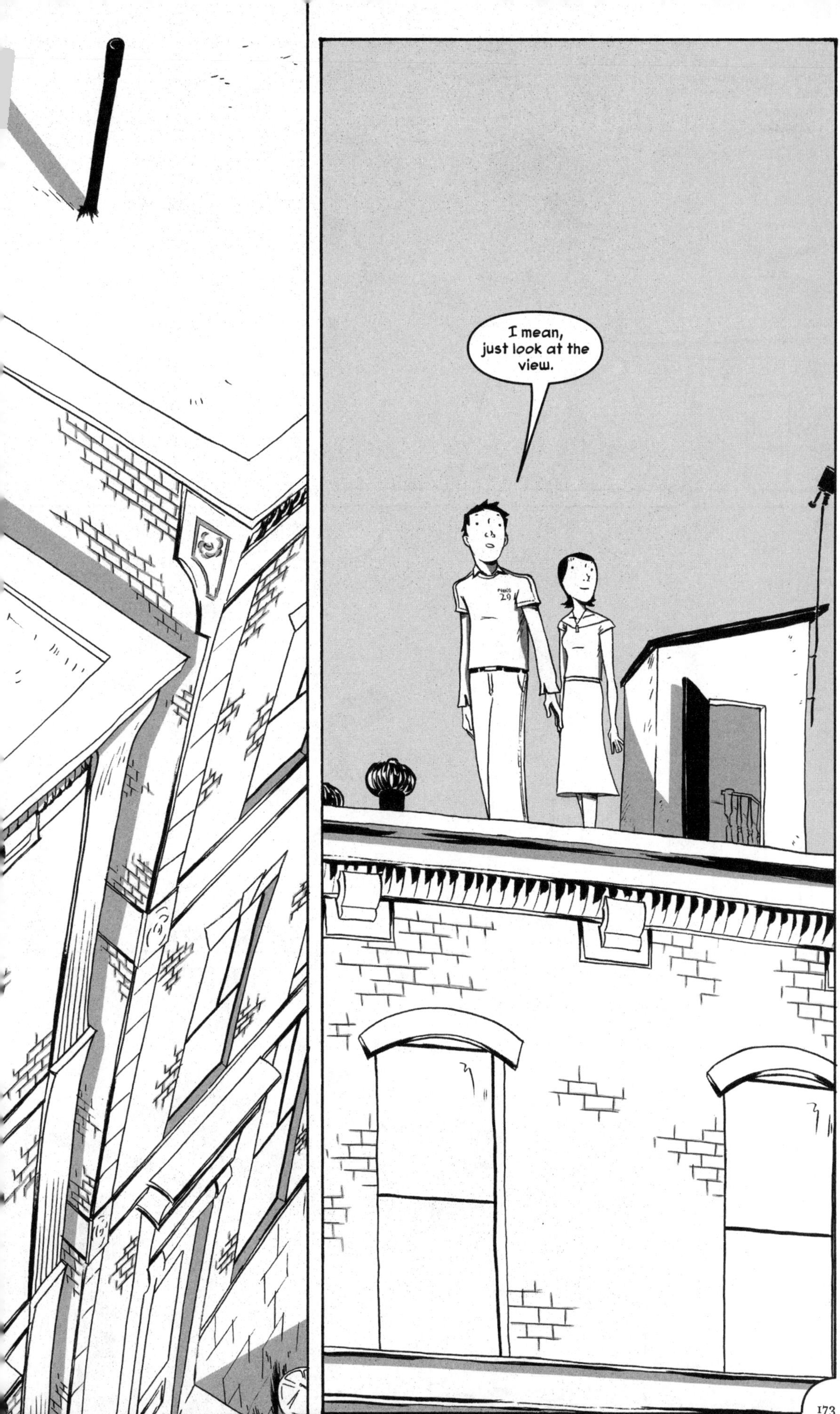
I mean, just look at the view.

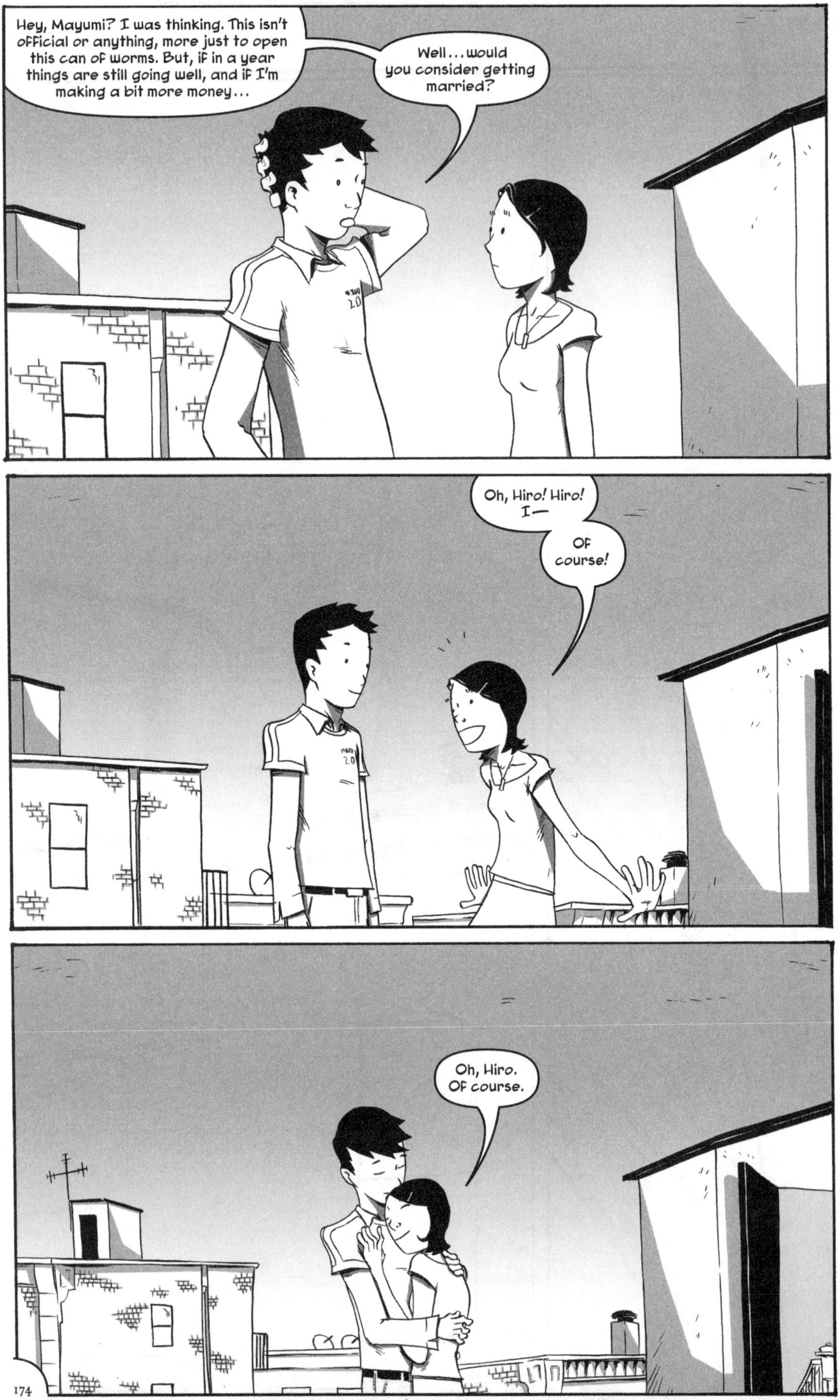
Hey, Mayumi? I was thinking. This isn't official or anything, more just to open this can of worms. But, if in a year things are still going well, and if I'm making a bit more money...
Well...would you consider getting married?
Oh, Hiro! Hiro! I—
Of course!
Oh, Hiro. Of course.

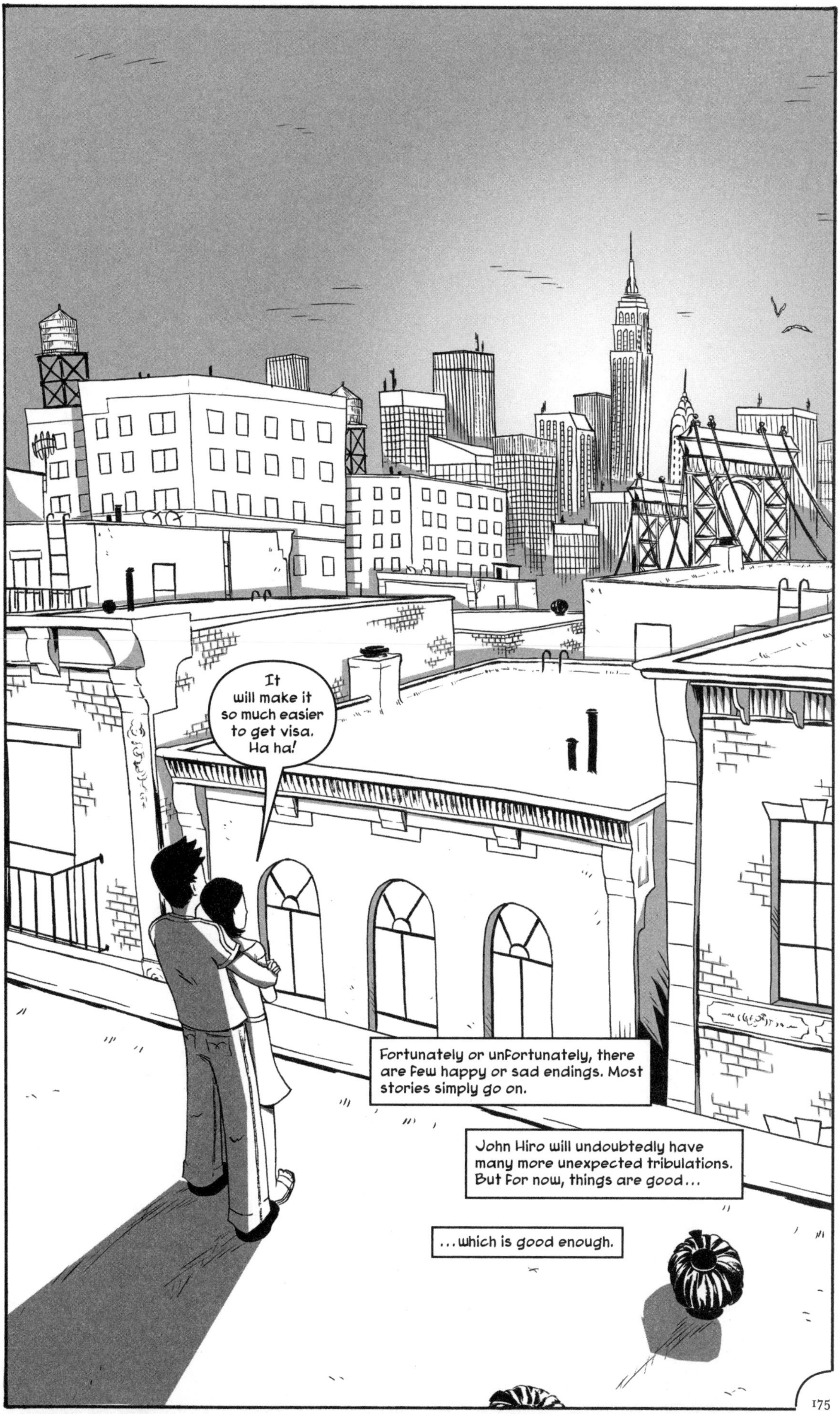
It will make it so much easier to get visa. Ha ha!
Fortunately or unfortunately, there are few happy or sad endings. Most stories simply go on.
John Hiro will undoubtedly have many more unexpected tribulations. But for now, things are good...
...which is good enough.

とくべつへん

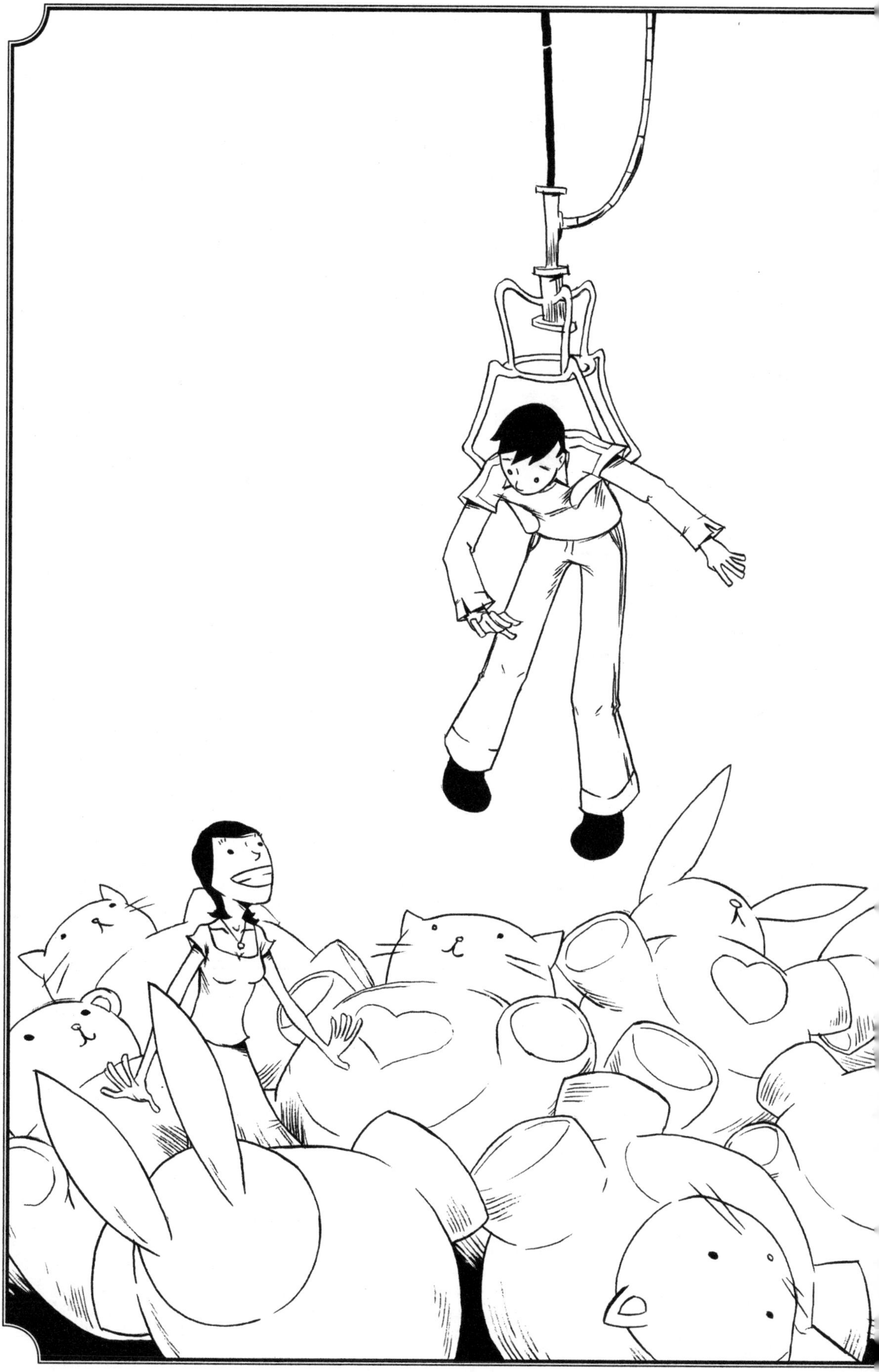

Fantastic Voyage

{ with Johnny Hiro and Coolio }

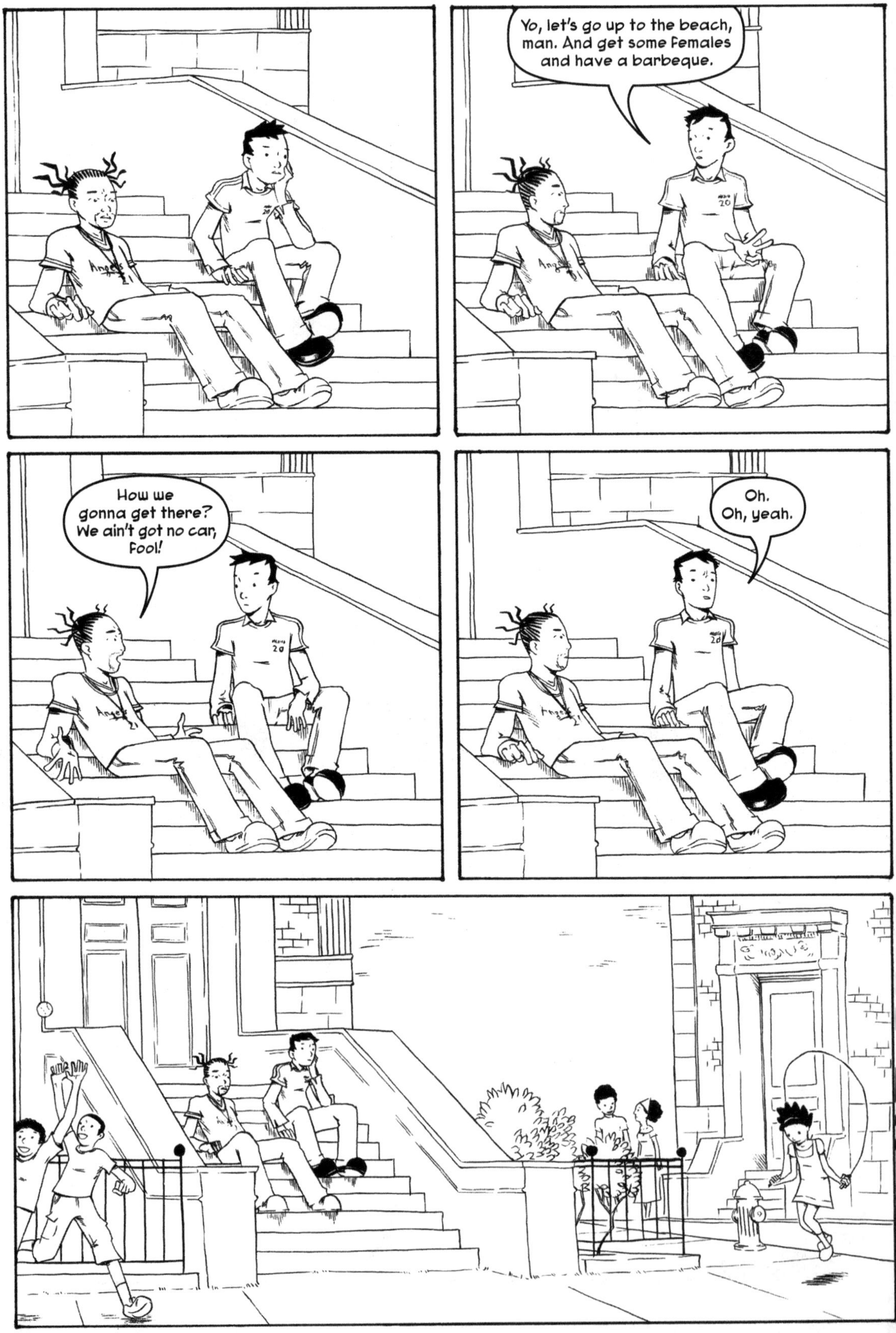
Yo, let's go up to the beach, man. And get some females and have a barbeque.
How we gonna get there? We ain't got no car, fool!
Oh. Oh, yeah.

Lets Go Shopping!

{ with Johnny Hiro and Mayumi Murakami }

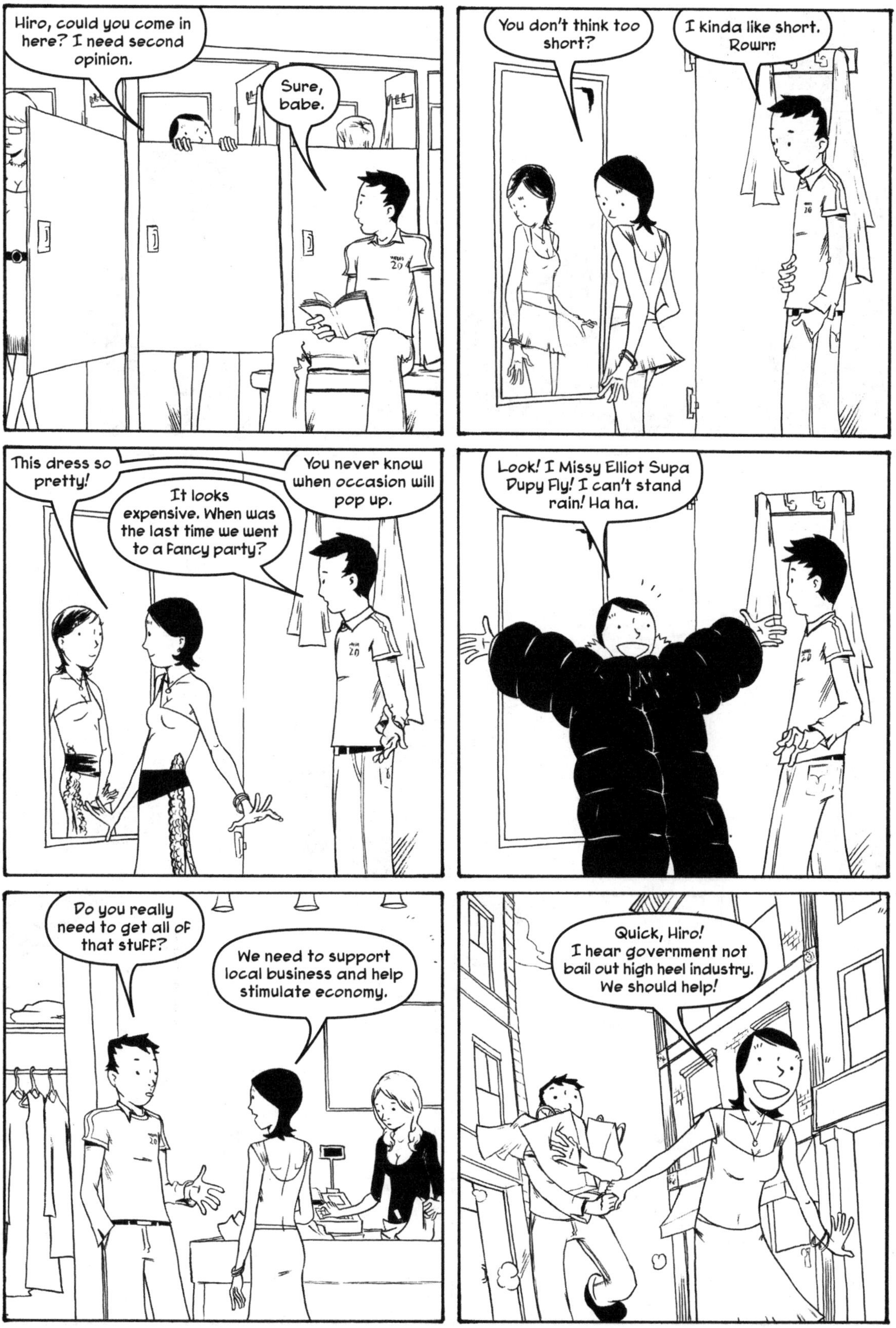
Hiro, could you come in here? I need second opinion.
Sure, babe.
You don't think too short?
I kinda like short. Rowrr.
This dress so pretty!
It looks expensive. When was the last time we went to a fancy party?
You never know when occasion will pop up.
Look! I Missy Elliot Supa Dupy Fly! I can't stand rain! Ha ha.
Do you really need to get all of that stuff?
We need to support local business and help stimulate economy.
Quick, Hiro! I hear government not bail out high heel industry. We should help!

Snacking Before Bedtime

{ with Johnny Hiro }

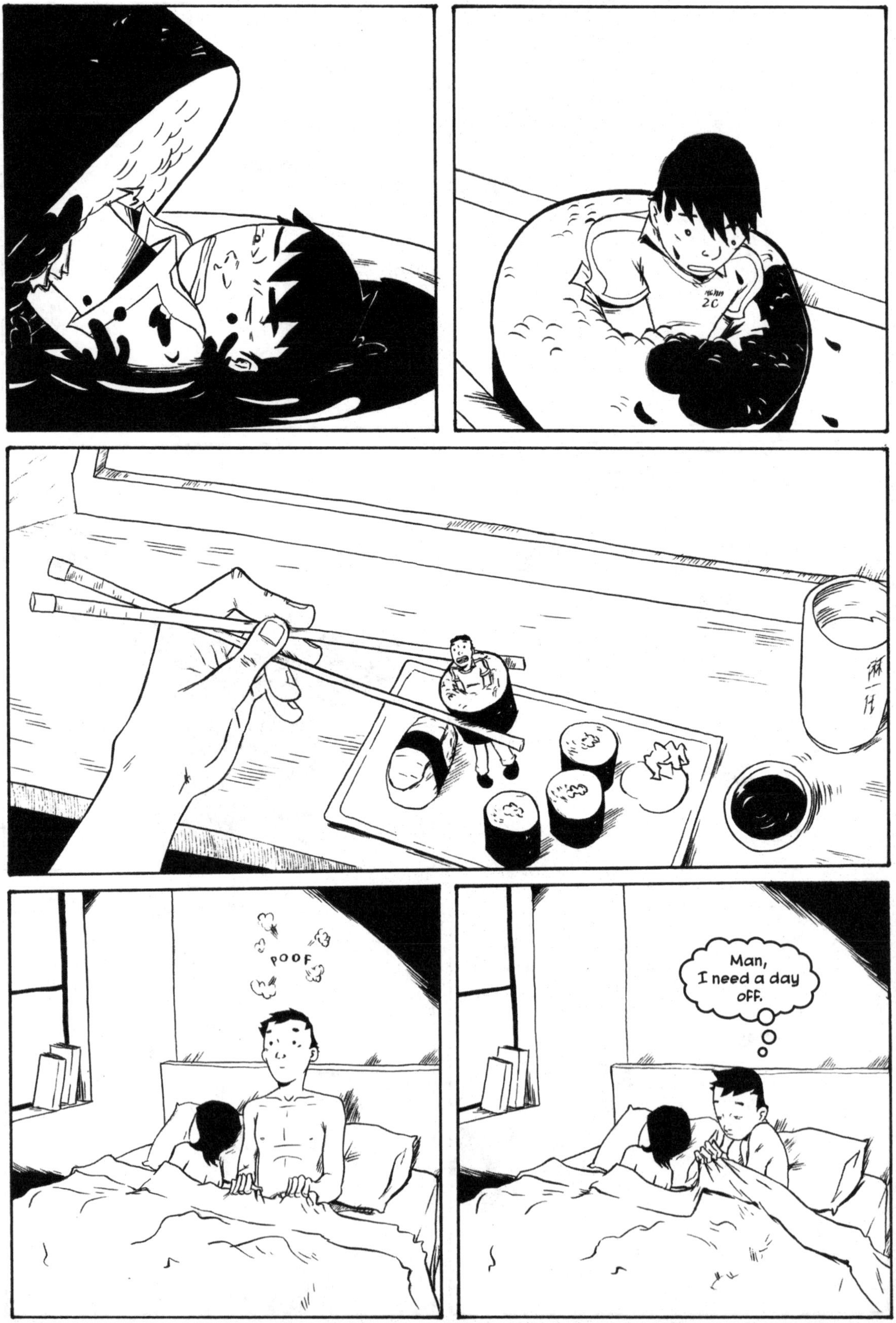
POOF
Man, I need a day off.

Jeopardy

{ with Johnny Hiro and Alex Trebek }

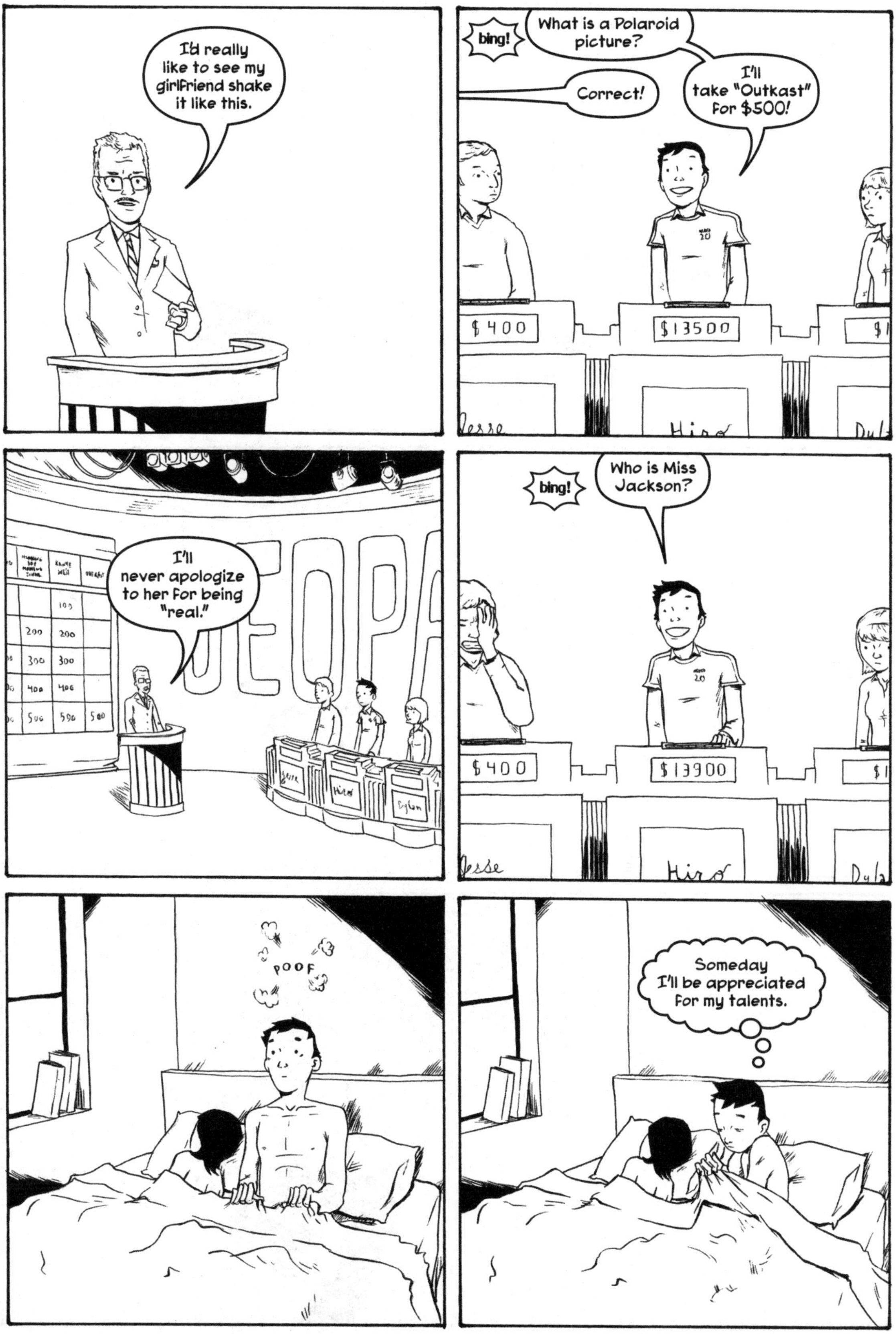
I'd really like to see my girlfriend shake it like this.
bing!
What is a Polaroid picture?
Correct!
I'll take "Outkast" for $500!
$400
$13500
I'll never apologize to her for being "real."
bing!
Who is Miss Jackson?
$400
$13900
POOF
Someday I'll be appreciated for my talents.

Tomo Saito

{ all waiter, all hero }

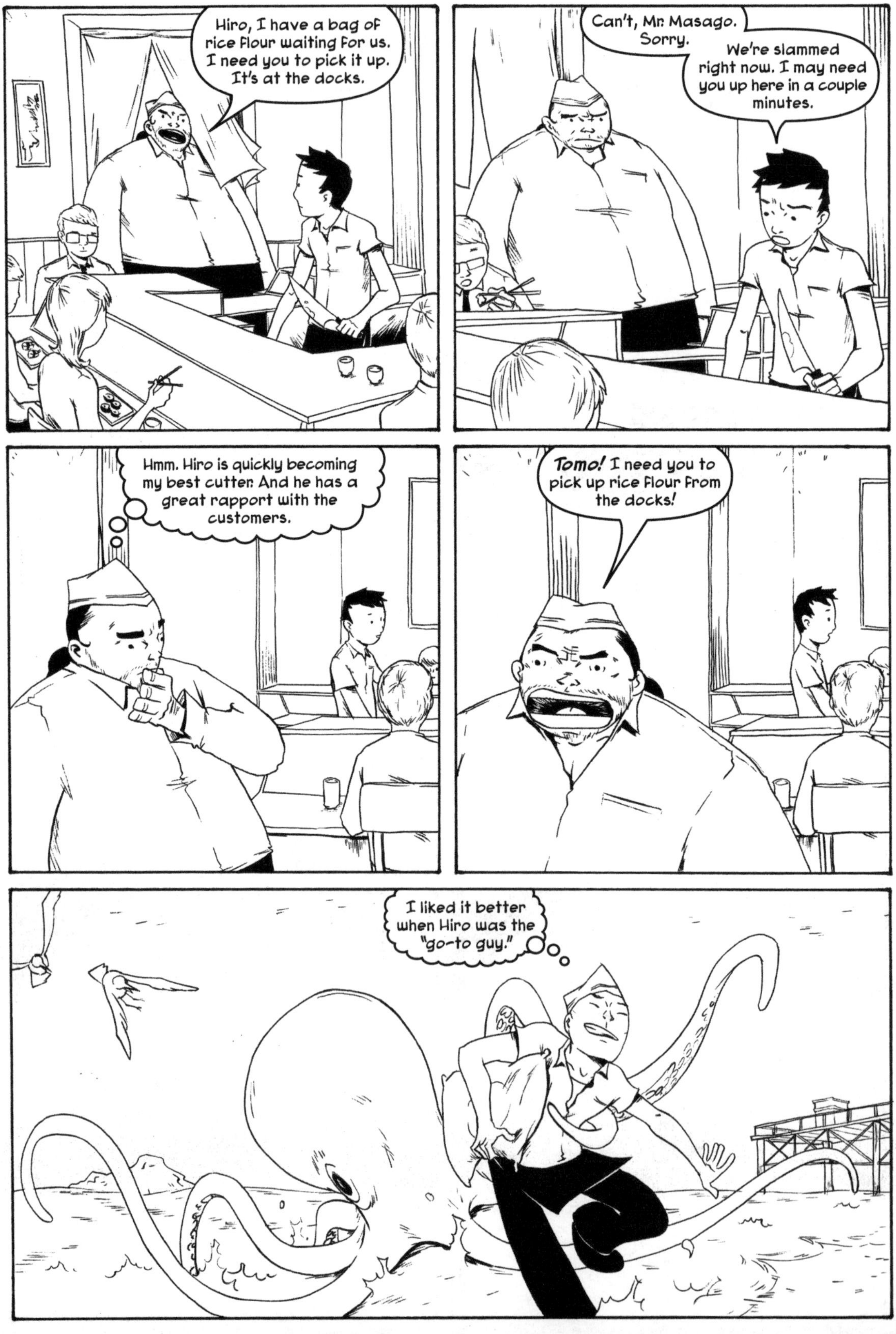
Hiro, I have a bag of rice flour waiting for us. I need you to pick it up. It's at the docks.
Can't, Mr. Masago. Sorry.
We're slammed right now. I may need you up here in a couple minutes.
Hmm. Hiro is quickly becoming my best cutter. And he has a great rapport with the customers.
Tomo! I need you to pick up rice flour from the docks!
I liked it better when Hiro was the "go-to guy."

Big Hug Time

{ with Hello Bunny and Ha-Ha Kitty }

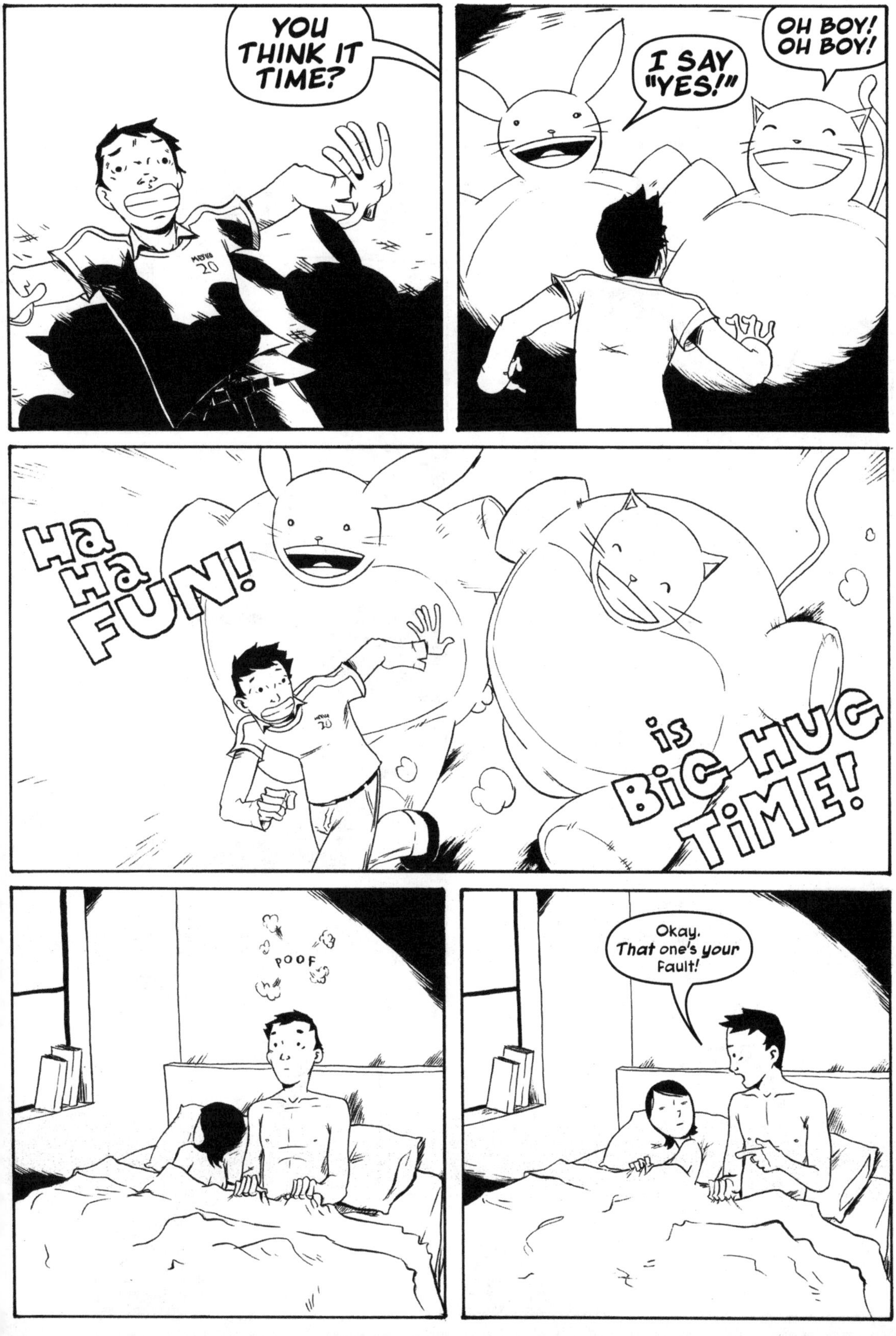
YOU THINK IT TIME?
I SAY "YES!"
OH BOY! OH BOY!
Ha Ha FUN!
is BIG HUG TIME!
POOF
Okay. That one's your Fault!

Nine to Five

{ with Johnny Hiro }

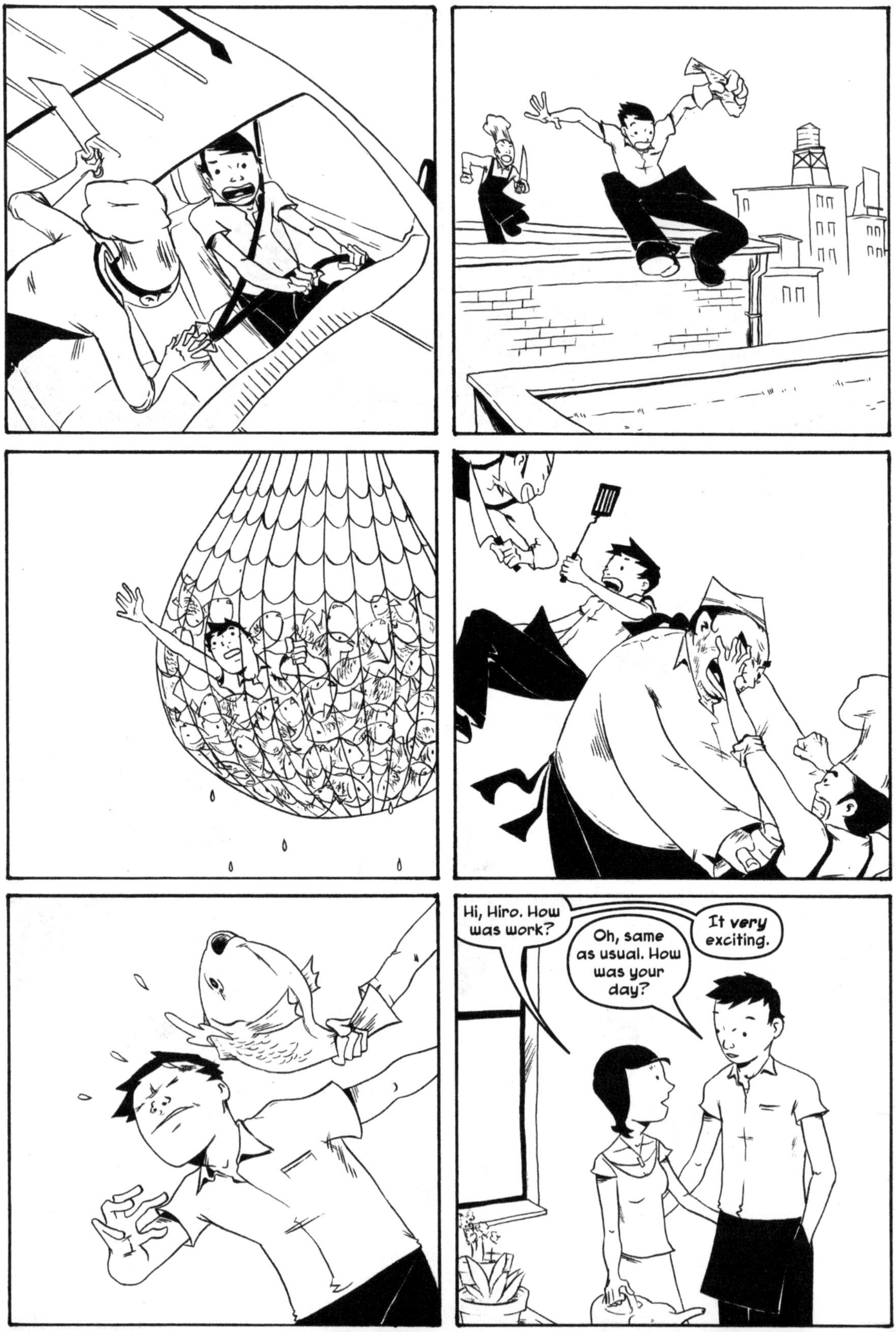
Hi, Hiro. How was work?
Oh, same as usual. How was your day?
It *very* exciting.

Bunny Slippers

{ with Johnny Hiro and Mayumi Murakami }

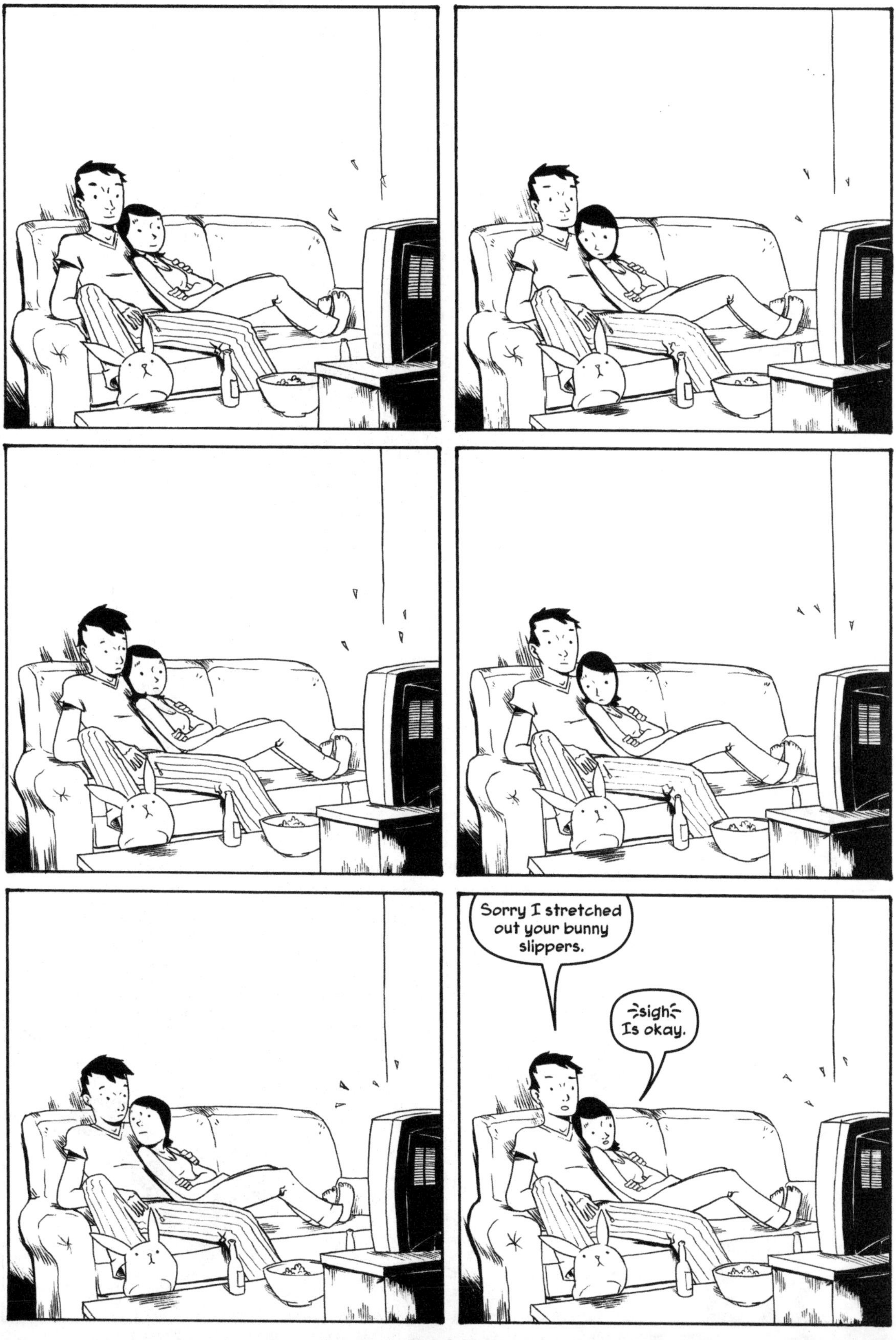
Sorry I stretched out your bunny slippers.
sigh
Is okay.

Food Fight

{ with Fred Chao and Alton Brown }

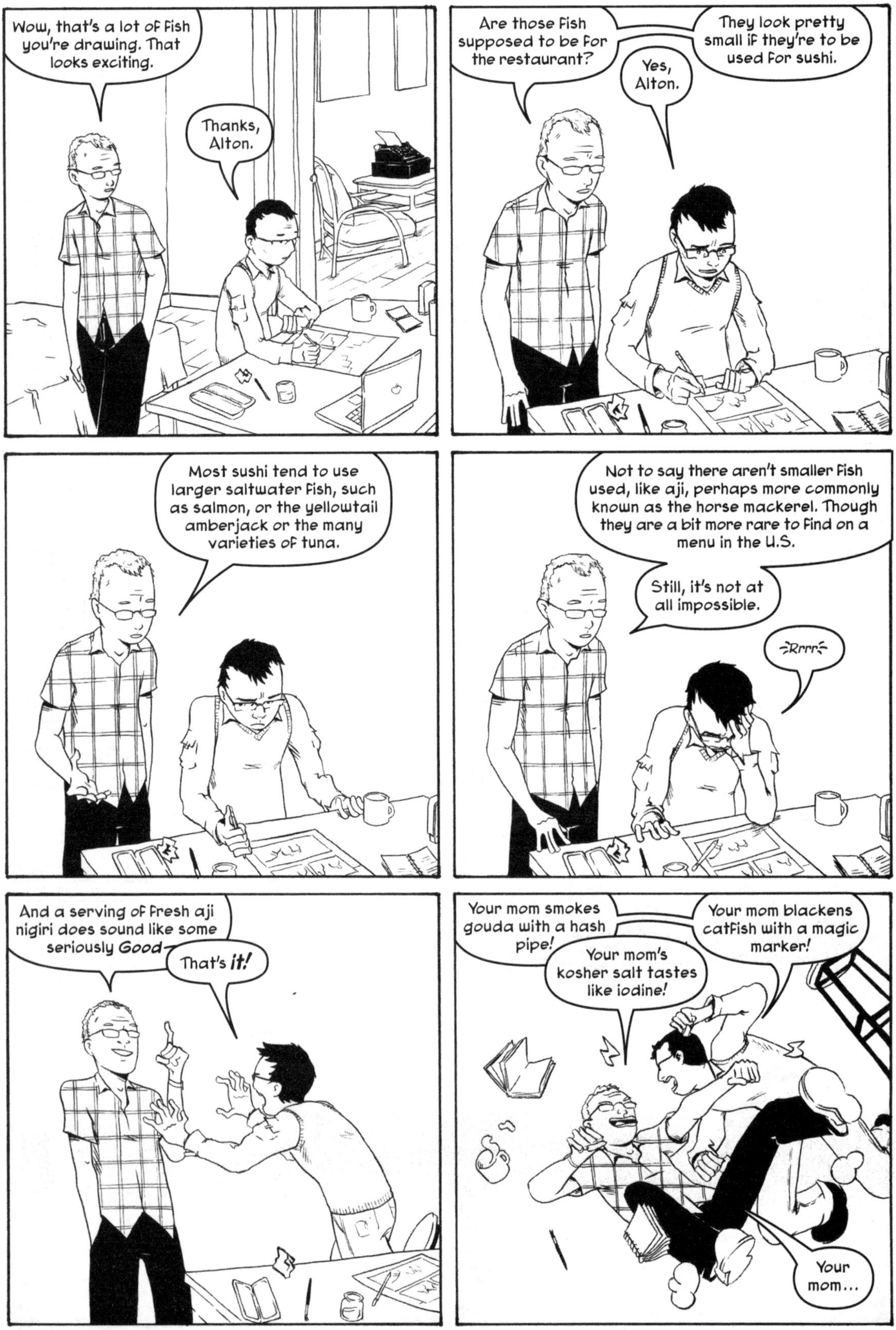

Wow, that's a lot of fish you're drawing. That looks exciting.
Thanks, Alton.
Are those fish supposed to be for the restaurant?
Yes, Alton.
They look pretty small if they're to be used for sushi.
Most sushi tend to use larger saltwater fish, such as salmon, or the yellowtail amberjack or the many varieties of tuna.
Not to say there aren't smaller fish used, like aji, perhaps more commonly known as the horse mackerel. Though they are a bit more rare to find on a menu in the U.S.
Still, it's not at all impossible.
Rrrr
And a serving of fresh aji nigiri does sound like some seriously Good—
That's it!
Your mom smokes gouda with a hash pipe!
Your mom blackens catfish with a magic marker!
Your mom's kosher salt tastes like iodine!
Your mom...

Road Trip!

{ with Johnny Hiro and Mayumi Murakami }

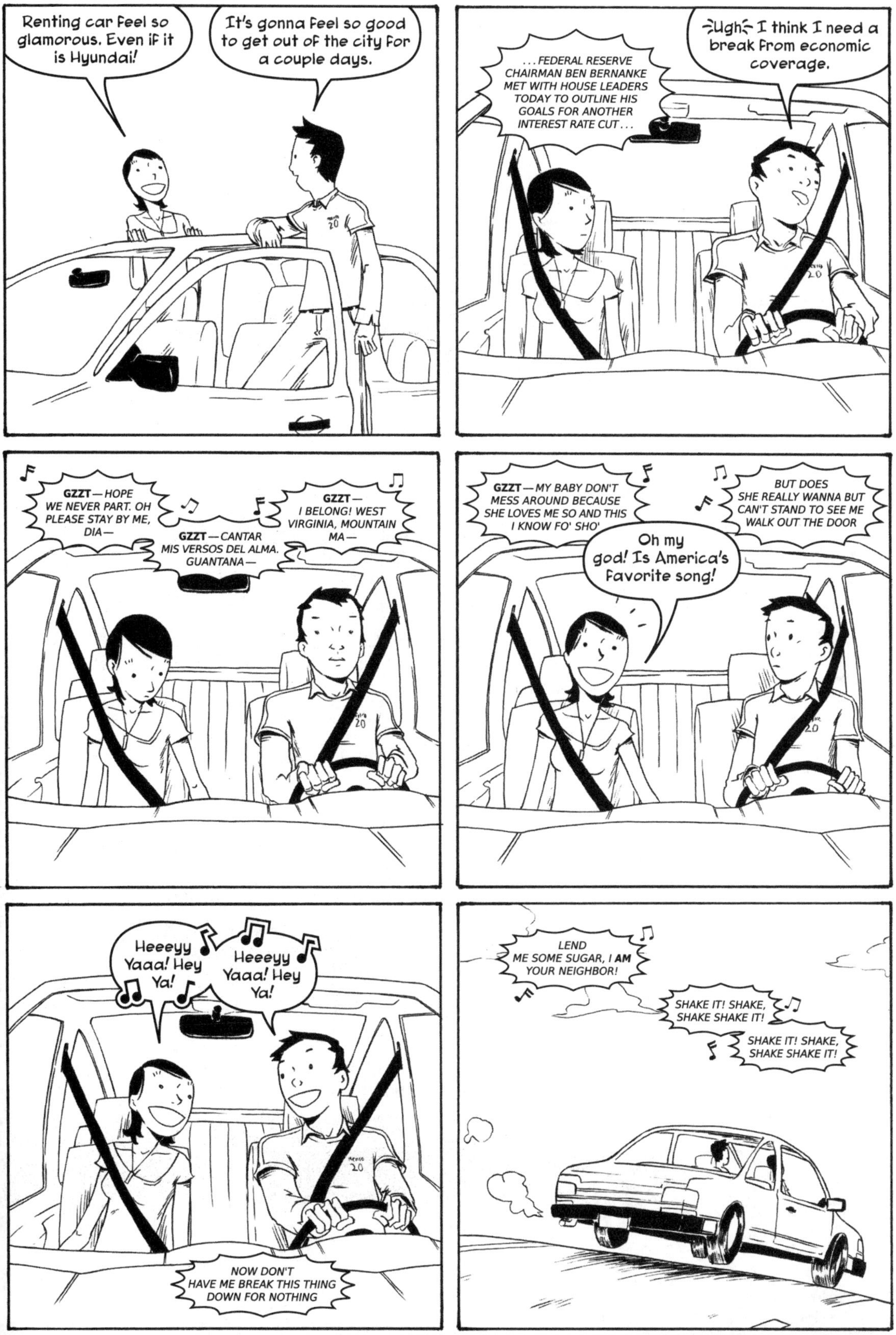

Renting car feel so glamorous. Even if it is Hyundai!
It's gonna feel so good to get out of the city for a couple days.
. . . FEDERAL RESERVE CHAIRMAN BEN BERNANKE MET WITH HOUSE LEADERS TODAY TO OUTLINE HIS GOALS FOR ANOTHER INTEREST RATE CUT . . .
Ugh I think I need a break from economic coverage.
GZZT—HOPE WE NEVER PART. OH PLEASE STAY BY ME, DIA—
GZZT—CANTAR MIS VERSOS DEL ALMA. GUANTANA—
GZZT—I BELONG! WEST VIRGINIA, MOUNTAIN MA—
GZZT—MY BABY DON'T MESS AROUND BECAUSE SHE LOVES ME SO AND THIS I KNOW FO' SHO'
BUT DOES SHE REALLY WANNA BUT CAN'T STAND TO SEE ME WALK OUT THE DOOR
Oh my god! Is America's favorite song!
Heeeyy Yaaa! Hey Ya!
Heeeyy Yaaa! Hey Ya!
NOW DON'T HAVE ME BREAK THIS THING DOWN FOR NOTHING
LEND ME SOME SUGAR, I AM YOUR NEIGHBOR!
SHAKE IT! SHAKE, SHAKE SHAKE IT!
SHAKE IT! SHAKE, SHAKE SHAKE IT!

Acknowledgments

None of this could have been done without my family—Mom, Dad, Shirley, and Katherine—whose seemingly endless love and support have carried me further than they could possibly know.

As well as my extended family—San shu gong, Jiu jiu, Gu po, Gong gong, and everyone else in the Chao and Wang families. And Ye ye and Nai nai, who would have loved this.

For accompanying me through so many of the stupid/crazy experiences that eventually led to making comics, I am incredibly grateful for the friendships of Seth Brindis, Peter Chow, Scott Edmonds, Ethan Herr, Mike Plann, and Jeff Sammis.

Also to my doggs—Beth Bayley, Nate Gibson, Tracey Long, Kathe McKenna, Opus Moreschi, Davy Rothbart, Michelle Sarrat, Peter Muelenbrook, Stephen Shipps, and Thomas Turnbull.

More recently, I've met so many wonderful people in and around comics who have inspired me to keep at the desk writing and drawing—Josh Cotter, Robert Goodin, Laura Hudson, Tim Leong, Matthue Roth, Jamie Tanner, and GB Tran.

This comic would have taken so much longer without the support of Sean Boggs, Rick Farley, Joe Merkel, John Sazaklis, and Tom Starace. Good part-time employment is hard to come across.

And many thanks to Dylan Babb and Jesse Post—whose efforts and dedication have made this comic far richer.

For this edition, I owe so much to the support of Tom and Amy Adams, Seth Fishman, and Steven Padnick.

And of course, Chris Pitzer.

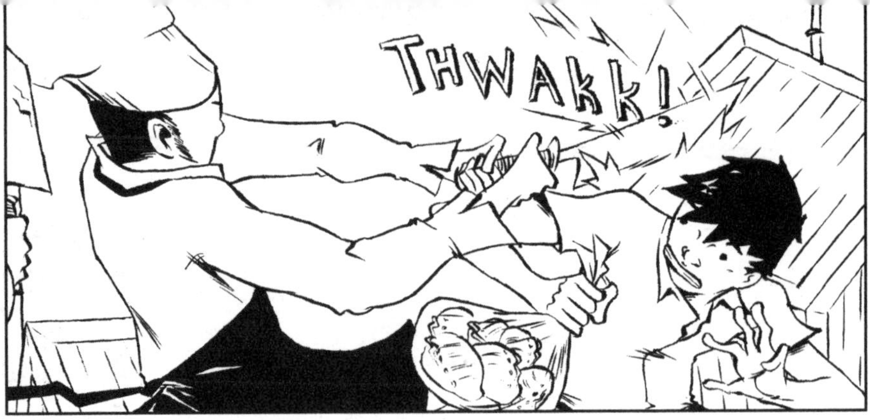
THWAKK!

Coming Summer 2013:

JOHNNY HIRO

{ The Skills to Pay the Bills }

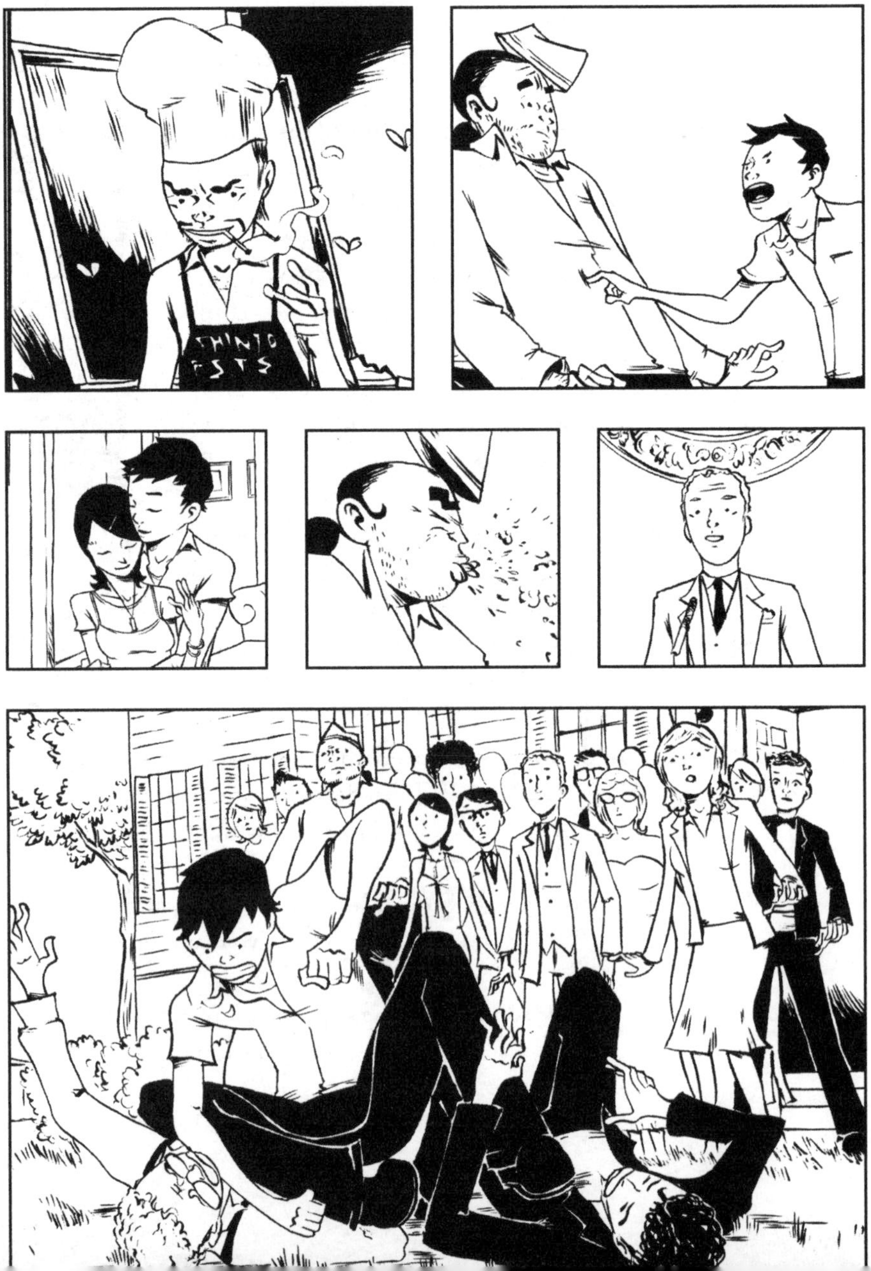

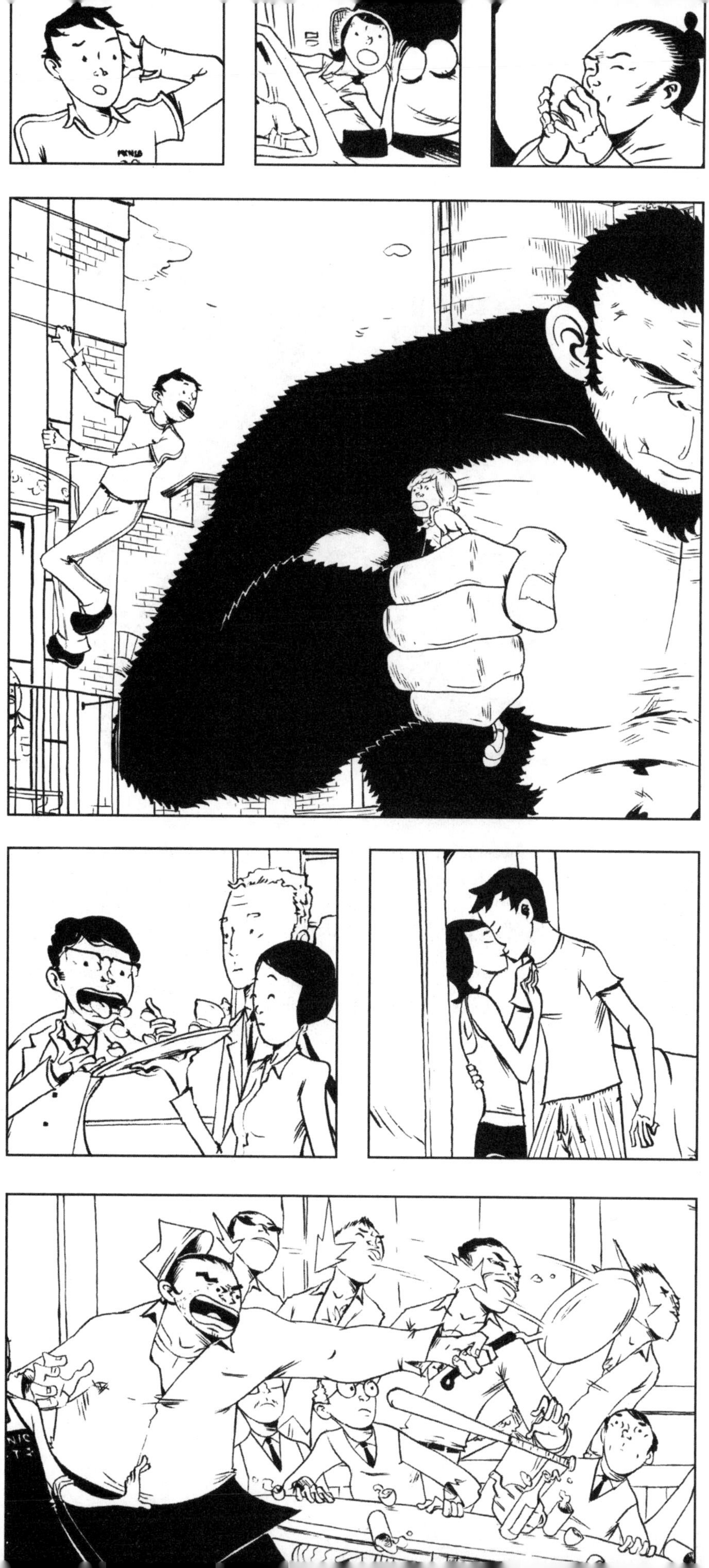

FRED CHAO was born in 1978 in San Francisco, California.
His comics have appeared in *Found: Requiem for a Paper Bag*.

This is his first graphic novel, parts of which appeared in
The Best American Comics 2010.

He lives in Brooklyn. He has no cats.